HELLENIC RELIGION AND CHRISTIANIZATION
C. 370-529

DATE DUE

HELLENIC RELIGION
AND CHRISTIANIZATION
C. 370–529

FRANK R. TROMBLEY

VOLUME 1

SECOND EDITION

BRILL ACADEMIC PUBLISHERS, INC.
BOSTON • LEIDEN
2001

Library of Congress Cataloging-in-Publication Data

Trombley, Frank R.
  Hellenic religion and Christianization c. 370–529/by Frank R. Trombley.
    p. cm.
  Originally published: Leiden: E.J. Brill, 1993–94, in series: Religions in the
Graeco-Roman world.
  Includes bibliographical references and index.
  ISBN 0-391-04121-5
  1. Christianity and other religions—Greek. 2. Christianity and other
religions—Roman. 3. Church history—Primitive and early church,
ca. 30–600. 4. Rome—Religion. 5. Greece—Religion. 6. Middle East—
Religion. 7. Egypt—Religion. I. Title.

BR128.G8 T76 2001
261.2′2′09015—dc21

                                                              2001043489

ISBN 0–391–04121–5

For
Mary Kay

Beside the white sparkling marble quarries of Thasos
Amidst the red walls and towers of Anastasioupolis
Through the winding curves of the Nestos valley
Beneath Azoros' bleak akropolis walls
Among the minaret spires of Xanthi
Over sun-baked Via Egnatia looking west
And a world away in the damp twilight of
London.

CONTENTS

Preface ix

Abbreviations xiv

I. The Legal Status of Sacrifice to 529 1
  1. The Sacrifice in Late Hellenic Religion 3
  2. The Status of the Hellenic Cults in the Theodosian
     Code 10
  3. The Varieties of Hellenic Religion 35
  4. The Legislation against Sorcery 59
  5. The Transformation of the Law after 438 72
  6. The Quasi-Justinianic Laws of Zeno c. 481–484 81
  7. Conclusion 94

II. Christianization 98
  1. Christianization and the Transformation of Local
     Gods 99
  2. The Social Context of Temple Conversions 108
  3. Temple Conversions at Apamea, Alexandria and
     Palmyra 123
  4. Christianization of Rite 147
  5. Christianization of the Decurion Class 168
  6. Conclusion 181

III. Gaza
  1. The Cults of Gaza in 395 188
  2. The Urban Pagan Establishment 191
  3. The *Territorium* of Gaza 204
  4. The Destruction of the Temples in 402 207
  5. The Growth of the Gazan Church 223
  6. The Church Establishment 234
  7. Conclusion 243

Appendix I: The Priority and Historicity of the Greek
             Version of Mark the Deacon's Life of
             Porphyrius of Gaza 246

IV. Athens and Attica 283
    1. The Christianization of Attica and the Epigraphy 284
    2. Hellenic Religion c. 400 292
    3. The Mid-Fifth Century 307
    4. The Social Background to the Survival of the
       Athenian Cults 324
    5. Conclusion 329

Appendix II : Did John Chrysostom Visit Athens in
              367/8? 333

Appendix III: The Closure of the Asklepieion and
              Parthenon in 481–484 342

INTRODUCTION

Hellenic Religion and Christianization c. 370–529 was first published in 1993. It was begun at a time when the problem of Christianization was just beginning to receive attention.[1] Much had already been written on the decline of the pre-Christian religions of the Mediterranean basin and its hinterlands, going back to Johannes Geffcken's *Der Ausgang des griechisch-römischen Heidentums* (Heidelberg 1929). There were few scholarly canons for discussing the other side of this question, the gradual displacement of the older religious culture with the new forms of Christian monotheism. It was often supposed that tracing the Christianisation of culture was a satisfactory way of resolving this.[2] My own preference was to confine the discussion to purely religious phenomena, or to the features of the Greek *paideia* that influenced them in the fourth to sixth centuries.

It became obvious right from the start that the project had taken a line of analysis that few had anticipated. It was suggested to me, for example, that there was no paganism, and that it would be more profitable to fit Christian behavioral patterns into the structures suggested by anthropology.[3] In the end it came down to a small number of parameters. It was taken as a given that the laws of the emperors prescribing punishments for pagan sacrifice reflected a historically "real" social pattern, and that a term first suggested by Ernst Kirsten, *Ritenchristianisierung* (Christianization of rite), signified the final phase of the process implicitly demanded by the imperial edicts. It then became a matter of tracing it through the literary sources of the period between the death of Julian the Apostate in 363 and the law of Justinian published in 529. The variety of sources proved to be immense: the great ecclesiastical histories of Sozomen, Socrates and Theodoret, hagiographic texts, the epigraphic collections, the Greek anthology, the letters of Isidore of Pelusium and Nilus of Ankyra, the Greek magical papyri, a small number of recent archaeological reports on the destruction of temples. Many texts already existed in translation, but most of these were completed before the systematic terminological analysis done in A.H.M. Jones' *Later Roman Empire*, a work that among other things identified the "real" social conditions

---

[1] R. MacMullen, *Christianizing the Roman Empire (A.D. 100–400)* (New Haven 1984).
[2] G. Bowersock, *Hellenism in Late Antiquity* (1990).
[3] Oral communication, Peter Brown, November 1985.

lying behind the laws found in the Theodosian and Justinian codes.

Hellenic Religion and Christianization c. 370–529 was for the most part favorably reviewed.[4] Ramsay MacMullen has elsewhere integrated the results of the book into his own discussion of the problem of Christianization.[5]

It was necessary for me to take a position in this work on certain texts where definitive conclusions were not always possible to achieve. Among these is the law at *Codex Iustinianus* 1.11.9–10 whose prescript is missing. Prescripts were normally attached to new laws giving the date of issue, the recipient, and the name of the reigning emperor.[6] It is unlikely that the jurists in charge of the codification would have omitted the prescript of a recent law by Justinian, since the latter had begun to rule as sole emperor only a few years before the commission started its work. The law seems to me to be directed against the Hellenists who supported Illus' rebellion against emperor Zeno in 481–88. Commentators have offered no serious proof that the law is Justinianic and have reaffirmed the older, received interpretations.

The years 481–488 quite probably saw the destruction of the Aphroditeion in Aphrodisias, the removal of Pheidias's chryselephantine Athena from Parthenon, and the conversion of the Asklepieion in Athens into a Christian shrine dedicated to the healing cult of St. Andrew, all of them important Hellenic religious shrines. There is some additional evidence suggesting that the civil war took a dangerous pagan-Christian ideological colour in the early going, the casting political horoscopes favourable to emperor Zeno's cause. These horoscopes were put together by a pro-imperial astrologer and showed that the rebellious leaders Pamprepius and the usurper Leontius proclaimed by Illus were fated to be defeated.[7] It remains an open question whether these documents were concocted with a view to gaining public support in 484 or were *vaticinia ex eventu* designed to demoralize remnants of the political opposition after Zeno's victory.[8]

---

[4] F. Graf, *Museum Helveticum* 51 (1994). N. Zeegers, *Revue d'histoire écclésiastique* (1994), 660–63. G. Clark, *The Classical Review* 45 (1995), 76–79. O. Ballériaux, *Kernos* 8 (1995), 299–303. R. Hošck, *Byzantinoslavica* 58 (1997), 175–83.

[5] *Christianity & Paganism in the Fourth to Eighth Centuries* (New Haven 1997), 17, 136f., etc.

[6] See below, Chapter I, pp. 81–94.

[7] D. Pingree, "Political horoscopes from the reign of Zeno," *DOP* 30 (1976), 136, 139–149.

[8] A recent review of the evidence on Illus' rebellion is found in *The Chronicle of Pseudo-Joshua the Stylite*, trans. F. Trombley and J. Watt (Liverpool 2000), 13–16. The ideological character of the struggle is also emphasized by C. Haas, "Patriarch and people: Peter Mongus of Alexandria and episcopal leadership in the late fifth century," *Journal of Early Christian Studies* 1 (1993), 310–15.

Is it likely that Zeno would have destroyed the shrines of the dissident groups being courted by Illus in 484 when the "cold war" with the emperor ended and the actual fighting began? The answer is a conditional "yes." In the same year Zeno ordered the destruction of the Samaritan temple on Mt. Gerizim and subsidized the construction of a new church there dedicated to the *theotokos*.[9] We do not know for certain if Illus approached the Samaritans, but the incident is a peculiar and seems to parallel events elsewhere. As to the closure of the Aphroditieon in Aphrodisias, the excavations have begun to produce stratified numismatic evidence that the destruction took place at a date after 450, provisionally corroborating the chronology suggested in Chapter VI.[10]

It is to be assumed that new evidence about pagan dedications and sacrifices between 363–529 will continue to turn up, and that earlier views will be revised. One thinks, for example, of the bronze Hekateion of Flavios Gerontios excavated in the Mithraion of Sidon, which Ernest Will redated to A.D. 389, providing an archaeological reference frame for the ongoing use of the temple and the cult of Hekate.[11] More startling are the inscriptions commemorating an unofficial sacrificial cult of the ironworkers in Hermonthis in Thebais II (Egypt). Dated inscriptions record the celebration of sacrifice on 27–28 December in 324, in 333/4 or 347/8, and in 357, *all of them painted in the same hand*, probably that of Atres son of Horion the secretary (*grammateus*) named in the dated inscriptions.[12]

It is recognized that Hellenic and Christian religious experience is a subject deserving much greater attention than it has received in *Hellenic Religion and Christianization*. The need to introduce sociological, psychoanalytic, and anthropological reference frames makes it a complex task, which will require a great deal more work before definitive results can be achieved.[13]

A continuing controversy surrounds the historicity of the life of Porphyrius bishop of Gaza written by Mark the Deacon, which is discussed in Appendix I below. The future of the debate lies in the hands of the translators who are preparing translations of the Greek

---

[9] A.M. Schneider, "Römische und byzantinische Bauten auf dem Garizim," *Zeitschrift der Deutschen Palästina Verien* 68 (1951), 212, 217f. R.T. Anderson, 'Mount Gerizim: navel of the world,' *Biblical Archaeologist* 43 (1980), 217–21.

[10] Unpublished paper of C. Ratté, "Strategies for urban research at Aphrodisias, Turkey," read at Late Antique Archaeology 2001: New Research, Method and Practice, Trinity College, Oxford, 17–18 March 2001.

[11] E. Will, "La date du Mithréum de Sidon," *Syria* 27 (1950), 261–69.

[12] *SEG* 41 (1991), nos. 1612–1615.

[13] E.g. F. Trombley, 'Religious experience in Late Antiquity: theological ambivalence and Christianization,' *Byzantine and Modern Greek Studies* 24 (2000), 2–60.

and Georgian texts with commentary for the *Translated Texts for Historians* series. I believe that the text will in the long run be rehabilitated as a relatively early account of a "real" bishop whose activities included the destruction of the temples of Gaza.

I must here state my disagreement with Ramsay MacMullen's nay saying in this connection. It should be noted that, in his *Christianizing the Roman Empire A.D. 100–400*,[14] MacMullen slavishly follows Paul Peeters's arguments in favor of the priory of the Georgian-Syriac recension. In consequence, there was no particular reason to consider what he calls "the arguments [he] proposed" in his book.[15] To refute Peeters is to refute MacMullen's argument *in toto*. Most of the discussions Peeters cites as proof for a post-534 date for the Greek version are merely passing comments, which pre-date my own analysis. I have never found "appeal to authority" convincing in the face of hard evidence.

Henri Grégoire's introduction to the Greek text is completely out of date and can no longer be trusted on points of lexicography. He states, for example, that the Greek word λησμονέω is "une κοινή vulgaire, mais d'un vulgarisme modéré ... Nous n'avons trouvé [le mot], en dehors de notre Vie, que dans un texte attribué faussement à Athanase, et qui parait daté du VIIIe siècle au plus tôt."[16] The word can, however, be found in Nilus of Ankyra's *Epistle* 2.175 (c. 430) and a pagan Greek inscription of third- to fourth-century date in Phrygia.[17]

Epigraphic data are important where literary material is lacking. Inscriptions are present in Asia Minor in overwhelming numbers, mainly for the period before A.D. 400. No complete understanding of the religious transformation there will be complete until all this data has been carefully dated and subjected to critical analysis.[18] Syria, Phoenicia and Arabia also have extensive epigraphic remains. The work done by Jacques Jarry in the Limestone Massif and other epigraphic material was overlooked in the first edition of *Hellenic Religion and Christianization*. I have reviewed the dated Greek and Syriac inscriptions in Jarry's collection, and find that the chronology of Christianization I suggested in Chapter X has not for the most

---

[14] See above, note 1.
[15] *Christianity and Paganism*, 174, note 68.
[16] Marc le Diacre, *Vie de Porphyre évêque de Gaza*, ed. and trans. H. Grégoire and M.-A. Kugener (Paris 1930), xliv–xlv.
[17] *SEG* 6.250.
[18] See S. Mitchell, *Anatolia* 2 (Oxford 1993). The author often fails to understand other scholars' work, e.g. pp. 117, note 69; 118f. and note 78; 145, note 104.

part been affected by these omissions.[19] Similarly a considerable number of Late Roman inscriptions in the Provincia Arabia came to light since the findings of the Princeton University Expeditions of 1904–5 and 1909 were published in 1921, including a small corpus in *SEG* 7 in 1934.[20] The latter consists mostly of funerary inscriptions and does not at first sight seem to contradict the overall chronology of Christianization in Arabia, but I have not had the opportunity to review this material systematically. The existence of early Christian basilicas in the Arabian towns in the first half of the fifth century is important, but cannot be taken as proof of the adherence of the populations of their *territoria* to the new religion.[21] The latter is a demographic question that can best be solved by studying the epigraphy.[22]

University of Wales, Cardiff
23 July 2001

---

[19] J. Jarry, 'Inscriptions arabes, syriaques et grecques du Massif du Bélus en Syrie du Nord,' *Annales islamologiques* (= *AI*) 7 (1967), 139–220; 9 (1970), 187–214. 'Inscriptions de Syrie du Nord relevées en 1969,' *AI* 9 (1970), 215–221. 'Nouvelle inscriptions de Syrie du Nord,' *Zeitschrift für Papyrologie und Epigraphik* (= *ZPE*) 47 (1982), 73–103. 'Nouveaux documents grecs et latines de Syrie du Nord et de Palmyrène,' *ZPE* 60 (1985), 109–115.
[20] *SEG* 7 (1934), nos. 935–1232.
[21] R. Donceel, 'L'évêque Épidore et les basiliques de Kanatha d'après une inscription greque inédite,' *Le Muséon* 100 (1987), 67–88. P. Donceel-Voûte, 'À propos de la grande basilique de Soueida-Dionysias et de ses évêques,' *Le Muséon* 100 (1987), 89–100.
[22] F. Trombley, 'Demographic aspects of adhesion to Christianity under the Constantinian dynasty, c. 306–363 A.D.,' *The Power and the Glory: The Legacy of Constantine* (University of Exeter Press). No other publication details available.

ABBREVIATIONS

Bury, LRE	John B. Bury, *History of the Later Roman Empire from the Death of Theodosius 1 to the Death of Justinian*, 2 vols. (London 1923).
Cod. Iust.	*Codex Iustinianus* in *Corpus Iuris Civilis*. Ed. P. Krueger, 2 (Berlin 1929).
Cod. Theod.	*Theodosiani Libri XVI cum Constitutionibus Sirmondianis*. Ed. T. Mommsen, P. Krueger, and P.M. Mayer. 2 vols. in 4 (Berlin 1905).
DACL	*Dictionnaire d'archéologie chrétienne et de liturgie*. Ed. F. Cabrol and H. Leclercq (Paris 1903–50).
IG	*Inscriptiones Graecae* 1–14. Ed. A. Kirchoff et alii (Berlin 1873–90).
ILCV	*Inscriptiones Latinae Christianae Veteres*. Ed. E. Diehl 1–3 (Berlin 1925–31).
Jones, Later Roman Empire	*The Later Roman Empire 284–602: A Social Economic and Administrative Survey* 1–3 (Oxford 1964).
MAMA	*Monumenta Asiae Minoris Antiqua* 1–6 (Manchester 1928–39).
OGIS	*Orientis Graeci Inscriptiones Selectae*. Ed. W. Dittenberger 1–2 (Leipzig 1903–5).
PG	*Patrologia Cursus Completus*, Series Graeco–Latina. Ed. J.P. Migne (Paris 1857–).
PGM	*Papyri Graecae Magicae: Die griechischen Zauberpapyri*. Ed. Karl Preisendanz *et alii* 1–2 (Stuttgart 1973–74).
PL	*Patrologia Cursus Completus*, Series Latina. Ed. J.P. Migne (Paris 1884–).
SEG	*Supplementum Epigraphicum Graecum*. Ed. P. Roussel *et alii*. (Leiden 1923–).

CHAPTER ONE

THE LEGAL STATUS OF SACRIFICE TO 529 A.D.

The compilation and promulgation of the Theodosian Code, which was formally effected in 438, put the Hellenic cults of the Eastern Roman Empire on a new footing.[1] Previous imperial edicts and rescripts on that subject had until that date been directed to the *officium* of a single Praetorian Prefect.[2] On other occasions such local officials received them as the Prefect of the City (Rome), the Dux of Osrhoene, the Augustal Prefect and Count of Egypt, the Vicar of the Five Provinces of Spain, and the Proconsul of Africa.[3] The inclusion of the rescripts on pagans and Hellenic cult practices within the codification is emphatic proof that the rescript of 9 April 423, which made reference to the "pagans who have survived, although we believe that there be none left," had been formulated on the basis of inadequate data.[4] The earliest law against the pagan sacrifice dated from the reign of Constantine the Great (17 December 321).[5] This law, with all subsequent enactments, had the force of edicts or an imperial law of general force (*edictorum vires aut sacra generalitas*), as the prolegomenon to the Theodosian Code states.[6] It adds that all new laws should be valid in both halves of the empire after the transmission of suitable imperial letters and their publication by the bureaus.[7]

The incorporation of anti-pagan legislation into the new code indicated the intention of the imperial government to systematize a struggle which many urban bishops and rural monks had waged

---

[1] *Theodosiani Libri XVI cum Constitutionibus Sirmondianis*, ed. Theodor Mommsen, Paul Krueger, and Paul M. Mayer, 2 vols. in 4 (Berlin 1905). Cf. *The Theodosian Code and Novels and the Sirmondian Constitutions*, tr. C. Pharr *et. al.* (Princeton 1952). See also: Periklès-Pierre Joannou, *La legislation impériale et la christianisation de l'empire romain (311–476)* (Rome 1972). The last named work provides a chronology of the imperial decrees relating to sacrifice and Hellenes.

[2] *Cod. Theod.* 16.10 passim.

[3] *Cod. Theod.* 16.10.3, 8, 11, and 15.

[4] Paganos qui supersunt, quamquam iam nullos esse credamus. *Cod. Theod.* 16.10.22.

[5] *Cod. Theod.* 16.10.1.

[6] *Cod. Theod., Gesta Senatus Romani de Theodosiano Publicando* (Mommsen-Krueger, 2, lines 4–7).

[7] Ibid., lines 33–39.

against the pagans of their communities for many decades. The life
of Porphyrius of Gaza, written by Mark the Deacon, most fully
documents the dynamics of this conflict, which often found bishops
deadlocked with wealthy urban dynasts who adhered to the old
religion.[8] These latter used their control of the magistracies and
large funds of manpower in town and countryside to resist the
efforts of the local churches to catechize the urban artisans and
poor, as well as the villages of agriculturalists inside the city's
territorium or rural administrative zone. Where opposition was
strong, a bishop like Porphyrius had to procure a special rescript to
pursue his program, which in this case included the destruction of
the Marneion, the great temple of the Cretan-born Zeus Marnas.
This occurred, it should be added, well before two early edicts of
Arcadius and Theodosius II (15 November 408 and 30 August 415)
had come out.[9] The Theodosian codification left little doubt about
the legal remedies available to bishops who had the ambition to
Christianize their towns by force. It must be borne in mind, however, that this power accrued to the churches gradually and only
through the dispensation of the secular arm. The fate of Marcellus,
metropolitan of Apamea in Second Syria, demonstrates what was
in store for those who overlooked this reality.[10]

The laws against paganism collected in the sixteenth book of the
Theodosian Code extend from 8 March 321 to 14 November 435.
They contain accurate if brief statements about all the proscribed
social conditions by reason of legal necessity, for a magistrate
cannot rule against a practice which is not described in typologically accurate terms in his law book under the code (as opposed to the
common law) system. Hence the need of the Theodosian Code for
precision and comprehensive coverage of all possible cases. There
is a second consideration brought forward by A.H.M. Jones,
namely that the existence of a law does not presuppose widespread
public obedience to it, but rather often reflects simply the "pious
aspiration" of the magistrate.[11] It will be seen in due course that
Jones' dictum that the "laws were intermittently and sporadically
enforced" applies accurately to the repression of Hellenic religion.
The stiff penalties attached to certain offenses suggest, if anything,
rather frequent violations.

---

[8] Infra, Ch. III, Sect. 2 and 4.
[9] *Cod. Theod.*16.10.19 and 20.
[10] Infra, Ch. II, Sect. 3.
[11] A.H.M. Jones, *The Later Roman Empire 284–602: A Social, Economic and Administrative Survey* (Oxford 1964), viii. This work is hereinafter cited as Jones, *Later
Roman Empire.*

I. The Sacrifice in Late Hellenic Religion

The inclusion of the earliest laws in the codification of 438 reflects the existence of ongoing social and cultural conditions. The overriding concern of successive emperors and magistrates lay in the persistence of the pagan sacrifice (θυσία), which sought to achieve the favor of the gods on the principle of *do ut des* by the consumption of a "victim", whether of animal or vegetable origin, by fire and a subsequent common meal (ἱερὸν δεῖπνον).[12] The sacrifice was a symbol of public solidarity in the pre-Christian urban or agricultural community. The officers of the sacrifice and their functions are known mainly from inscriptions of pre-Christian antiquity. Officers included public masters of ceremonies, official recorders of sacrifices, temple sweepers and cleaners (διάκονοι), priests, official woodcutters, and officers of the subsequent banquet, which included harpists, trumpeters, cooks, and wine pourers. At oracular temples like those of Apollo at Delphi and Klaros there were seers (μάνται) who made oracular pronouncements, whereas at the celebration of mysteries there might be a leader who interpreted symbol and myth (ἐξηγητής). The city council might elect them to office, but some priesthoods, like those at Eleusis in Attica and Philae in Upper Egypt, were hereditary. Others yet could be purchased. These men took oaths that they would perform the rites in the regularly ordained fashion.[13] Institutions of this sort certainly persisted through the reigns of Julian the Apostate (361–363) and Valens (364–378) in the Greek East, under whom the previous legislation against sacrifice became largely a dead letter.[14] The real repression of sacrifices and the cadres of their officiants began with the law of 21 December 381 given by emperor Theodosius I.[15]

The rites of the public sacrifice varied from place to place. Accurate descriptions of their practice from Late Antiquity are generally lacking, except the account of a nocturnal camel sacrifice which the pagan Arabs of Sinai performed,[16] and the more general treatment found in the sections of Ammianus Marcellinus' *Histories* pertaining to the stay of Julian the Apostate at Antioch.[17] The

---

[12] See the detailed description of the Panathenaia, the sacrifice, and the distribution of meats in: *Sylloge Inscriptionum Graecarum*, ed. W. Dittenberger, 3rd ed., vol. 1 (Leipzig 1915), no. 271, line 24f.

[13] Royden K. Yerkes, *Sacrifice in Greek and Roman Religions and Early Judaism* (London 1953), 74–80.

[14] Infra, Ch. II, n. 46.

[15] Infra, Ch. I, Sect. 2.

[16] Yerkes, *Sacrifice*, 81. Nilos of Ankyra, *Narrationes*, PG 79, 613A–C.

[17] Ammianus Marcellinus, *Res Gestae* 22.13.3 (wax tapers and a votive image of

desired precision is found in a much earlier document, an inscription attached to the peace treaty concluded between Miletus and Magnesia-on-Maeander concluded in 196 B.C.:[18]

> The stewards in office are to purchase the best bull [obtainable] in the month of Heraion at the annual fair. They are to exhibit it to Zeus at the beginning of seedtime on the first of the month Kronion with the priest and priestess of Artemis Leukophryene, the *stephanophorus*, the sacred herald, and the public sacrificer in the city. The officers of the boys are to send nine boys, each with both parents living. The officers of the girls are to send nine girls, each with both parents living.
>
> At the exhibition of the bull the sacred herald is to pray, with the priest and priestess, the stephanophorus, the boys and girls, the military officers, the cavalry officers, the stewards, the secretary of the council, the auditor and the general, for the safety of the city and the land, the women and children and all the inhabitants of the city and the land, for peace and wealth and bearing of grain and all other fruits and possessions.

The last several phrases succinctly sum up the idea of the peace of the gods. The inscription continues:

> The permanent stephanophorus, with the priest and priestess of Artemis Leukophryene, lead the procession on the twelfth of the month Artemision and sacrifice (θύειν) the exhibited bull.
>
> In the procession with them are to be the senate, the priests, the appointed and lottery-chosen magistrates, the young men, the youths, the boys, those who have won the competitions in the Leukophryene, and all others who have won crown competitions.
>
> The stephanophorus, leading the procession, is to bring the wooden images of all the twelve gods in their finest attire. He is to erect a tholos in the agora at the altar of the twelve gods. He is to prepare three beds, as fine as possible. He is to furnish players, a flutist, a piper, and a harpist.
>
> On the twelfth of the month Artemision the stewards are to furnish three victims which they are to sacrifice to Zeus Sosipolis, to Artemis Leukophryene, and to Apollo Pythios; for Zeus a ram, the finest obtainable, for Artemis a goat, and for Apollo a he-goat, sacrificing to Zeus on the altar of Zeus Sosipolis, to Artemis and Apollo on the altar of Artemis. The priests of these gods are to have the customary portions.
>
> When they sacrifice the bull they are to distribute to all the participants in the procession.

Dea Caelestis), 22.14 (sacrifice to Zeus on Mount Casius), and especially 22.12 (... *Iulianus ... victimasque innumerabiles caedit*).

[18] *Die Inschriften von Magnesia am Maeander*, ed. Otto Kern (Berlin 1900), 98. The translation given here is borrowed almost completely from Yerkes, *Sacrifice*, 75f., as this version is practically definitive.

The ram, the she-goat, and the he-goat they are to distribute to the stephanophorus, the priestess, the polemarchs, the presiding magistrates, the temple wardens, the magistrates, and those who have rendered public service. The stewards (*oikonomoi*) are to distribute these portions.

When the stewards have exhibited the bull, they are to farm him out that he may be nourished by a contractor. The contractor is to lead the bull to the agora; he is to collect from the grain merchants and other merchants what is fitting for its nourishment. It is better for those who give.

The stewards are to record this vote at the temple of Zeus.

The splendor of these events will have declined by the late fourth century A.D., and particularly from the time of Theodosius the Great (379–395) onward. The later narratives found in the Christian biography of Porphyrius of Gaza (c. 400) and the pagan life of Proclus the Neoplatonist (c. 430–485) suggest hardly anything about public ritual. The Christian writer no doubt suppresses whatever information he had, but the pagan writer, Marinus of Neapolis, makes it clear that public cult consisted of little more than the traditional litanies or processions, but without sacrificial ritual. The Hellenes of Proclus' circle observed private sacrifice with all its ramifications and variations and talked publicly about their activities.[19] This circumstance suggests that the private religious sacrifice remained largely above the law, particularly in cities like Athens which had kept a relatively large pagan population through the mid-fifth century.

The legislation compiled in the Theodosian Code, then, aimed more at suppressing public ceremonial than interfering with private conscience. A variety of sources including Libanius' oration in behalf of the temples and Damascius' life of Isidore the sophist confirms this dictum, as does a systematic analysis of the provisions of the Theodosian Code relating to sacrifice and Hellenism. The sacrifice connected with magical arts, on the other hand, did not belong to the realm of private conscience, inasmuch as it included devices widely believed in during this epoch and designed to manipulate the behavior and damage the health of private individuals. It therefore constituted an illegal sacrifice *alius generis* which, if its efficacy were proven by the standards of the day, required legal penalties, including the death penalty.[20]

---

[19] Infra, Ch. IV, Sect. 3.

[20] For texts, see: *Papyri Graecae Magicae: Die griechischen Zauberpapyri*, ed. Karl Preisendanz *et. al.*, 2 vols. (Stuttgart 1973–74). Numerous other examples, inscribed on all sorts of media, have appeared in the recent numbers of *Supplementum Epigraphicum Graecum*. Cf. the erotic charm composed in a lead tablet (Antinooupo-

The character of the Hellenic sacrifice as popularly practiced
emerges most clearly in the Oration 30 of Libanius, the *Pro Templis*,
which belongs apparently to the year 386, over half a decade before
the comprehensive law of Theodosius the Great which banned all
forms of public cult and processional, even those which did not
entail animal sacrifice but consisted merely of offerings in incense,
the hanging of garlands, and so forth.[21] The oration *Pro Templis*
dealt with the ravages of monks not only against temple buildings,
but also against the pious behavior of rustic pagans who made
offerings to the tutelary deities of the land when they sat down to
eat. If we may trust Libanius' understanding of the legal issue, such
acts of religion had not been comprehended within the laws against
sacrifice to date, which had public ceremonial in mind. Libanius
not only describes the phenomena of Hellenic cult, but provides a
brief history of the legislation on that subject since the death of
Julian the Apostate in 363. These data are of vital significance for
understanding the character of popular pagan religion in the subsequent century, as the law demonstrably worked only sporadically
against this cultic substrate.

Libanius sets forth the traditional argument that the "peace of
the gods" (*pax deorum*), or, as he puts it, the goodwill of the gods
toward men (θεῶν . . . εὔνοια τοῖς ἀνθρώποις),[22] including the

---

lis, Egypt, 3rd–4th c.), SEG 26 (1976–77), no. 1717. For an anthropological
discussion and suggested paradigms, but no treatment of Late Antique sorcery
and magic, see the essays collected in *Witchcraft and Sorcery*, ed. Max Marwick
(London 1982). For the Latin context in Late Antiquity, see: Richard Kieckhefer,
Magic in the Middle Ages (Cambridge 1989), 19–42. Kieckhefer argues elsewhere
that the magic of invoking *daimones* is in fact a "religious" phenomenon to be
distinguished from "natural" magic. He also concedes that "popular" or folk
sorcery ultimately worked its way into high culture. Ibid., 1f. This supposition
agrees with my own discussion of theurgy. Infra, Ch. I, Sect. 3 and 4. It is perhaps
at variance with Peter Brown's thesis expounded in: *The Cult of the Saints: Its Rise
and Function in Latin Christianity* (Chicago 1981), 17–20. Kieckhefer's arguments
have the merit of being both empirically and theoretically grounded.

[21] Libanius, *Or.* 30 ("To the Emperor Theodosius, For the Temples") in *Selected
Works*, tr. A.F. Norman, 2 (London 1977), 92–151.

[22] Ibid., 102f. This concept of the "peace of the gods" has prevailed in many
cultures, ancient and modern. Cf. the implicit formulation found in Origen *Contra
Celsum* 5.26–28. See also the comments of Henry Chadwick (tr.), *Contra Celsum*
(Cambridge 1965), xv. Augustine of Hippo was aware of a similar rationale to that
of Libanius in the years after the sack of Rome by the Visigoths in 410: "And the
first duty that presented itself [to me] was to reply to those who hold the Christian
religion responsible for the wars with which the whole world is now tormented,
and in particular for the recent sack of Rome by the barbarians. They ascribe this
to the Christian prohibition of the offering of abominable sacrifices to demons." *De
Civitate Dei* 2.2. Translation cited from Augustine, *Concerning the City of God against
the Pagans*, tr. H. Bettenson (London 1972), 49. There are twentieth-century
examples of accusations against the Christian religion for upsetting the peace of

maintenance of Roman imperial power,[23] depended on the traditional sacrifices. As he puts it: "One god contends for the might of
Rome, another protects its tutelary city, another yet sustains an
estate, providing it with good production" (ὁ μέν τις τῷ σκήπτρῳ
τῷ τῆς Ῥώμης συναγωνίζεται, ὁ δὲ ταύτῃ σώζει πόλιν ὑπήκοον,
ὁδέ τις ἀγρὸν ἀνέχει παρέχων εὖ πράττειν).[24] Periodic shortfalls
in local cereal production left the cities and their *territoria* liable to
starvation and dependant on the grain of Egypt, which the educated Hellene saw as the gift of Sarapis, even though carried in
regular shipments by an imperial merchant marine administered
and manned by Christians:[25]

> And it is not only in Rome that sacrifice has been maintained. They
> are also performed in the great and mighty city of Sarapis, with its
> fleet of ships whereby it makes the produce of Egypt common to all
> mankind. Egypt is the work of the Nile, and offers feasts to the Nile
> inducing him to flood the fields, and if these are not performed in due
> season and by due persons, he too would refuse. I feel that, in
> awareness of this, the eager supporters of abolition [of sacrifices]
> have refrained from abolishment of them, but have allowed the river
> to be feasted in the time-honored ritual for the customary reward.
>   What, then? Since there is not a river on every estate bestowing the
> blessings of the Nile upon the land, must the temples in them cease to
> exist and be misused in whatever way these splendid fellows [the
> monks] decide? I would like to put this question to them. Will they
> dare come forward and propose the abolition of the Nile feast, and
> with it the banning of the land from partaking of it, and from the
> sowing and reaping and production of grain and all its products and
> their transportation to all the world as now?

Libanius thus makes a Mediterranean-wide analogy of the goodwill
of the gods and applies it to the highly localized conditions which
prevailed in the *territorium* of Antioch. His description of the Nile
cults provides an accurate summary of those which persisted in the

---

the gods. The manifesto of the Boxer rebellion of 1900 in China contained a clause
dealing with this: "The Catholic and Protestant religions being insolent to the
gods and extinguishing sanctity, rendering no obedience to Buddha, and enraging
Heaven and Earth, the rain-clouds no longer visit us. . . ." Peter Fleming, *The
Siege at Peking* (New York 1959), 35. The importance of ongoing sacrifices is
recognized in late Vedic Indian religion as well: "The world began with a
stupendous sacrifice performed by the gods. To maintain it in good working order
constant repetitions of that original sacrifice are necessary. Otherwise the universe
would quickly degenerate and chaos would come again." This led to the brāh-
mans' powerful position, for only they were qualified by their knowledge of ritual
to carry through the requisite sacrifices. A.L. Basham, *The Sacred Cow: The
Evolution of Classical Hinduism* (London 1989), 30f.

[23] Quoted from Libanius, "For the Temples" (Norman 2, 128f.).
[24] Ibid., 130f.
[25] Ibid., 130–133.

Nile river valley at least through the mid-fifth century, from Canopus in suburbicarian Alexandria to the environs of Shenute of
Atripe's White Monastery near Antinoupolis, and beyond to the
temple of Isis at Philae near the southern extremity of the Roman
frontier.[26] The seemingly archaic ring of this argument on behalf of
the private sacrifice held sway in numerous localities in Syria and
Asia Minor too, as the criticism of local texts and inscriptions
demonstrates.[27]

Libanius provides the lengthy description of a typical offering to
the tutelary gods of the land. The orator carefully distinguishes the
licit from forbidden rituals:[27a]

> So what basis is there for the charge, save the mere assertion that
> they have performed an illegal sacrifice? But this sort of argumenta-
> tion will not suffice for the emperor.
> "They did not sacrifice, then?" will be the comment. Of course
> they did, but for a banquet, a dinner, a feast, *and the oxen were
> slaughtered elsewhere, no altar received the blood offering, no part of the victim
> was burned, no offering of meal began the ceremony, nor did libations follow it.*
> If people assemble in some beauty spot, slaughter a calf or sheep, or
> both, and boil or roast it, and then lie down on the ground and eat it,
> I do not see that they have broken the laws at all.
> You, O emperor, have put no legal ban on these acts. By banning
> the performance of one specific action you automatically permit
> everything else. So even if they were in the habit of drinking together
> amid the scent of every kind of incense, they broke no law, nor yet if
> in their toasts they sang hymns and invoked the gods, unless indeed
> you intend to use a man's private life as grounds for accusation.
> It used to be the custom for country folk to assemble in large
> numbers at the homes of village notables at festival time, to make a
> sacrifice and then hold a feast. This they did while ever it was
> permitted to do so, and therefore all the rest, with the exception of
> sacrifice, remained permissible. *So, summoned on the customary day, they
> dutifully honored it and the shrine in a manner that involved no legal risk.* That
> they also saw fit to offer sacrifice no single person has ever said or
> heard, alleged convincingly or believed. Nor yet could any of their
> enemies assert that he either had personally witnessed a sacrifice or
> could produce an informant about one. But if he had these proofs, or
> even one of them, who would have put up with arrests, a hue and cry,
> and charges made by these people, not in Flavianus' [patriarch of
> Antioch] court but in a real court of law?

Burnt offerings, particularly those in which the bloody parts of
victims were tossed onto the altar as first fruits to the gods, were
repudiated by the existing legislation (βωμοῦ δὲ οὐδενὸς τὸ αἷμα

---

[26] Infra, Ch. IX, passim.
[27] Infra, Ch. VII and VIII.
[27a] Quoted from Libanius, "For the Temples" (Norman 2, 117f.) (my italics).

δεχομένου οὐδὲ μέρους οὐδενὸς καομένου), as was the scattering of cereal or meal and the pouring of wine libations. The scent of burning animal flesh was thought by Hellenes like Porphyry of Tyre (ob. 301) to attract bad *daimones* (πονηροὶ δαίμονες), which caused disease, "possession" in the form of insanity, and other phenomena considered harmful to humans, particularly in connection with soliciting oracles.[28] On the other hand, no jurist— if one believes Libanius—construed the law in such a manner as to ban hymning and invoking the gods with incense-burning (but not alight on an altar) amidst the consumption of food and drink. The principle that banning one act permitted all else (ἓν εἰπὼν δεῖν μὴ ποιεῖν τἄλλα πάντα ἀφῆκας) provided the legal technicality necessary to avert prosecutions for sacrifices where circumstantial evidence suggested their performance, but where the absence of witnesses and in particular the absence of altars left the case moot. The monks who broke up these festivities with the tacit approval of patriarch Flavian I of Antioch (381–404) did not recognize the nicities of legal form, and it must be admitted that Libanius had much to hide in making these arguments, being likely to understate the clear prevalence of pagan cultic activity in the *territorium* of Antioch. The limitations set on the rituals requisite for Libanius' *legal* cultic banquet seems a bit formulaic, and to belong more to the ethos of urban dinners where Christians might be present and inclined to report illegal activities. It remains difficult to see how a convinced Hellene or rural pagan, if free from hostile observation, would not toss some few bits of the repast onto a fire on a makeshift altar in honor of the local deities. One could hardly have expected less educated or illiterate rustics to engage in such legal sophistries in closed groups. Nor does Libanius' argument that the failure to prosecute those who allegedly sacrificed in these situations in the regularly constituted law courts prove that sacrifices were not offered.[29] His argument rather more suggests that civil society, as opposed to the monastic, populated with many recent converts, felt an easy tolerance for its previous coreligionists, and that, as in most other situations, inertia governed the behavior of men more often than religious fanaticism.

It should be added that urban Hellenes who knew the *paideia* will have found—as Julian the Apostate did—exceptionally detailed examples of sacrificial ritual capable of easy imitation in the Homeric poems and other texts. Proclus, head of the Neoplatonist

---

[28] Infra, Ch. II, Sect. 1.
[29] Libanius, "For the Temples" (Norman 2, 118f.).

school in fifth-century Athens, certainly knew this lore in great detail, in addition to many arcane theologies and theurgies. In the countryside rustic common sense, fear for the good harvest, and awe of the divine seen in the forces of nature will have informed the non-Christian as to what rituals and first-fruit offerings the gods required. It remains to be seen how the legal system through the Theodosian codification of 438 sought to restrict the forbidden cult practices and what their precise state was in the first four decades of the fifth century.

II. The Status of the Hellenic Cults in the Theodosian Code

The Theodosian Code, as assembled, edited, and published in 438, constituted a blanket statement of the government of Theodosius II (408–450) on how it intended to deal with the extant Hellenic cults. It proves that the reality of ongoing sacrifices and other manifestations of the old religion c. 438 was patent. No reason otherwise existed to revive the imperial edicts of the previous century dating back to the reign of Constantius II (337–361) except to lend force to the argument that Christian emperors had *always* forbidden sacrifice and that it had become expedient once again to reaffirm those prohibitions. These documents, meant for jurists noted for their brevity in rhetoric and contempt for irrelevancy, necessarily dealt with the phenomena that a provincial governor and the notaries of his *officium* might encounter in the course of a year's duties. Abundant evidence exists to prove that, while the public sacrifices in the cities had ceased by the early fifth century, private worship of the sort described in the previous section of this chapter proved to be ineradicable even by the most stringent penalties. It is not so much our task here to trace the legal disabilities laid on those convicted of sacrifice as it is to test the mentality of the government toward the cultural and demographic reality of this phenomenon.

The codification made edicts originally published in light of conditions in circumscribed localities such as Proconsular Africa, Osrhoene, and Egypt binding throughout the empire. This act demonstrates not so much a thirst for the eclectic or some such misapprehension, for example, that African cults existed in identical form in ethnically different parts of the empire, as the desire to make known a set of *principles* embodied in the diverse imperial laws. They presuppose that a judge with a sense of discretion could easily apply this corpus of past edicts during his deliberations in a given case. It was not so much a matter of misinterpreting or misapplying the conditions found in one locality with reference to those in another as it was of trying cases with a set of established, if flexible, principles.

The laws of Theodosius II (408–450), particularly those published most recently prior to the codification in 438, reflect a certain grudging realism about the survival of Hellenes and their ineradicable sacrifices. A law of 9 April 423 given at Constantinople calls upon "the pagans who have survived" (*paganos qui supersunt*) to heed all recent legislation. The law adds the clause: "although we would like to believe there be no [pagans] left any longer" (*quamquam iam nullos esse credamus*).[30] One can account for this notion only in light of the fact that Theodosius, who ran the palace like a monastery and recited the psalms daily with his imperial sisters, was much divorced from the realities of provincial affairs.[31] This pious hope must have drawn cynical smiles from the quaestor and his staff of notaries who drew up the law, for cities such as Aphrodisias in Caria and Athens, to cite two examples, had many wealthy and influential Hellenes among their *curiales* or members of the city council even decades later.[32]

Another law, coming a decade later (14 November 435), reflects a greater sense of reality:[33]

> We interdict all persons of a hardened pagan mind because of the accursed immolation of victims and the condemned sacrifices and the other acts forbidden by the authority of the ancient *sanctiones*. We order all their groves, temples, and precincts, *if they remain intact even now*, to be destroyed by the decree of the magistrates [of the cities] and cleansed by the erection of the revered sign of the Christian religion [the cross].

The law prescribes the death penalty for anyone who flouts its provisions. Addressed to Isidore, the praetorian prefect of Oriens (c. 29 January 435–4 August 436),[34] the emperors' decree had in view rural groves, temples, precincts, and sites of sacrifice (*fana templa delubra*) of a sort frequently attested in the sources of the period: groves and other places sacred to Artemis in "inner Bithynia" (c. 443–446),[35] and the temples of the Syrian villages, which the monks had begun to penetrate in large numbers only during the episcopate of Flavian I of Antioch (381–404).[36] Some temples

---

[30] *Cod. Theod.* 16.10.22.
[31] Jones, *Later Roman Empire*, 173.
[32] Infra, Ch. IV and VI.
[33] *Cod. Theod.* 16.10.25.
[34] Venance Grumel, *Traité d'Études byzantines I: La chronologie* (Paris 1958), 367.
[35] Infra, Ch. VII, Sect. 1.
[36] Infra, Ch. VIII.

remained open and accessible to persons who sacrificed in spite of
the law: at the Asklepieion in Athens, where private sacrifice seems
to have accompanied incubation for the cure of maladies until the
480's; in the temples at Carrhae-Ḥarrān where the solar, lunar, and
planetary cults were practiced with impunity; and in the Isis temple at Philae where, even if the maintenance of the cult was guaranteed by a treaty with the barbarian Blemmyes and Nobadae, many
Hellenes came to worship openly.[37] Many temples had been "destroyed by the command of the magistrates" (*praecepto magistratuum
destrui*) by this time, but possibly more often than not by the
connivance or direct action of bishops like Marcellus of Apamea (c.
388) and Porphyrius of Gaza (in 402) who supervised the literal
pulverization and burning of the urban temples.[38] Other buildings
continued to stand, however, to which an enterprising Hellene like
the younger Asklepiodotus of Alexandria might gain access. The
latter sacrificed at the closed temple of Isis at Canopus in the 480's.
The place had kept its statuary right under the nose of the patriarch of Alexandria and remained a mecca for the practitioners
of sundry acts of divination and incubation, keeping a Mediterranean-wide reputation, but particularly at Athens, through the
480's.[39] The "destruction" of temples often meant no more than the
removal or storage of the cult effigies, altars, and ornamental
statuary, and in some instances the sealing off of the interior, but
this rule did not apply to the splendid temples in Athens until half a
century after the publication of the law of 435. The bishops or
magistrates often erected the cross to purge such temple buildings
from the taint of the old cults (*conlocatione venerandae Christianae
religionis signi expiari*), as the archaeological record makes clear.[40]
This proved to be a simple expedient in the urban ethos, but in the
countryside, where numinous powers were often thought to inhere
in groves, springs, and stones, monks strode about not only burning
trees and incising crosses on objects of every kind, but physically
making the sign of the cross with a movement of the hand upon
themselves and all who came to them for help, and instructed
persons to perform this act when they passed sites of pagan religious awe.[41] To put it briefly, many shrines "remained intact even

---

[37] Infra, Ch. IX, Sect. 3 (Philae). Ch. IV, Sect. 3 (Athens). On Ḥarrān in
general, see: J.B. Segal, "Pagan Syriac Monuments in the Vilayet of Urfa,"
Anatolian Studies 3 (1953), 97–119. For a translation of Jacob of Sarug's sermon on
the fall of the idols, see: Ibid., 109.
[38] Infra, Ch. II, Sect. 3, and Ch. III, Sect. 4.
[39] Infra, Ch. IV, Sect. 3, and Ch. V, Sect. 2.
[40] Infra, Ch. II, Sect. 2.
[41] Infra, Ch. VII, Sect. 1.

now" (*qua etiam nunc restant integra*) in the phrase of the law, in a material and cultural sense, just as the cross had begun in equal measure to invade the material and cultural ethos of the old cults.

The circumstances of Hellenic cult adumbrated by these recent laws of 423 and 435 had a history of regulation since the times of Constantine the Great (324–337 in the East). The purport of all the earlier legislation is summed up in the comprehensive law of the co-emperors Theodosius the Great, Arcadius, and Honorius given at Constantinople 8 November 392.[42] Although issued to Rufinus, Praetorian Prefect of Oriens (392–395), it was circulated throughout the empire. It proscribed even private sacrifices of devotion—as opposed to those performed for magical purposes—in comprehensive fashion:[43]

> No person of any class or order whatsoever . . . shall sacrifice an innocent victim to senseless images (*carentibus simulacris*) in any place at all or any city. He shall not in secret wickedness kindle lights with fire to a household deity (*lar*), with a wine libation (*merum*) to his genius, with incense to his *penates*, lay incense, or hang garlands, (*serta*).
>
> If anyone bent on sacrifice dares to immolate a victim (*hostia*) or to consult quivering entrails (*spirantia exta*), let the party who was informed against by an accusation permitted to all persons receive the sentence appropriate for treason (*maiestas*), even though he sought nothing contrary to, or against, the welfare of the emperors. For it suffices to constitute an enormous crime that any person should wish to break down the very laws of nature to investigate forbidden matters, to disclose hidden secrets, to attempt forbidden practices, to seek to know the end of another's life, or to promise the hope of another's death.

Penalties for treason were laid on those who sacrificed, the assumption being that where devotional sacrifices existed, the more dangerous, politically motivated sacrifices designed to reveal the names of future monarchs might also crop up or even flourish.[44] The ageing Theodosius the Great can hardly have failed to reckon on the possibility of plots against his young sons, the co-emperors named in the prologue to the law, particularly by persons who used divination as a tool to rally support to a given candidate. This was not, however, the senior emperor's sole intention, for *humiliores*—persons below the legal standing of senators, soldiers, *curiales*, and bishops—who could hardly expect to rise to power, fell under ban as well. Nor can most persons who lit candles, scattered incense or

---

[42] *Cod. Theod.* 16.10.12.
[43] *Cod. Theod.* 16.10.12, *prooem.* and 1.
[44] Infra, Ch. I, Sect. 3.

poured libations to tutelary deities, except certain prominent Hellenes, have often been viewed as potential conspirators. The law is remiss in one sense of its characterization of images: while some Hellenic philosophers and Christian bishops regarded cult effigies as purely material objects, many others of the same ilk regarded them as inhabited by the *numen* of the deity worshipped (pagans) or as the haunt of a bad *daimon* (Christians).[45] For these latter idols were anything but "senseless" or devoid of divine force. The crime of treason theoretically left the perpetrator's life and property forfeit, but its enforcement had gradations of severity which the second section of the law outlines, namely the confiscation of the building where the acts of sacrifice took place.

The second section of the law of 392 provides direct evidence of the Hellenic cults' energetic character in the last decade of the fourth century, as a careful reading reveals:[46]

> But if any person should venerate, by placing incense before them, images made by the work of mortals and destined to suffer the ravages of time, and if, in a ridiculous manner, he should suddenly fear the effigies which he himself has shaped, or should bind a tree with fillets, or should erect an altar of turf that he has dug up, or should attempt to honor vain images with the offering of a gift, which even though it is humble, still is a complete outrage against religion, such a person, as one guilty of the violation of religion, shall be punished by the forfeiture of that house or landholding in which it is proved that he served a pagan superstition. For we decree that all places shall be annexed to our fisc, if it is proved that they have reeked with the vapor of incense, provided, however, that such places are proved to have belonged to such incense-burners.

With the closure of many temples and cessation of the public sacrifices, private individuals, including the *curiales* who held the traditional priesthoods, transferred the cults to their own estates. Where marble altars at the entrances of temples had ceased to exist, men were now erecting turf altars (*erecta effossis ara cespitibus*), often, it seems, near sacred trees which were decorated with fillets (*redimita vittis arbore*).[47] That Hellenes were still buying cult images from the appropriate craftsmen is implicit in the grammar of the law: "if someone should . . . suddenly fear the images which he himself has fashioned" (*Si quis . . . metuens subito quae ipse simulaverit*), the

---

[45] On the subject of animate images, see: Edwyn Bevan, *Holy Images: An Inquiry into Idolatry and Image-Worship in Ancient Paganism and in Christianity* (London 1940), 24–27 and 91–93.

[46] *Cod. Theod.* 16.10.12.2. Quoted mainly from Pharr, *Theodosian Code*, 474.

[47] Cf. the siting of altars in proximity to sacred trees in early Greek, Semitic, and Vedic religion. Mircea Eliade, *Patterns in Comparative Religion* (New York 1958), 269f. and 279f.

fashioner being the person who commissioned the making of the image, although many members of the priesthoods may have cultivated artisan talents in that direction.[48] This fact hardly brings surprise. Marinus of Neapolis indicates that the protagonist of his biography, the Neoplatonist Proclus (ob. 485), sponsored the manufacture of images, and refers to another phenomenon mentioned in the law, the sacrifice of more "humble" offerings (*humiliore licet muneris praemio*) if the cost of animals were prohibitive, as for example incense, whey, and *potana* cakes.[49] The government would discover the difficulty of controlling private sacrifices in the coming centuries, the few cases which crop up in the sources being only the tip of the proverbial iceberg.[50] Even the threat of confiscating buildings and estates would not deter the determined "incense burners" (*turificantes*).

The coemperors regarded those who stole into public temples and their precincts, or the private property of others, to sacrifice, as particularly infamous, as the third section of the law of 392 indicates, probably because access to rural temples, famous and locally known alike, proved difficult to control (*Sin vero in templis fanisve publicis aut in aedibus agrisve alienis tale quispiam sacrificandi genus exercere temptaverit*).[51] A rural Bithynian diviner of the fifth century (c. 443–446) advised his clients to sacrifice at the local idol-temple (εἰδωλεῖον) in order to gain a hearing for their petitions, and practically anyone could gain clandestine admission to the great Isis temple at Canopus near Alexandria after its closure, down to the 480's.[52] Many ancient temples must have stood on the rural estates of landed magnates, *curiales*, and senators. The law provided that scrupulous care be taken to ascertain whether the owner of the property connived at the sacrifice (*si ignorante domino usurpata constiterit*), and only if this proved to be the case was the fine of 25 pounds in gold (1800 *solidi*) to be assessed of the owner, and in

---

[48] I take "fearing" (*metuens*) to mean "manifesting religious awe" in the sense of feeling the necessity to propitiate the divinity represented by the image with sacrifices to preserve the "peace of the gods". There is substantial evidence to suggest that the image at times provoked physical fear as well, because of the *daimon* or *numen* thought to reside within it. The worshipper thus had to "soothe" the divinity with sacrifices in order to avoid provoking a hostile kratophany ("manifestation of power"), or, put another way, its "daimonic rage". Infra, Ch. VII, Sect. 1 (Zeus Bronton?) and Ch. VIII, Sect. 2 (evidently the local Syrian *ba'al*).

[49] Infra, Ch. IX, Sect. 2.

[50] A series of sixth-century examples of this phenomenon are treated in Frank R. Trombley, "Religious Transition in Sixth-Century Syria," *Proceedings of the UCLA Byzantinists' Colloquium*, Sect. 2 (publication data not yet available).

[51] *Cod. Theod.* 16.10.12.3.

[52] Infra, Ch. VII, Sect. 1, and Ch. IX, Sect. 2.

equal measure on the persons who actually perpetrated the ritual.
The amount was, needless to say, quite a small fee to pay in order
to assure the free practice of one's religion for a senator or *curialis*,
whose annual income might be computed in hundreds of thousands
of *solidi*,[53] especially if he gave thought to the relationship between
the peace of the gods and the good harvest. The law betrays the
tendency, on the other hand, for men to borrow the buildings and
lands of others for cultic purposes. One can hardly doubt that
pagan or partially Christianized renters and smallholders at times
made use of a Christian landlord's properties and buildings to
perform sacrifice. Such acts could be used to discredit one's enemies in prefectural, provincial, and urban political infighting, but
the issue of doubt about finding the responsible party hardly viti-
ates the clear purport of the law that clandestine sacrifices were
common c. 392.

The last section of the law of 8 November 392 lodges the respon-
sibility of enforcing its provisions with the governors of the provinces (literally *iudices* here, as they handled cases of criminal
litigation), the city councils, and the defensors of the cities (*iudices ac
defensores et curiales singularum urbium*).[54] Local political conglomer-
ates often had the power to suborn these officials through bribery or
hints to them to look the other way: the law refers to this as
"favoritism" (*gratia*) and "carelessness" (*incuria*), a truly euphemis-
tic characterization. At any rate, the law prescribed a fine with
"judicial action" of unspecified character to punish them, the sum
being 30 pounds in gold or 2160 *solidi*. The toleration of the Olympia with its attendant private sacrifices at Chalcedon by its
archbishop Eulalius and the connivance of the Prefect of the City of
Constantinople Leontius (c. 434–35) suggest that this fine troubled few persons even in ostensibly Christian cities. It was left to
the monks of rural Bithynia, as in the *territorium* of Antioch, to break
up these proceedings. The threat of St. Hypatius of the monastery
at Rufinianae to attack the prefect physically with his fellow archi-
mandrites sufficed to secure the cancellation of the games and
festival.[55] A fine of 30 pounds in gold (2160 *solidi*) fell on a provincial governor who deferred litigation on such matters in the hope of
allotting the case to the "circular file". His *officium* became liable for
that fee collectively as well, presumably if it failed to report his

---

[53] An income of 120,000 *solidi* per annum or above 1,600 pounds in gold was not
uncommon, belonging to the middle range of senatorial incomes. Jones, *Later
Roman Empire*, 554f.

[54] *Cod. Theod.* 16.10.12.4.

[55] Infra, Ch. VII, Sect. 1.

connivance, a potentially serious hardship for low-level bureau-crats even if shared out proportionately to their salaries.

The law of 8 November 392 largely reaffirmed the previous legislation of Theodosius the Great, a series of edicts and rescripts issued over the previous decade between 381–391. They had apparently received little public cooperation. These earlier enact-ments are worth reviewing insofar as they treat the phenomena of cult which persisted into the next century. The first of these pro-scribed diurnal and nocturnal divinatory sacrifices by the "consul-ter of uncertain events" (*incertorum consultor*), who at times did so in sacred precincts and temple buildings.[56] Issued in the names of the co-emperors Gratian, Valentinian II, and Theodosius on 21 De-cember 381 at Constantinople, it reflects the concerns of the last-named, the eastern emperor at the time, and perhaps relates to fear of conspiracies similar to those which gained notoriety in the time of Valens (364–378).[57]

Imperial decree at times allowed temples to remain open as a specific exception to the usual rule if their use was tied to tradi-tional civic festivals, so long as public sacrifice was eschewed. This rule goes back to the law of 30 November 382 issued by Gratian, Valentinian II, and Theodosius to Palladius, *dux* of Osrhoene, the Transeuphratesian province which had Edessa as its capital:[58]

> By the authority of the imperial consistory (*publicum consilium*) we decree that the temple shall be continually open that was formerly dedicated to the assemblage of throngs of people and now also is for the common use of the people, and *in which images are reported to have been placed which must be measured by the value of their art rather than by their divinity*. We do not permit any imperial response that was surrepti-tiously obtained to prejudice this situation. In order that this temple may be seen by the assemblages of the city and by frequent crowds, your experience shall preserve all celebrations of festivities, and by the authority of our imperial response, *you shall permit the temple to be open, but in such a way that the performance of sacrifices forbidden therein may not be supposed to be permitted under the pretext of such access to the temple.*

The address of the law to Palladius, *dux* of Osrhoene, implies that a pious Christian soldier in command of the provincial cavalry *arith-moi* might, on occasion, have interfered with such public ceremonial on the ground that it violated the laws against sacrifice, despite the fact that the provincial governor had jurisdiction over criminal affairs. The primary and initial purpose of the law, therefore, may

---

[56] *Cod. Theod.* 16.10.7.
[57] *Infra*, Ch. I, Sect. 3.
[58] *Cod. Theod.* 16.10.8. Adapted from Pharr, *Theodosian Code*, 473.

have been to resolve conflicts between the civil and military jurisdictions in Osrhoene, having emerged as it did from a resolution of
the imperial consistory (*publici consilii auctoritate*). The civic festivals
of Edessa reveal traces of the survival of the temples and processions mentioned here even in the early sixth century.[59]

The traditional procession of the effigy of Athena in the sacred
boat from the Piraeus to the Akropolis whose survival is attested by
a late fourth-century inscription, probably went on in the next
century as well. Plutarch, son of Nestorius, who appears in the
inscriptions alternately as sophist and philosopher, and who
apparently endowed the Neoplatonic school with considerable
properties, personally funded the Panathenaic procession on three
occasions before his death in 410 (ὃς καὶ τρὶς ποτὶ νηὸν
Ἀθηναίης ἐπέπλασσεν ναῦν ἐλάσας ἱερήν):[60]

> The *demos* of Erechtheus have set up a [statue of] Plutarchos, king of
> [rhetorical and philosophical] discourses, who thrice sailed the
> sacred ship and moored it at the temple of Athena, having poured out
> great wealth.

The occasion certainly required lavish preparations apart from the
construction of the processional vehicles, including meat, wine, and
possibly specie for the participants and onlookers. If no hint of
public sacrifice survives in the inscription, the performance of
private offerings can hardly be doubted, particularly as such personal acts are well attested in Marinus' life of Proclus for the
middle of the next century.[61] The three Panathenaia mentioned in
the inscription probably belong to the last two decades of Plutarch's life, c. 390–410, and most likely well after the promulgation
of the law of 392, which did not derogate the earlier law of 382
concerning non-cultic processions to temples.

Himerius, an Athenian sophist who lived in the reign of Julian
the Apostate (361–363) and died in the 390's, provides a detailed
contemporary description of the Panathenaic procession in his
oration "To Basileios on the Occasion of the Panathenaia at the

---

[59] The chronicle of Joshua the Stylite reports the persistence of a festival at
Edessa "at which the heathen tales were sung" in 497/8 A.D. No sacrifices are
reported, but there took place processions with lit candles, the burning of incense,
vigils, singing, and so forth. Joshua the Stylite, *The Chronicle*, tr. W. Wright
(Cambridge 1882), 20f. Other ceremonies are reported. Ibid., 18, 23, and 35. The
general situation in Syria at this time makes it most probable that private sacrifice
persisted. Supra, Ch. I, n. 50.
[60] *Inscriptiones Graecae 3/2: Inscriptiones Atticae Aetatis Romanae*, ed. W. Dittenberger
(Berlin 1882), no. 3818. On the date, see: H.J. Blumenthal, "529 and Its Sequel:
What Happened to the Academy?" *Byzantion* 48 (1978), 373f.
[61] Infra, Ch. IV, Sect. 3.

Beginning of Spring." Written for Basileios, who as "proconsul" must have been the civil governor of Achaea, this oration, if idealized, represents the kinds of furbishment that a wealthy man like Plutarch will have striven for and devised:[62]

> I wish to relate to you a detailed account about the custom of the city and *panegyris* to which you are coming. It is pleasant and admirable not only to see the Panathenaia for oneself, but even to say something about the Hellenes when the Athenians send the Sacred Trireme to the goddess in this *panegyris*. The ship begins by putting to sea out of the gates as if from some calm harbor. [The Trireme], being moved from there as if against a sea without waves, is pulled through the middle of the thoroughfare, which comes down straight and level from the upper parts [of the city] and separates the stoas arrayed on either side of it, where the Athenians and other folk conduct business [the Agora]. Priests and priestesses, all of them Eupatrids, crowned with garlands, some of gold, others of flowers, are the complement of the ship.
>
> The ship, stately and high in the air, is led in circles as if with sea waves lying beneath, and the priests and priestesses, equipped with many wooden poles athwart, lead the ship (τὸ σκάφος) without hindrance to the hill of Pallas, [the Akropolis]. From there, I think, the goddess overlooks the *panegyris* and the entire holy time of the month (ἱερομηνία). An ode will release the ship's cables, which ode the Athenians sing as a sacred chorus, summoning the wind for the ship that it would be present and fly in the manner of a sacred ship. And the chorus, I surmise, knowing the Kean ode which Simonides set forth in the middle of the sea, follows it directly with lyric poetry (τοῖς μέλεσι), and, as if sending a fair wind, blows against the stern and thus drives the ship (τὴν ὁλκάδα) by the breeze.
>
> There is a story about the Egyptian river Nile that, when the sun rides in the middle of the sky and brings about the summer season, and when [the Nile flood] pours over the land of Egypt and hides the tilled fields, Egypt appears to be the high sea, navigable and fit for ships. But the Sacred Trireme of the Parthenon, not bound by some incredible Egyptian flood, sets forth across dry earth. But clear-voiced breezes from Attic flutes, resounding clearly, drive the ship onward.

Such civic observances as these easily passed the test of the law on processions to temples. No hint of sacrifice exists, and Himerius' view that Athena, a deity often invoked by Proclus a century later, oversees the procession from the Akropolis, is expressed in terms divorced from cult. Such well-turned phrases as these can hardly have evoked the charge of sacrificing to a female *daimon* from a Christian critic. The sponsor of the Panathenaic procession had to provide the monies for building the Sacred Trireme, the timber

---

[62] Himerius, *Declamationes et Orationes*, ed. Aristides Colonna (Rome 1951), 194f.

needed for the poles to push the vessel, the gold and floral garlands, and the musical instruments. It seems that the Eupatrid priests and priestesses, obviously members of the curial class, also formed the chorus, with their education in the Greek *paideia* assisting the task of lyric recitation. The sponsor of the festival presumably funded a public banquet as well, a survival of the old liturgy connected with public sacrifice. One can hardly imagine interference with private acts of sacrifice amidst the crowding of the inner city during the Panathenaic procession. It seems probable that ordinary pious Christians could and did participate in the festivities as onlookers. Nor can it be doubted that Christian Athenian Eupatrids, men and women of curial rank, would feel a degree of social pressure and personal longing to participate in these doings, tied as they were to the Greek *paideia*. This rule would apply particularly to recent converts.[63] Himerius not only sums up Simonides' Kean ode, but also quotes a phrase, "most beautiful of all stars" (ἀστέρων πάντων ὁ κάλλιστος), from Sappho, Fragment 133, in his oration.[64]

To return to the law of 30 November 382, an urban community known for its avoidance of sacrifice such as Edessa could easily rely on imperial favor in keeping its temples open. In places where the old cults were deeply entrenched like Athens, little choice existed except to tolerate the public ceremonial in the pious hope that private sacrifices would be kept to the minimum.[65] The statues were themselves to be contemplated as works of art rather than as the antitypes of deities wherein the *numen* might reside (*simulacra feruntur posita artis pretio quam divinitate metienda*). Even the traditional public vows (*vota*) at temples, an annual ceremony of Roman Republican origin, might be celebrated so long as sacrifices did not vitiate established law (*omni votorum celebritate servata auctoritate nostri*). This law remained in general force as a result of the Theodosian codification despite the provisions of the comprehensive law of 8 November 392, which seem to contradict it.

The essence of the three other early laws of Theodosius the Great put in the codification of 438 require notice primarily because of the ongoing phenomena of which they provide an adequate description. Thus the law of 25 May 385, given at Constantinople, was included because of the continuing Etruscan practice of examining the livers of sacrificial victims:[66]

---

[63] For the Christian Eupatrids of Athens, cf. infra, Ch. IV, Sect. 1.
[64] Himerius (Colonna, 195).
[65] On the control of civil life in Athens by prominent Hellenes, cf. infra, Ch. IV, Sect. 2 and 4.
[66] *Cod. Theod.* 16.10.9. Quoted from Pharr, *Theodosian Code*, 473.

No mortal shall assume the audacity of performing sacrifices, so that by the inspection of the liver and the presage of the entrails of the sacrificial victims, he may obtain the hope of a vain promise, or, what is worse, he may learn the future by an accursed consultation. The torture of a very bitter punishment shall threaten those persons who, in violation of our prohibition, attempt to explore the truth of present or future events.

The rhetoric is striking. The second of these laws, that of 24 February 391, given at Milan, simply takes up the issue of sacrificing an innocent victim (*insontem victimam*) and of entering a temple "whether on the road or in a city for the purpose of adoration" (*vel in itinere vel in urbe adoraturus*). This phrase points once again to the frequenting of rural temples, as if in the mind of the Hellene sacrificing outside the city limit somehow mitigated the offense. The law stipulated a fine of 15 pounds in gold.[67] The later comprehensive law of 8 November 392 erased this penalty and indicated the less precise but more dangerous "competent sentence according to the precedent of treason" (*ad exemplum maiestatis . . . sententiam competentem*), which might entail the execution of the criminal.[68]

The third law, published 16 June 391 and sent to Evagrius the Augustal Prefect of Egypt and Romanus Count of Egypt, had more specific conditions in view:[69]

Let the power of sacrificing be granted to no one, let no one make the rounds of the temples, let no one honor shrines. Let them recognize that profane access is restricted for them by the obstacle of our law to the extent that, if someone contrives anything at all concerning the gods or things sacred contrary to our prohibition, he deprives himself of any acts of mercy (*indulgentiis*). If any governor or nome official (*iudex*) enters polluted places (*polluta loca*) during the tenure of his administration, sacrilegious defiler that he is, he shall be compelled to pay our fisc (*aerarium*) fifteen pounds in gold, and his *officium* an equal sum, unless they resisted him with their combined force.

Conditions in Egypt following this date, and that of the codification of 438, turn all this rhetoric into something of a joke. Neither this law nor later edicts set up any such obstacle (*nostrae legis obstaculum*), except in some unusually sensational cases. Persons still made the rounds of the temples (*nemo templa circumeat*)—an ironic phrase—even in the 480's, for access to the Isis temple at Canopus proved

---

[67] *Cod. Theod.* 16.10.10.
[68] *Cod. Theod.* 16.10.12.1.
[69] *Cod. Theod.* 16.10.11.

easy despite its closure.[70] The Nile river winds some 200 miles
between Canopus on the doorstep of Alexandria and the southern
terminus of the province of Aegyptus, where the Thebaid begins.
The Augustal Prefect and his *officium* resided at Alexandria, a city
with a fair measure of political, ecclesiastical, and administrative
headaches.[71] It must have fallen to the Count of Egypt to police
sectors outside the Delta, but he can hardly have acted except in
response to specific complaints, the frequency of which is unknown,
due to the distances over which he operated. The law seems to have
been a retroactive confirmation of the behavior of Theophilus,
patriarch of Alexandria (385–412), who led the urban *demos* in the
destruction of the Serapeum earlier that year, the great temple of
Sarapis which had given the city, in the phrase of the Hellene
Eunapius of Sardis, "the semblance of a sacred world" (ἱερά τις ἦν
οἰκουμένη).[72] The Greek ecclesiastical historians of the next century, Sozomen, Socrates, and Theodoret of Cyrrhus, treated this
act as if it were the end of the pagan cults of Aegyptus proper by
simply defaulting on the discussion of later cases. Canopus aside,
entirely different conditions prevailed up the river in First and
Second Thebais, where Shenute of Atripe, hegumen of the White
Monastery, led a truly popular war of great intensity against the
temples and priesthoods there during the next century.[73]

   The law of 391 appears to represent an attempt to mop up the
resistance of the Hellenes to the *fait accompli* of the destruction of the
Serapeum in Aegyptus only, the business of the Thebaic provinces
being left to future edicts which never came or to existing laws. The
Hellenes of Alexandria had apparently in the meantime taken their
business to other temples in the Delta region, like the temenos of
Isis at Canopus, which were outside the immediate grasp of patriarch Theophilus and the mob of monks and secular zealots who
had participated in the mayhem and demolitions of 391. Theophilus later led his retainers out to Canopus, some 14 kilometers
north-northeast of Alexandria, inflicted some damage on the temenos, and dispersed the Hellenes there. The Canopic temple had
apparently become the cult center and rallying point of the Alexan-

   [70] For detailed analysis of urban and rural Egypt, see infra, Ch. II, Sect. 3,
Ch. V, and Ch. IX.
   [71] *Praefectus Augustalis* is for some reason not indexed in Jones, *Later Roman
Empire.*
   [72] Eunapius of Sardis, *Lives of the Philosophers and Sophists,* tr. Wilmer C. Wright
(London-Cambridge, Mass. 1921), 420, lines 2f. For the date, see John B. Bury,
History of the Later Roman Empire from the Death of Theodosius I to the Death Justinian, 1
(London 1923), 368f. This work is hereinafter cited as Bury, LRE 1.
   [73] Infra, Ch. IX, Sect. 1.

drian Hellenes, but had a prestigious reputation throughout the Mediterranean world and received many visitors.[74] Theophilus' liquidation gangs did not finish the job, as the idols, a rudimentary priesthood, and the repute of the place survived for nearly another century, until its final incineration during the patriarchate of Peter III Mongus (482–489).[75] The decline of the cults in the Nile delta and basin owed more to the unofficial war in the countryside conducted by the patriarch and his monks against the temples and to the general decline in Hellenic belief than to imperial edicts, which in this instance merely underwrote a process already under way with the promise of civil and military support.

There remains the task of examining the legislation of the co-emperors Arcadius and Honorius, and of their successors. This aimed to supplement that of Theodosius the Great which, as has been seen, was embodied most fully in the comprehensive law of 8 November 392.[76] Apart from the two very late laws of 423 and 435 that were considered at the beginning of this section, there were *eleven* laws issued on the problem of ongoing sacrifice and other phenomena of late Hellenism between 7 August 395 and 8 June 423. Of these, probably seven were given at either Rome or Ravenna, and applied to conditions prevailing in the western provinces, including Africa and Spain. Every one of these laws was issued in the names of the co-emperors East and West, and had binding force throughout the Roman *oikoumene*. The commission which codified the imperial edicts at Constantinople in 438 perhaps saw the relevance of these laws to conditions in the East and included them in the selection, but caution is indicated here, as the codification was intended to be comprehensive rather than selective, and was completed with a view to its eventual ratification by the Senate at Rome and the western emperor Valentinian III (425–455). On balance, one is inclined to treat the laws addressing conditions in Italy, Africa, and Spain with some skepticism when looking for evidence about the state of affairs in the eastern provinces, except where such phenomena have a universal attestation or are inherently probable. The problems of interpretation connected with these suppositions are considerable.

The earliest of these eleven laws, given 7 August 395 at Constantinople, aimed at tightening up the enforcement of existing laws

---

[74] Rufinus of Aquileia, *Historia Ecclesiastica* 2.26. The incident is discussed in detail infra, Ch. II, Sect. 3. For the edition of this text used, cf. infra, Ch. II, n. 135.

[75] Infra, Ch. IX, Sect. 2.

[76] *Cod. Theod.* 16.10.12.

respecting heretics as well as pagans. After indicating that the
latter had continued to enter temples and perform sacrifices, the
law requires provincial and urban officials to enforce the laws of
Theodosius the Great, including the imposition of fines, confiscations, and executions. The law prescribes capital punishment for
provincial governors (*moderatores*) remiss in diligence.[77] These officials had to contend with wealthy, powerfully entrenched local
factions, and the choices proved to be difficult, but no evidence has
come to light in this inquiry to suggest that any governor was
actually punished for such negligence, nor is it probable in light of
the cases of Gaza and Carrhae-Ḥarrān, whose cults enjoyed tacit
imperial toleration after 395.[78] One could hardly convict provincial
governors of complicity with the local Hellenes if the government in
Constantinople itself turned a blind eye to these abuses. The unofficial pretext for tolerating the cults of Gaza lay in the emperor
Arcadius' concern for its revenues.[79] The reasons in the case of
Carrhae-Ḥarrān are unknown.

The priesthoods of the urban Hellenic elites survived until this
time. The law of 7 December 396 given at Constantinople revoked
the privileges given them by previous emperors:[80]

> Let the privileges which were conceded by ancient law to the minis-
> ters, prefects, and hierophants of sacred mysteries, or by whatever
> name they are called, be altogether abolished. Let them not con-
> gratulate themselves that they are fortified by a privilege whose
> profession (*professio*) is known to be condemned by law.

The origin and nature of these privileges is difficult to trace, but
some must have derived from the not so long-past reign of Julian

---

[77] *Cod. Theod.* 16.10.13.
[78] Infra, Ch. III, Sect. 2. This is not the place to cite the very extensive
literature about the survival of Semitic polytheism at Carrhae-Ḥarrān. For a
relatively recent summary with bibliography, see: Ilse Rochow, "Zu einigen
oppositionellen religösen Strömungen," *Byzanz im 7. Jahrhundert: Untersuchungen zur
Herausbildung des Feudalismus*, ed. F. Winkelmann (Berlin 1978) 233–236. Cf. J.B.
Segal, "Pagan Syriac Monuments in the Vilayet of Urfa," *Anatolian Studies* 3
(1953), 97–120. Idem, "The Sabian Mysteries. The Planet Cult of Ancient Har-
ran," *Vanished Civilizations*, ed. E. Bacon (London 1963), 201–220. For an early
sixth-century Christian polemic against the cults of the city, see: J.P. Martin,
"Discours de Jacques de Sarroug sur la chute des idoles," *Zeitschrift des Deutschen
Morgenländischen Vereins* 29 (1875), 107–147. For an overview and digest of several
decades of research, see: Han Drijvers, "The Persistence of Pagan Cults and
Practices in Christian Syria," *East of Byzantium: Syria and Armenia in the Formative
Period*, ed. Nina G. Garsoian et alii (Washington, D.C. 1982), 35–43, with the
standard bibliography.
[79] Infra, Ch. III, Sect. 2.
[80] *Cod. Theod.* 16.10.14.

the Apostate (361–363), whose imprint still lay heavily on the
Roman state, as with the still enforced reunification of Christian
Maiuma and pagan Gaza.[81] It is conceivable that Julian's grant of
grain and wine from the imperial estates in Asia Minor to the
priesthood of Kybele at Pessinus in Second Galatia was still in
force, particularly as it contributed to the public welfare.[82] The
Christianization of parts of Galatia may have lagged behind for this
reason. The mention of hierophants, that is the priesthoods of
mystery cults like that of the Eleusinian Demeter and Persephone,
suggests the continuation of a viable priesthood there, notwithstanding the statement of the pagan historian Eunapius of Sardis
that the ancient Eumolpid family, the repository of the cult, had
died out, leaving the office to a candidate from Thespiae.[83] The
learned Hellene doubtless disliked the lowered tone of the Eleusinian cult and found the change of dynasty after a millenium tanta-
mount to the extinction of the cult. The temenos apparently
suffered extensive damage shortly before the enactment of the law,
in 396, as a result of Alaric's Goths' having plundered Attica.[84] Not
surprisingly, our biased and, in this instance, dubious authority
Eunapius has it that monks accompanying the barbarians caused
this destruction.[85] The privileges granted to Eleusis apparently
dated from the reign of the tolerant co-emperors Valens and Valentinian I (c. 364–375), who permitted the continuation of the
Eleusinian mysteries after the proconsul of Achaea made the plea
that their suppression would cause the Greeks to find life not worth
living.[86]

Three edicts issued in the West in 399 pertaining to the disposition of temple buildings had sufficient relevance to general conditions to merit being included in the Theodosian Code some forty
years later. The first of these, given at Ravenna on 29 January 399
and sent to the Vicar of Spain and the Five Provinces, forbade
private persons to dismantle the ornamental blocks of public buildings (*publicorum operum ornamenta*), that is the pagan temples which
had reverted to the *res privata* of the emperors. Those who performed such acts of spoliation probably belonged to the curial class

---

[81] Infra, Ch. III, Sect. 1.
[82] Infra, Ch. II, Sect. 5.
[83] The man from Thespiae held the hieratic rank of *pater* in the cult of Mithra at
the time of his succession to the Eumolpids. Eunapius, *Lives of the Philosophers*
(Wright, 436f.).
[84] Bury, LRE 1, 119f.
[85] Ibid., 370, Eunapius, *Lives of the Philosophers* (Wright, 438f.).
[86] Bury, LRE 1, 368, Infra, Ch. I, Sect. 4.

and wished to embellish their townhouses and country estates. The law required "dug-up documents of whatever kind" (*erutae huiusmodi chartae*) to be produced in order to verify one's right to dismantle a temple.[87] It is worth noting in this connection that Porphyrius, bishop of Gaza, proceeded against the temples of his city around this time only after arming himself with imperial rescripts that he could present to the provincial governor, the duovirs of Gaza, and the city council.[88]

The second western law of 399, given at Patavium on 20 August and addressed to the governor of Africa Proconsularis, indicates that certain parties were demolishing empty temples on the ground that persons had entered them and performed sacrifice. The authors of these acts were probably bishops, unless they were decurions looking for a pretext to get decorative materials for their own private buildings. The co-emperors ruled that, if the structure of the temple buildings proved to be sound (*ut aedificiorum quidem sit integer status*), and no real justification thus existed for dismantling the building, it should be left intact and the perpetrators of the sacrifice be prosecuted after the idols had been removed and deposited with the local authorities (*depositis sub officio idolis*), the idols "on which it is clear that the cult of vain superstition depends *even now*" (*quibus etiam nunc patuerit cultum vanae superstitionis impendi*).[89] The law speaks well for the importance of images in pagan cult c. 400. It sets up the implicit rule, *mutatis mutandis*, that idols might only be removed if sacrifice in front of them could be proven. The Hellenes of Athens undoubtedly owed the long preservation of the images of Asklepios and the chryselephantine Athena in the Asklepieion and Parthenon as late as the early 480's to the scrupulous observance of the rule against clandestine sacrifice at temples.[90] The surviving priesthoods of some cities will have policed the precincts of their temples against such violations of the law.

The third law of 399, given on 10 July to Eutychianus, Praetorian Prefect of Oriens, gave up rural temples to random destruction:[91]

> If there are temples in the countryside (*in agris templa*), let them be demolished without mobs and riots (*sine turba ac tumultu*). For after they have been cast down and levelled, every occasion for superstition will be destroyed.

---

[87] *Cod. Theod.* 16.10.18.
[88] Infra, Ch. III, Sect. 4.
[89] *Cod. Theod.* 16.10.18.
[90] Infra, Ch. IV, Sect. 2 and 3.
[91] *Cod. Theod.* 16.10.16.

The law presumably had it in mind that civil officials should publicly notify villagers and estate owners, and thereby forbid any resistance to the destruction of their shrines, even when the demolition gangs consisted of bishops or monks. One thinks here of Marcellus, archbishop of Apamea, the metropolis of Second Syria, who initiated what amounted to a war in the *territorium* of his city c. 388 and was finally killed while directing a band that included gladiators against a rural temple at Aulon.[92] The survival of rural temples, groves, sacred stones, *daimon*-inhabited springs, altars beside numinous trees, and so forth certainly gave life to the local cults. The accounts of such places being destroyed in the fifth century are all consistent in reporting the complete absence of resistance by villagers to the forays of monks and clerics against their shrines in Bithynia, northern Syria, and the Nile valley.[93] One partial exception to this rule concerns Hypatius, hegumen of the monastery at Rufinianae in Bithynia, who hesitated to send his usually vigorous monks against a building (οἶκος), probably an abandoned temple, which housed some forty men who performed sacrifices (c. 443–446). The monks, who perhaps anticipated resistance and could not rouse the partially Christianized peasantry to action, prudently waited to dismantle the place until its occupants had abandoned it. The latter had on one occasion badly beaten a Christian and probably outmatched their Christian monastic counterparts in numbers and physical strength.[94]

Three of the edicts incorporated into the Theodosian Code have a strictly local context, but ended up there because of a certain general relevance. The first of these, addressed to Curtius, Praetorian Prefect of Italy, Africa, and Illyricum and given at Rome, took away the *annonae*, that is the imperial donations of grain, from the temples on the grounds of military necessity, the grants being transferred to the soldiery.[95] The existence of these grants at the late date of this edict, 15 November 408, is plausible in Italy because of traditionalist senatorial opinion, which had by this time obtained many concessions for the old cults,[96] and perhaps in

---

[92] Infra, Ch. II, Sect. 3.
[93] Infra, Ch. VII–IX.
[94] Infra, Ch. VII, Sect. 1.
[95] *Cod. Theod.* 16.10.19 *prooem.*
[96] Jones, *Later Roman Empire*, 33. The emperor Gratian is said to have ordered the confiscation of the revenues (but not of the estates themselves) of the Vestal Virgins in 381, but this information does not derive from an imperial edict. Ibid., 163. Later petitions of pagan senators for the restoration of these incomes were brushed aside. Ibid., 168. One of the concessions planned to gain the support of pagan senators during the rebellion of Eugenius and Arbogast was the reopening of this question. Ibid., 168f.

Africa. Temples which looked after the public welfare, as for example
the *hieron* of Kybele at Pessinus, constituted a class of institutions
which may have kept their *annonae* until this time.[97] The record for
Africa stands in a vast array of sources which lie beyond the scope of
this study to examine. It seems that the local landowners there had
great power,[98] perhaps sufficient to influence the Praetorian Prefect to
maintain the *templorum annonae*. Nor had the old opinions died out.
One hears of Possidius, bishop of Calama, attempting to break up a
"traditional procession" in 408, the same year as this law, and nearly
being killed in the riot which followed.[99] The words of Augustine
suggest something more virulent:[100]

> Accept in a few words [my account] of what happened, and discern
> for yourself the guilty from the innocent.
> Contrary to the most recent laws, a sacrilegious ceremony of the
> pagans was roused on the sixth Kalends of June, with no one attempt-
> ing to prevent it (*nemine prohibente*). With great daring such as never
> occurred in the times of Julian [the Apostate], a threatening crowd of
> leaping people directly passed the gates of the church in the same
> town (*in eodem prorsum vico fores transiret ecclesiae*). When the clerics tried
> to prevent this most illegal and undignified business the church was
> stoned. Then, eight days later, after the bishop had put the well-
> known law into effect and while the matter was being litigated, the
> church was stoned again, as though those people were not disposed to
> carry out the provisions of the law.
> On the next day . . ., as if they had been put in a state of fear by
> some divine power (*ut vel divinitus terrerentur*), the mob returned in
> large numbers with rock-throwings (*lapidationibus*). After carrying
> this out, they brought about a third rock-throwing incident on the
> spot, and after that set fire to the church buildings and attacked our
> own men. They killed one of the servants of God who happened to
> come upon those of the mob. While some others hid where they were
> able and others fled, the bishop, driven by force and hard-pressed,
> hid himself in a certain place where he could hear the voices of those
> people screaming for him and calling for his death, because they had
> gratuitously perpetrated a crime greater than can be imagined [and
> wanted no witness].
> Not one of those whose authority carries weight (i.e. the *curiales*)
> tried to help, except a certain non-resident [of Calama] (*peregrinus*),
> through whom many of the servants of God (i.e. the clergy) were
> freed from the hands of men trying to kill them, and also many
> objects taken by those plunderers. He also made it clear that such
> things ought not to be done readily or at all, that they should desist
> from what had been begun if they were citizens [of Calama], and that
> the decurions (*primates*) forbid any more of this being done.

---

[97] Infra, Ch. II, Sect. 5.
[98] Peter Brown, *Augustine of Hippo* (Berkeley 1967), 420.
[99] Brown, *Augustine of Hippo*, 287f.
[100] Augustine, *Epistle* 91, 8–10, PL 33, 317f.

Augustine adds that the whole lot of the rioters were pagans (*ipsos paganos*).[101] The fact that no one intervened to prevent the procession (*nemine prohibente*) suggests that the town council (*primates*) and urban population of Calama had at very least a considerable pagan minority, as does the fact that, as Augustine puts it, "in that entire city, you cannot distinguish the innocent from the guilty, but perhaps only the less guilty from the guilty."[102] This event roughly coincided with, and resembles, the pagan riot against Porphyrius and the Christian churches of Gaza, a city in which the Christians remained a distinct minority even in the first quarter of the fifth century.[103]

The law of 408 goes on to discuss the usual business of pulling down cult images to their bases (*simulacra . . . suis sedibus evellantur*), destroying altars (*arae*), and the transfer of temple buildings to other uses. The third clause of the law sets forth a stricture concerning public funerary rites:[104]

> It shall not be permitted at all to hold convivial banquets in honor of a sacrilegious rite in places defiled by tombs or to celebrate any religious rite. (*Non liceat omnino in honorem sacrilegi ritus funestioribus locis exercere convivia vel quicquam sollemnitatis agitare.*)

The bishops were supposed to enforce the law and provincial governors were to be fined twenty pounds in gold for negligence in adjudicating such practices. They were evidently quite common, as pagans and Christians had burial grounds and *nekropoleis* in every city, and sometimes shared the same funerary places. Priests would sometimes officiate at the Hellenic rites, as an epigram of Gregory of Nazianzus (ob. c. 390) indicates. The district was Cappadocia and the Armenian borderlands:[105]

---

[101] In *Ep.* 91, 10, Augustine refers to the perpetrators of the assault at Calama as "the pagans unaided" or "the pagans for their part" (*ipsos paganos*). F. van der Meer has discussed the African pagans of Augustine's experience in exceptional detail, referring to them as a "dwindling minority". *Augustine the Bishop*, tr. B. Battershaw and G.R. Lamb (New York-London 1961), 29–75. To this magisterial account might be added the statements of Augustine himself about adult conversions in the *De Civitate Dei* 1.38 and 22.8. The latter passage names a physician and an actor from the village of Curubis as recent recipients of baptism.

[102] Augustine, *Ep.* 91,9. PL 33, 317.

[103] Infra, Ch. III, Sect. 2.

[104] *Cod. Theod.* 16.10.19.3.

[105] *Greek Anthology* 8.175. The text used hereinafter is that found in *The Greek Anthology*, tr. W.R. Paton, 5 vols. (New York-London 1916–18). I am unable to agree with Georg Petzl that this epigram and those following were specifically intended to reflect the monuments at Nimrud Dag in Cappadocia. "Die Epigramme des Gregor von Nazianz über Grabräuberei und das Hierothesion des

They solemnly celebrate unclean banquets to *daimones*, as many as wished in former times to perform service for *daimones*. We Christians found release from this business, and established spiritual meetings with our martyrs. But now a certain dread grips me. Listen, revellers, you desert us for daimonic figures carved in relief.

The last line of the epigram contains a pun, with "daimonic figures carved in relief" (τοὺς δαιμονικοὺς τύπους) having the additional sense of "acts of pagan religion". The epigram is addressed "to those who feast luxuriously in martyr-chapels" (πρὸς τοὺς ἐν μαρτυρίοις τρυφῶντας), recently converted Hellenes who persisted in the old funerary customs. Their practices provide a not so dim idea of what phenomena the law of 408 had in mind. The celebrants (νεκροκόμοι) might invite a priest of the old religion (θυηπόλος) to funerary services in *nekropoleis* of mixed cult:[106]

Thrice worthy of death! You have mixed the bodies of the unclean with martyrs, and the tombs have a priest somewhere about.

The learned Gregory sums up the business of funerary *convivia* in terms which apply to both Christians and Hellenes:[107]

If the contests [of martyrdom] are dear to dancers, then let debauchery be dear to martyrs. But these things are opposite. As it is, contests are not dear to dancers, nor is debauchery to martyrs. How is it, then, that you bring silver, wine, food, and belchings as gifts to martyrs?

Or again:[108]

I witness, O martyrs! The belly-lovers have made your honor an insult. You seek neither a fine-smelling table nor cooks!

The relevance of the edict of 15 November to the social tendencies of Hellenic religion can thus be seen. The continuation of these practices in that milieu explains the inclusion of that law in the codification of 438.

The second law of this African group, given at Ravenna on 30 August 415, provides considerable information about the social and economic underpinnings of cults. It repeats the rule that temples and their lands assigned to the imperial fisc or *res privata* be repos-

---

kommagenischen Königs Antiochos I.," *Epigraphica Anatolica* 10 (1987), 121f. Grave-breaking and funerary sacrifice were a common enough social phenomenon to be addressed without reference to this site.

[106] *Greek Anthology* 8.170. John Callahan, Professor Emeritus of Classics at Georgetown University and a participant in the Dumbarton Oaks Gregory of Nyssa project, was kind enough to discuss the philology of this passage with me.

[107] *Greek Anthology* 8.166.

[108] *Greek Anthology* 8.169.

sessed from illegal usufruct arrangements. This principle was to be observed not only in Africa, but "throughout all the regions situated in our world" (*per omnes regiones in nostro orbe positas*), that is all parts of the empire, for the decree came in the name of the co-emperors Honorius and Theodosius II.[109] Certain cultic officials are also named. In the first instance, the Frediani, Dendrophori, and other pagan cult guilds (*professiones gentilicae*) are spoken of as a thing of the past.[110] One thinks, for example, of the guild of the cult of Kybele ("Mother of the Gods") attested at Tomi, later in the province of Scythia Minor, in the third century, where the deity is called "Mother of the Dendrophoroi" (μήτηρ δενδροφόρων).[111] A later section of the law, however, mentions the continuing existence of Chiliarchs and Centonarii, cultic officials who perhaps supervised the distribution of sacrificial meats to the public.[112] The edict attached capital punishment even to assuming these titles, irrespective of the actual performance of sacrifice, whether public or private. One other section of the law prescribes the removal of cult images—as opposed to mere statuary—from bath-houses and other places of public association (*ab usibus lavacrorum vel publicis affectibus*) on the ground that they offered fresh cause for error.[113] Any image which had been the object of sacrifices thus might, in theory, provoke new ones, whether clandestinely at the site or later in private. This regulation did not interfere with the effigies still kept in temples, like the chryselephantine Athena in the Parthenon which was apparently not dismantled until the 480's.[114]

A final group of laws deals with the persons of the Hellenes, both those who continued to sacrifice and those who eschewed such acts. The first of these, given at Constantinople on 7 December 416 to Aurelianus, Praetorian Prefect of Oriens for the third time, provides that "those persons polluted with the defiled error of pagan rite or crime, that is pagans" (*qui profano pagani ritus errore seu crimine polluuntur, hoc est gentiles*), not be admitted to military office (*militia*) or administrative positions such as provincial governorships.[115] Governors who sacrificed could hardly be expected to enforce the imperial edicts proscribing those rites. Catechumens filled many low-level administrative posts in Constantinople, as the biography

---

[109] *Cod. Theod.* 16.10.20.1.
[110] *Cod. Theod.* 16.10.20.2.
[111] *Inscriptiones Graecae ad Res Romanas Pertinentes*, ed. R. Cagnat *et al.* I (Paris 1911), no. 614.
[112] *Cod. Theod.* 16.10.20.4.
[113] *Cod. Theod.* 16.10.20.3.
[114] *Infra*, Appendix III.
[115] *Cod. Theod.* 16.10.21.

of St. Hypatius of Rufinianae indicates.[116] The force of the edict
concerned not non-Christians in general or Hellenes who played at
the catechumenate for reasons of professional advancement, but
only those who made a practice of sacrificing. The law thus arti-
ficially narrowed the definition of the so-called *gentiles*.

The fundamental failure of coercive measures against sacrifice to
affect public behavior at large finds its fullest expression in the law
of 8 June 423 given at Constantinople:[117]

> The confiscation of goods and exile (*bonorum proscriptio ac exilium*) will
> coerce the pagans who have survived (*paganos qui supersunt*), if they
> are at any time caught in sacrifices to the pagan gods, although they
> deserve capital punishment.

The relative leniency of this regulation stands parallel to another
edict also given at Constantinople on the same date:[118]

> But we especially command those persons who are truly Christians or
> are said to be, that they shall not abuse the authority of religion and
> dare to lay violent hands on Jews and pagans who are living quietly
> and attempting nothing disorderly or contrary to the law. For if such
> Christians should be violent against persons living in security or
> should plunder their goods, they shall be compelled to restore not
> only that property which they took away, but after suit they shall also
> be compelled to restore triple or quadruple that amount which they
> robbed. Also the governors of the provinces and their office staffs and
> the provincials shall know that if they permit such a crime to be
> committed, they too shall be punished in the same way as the
> perpetrators of the crime.

Acts of violence against pagans on the pretext of religion are
attested mainly in connection with the destruction of temples.[119]
Yet the attacks of the monks which Libanius attests against groups
allegedly performing sacrifices in the *territorium* of Antioch must
have gone on indefinitely, as is confirmed by this edict.[120]

Examples of such behavior in the cities are for the most part
lacking. An attack upon Jews and at least one Hellene occurred at
Alexandria in Egypt in March 415.[121] The latter was Hypatia,
daughter of Theon the mathematician. This exceptional woman
expounded the Neoplatonic philosophy of Plotinus, and numbered
Synesius of Cyrene among her pupils.[122] Palladas, her contempo-

---

[116] Infra, Ch. VII, Sect. 1.
[117] *Cod. Theod.* 16.10.23.
[118] *Cod. Theod.* 16.10.24, mainly quoted from Pharr, *Theodosian Code*, 476.
[119] Infra, Ch. II, Sect. 3. Ch. III, Sect. 4.
[120] Libanius, *Or.* 30 *Pro Templis* (Norman 2, 106–111).
[121] Bury, LRE 1, 217–220.
[122] Ibid., 218, n. 1.

rary, a poet and Hellene of Alexandria, wrote near doggerel verse in praise of her,[123] a feeling commensurate with her public renown in the city. She enjoyed close relations with Orestes, the Augustal Prefect of Egypt. Orestes had a Nitrian monk executed after the latter had heaved a stone at him in the wake of the anti-Jewish riot and the subsequent controversy between the Prefect and Cyril, patriarch of Alexandria (412–444), over the latter's order to the populace to expel the Jews and plunder their property. In reprisal, the *parabalani* of the see of Alexandria, laymen who tended the sick, waylaid Hypatia and murdered her with malicious violence, stripping her and then tearing off her skin with sharpened potsherds (ὀστράκοις ἀνεῖλον), this in the church called the Kaisareion. After this act of desecration, the Christians "or those who are called such", to borrow a clause from the edict under consideration (*Christianis, qui vel vere sunt vel esse dicuntur*), dismembered her body and burned the parts at a site called the Kinaron. Even our Christian authority for these transactions, the fifth-century ecclesiastical historian Socrates, recoils in horror at the deed.[124] The Augustal Prefect Orestes claimed to be himself a Christian. When the Nitrian monks accused him of idol-worship and of being a Hellene, and used other select epithets, he reminded them of his baptism by Atticus, patriarch of Constantinople (406–425).[125] Orestes was despite this suspected of cryptopaganism, perhaps because of his association with Hypatia, perhaps for more factual reasons. His baptism had taken place only recently, during the first nine years of Atticus' episcopate. As Orestes will have been well advanced in years by then, the monks may have interpreted this act as one dictated by expediency and for the sake of career advancement. At any rate, even Hellenes like Hypatia who punctiliously avoided sacrifice risked injury, as did Christian officials suspected of such acts.[126] Doubtless few assaults on ordinary Hellenes had the heinous character of those perpetrated by the *parabalani* of Alexandria, but they persisted until the time of the law of 423 and beyond to 438, the year of the Theodosian codification.

The status of the Hellenic cults *circa* 438 appears, in the light of the collected edicts of the Theodosian Code, to have changed little qualitatively since the early fifth century. The temples, with some exceptions like the Parthenon and Asklepieion in Athens, or the shrine of Isis at Philae, had been closed, dismantled, or converted

---

[123] *Greek Anthology* 9.400. Cf. Bury, LRE 1, 217, n. 1.
[124] Socrates, HE 7.15 (PG 67, 768A–769A).
[125] Socrates, HE 7.14 (PG 67, 765B).
[126] For some reason Bury regards Orestes as an out and out pagan. LRE 1, 218.

to other uses, including employment as Christian churches. The
public sacrifice of ancient tradition had finally disappeared, but the
processions that accompanied them endured much longer. Private
sacrifice persisted despite all penalties. Its frequency dictated
leniency, as the confiscation of real property and exile, that is
exilium, which had a legal limit of ten years, were substituted for
capital punishment in one of the laws of 423.[127] Quantitatively,
however, much had changed. The fact that emperor Theodosius II
had supposed in the edict of 9 April 423 that no pagans survived
within the empire suggests the *visible Christianization of the cities*, and
such an impression was not far off the mark.[128] The casual observer
might even have taken Gaza in First Palestine for a Christian city
around the year 410. The oecumenical cult of the Cretan-born Zeus
Marnas had seemingly perished with the demolition of the Marneion and the reuse of the temenos for the Eudoxiana, a Christian
church, but the surviving pagans constituted the great majority of
the urban population there, and revered the blocks despoiled from
the shrine used to pave the courtyard in front of the new basilica.[129]
Appearances sometimes deceived.

The Christian religion had made even fewer inroads into the
countryside. In isolated districts villages remained pagan even at
the end of the sixth century, as the epigraphic evidence from the
eastern Hauran plain in the province of Arabia suggests.[130] In other
parts of Syria and Asia Minor, the process of Christianization was
completed only in the mid-sixth century.[131] Rural districts in the
territoria of the great Christian cities sometimes accepted the new
religion quickly. For the Limestone Massif east of Antioch, the
period of Christianization was circa 365–425, quite an early date,
but the failure of resurgent Hellenism under Julian the Apostate
within close proximity partially explains this phenomenon. The
villages there were rebuilt in the fourth century and after, to be
settled by prosperous folk, literate in Greek, who profited from
increased olive-oil production and its sale in Antioch. Across the
cultural frontier of this complex came stonecutters with their urban
architectural techniques, retired Christian civil servants who

---

[127] Carl Schneider, "Leibestätigkeit als Strafe: Bemerkungen zu einer Inschrift
an Sardis," *Polychordia: Festschrift Franz Dölger zum 75. Geburtstag*, ed. Peter Wirth
(Amsterdam 1966), 284–289.
[128] *Cod. Theod.* 16.10.22.
[129] Infra, Ch. III, Sect. 4.
[130] Infra, Ch. XI.
[131] Frank R. Trombley, "Paganism in the Greek World at the End of Antiquity:
The Case of Rural Anatolia and Greece," *Harvard Theological Review* 78 (1985), 328,
n. 3.

bought lands and dominated the local religious of life of the communities in which they settled.[132] In more remote districts like Bithynia and the middle Nile basin, the religious transformation took longer, as it was left in the hands of the monks and was less in touch with the rapid changes in urban religiosity.[133] This interaction was still in progress during the mid-fifth century. The edicts included in the Theodosian Code in 438 are fully consistent with a process of Christianization that had much local variation and was much protracted. It remains to analyse the phenomena of Hellenic religion in the individual cities and tracts of countryside where a detailed record exists.

III. The Varieties of Hellenic Religion

If the sacrifice to celestial and chthonic deities proved to be the most important and least eradicable feature of Greek and Semitic religiosity in the fifth century, there were many other *foci* round which belief, cult practices, and a sense of religious awe gravitated. Most of these *foci* and their attendant phenomena have vanished from human recollection because no writer found them worth recording. Exceptions exist. The outward forms of ancient aetiologies and rituals turn up in later Christian rite after their modification to conform to the new religion. Hagiographic texts abound with such data, and many features of "Christianization of rite" (*Ritenchristianisierung*) are discussed in the following chapter.[134] Our concern here is with unmodified Hellenic cult.

The dearth of good evidence is to some extent compensated for in the traditions about the fifth-century sophists and philosophers recorded by Damascius in his *Life of Isidore*, a work surviving only in fragments.[135] The religious phenomena noted in a work about the lives of philosophers owe their inclusion in part to the ongoing synthesis of Greek philosophy with theurgy, that is divine magic, which gained respectability with Iamblichus (ob. 325–330) and his successors such as Maximus of Ephesus (ob. 371), a real charlatan who even beguiled Julian the Apostate.[136] Another factor contributing to the inclusion

---

[132] Infra, Ch. X and XI.

[133] See the arguments in Trombley, "Paganism in the Greek World," and infra, Ch. VII–XI.

[134] Trombley, "Paganism in the Greek World," 327f., 337, and 345.

[135] Damascius, *Vitae Isidori Reliquiae*, ed. Clemens Zintzen (Hildesheim 1967). Cf. *Das Leben des Philosophen Isidoros von Damaskios aus Damaskos*, tr. Rudolf Asmus (Leipzig 1911).

[136] Cf. E.R. Dodds, "Theurgy," *The Greeks and the Irrational* (Berkeley-Los Angeles 1951), 283–311. C. Zintzen, "Die Wertung von Mystik und Magic in der neuplatonischen Philosophie," *Rhenisches Museum* 108 (1965), 71–100.

of this data in Damascius' work was the study of local Greek cults
and theologies initiated by philosophers like the Neoplatonist Proclus of Athens (ob. 485), whose well-honed religious sensibilities
caused him to note and systematize all the cases of religious lore
that came to his attention, even those which emerged from a
stratum of "popular" belief and practice.[137] "Popular" Hellenic
religion was not so much superstition or magic as the set of beliefs
and practices that arose outside the context of the temple cults,
which had a normative effect on how men approached the resident
deities.[138] These normative patterns perished with the end of public
sacrifice, the closure of the temples, the destruction of images, and
the withdrawal of the privileges held by the priesthoods, all this
amidst numerous conversions to Christianity. Yet men and women
continued to approach the old deities, particularly the chthonic sort
thought to bring about the hydrological and meteorological conditions favorable to the good harvest, those spirits which aided diviners in predicting future events and finding lost articles, and many
lesser *daimones* with other functions. The fifth-century Hellenes who
saw the old cults perishing everywhere studied this lore with avid
interest, recorded it in their theological treatises, and even incorporated it into their own cult practices. In their hands it became
certifiably "Hellenic", even if it was emergent from Semitic, Egyptian, or even Indic subcultures and religiosities. Some of the data
given by Damascius reflect a seeming antiquarianism in these
philosophers. One must bear in mind in this connection that the
"antiquarian" data transmitted by these writers often reflects not
so much the absence of such beliefs and practices in fifth-century
"popular" religion as it does a conscious attempt to stylize them in
the current Hellenic mode.[139] The critic must therefore attempt to
see these phenomena in their protean state, before the Hellenes
adapted them to their own philosophical tastes. Let us consider,
then, what modes of "popular" religiosity might be extracted from
Damascius' life of Isidore.

---

[137] Infra, Ch. IV, Sect. 3.

[138] Frank R. Trombley, "Popular Religion," *Oxford Dictionary of Byzantium*, ed.
Alexander Kazhdan *et al.*, (New York-Oxford 1991), 1695f.

[139] The reuse of seemingly archaic Hellenic devotions in a more recent context
and with some modification implies the ongoing relevance of these cults to
contemporary (in this case, fifth-century) religious concerns. Jacob Neusner has
demonstrated a similar connection with the continual reexamination of, and
commentary on, rabbinic literature by the redactors of the Midrash, Babylonian
Taimud, and other Late Antique Jewish texts. Cf. *Talmudic Judaism in Sassanian
Babylonia* (Leiden 1976), 10–12. *The Bavli and Its Sources* (Atlanta 1987), 1ff. and
177ff.

The regulations recapitulated in the Theodosian Code make it emphatically clear that urban Hellenes and rustic pagans continued to visit the temples and sacrifice. Damascius attributed these practices to the late fifth-century Hellenes as well. For example, Asklepiades (late 5th c.), son of Horapollon the elder, made his "soul to dwell in shrines on every occasion and in temples where initiatory rites were practiced" (ἐν ἀδύτοις ἑκάστοτε καὶ τελεστηρίοις). He performed the ancestral rites (τὰς πατρίους τελετάς) not only in Egypt, but also "in foreign [territory], whatever might have survived of such customs" (εἴπου τι κατελέλειπτο τῶν τοιούτων)."[140] Asklepiades, with his exceptional knowledge of Egyptian cultic lore (ἡ Αἰγυπτίων σοφία), crossed the frontiers as well.[141] The local rites and temple customs were rapidly being forgotten even in the limitrophic zone, a consequence of the financial woes of the temples and of conversions to Christianity. Acts of sacred pilgrimage nevertheless went on, and the memory of ancient ritual and theology lasted among the surviving priests. This fact stands out from the epigraphy of Philae on the Upper Nile as late as c. 460, and in that of Arabia as well.[142] One sophist was said to have recognized in the latter province the Arabian deity Theandrites, "a masculine-faced god who breathed pre-suckled life into souls," a formulation that owes something to Neoplatonic Hellenism superimposed on Semitic belief (ἔγνω δὲ Θεανδρίτην ἀρρενωπὸν ὄντα θεόν).[143] The locals at the village of Bosoa on the eastern Hauran plain rebuilt a temple to this deity (θεονδρίτιον) in 387 A.D.[144] Many villages of Provincia Arabia show no signs of Christianization even in the sixth century, when Damascius composed his biography of Isidore. The same traveller Asklepiades, who passed through Bostra, the metropolis or provincial capital of Arabia,[145] should thus have observed cult practices at the rural temples, or at any rate surviving statuary. Dusares, another Arabian deity, was remembered at this time as well. The Hellenes equated him with Dionysus.[146] The statuary, temples, and inscriptions littered the

---

[140] Damascius, Fr. 163 (Zintzen, 137).
[141] Damascius, Fr. 161 (Zintzen, 135).
[142] Infra, Ch. IX, Sect. 3, and Ch. XI.
[143] Damascius, *Epit. Phot. 198* (Zintzen, 272).
[144] Infra, Ch. XI, Sect. 1.
[145] Damascius, *Epit. Phot. 196* (Zintzen, 270).
[146] Damascius, Fr. 342 (Zintzen, 273). The theophoric personal name Dousarios (from Dushara) survived in Christian nomenclature into the sixth century. *Inscriptions grecques et latines en Grèce et en Asie Mineure*, ed. W.H. Waddington, 3/1 (Paris 1870), no. 1916. See the remarks of Henri Leclercq, "Hauran," DACL 6/2 (Paris n.d.), 2076f. The man in question was probably a recent convert to the new religion. The date was 539 A.D.

countryside of Arabia everywhere, but particularly in Djebel
Hauran, even at the time of the Princeton expedition in the early
twentieth century.[147] A Hellene determined to know all will have
found the temples easily accessible and completely intact in this
administrative backwater.

To return to Asklepiades: His travels stemmed from an interest
in theology common to the Hellenic philosophers from the time of
Proclus onward. Asklepiades accompanied Isidore, the *diadochos* or
president of the Neoplatonic school at Athens, to Phoenicia and
Syria-Palestine as well. At Heliopolis-Baalbek in Phoenicia
Libanensis they saw many *baityloi*,[148] or meteoric stones thought to
be sacred because of their unusual geomorphic characteristics and
the flashes in the sky that accompanied their entry into the earth's
atmosphere.[149] Asklepiades, who came from a priestly family,[150] is
said to have lit the altars he found there with holy fire (ἀνέκαιον
ὁσίῳ πυρὶ τοὺς βωμούς) in the company of Isidore, presumably in
the more remote parts of the district. Furthermore he resided in the
temples, seating himself before the cult images even then in existence (τάττεται δὲ καὶ ἐπὶ τῶν ἀγαλμάτων) and incubating on the
floor of the cella (λέγεται δὲ ἕδος καὶ τὸ ἔδαφος τοῦ νεώ).[151] The
categorical inference stands that sacrificial offerings went onto the
flaming altars, although Damascius leaves their character unstated, whether wheat cakes, whey, wine, or even animal meat.
Damascius implies that Asklepiades did the same at the Nilotic
shrines of Egypt, "where he furnished all things necessary to the
temples to the point of excess."[152] An Asklepieion perhaps survived
at Berytus, for Asklepiades noted in passing through the town that
the local Asklepios had a distinct, Phoenician origin (ἀλλὰ τις
ἐπιχώριος Φοῖνιξ), being different from the Greek or Egyptian
one.[153] Surviving statuary may have convinced him of this.

The real question about this evidence, which lacks a definitive
answer, is the extent to which the rustic locals of Syria and Arabia
frequented the temples. One suspects that, as with the Bithynian
peasants whom a local diviner told to offer an animal at the
idol-temple to gain an answer,[154] many an Arabic- or Aramaic-
speaker experienced no more hindrance to entering the same

[147] Infra, Ch. XI.
[148] Damascius, *Epit. Phot. 93* (Zintzen, 138).
[149] Infra, this section.
[150] Damascius, *Epit. Phot. 95* (Zintzen, 140).
[151] Damascius, Fr. 167 (Zintzen, 141).
[152] Damascius, Fr. 162 (Zintzen, 137).
[153] Damascius, Fr. 348 (Zintzen, 283; Asmus, 124).
[154] Infra, Ch. VII, Sect. 1.

shrines than did Isidore and Asklepiades. One could easily then light a sacrificial fire on an altar. Damascius, as usual, only informs us about the behavior of learned Hellenes. One example of this was a certain Antonius of Alexandria, who seems to have become a member of the city council of Gaza, "having taken up its political problems":[155]

> He became most pious toward the truth and kept his soul eager for the service of God, both publicly and even more privately, so that he rendered Gaza much more sacred than it had been before.

The innuendoes of the Greek leave this text almost untranslatable without commentary. The principal deity of Gaza, the Cretan-born Zeus, but usually called Zeus Marnas, still evidently retained a following in the late fifth century, to judge from Marinus of Neapolis' biography of Proclus the Neoplatonist (ob. 485), for the author mentions Proclus' devotion to Zeus Marnas, in connection with other deities whose cults certifiably survived until that time, certainly that of Isis at Philae and most probably that of Theandrites in Arabia.[156] The inference stands that, late in Proclus' life, Zeus Marnas still had adherents in Gaza. Antonius' "service of God, both public and even more in private" (πρὸς θεοῦ θεραπείαν, τήν τε δημοτελῆ τήν τε ἀπορρητοτέραν) provides the clue. The Marneion, destroyed in the first decade of the fifth century, remained a site of religious awe through the spolia taken from it to pave the courtyard of the new Eudoxiana cathedral erected on the site, for the Hellenes continued to revere those blocks.[157] Public behavior proves to be the aperture through which the wide span of private cult becomes visible. Damascius' Greek words allude in fact to sacrifice "performed at public expense" (θεραπεία δημοτελής). The reference to the "more ineffable service" suggests through parataxis with "public" the more common forms of liturgy connected with secret sacrifice when new edicts, like the Theodosian codification of 438, disrupted the complacency of provincial governors and bishops about the continuing consumption of burnt offerings. Gaza still had a much larger pagan population than Christian even by c. 420, if one can believe the figures for conversions given by Mark the Deacon in his biography of bishop Porphyrius.[158] It follows that many of the imperial edicts which

---

[155] Damascius, Fr. 186 (Zintzen, 159–161).
[156] Marinus of Neapolis, *Vita Procli*, 19, ed. Iohannes F. Boissonade (1814; repr. Amsterdam 1966), 16.
[157] Infra, Ch. III, Sect. 4.
[158] Ibid., Sect. 5.

reaffirmed the prohibition of sacrifice had places like Gaza in mind, where a strong pre-Christian subculture prevailed. All this inclines one to greet Mark the Deacon's assertion that Porphyrius crushed the urban cults with great skepticism. Antonius was, perhaps, only one of many adherents of the old cults of Gaza, but Damascius' preoccupation with sophists and philosophers obscures the social, cultural, and demographic context of late Semitic Hellenic paganism. It is possible, in any case, that temple spolia in some instances provided sufficient focus for the old beliefs to persist in an atmosphere of alternatingly zealous and passive Christianization.

Other temples remained in integral or at least identifiable condition in the late fifth century. The *baitylos*-worshipper Eusebius observed the fall of a meteoric stone near the splendid and very ancient temple of a female fertility deity—Damascius calls her Athena—which lay on a mountain outside the city of Emesa in Phoenicia (σχεδὸν ὡς πορρωτάτω πρὸς τὸ ὄρος αὐτό, ἐν ᾧ τῆς Ἀθηνᾶς ἵδρυται νεὼς ἀρχαιοπρεπής).[159] The temple need not have lost its importance to local Hellenes and rustic pagans, even if in bad repair or devoid of a priesthood, nor need we necessarily conclude that its cult images had been carted off. It is worth adding that the monk Abraames, a native of the *territorium* of Cyrrhus, converted a village on the Mount Lebanon massif in the countryside around Emesa in the early fifth century.[160] Christianity had made inroads into the rural areas there around the time Eusebius picked up his *baitylos*.

The cult images of the Greek, Semitic, and Egyptian gods in some instances survived the destruction of cultic statues mentioned in the Theodisian Code and other texts. Thus, Asklepiodotus of Aphrodisias in Caria used to "perform the ancestral sacred devices of a proper nature by decorating images [of the gods] and composing hymns" (εἰς τὰ ἱερὰ τῆς οἰκείας φύσεως ἔκγονα μηχανήματα, ἀγάλματά τε διακοσμῶν καὶ ὕμνους προστιθείς).[161] This behavior had, of course, become illegal under the law which forbade the ceremonial use of garlands.[162]

Of greater interest for Hellenic theological ideas was the attitude

---

[159] Damascius, *Epit. Phot. 203* (Zintzen, 274f.; Asmus, 121f.).
[160] Infra, Ch. VIII, Sect. 2.
[161] Damascius, Fr. 209 (Zintzen, 179, lines 5–7). There is more than a little information on Hellenic hymnography during this period. Cf. the Stoic hymn on the creation of the world found at Monte Fortino, Italy (2nd-3rd c. A.D.). SEG 32.1020. There is also a hymn to the goddess Hera (Samos, 4th c. A.D.). SEG 30.1082. On the compositions of Proclus of Athens, see infra, Ch. IV, Sect. 3.
[162] *Cod. Theod.* 16.10.12. *prooem.*

toward the sacred statues of the gods held by Heraiskos, who believed many of them to be animate:[163]

> Heraiskos became able to distinguish between animate and non-animate sacred statues, for in looking upon them he was wounded in the heart by divine frenzy and he leapt up in body and soul, as if seized by the god. If he was not moved in such a way, the statue was inanimate and bereft of divine conception. Thus he discerned that the ineffable statue of Aion was gripped by the god, whom the Alexandrians worshipped, along with Osiris and Adonis who were just as truly in the mystic divine mingling.

The difference between animate and inanimate (ἄψυχον) images (τῶν τε ζώντων καὶ τῶν μὴ ζώντων ἱερῶν ἀγαλμάτων) seems to have lain in the "divine conception" (θεία ἐπίνοια) of the sculptor when he produced the work. Such a work of art caused the religious Hellene to be gripped by divine frenzy (ὑπὸ τοῦ θειασμοῦ). A deity like Aion might then seize the viewer (ὑπὸ τοῦ θεοῦ κατεχόμενον). Damascius, or least his excerptor, leaves the precise operation by which the divine conception inhering in the idol gripped Heraiskos unclear, that is, whether the deity acted from inside the image, or whether the emotion of the viewer caused a descent or overshadowing of the god from, as it were, the celestial realm. Christian writers like Mark the Deacon, who imagined that the *daimon* or pagan god inhered in the cultic statue of the Semitic Aphrodite of Gaza, were thus not so much engaging in anti-pagan propaganda as giving the Christian interpretation of a belief common among Hellenes. Thus, as Mark had it, the statue of the female deity shattered at the approach of the cross and prayer of the bishop, and not from the imposition of the hammer.[164] Many a pagan might have agreed with this, inasmuch as epiphanies of deities were thought to flee before the sign of the cross, because of its association with death and the consequent ritual pollution, as Hypatius of Rufinianae claimed and even Julian the Apostate is said to have admitted.[165] This belief explains the frequent incision of crosses on the walls of temples and on statuary,[166] and their

---

[163] Damascius, Fr. 174 (Zintzen, 147). Se Zintzen's note on other texts describing animate images. Edwyn Bevan has collected many references to these in: *Holy Images: An Inquiry into Idolatry and Image-Worship in Ancient Paganism and in Christianity.* Among the themes discussed are: a Hermetic text on Asklepios c. 260–310 (24f.), a Hellenistic automaton (25), the ritual animation of an image, with Hindu examples (31f.), the implantation of a *daimon* inside an image (34), and the image as an abode or instrument of a divinity (36f. and 39).

[164] Infra, Ch. III, Sect. 4.
[165] Infra, Ch. V, Sect. 4.
[166] Infra, Ch. II, Sect. 2.

erection everywhere when a monastery supplanted the temenos of a local deity.[167] Heraiskos' experience provides a single fifth-century instance of the phenomenon Christian writers and preachers sought to suppress.[168]

Many aniconic chthonic deities thought to move and exist within the forces of nature, such as rivers, rain clouds, and hail storms, survived in popular imagination and religiosity well after the fifth century.[169] Sky-gods like Apollo-Helios, Zeus, and the innumerable Baals of the Hellenized East were thought at times to control such lesser gods or *daimones*, as an incident in the life of Asklepiodotus of Aphrodisias reveals:[170]

> He [Isidore] and Asklepiodotus, who was formerly his tutor, went down to the channel of the Maeander river to swim. The Maeander, taking them back in its eddies, submerged them, until Asklepiodotus raised himself enough so that the sun could be seen, and cried: "We are dying!" He was unable to utter anything [else], hardly an indistinguishable word. Then, suddenly, out of no apparent forethought, they lay upon the bank of the river half-dead. They thereupon recovered their breath and went up from the torrents of Hades. Thus Asklepiodotus owned god-inspired power and these things are still with his body.

Local credence pictured the Maeander with a strong-willed personality, which in this case relented at the command of the sun. Strabo relates that when, on one occasion, the Maeander shifted its course and undermined tilled fields, the Phrygians fined the river under religious law in the form of a crossing toll, which evidently went into a local temple treasury.[171] A sixth-century Christian monk, Theodore of Sykeon, clung to the earlier belief of the Galatians west of Ankyra in the ill-tempered and erratic nature of the Sangaris river, when he inserted crosses on its bank to prevent the erosion of the monastery's tilled lands.[172] In the transformed Christian ethos, the cross was thought to make the river deity more tractable than the fines and other devices of the old religion.

The early chthonic Anatolian deities exerted a powerful influence on the popular imagination. Among them was Kybele or the Great Mother of the Gods, whose powers were thought to

---

[167] Cf. the example of Nikertai in the *territorium* of Apamea in Second Syria. Infra, Ch. VIII, Sect. 2.

[168] A later example of the *daimon* of Aphrodite dwelling in a mosaic depiction of her life turns up in the sixth-century life of Eutychius of Constantinople. PG 86, 2333D–2336A.

[169] Trombley, "Paganism in the Greek World," 340f.

[170] Damascius, *Epit. Phot. 116* (Zintzen, 156).

[171] Strabo, *Geogr.* 12.8.19.

[172] Supra, Ch. I, n. 169.

produce all good things from the soil.[173] Her worship was deeply
rooted and was still practiced in the isolated mountain districts of
eighth-century Caria.[174] The sophist Asklepiodotus of Aphrodisias
(5th c.) celebrated her cult in a theologically upgraded form. Once,
in Laodicea-Hierapolis in Phrygia, he dreamed that he had completed a festival of hers called the Hilaria after a vision of Attis, her
consort (καὶ μοὶ ἐπιτελεῖσθαι παρὰ τῆς μητρὸς τῶν θεῶν τὴν τῶν
Ἱλαρίων καλουμένην ἑορτήν).[175] If the Basket of Artemis survived among the rural population of "inner" Bithynia c. 443–448,
one can hardly doubt that the unchristianized rustics of other
localities, and in this case Phrygia, celebrated the annual rites of
their own Mothers of the Gods, whose earlier votive offerings (2nd
and 3rd centuries A.D.) recorded in inscriptions reveal many local
epithets.[176] Sites of religious awe remained holy to the Mother of
the Gods in Asklepiodotus' lifetime, as for example the so-called
Ploutoneion or Charoneion at Laodicea Hierapolis, a subterranean
descent (βόθρος) under the temple of Apollo which gave off deadly
fumes, probably sulfide gases, that were fatal to all who entered.[177]
It was said that only the Galloi, the castrated initiates of the Great
Mother, could avoid harm in the deepest recesses of the chasm
(τοῖς δὲ τετελεσμένοις . . . δυνατόν).[178] Damascius' use of the
perfect tense suggests that Galloi were still about, just as they were
on the authority of Cosmas of Jerusalem in the eighth century.[179]
None of them seems to have accompanied Asklepiodotus on his
own descent there nor does he seem to have desired to pay the price
of becoming an initiate. The epigraphy reveals that Laodicea had
become a largely Christian city in the fourth century, and that its
territorium in the Axylon steppe had mostly gone over to the new
religion by the last quarter of the same century.[180] At any rate, in
his early youth, with the sure empiricist sense of a Hellene, Asklepiodotus went down into the depths of the Charoneion in the
manner of an "initiate-descender" (ὁ καταιβάτης):[181]

---

[173] See the rather general remarks of John Ferguson, *The Religions of the Roman
Empire* (Ithaca 1970), 15f.
[174] Trombley, "Paganism in the Greek World," 344.
[175] Damascius, *Epit. Phot. 131* (Zintzen, 176; Asmus, 78).
[176] Infra, Ch. VII, Sect. 2.
[177] Damascius, *Epit. Phot. 131* (Zintzen, 176f.; Asmus, 78 and 174).
[178] Ibid., Zintzen, 176.
[179] The translation runs; "Certain irrational pagans in the mountains of Caria
practice self-castration even until the present day, as the story goes, gripped by
this ancient custom." Cosmas of Jerusalem, *Scholia in Gregorii Nazianzeni Carmina*
PG 38, 502.
[180] Infra, Ch. VII, Sect. 2.
[181] Damascius, *Epit. Phot. 131* (Zintzen, 178).

For as a young man he said he went to this place and made a trial of its nature. Twice and thrice he folded his garment over his nostrils, that he might breathe often yet not inhale the destructive and malignant air, but rather safe and harmless air. Having wrapped safe air in his garment, he brought it inside, and having done thus he went within the declivity following the efflux of the hot waters to the uttermost end of its innermost and least accessible nook, but did not arrive at the end of the descent. For the route broke away to great watery depths and was inaccessible to men. But the initiate, being divinely enthused, bore himself to the limit.

In all this one can see the claim of the fifth-century philosophers to primacy over the older priesthoods. Here the rationalism of the youthful Hellenist Asklepiodotus allowed him to penetrate mysteries accessible only to the initiates of the old cult. Damascius takes even this to be a "miracle" (θαῦμα), that is, a wonder of the divine virtue found in the man. The emission of deadly fumes from the subterranean waters was taken to be the hierophany of the Mother of the Gods, whose power over life-giving water equalled her ability to bring death, all from the same source.

The *Nachleben* of Christian belief and ritual surrounding this site is unknown, but we should not err too far in supposing that it was regarded as the haunt of destructive subterranean *daimones*, which appear in pre-Christian parlance as the "katachthonic deities" (καταχθόνιοι θεοί),[182] the kind whose presence one could smell in the air. Some natural phenomena, such as sacred springs and stones, lent themselves to Christian aetiologies only gradually, and saw the impress of the new religion only later, as for example the sacred black volcanic stone on a mountain peak outside Miletus in the tenth century.[183] To cite another example, the memory and worship of Attis, the consort of the Mother of the Gods, persisted in popular memory as well. Its strength may be gauged by the fact that his iconography was occasionally transferred to Michael the archangel, the archistrategos of the heavenly army, a Christian spirit often invoked in later centuries at the sacred spring at Colossus-Chonae, where the cult of an earlier katachthonic deity, perhaps Attis himself, had prevailed.[184]

Less information has survived about the state of Hellenic ritual, apart from the actual performance of sacrifice. Marinus of Neapolis records the specific practices of the Neoplatonist Proclus (ob. 485), but these belong largely to the local Athenian context.[185] The

---

[182] Infra, Ch. VII, Sect. 2.
[183] Trombley, "Paganism in the Greek World," 333–339, 345.
[184] Infra, Ch. II, Sect. 4.
[185] Infra, Ch. IV, Sect. 3.

fifth-century philosopher Heraiskos, who as mentioned above became gripped by divine frenzy when in the presence of a cult image
of "divine conception", adhered like Proclus to strict rules of ritual
purity. Heraiskos' inspired, or perhaps hypersensitive, nature was
said to cause him headaches whenever he heard the utterance of a
menstruating woman, who in that state was of course in a condition
of ritual contamination.[186] Philosophers constantly in a state of
spiritual emulation were supposed, like Heraiskos, always to respond in this manner, and not only when sacrificing. Like Proclus,
Asklepiades composed liturgical hymns to the Egyptian gods (ἀπό
τε τῶν ὕμνων, ὧν συγγέγραφεν εἰς τοὺς Αἰγυπτίων θεούς).[187]
These were doubtless a pale reflection of the recitative mode of
ordinary pagans. The traditional funerary rites lasted until the late
fifth century, as Marinus' account of Proclus' obsequies reveals.[188]
These ceremonies had a true liturgical character. To cite an example from the later fourth century, Ammianus Marcellinus observes
concerning the funeral procession of a certain Heliodorus c. 371/2
that "persons preceded the ill-omened bier of the body-snatcher to
the sepulchre, marching with bared heads and feet, some also with
folded hands."[189] The ritual usually included singing and music.[190]
Upon the death of Heraiskos, his friend the Hellene Asklepiades
provided him with a shroud of Osiris:[191]

> After the customary rites had been performed by the priests, Askle
> piades provided the dead man with the other [usual tributes], includ
> ing the garments of Osiris for his body. They were everywhere
> illuminated with the ineffable letters of shrouds and around them
> were seen the god-like shapes of apparitions, who exhibited [Herais
> kos'] soul palpably, so great a hearth-sharer had he become with the
> gods.

One is reminded here of the mummy portraits in which the god
Horus exhibits the soul of the deceased beside his sarcophagus, the
latter bearing his likeness in death, the former his personality in the
afterlife.[192] The "ineffable letters" (ἀπόρρητα διαγράμματα) were
undoubtedly modelled on the hieroglyphic script, which had re-

---

[186] Damascius, Fr. 174 (Zintzen, 147).
[187] Damascius, Fr. 164 (Zintzen, 137f.).
[188] Infra, Ch. IV, Sect. 3.
[189] Ammianus Marcellinus, *Res Gestae* 29.2.12–15. Infra, this section.
[190] Cf. Johannes Quasten, *Music and Worship in Pagan and Christian Antiquity*, tr.
B. Ramsey (Washington, D.C. 1983), 148–160.
[191] Damascius, Fr. 174 (Zintzen, 147).
[192] There are three examples of burial shrouds that show the deceased between
a mummiform Osiris and the funerary deity in: K. Parlasca, *Mumienporträts und
verwandte Denkmäler* (Wiesbaden 1966), Tafel 12/1, 35/1, 61/2.

mained in cultic use at Philae until at least 394 A.D.[193]

A somewhat different set of beliefs surrounded the *baityloi* or meteoric stones, on which a considerable literature exists.[194] This cult, initially a Semitic one, had penetrated the Greek world at some indeterminate point. The collection of *baityloi* formed one part of the religious experience of a Hellene named Eusebius, who resided near Emesa in Phoenicia Libanensis:[195]

> The name of the *baitylos*-worshipper was Eusebius, who said that an unconsidered yearning had come over him to wander nearby, outside the city of Emesa in the middle of the night, directly in front of the mountain on which is built a time-honored temple of Athena. He went quickly to the foot of the mountain and sitting there rested as if from the road. He saw a fire-ball suddenly leaping down from above, the constellation of the great Lion standing nearby next to the ball. At once it became invisible. He ran over to the extinguished fire-ball and discovered that it was a *baitylos*. He picked it up, and queried what god it might be. It appeared to be that of Gennaios, whom the Heliopolitans honor, having erected a statue of Zeus in the shape of a lion. Eusebius carried the *baitylos* home, covering, as he said, not less than 210 *stadia* in the same night. Eusebius was not a master of the movement of the *baitylos*, as other persons are of other phenomena, but he prayed and gave heed to its oracular answers.

The notion that *baityloi* could give oracular answers belongs to the ethos of late Hellenism. Eusebius took the spectacular fall of the meteor through the atmosphere (τὸν βαίτυλον διὰ τοῦ ἀέρος κινούμενον . . . σφαῖραν δὲ πυρός) as the hierophany of Zeus Gennaios, a local Baal of the temple complex at Baalbek-Heliopolis. Eusebius claimed the ability to get oracular answers from the meteorite which he once described; Photius, writing in the ninth century, observes:[196]

> Having said many foolish things, as though he were worthy of the *baitylia*, he describes the stone and its shape. He says: The sphere was exactly round and its color whitish. It was a span in size. But it was here and there greater or smaller, and at times purplish. He showed us letters written on the stone colored vermilion. He hammered on its side. Through this it rendered the oracle sought by the person inquiring, and it gave forth the sound of a delicate pan-pipe, which Eusebius interpreted.

---

[193] Infra, Ch. IX, Sect. 3.

[194] Henri Lammens, "Le cult des bétyles et les processions religieuses chez les Arabes préislamites," *Bulletin de l'Institut d'Archéologie Orientale, Cairo* 17 (1919–20), 39–101. See the brief discussion of Mircea Eliade, *Patterns in Comparative Religion*, 227–229.

[195] Damascius, *Epit. Phot. 203* (Zintzen, 274ff.; Asmus, 121f.).

[196] Ibid., Zintzen, 276.

The appearance of the stone with its unusual mineral content evoked wonder, but the magic lettering probably represents an attempt by Eusebius to improve on the seemingly miraculous coincidence of his finding the stone. The technique by which Eusebius got the stone to whistle will remain an object of uncertainty, whether by some mechanical means, or whether, because of an intricately and deeply pitted surface, it gave the sound of a flute when turned in the air or blown upon. Eusebius and the philosopher Isidore disputed the theological significance of the wonderful stone. While the former attributed it to the local divinity, the latter with evident satisfaction and a degree of cynicism assigned its attributes to the activity of a lesser *daimon* (δαιμόνιον), this attitude being consistent with late Hellenic attitudes toward mantic activity; Photius adds:[197]

> After relating the said marvels, this empty-headed man relates other myriad and even more fraudulent things about the *baitylos*: I think that the matter of the *baitylos* is divine, but Isidore argued to the contrary that it is daimonic. For a certain *daimon* activates it with neither harmful nor connected effects . . . One after the other of the *baityloi* are dedicated . . . to Kronos, Zeus, Helios, and other deities.

The deities listed belong to the solar and planetary cults. If the Christian Photius, writing in the mid-ninth century, had nothing but contempt for Eusebius' theological speculations, Isidore took them quite seriously, regarding them as a legitimate set of views within the mainstream of Hellenic religious thought. The cult of *baityloi* achieved a wider following in Greek religion at an indeterminate time, perhaps in Late Antiquity.[198] A remnant of this custom and belief survived in Boeotia and Phokis until at least the ninth century. A marginal note found in Manuscript A of the Photian Epitome of the life of Isidore, perhaps that of Photius himself, indicates the spread of this cult to rural Greece:[199]

> I have heard from the indigenous inhabitants of Greece about this kind of *daimonion* [the *baitylos*], which turns up in the Parnassos district. They say many other strange things about them, which ought sooner to be left in silence than talked about.

Would that the glossator had gone into greater detail about the other phenomena.

One divinatory practice with a long history of continuity through

---

[197] Damascius, *Epit. Phot. 203* (Zintzen, 276–278).
[198] I am unable to discover anything about the *baityloi* in Michael P. Nilsson, *Geschichte der griechischen Religion*, 2 v. (1955–61).
[199] Damascius (Asmus, 191).

all phases of religious transition was that of predicting the future
from cloud formations. A woman named Anthusa continued this
ancient art during the reign of emperor Leo I (457–474):[200]

> Wherefore one finds a woman in the days of Leo the Roman
> emperor who knew neither by sense of hearing nor by the ancient
> practices the art of divination by clouds. The woman came from
> Aigai in Cilicia, having come from the family of the Orestiadai who
> dwell on the mountain at Komana in Cappadocia. Her family went
> back to the Peloponnese. She took thought for a man entrusted with a
> military command who was sent with others to the war [against the
> Vandals] in Sicily. She prayed to foresee the future by dream and
> prayed facing the rising sun. Her father prescribed and commanded
> her in a dream to pray toward the west. When she prayed, a cloud
> from the upper air stood around the sun, and became enlarged and
> took the shape of a man. Another cloud sheared off and rendered
> itself of equal size and took the shape of a wild lion. It went into a
> great rage and, having made a great chasm, the lion swallowed the
> man. The human, cloud-made shape was like a Goth. A little more
> about the apparitions: Thereupon the emperor Leo slew Aspar him-
> self, the hegemon of the Goths [in Constantinople] and his children.
> From that time Anthusa has continued until now without interrup-
> tion to practice the custom of mantic prediction through clouds.

The Hellenic pedigree of Anthusa's family speaks for a pedigree of
cult as well. The dream vision of her father suggests family traditions that presumably or ostensibly went back to Peloponnesian
settlers who migrated to the Armeno-Cappadocian borderlands in
Hellenistic times. Thus, her father may have instructed her in the
techniques of cloud divination in early youth which came back to
her as a figment of the unconscious mind in her dream. Cloud
divination survived in Greek Christian culture until the time of the
canonist Balsamon in the twelfth century.[201]

The merging of theurgy and philosophy in the mainstream of
Hellenic religious thought seems to date from the time of Iamblichus (ob. 325–330). Maximus of Ephesus, an out-and-out charlatan who even convinced Julian the Apostate of his sincerity, gave
this strand of Greek religion an extremely bad name with Christians, although enlightened and even-handed Hellenes like the

---

[200] Damascius, *Epit. Phot. 69* (Zintzen, 98).

[201] The canonist reports: "They predict things unknown to many from the
clouds. For some gaze at the clouds, or rather, when they become fiery at sunset,
feign to learn the truth from them. For this cloud, when it takes the shape of a
dove, they say misfortune will come to the inquirer. From another cloud, when it
takes the shape of a sword-bearing man, they predict war. From another, when it
takes the shape of a lion, they predict the action of imperial edicts." Balsamon,
Syntagma tōn theiōn kai hierōn kanonōn, ed. G.A. Rhalles and M. Potles, vol. 2 (Athens
1852), 445.

historian Ammianus Marcellinus could call him a man with a great reputation for learning (*vir ingenti nomine doctrinarum*) and decry the injustice of his execution by order of Festus, proconsul of Asia.[202] The more biased Eunapius of Sardis (ob. 414) extols Maximus to the skies in his *Lives of the Philosophers*, despite recording the naked terror felt by Eusebius of Myndus at Maximus' precocity in summoning Hekate and allegedly causing her statue in her temple at Pergamum to smile and then laugh.[203] This was just the thing that Christians most feared of cult effigies, in which *daimones* were often thought to reside. Some statues, like that of Sarapis in the Serapeun of Alexandria, were hollow and emitted the disguised voices of the priests hidden within. This evoked terror in pagan and Christian alike. Thus the account of Eusebius of Myndus:[204]

> Eusebius said: "Maximus is one of the older and more learned students, who, because of his lofty genius and superabundant eloquence scorned all logical proof in these subjects and impetuously resorted to the acts of a madman. Not long since, he invited us to the temple of Hekate and produced many witnesses of his folly. When we had arrived and saluted the goddess: 'Be seated,' said he, 'my well-beloved friends, and observe what shall come to pass, and how greatly I surpass the common herd.' When he had said this, and we had sat down, *he burned a grain of incense* and *recited the whole of some hymn or other*, and was so successful in his demonstration that the image of the goddess first began to smile, then even seemed to laugh aloud'.
>
> "We were much disturbed at this sight but he said: 'Let none of you be terrified by these things, for presently even the torches which the goddess holds in her hands shall kindle into flame.' And before he could finish speaking the torches burst into a blaze of light. Now for the moment we came away amazed by that theatrical miracle-worker."

Unless this anectode be pure fantasy, one can hardly doubt that mechanical devices were at play here. It reveals in any case what people thought of cult images and theurgists.[205]

Maximus of Ephesus underwent execution c. 371–72 because of his failure to divulge his own knowledge of the THEOD oracle plot at Constantinople, which purported to signify the first four letters of the name of the emperor who would succeed Valens (364–378).

---

[202] Ammianus Marcellinus, *Res Gestae* 29.1.42.

[203] Eunapius, *Lives of the Philosophers* (Wright, 435).

[204] Quoted from ibid., 433f.

[205] See the recent discussion of temple automata designed by Hero of Alexandria, which caused the doors of the cella to open when a sacrificial fire was lit on an altar in front of the building in: Sigvard Strandh, *The History of Technology* (New York 1979), 34f. Cf. Albert Neuberger, *Die Technik des Altertums* (Leipzig 1919), and Curt Merkel, *Die Ingenieurtechnik im Altertum* (Berlin 1899; repr. 1969).

The perpetrators of the oracle recognized a certain Theodore, an imperial secretary who was later accused of inveterate ambition to acquire the imperial crown, as that successor.[206] The officials who conducted the seance constructed a sacred divination table (*mensula*) in the fashion of a Delphic tripod (*cortina Delphica*), and dedicated it with many incantations (*imprecationibus carminum secretorum*).[207] Our witness, Ammianus Marcellinus, continues the story, which he bases on the deposition of a certain Hilarius:[208]

> 30. [The tripod] was placed in the middle of a house purified thoroughly with Arabic perfumes; on it was placed a perfectly round plate made of various metallic substances. Around its outer rim the written forms of the twenty-four letters of the [Greek] alphabet were skilfully engraved, separated from one another by carefully measured spaces.
> 31. Then a man clad in linen garments, shod also in linen sandals and having a fillet wound round his head, carrying twigs from a tree of good omen, *after propitiating in a set formula the divine power from whom predictions come* (*litato conceptis carminibus numine praescitorum auctore*), having full knowledge of the ceremonial, stood over the tripod as priest and set swinging the hanging ring fitted to a very fine linen thread and consecrated with mystic arts. This ring, passing over the designated intervals with a series of jumps, and falling upon this and that letter which detained it, made hexameters corresponding to questions and completely finished in feet and rhythm, like the Pythian verses which we read, or those given out from the oracles of the Branchidae [the priesthood of Apollo at Didyma near Miletus].
> 32. When we then and there inquired, 'what man will succeed the present emperor?', since it was said that he would be perfect in every particular, and the ring leaped forward and lightly touched the two syllables ΘΕΟ, adding the next letter [a delta], then one of those present cried out that by the decision of inevitable fate Theodorus was meant. And there was no further investigation of the matter; for it was agreed among us that he was the man who was sought.

Ammianus tries the critic's skepticism by failing to mention the offering of a propitiatory sacrifice that went with the incantations recited by seer. Even if Maximus, then living in Ephesus, played no role in the mantic techniques that led to the THEOD oracle, his association with the principals in the affair and his reputation for the knowledge and practice of analogous forms of theurgy proved damning.

The circle of Isidore, successor of Proclus as director of the

---

[206] Ammianus Marcellinus, *Res Gestae* 29.1.5–44.
[207] Ammianus Marcellinus, *Res Gestae* 29.1.29.
[208] Quoted from *Ammianus Marcellinus with an English Translation*, ed. J.C. Rolfe 3 (London 1964), 205f.

Neoplatonist school in Athens (post 485), remembered Maximus of Ephesus' acts with a degree of fright:[209]

> Maximus—for this man was a Hellene in worship—sent off many glances of the eyes and used to see frightening and dangerous things, so that he repelled the gaze of those who beheld him . . . He was even the seer of apparitions which others could not see. He had the capability to dispatch destructive *daimones* and to summon those sent from elsewhere. Except that because of performing impious acts he was arrested at Constantinople and did not escape the justice of the sword.

The purported ability to dispatch destructive *daimones* and to re-direct those sent from elsewhere (ἱκανὸς δ' ἦν καὶ δαίμονας ἐπιπέμπειν φθοροεργούς, καὶ ἄλλοθεν ἐπιπεμπόμενους ἀναστέλλειν) and, indeed, the uncommon ability to perceive such daimonic presences in general, belonged to the regular stock-in-trade of the lowest criminal sorcerer. An almost identical set of talents, with a survey of the different varieties of acts of destruction perpetrated, such as plagues of locusts against tilled fields, poisoning, and *daimon*-possession, are attributed to a certain Theodore Kourappos, who resided in mid-sixth century Galatia at the village of Mazamia. The man had never been baptized, owned magic books with directions for imposing spells, claimed to converse with *daimones*, and evoked great popular fear. The local Christian hegumen Theodore of Sykeon eventually proved the sorcerer's powers to be impotent against the holy man, both as regards the dispatch of *daimones* and in his humanitarian ability to win over the rural population enthralled by religious awe.[210] If Isidore's biographer Damascius and many fifth-century Hellenes like him abhorred such acts with terror and disdain, they nevertheless believed them to be within the reach of the theurgist, whether he belonged to the Hellenic elite of philosopher-theologians or was an impoverished rural sorcerer. If few Hellenes chose to follow this path, these instances nevertheless provide another example of the systematization and recategorization of debased practices within high-cultural Greek theology.

Philosopher-theurgists in Isidore's circle of friends claimed to have performed such acts. For example, when Isidore accompanied Asklepiades to see the *baityloi* at Baalbek-Heliopolis below the Mount Lebanon massif, the latter supposedly "lit with fire the plain lying oyster-green with grape clusters below and he saw the crop turn entirely to ash" (καὶ τὸ ὑποκείμενον πεδίον

---

[209] Damascius, *Epit. Phot. 204* (Zintzen, 278).
[210] Trombley, "Paganism in the Greek World," 340.

στάχυσι βρύον τοξεύει πυρί, καὶ τὸ λήϊον πᾶν τέφραν ᾤετο γεγονέναι).[211] Modern speculation about a more material cause for such phenomena can hardly blunt the reality of the sense of fear with which both educated and illiterate superstition regarded the theurgist, who will more often than not have taken a fee for his services, unlike Asklepiades, for whom the alleged act was little more than a gratuitous display of power. One wonders, but can hardly discover, how many times Christian monks restored communal confidence in the good harvest by raising an apotropaic cross against sorcerers and the *daimones* thought to act at their behest. Asklepiades, at any rate, included destructive theurgy in the "harmony of all theologies" (τῶν θεολογιῶν ἁπασῶν ἡ συμφωνία) which he is said to have begun writing.[212]

This control of *daimones* which the Hellenic theurgists claimed to display theoretically gave them the power to perform exorcisms, a task of the earliest Christians clergy which monks like Hypatius of Rufinianae later coopted in the struggle to Christianize the Bithynian countryside in the 440's.[213] A pious Hellene like the sophist Theosebios might perform such an operation simply by calling upon deities known from his studies of theology without any real expertise in theurgy:[214]

> As a *daimonion* was not persuaded to go out of a woman by gentle words, Theosebios compelled it with an oath (ὅρκῳ) and did it without knowing how to practice magic or having studied theurgy. He adjured the rays of the sun, while stretching forth [his hand], and the God of the Hebrews. The *daimon* was driven off, crying out that it revered the gods and that it was ashamed even before him.

The incident bears a remarkable similarity to Christian exorcism, with the stretching forth of the hand, as the text implies, and the summoning of the Almighty God of the Jews, whom the monks regarded as one and the same as theirs. Hypatius would invariably seal the forehead of the victim possessed by the *daimon* (in the above instance a *daimonion* or lesser *daimon*) with holy oil and the sign of the cross (σφραγίς).[215] The philospher might, like the monk, "move all things", whether the *daimones* thought to cause mental disorders, rain clouds, locusts, the rise of rivers and even the rays of

---

[211] Damascius, Fr. 166 (Zintzen, 139).

[212] Damascius, Fr. 164 (Zintzen, 137f.).

[213] Infra, Ch. VII, Sect. 1.

[214] Damascius, *Epit. Phot. 56* (Zintzen, 82). Theodoret of Cyrrhus reports a strikingly similar, if more detailed, case of Christian exorcism in his *Historia Philotheos*. Infra, Ch. VIII, Sect. 5.

[215] Infra, Ch. VII, Sect. 1.

the sun.[216] In fifth-century Hellenic theology the rays of the sun, the hierophany of a great deity, were thought break the grip of lesser *daimones*, who revered him in a hierarchy reminiscent of the Neoplatonic *taxeis* of celestial beings.[217] At the same time the God of the Jews (ὁ Ἑβραίων θεός), often summoned for such purposes in magical texts, was thought to specialize in repelling *daimones*, and His cult thus became integrated in the Hellenic "harmony of all theologies". This behavior suggests the existence of an unsuspected avenue for conversion to Christianity and at the same time crypto-paganism, for a Hellene might as a catechumen revere the Jewish, or publicly Christian, God with a sincere respect for His unique powers, while keeping in mind the aretalogies of the Hellenic deities. The powers of the latter might eventually be seen to lapse with the failure of prayers to them and the closure of their temples. The catechumen might then keep the Jewish-Christian God as part of the bargain, and transfer his allegiance entirely if some wonder or cure was performed in His name. This behavioral model may explain some of the conversions of the pagan Constantinopolitans effected by Hypatius of Rufinianae.[218]

The manufacture and circulation of amulets (φυλακτήρια), apotropaic devices designed to ward off harm in all its manifestations, disease, bodily insult and injury, the evil eye, and the ubiquitous *daimones* of physical and mental illness, was a prominent feature of Greek, Semitic, and Coptic religion in its polytheistic, Judaic, Christian, and syncretistic varieties.[219] The manufacture and use of such objects developed as the logical consequence of, and as a countermeasure to, the magical devices of sorcery, which often aimed at seduction, the demolition of erotic relationships, and the physical injury of persons. Amulets often took the shape of rings, medallions, and folded metal sheets worn with one's personal effects and inscribed with prayers or adjurations to the protecting deity or *daimon*. It is hardly possible in the present survey to provide

---

[216] πάντα οὖν καλῶν ἐκίνει. Damascius, *Epit. Phot. 57* (Zintzen, 82).

[217] This supposition receives a fifth-century Neoplatonist basis and interpretation in Proclus' *Elements of Theology*, Prop. 143: "All inferior principles retreat before the presence of the gods" (πάντα τὰ καταδεέστερα τῇ παρουσίᾳ τῶν θεῶν ὑπεξίσταται). *The Elements of Theology*, ed. tr. E.R. Dodds, 2nd ed. (Oxford 1963), 127 and 275.

[218] For the problem of conversion, see infra, Ch. V, passim.

[219] See the full discussion and vast array of examples in Campbell Bonner, *Studies in Magical Amulets Chiefly Graeco-Egyptian* (Ann Arbor 1950). Also of general interest are: Henri Leclercq, "Amulettes," DACL I/2 (Paris 1907), 1784–1802, and Gary Vikan, "Art, Medicine, and Magic in Early Byzantium," *Dumbarton Oaks Papers* 38 (1984), 65–86.

a plausible summary of the variety of these objects, which continue to turn up in excavations and fortuitous finds. Damascius mentions an amulet, a Chaldaean ring of wisdom (τὸ τῆς σωφροσύνης δακτύλιον) owned by Theosebios, the philosopher who performed the aforementioned exorcism without having cultivated either magic or theurgy (καίτοι οὔτε μαγεύειν εἰδὼς οὔτε θεουργίασμά τε μελετήσας).[220] The name of the protecting deity is left unstated:[221]

> Theosebios, having furnished this man with the ring of wisdom which the Chaldaean had come and given to him, went to his wife and told her: "He once gave you a ring for the betrothed of a child-bearing marriage. Now I give one to you as a chastizer, to be present as a protector of wise housekeeping and its cares. She accepted it gladly, and lived with her husband the remaining time without bodily intercourse. This amulet had something efficacious not only for the wife but also for himself, as he used to relate a long time ago. For when he was a young man, he confessed, he contended in the *agon* of the *paideia* with enemies in his own generation, both those who attacked him from without and those who betrayed him from within.

The amulet was thought to assist the woman's housekeeping (ἐπίκουρον παρεσόμενον τῆς σώφρονος ἐπικουρίας), but also led to a philosophical style of cohabitation (ἄνευ σωματικῆς κοινωνίας). Although worn by the man's wife, the phylactery protected him in his own professional life as well, that is from his contemporaries (γενεσιουργοί) in the sophists' discipline. One gets the impression that the typical jealousies among scholars led them to mobilize the received knowledge of theurgy against their professional competitors, much like the more banal varieties that prevailed amongst the charioteers and wrestlers of the hippodrome.[222]

---

[220] Damascius, *Epit. Phot. 56* (Zintzen, 82; Asmus, 35).

[221] Damascius, *Epit. Phot. 311* (Zintzen, 87f.). Cf. the comment of R. Asmus, *Das Leben des Isidoros*, 156.

[222] For the legislation on acts of sorcery, see infra, Ch. I, Sect. 4. The life of George of Choziba, a seventh-century text, provides the striking example of a wrestler who ultimately found a cure with the Christian monk after having tried both pagan and Christian devices to defeat the effects of "sorcery": "There was a certain wrestler in Byzantium, a Cilician by birth, who was victorious in his art. His opponents, who were in difficulty because of his art, poisoned him, and he suffered. His friends brought him from chapel to chapel and from monastery to monastery, and were grieved for his sake. Finally, out of much folly, or rather madness, these so-called Christians brought him to sorcerers who rejected the saints for the sake of their own tricks. The sorcerers bound an evil spirit to him for two years. He was victorious in his art from the strength of his body and from the activity of the spirit." *Vita S. Georgii Chozibae a Antonio*, ed. C. Houze, *Analecta Bollandiana* 7 (1888), 114. Ancient varieties of sorcery correspond closely to those reported in the anthropological literature. Cf. E.E. Evans-Pritchard, "Sorcery and Native Opinion," *Africa* 4 (1931), 23–28, and idem, "Witchcraft (*Mangu*) amongst

It is instructive to consider some archetypal examples of amulets which, if dating from earlier centuries, reflect paradigmatic modes of regarding a sometimes threatening exterior world. Thus, a text from c. 200 A.D. composed "in a crude school hand . . . on a roll left blank after entering tax receipts" reflects issues of general concern:[223]

> Amulet. Great celestial one, who grasps the world, you who are the god Iao, lord pantokrator, [magic word] Ablanathalaabla, give, give, that I might possess a favor, the name of the great god in this amulet, and protect me from every evil (φύλαξόν μοι ἀπὸ παντὸς κακοῦ πράγματος), whatever some woman might beget, whatever some man might beget.

A papyrus from Egypt of fourth- or fifth-century date reflects concerns which affected Hellene and Christian alike:[224]

> XMΓ. [Magic words.] Iao, Sabaoth, Adonai, Eloe, Salaman. [Magic word.] I bind you, scorpion, Artemisian, 315 times. Protect this house with those living in it from every evil influence of the spirits of the air, and of the human [evil] eye, and of dangerous illness, and of the bite of the scorpion and snake through the power of the name of God most high. [Magic words.] Protect me, Lord, son of David according to the flesh, who are begotten holy highest God of the holy virgin Maria of the Holy Spirit. Glory to you, celestial king! Amen. A+Ѡ.Ᵽ.A+Ѡ . IXΘYC

As regards household concerns, a fragmentary amuletic prayer dating from the sixth or seventh century adjures an unknown deity or *daimon* to protect the bearer against the archetypal, particular, or bodily *daimon*—the sense is unclear—thought to cause pregnancy (διαφυλάξετε ἀπὸ τοῦ συλ[ληπτικοῦ] αὐτοδαίμονος) and against migraine. (πρὸς ἡμίκρανον).[225] A philosophical marriage without

---

the Azande," *Sudan Notes and Records* 12 (1929), 163–249. For extracts and modifications of Evans-Pritchard's groundbreaking theories, see: *Witchcraft and Sorcery*, ed. Max Marwick (London 1982). Scholars generally agree on several points about sorcery: that inveterate competitiveness often provides the motivation (as in the case of George of Choziba's wrester), that it entails the supposed dispatch of spirits, and that the *maleficium* requires the belief of the *victim* in its potency in order to produce the desired evil effect, which is often sympathetic, hysterical, or psychosomatic in nature. Ibid., 16, 31, and 52. The tendency to assume the operation of magic rather than natural causes in cases of illness is quite common in primitive societies. Bronislav Malinowski, *Magic, Science, and Religion and Other Essays*, ed. Robert Redfill (Garden City 1984), 15.

[223] *Papyri Graecae Magicae: Die griechischen Zauberpapyri*, ed. Karl Preisendanz, 2 (Stuttgart 1974), P.LXXI (203). In this and the following instances, I have deliberately selected some shorter illustrative texts for the sake of brevity. This source is hereinafter abbreviated as PGM.

[224] PGM 2, P3 (p. 210f.).

[225] PGM 2, P.LXV (p. 197).

sexual intercourse like that mentioned in connection with Theosebios' ring might generate an occasional migraine in the course of
reading and speculation, but quite clearly obviated any need for a
prophylactic amulet.

It remains to consider some of the phenomena of everyday life
that belong to the varieties of Hellenic religion practiced by persons
of a lesser philosophical bent than those named in Damascius'
biography of Isidore. Some of these phenomena lie in the sphere
of true religion, others in the realm of sorcery. Our source is
Ammianus Marcellinus, a soldier and Hellene of Antioch who
reports on the affairs of the eastern parts of the empire during the
last years of the emperor Valens in the final three books of his
histories (c. 371–378). A characteristic feature of this era was a
preoccupation with sorcery linked to the sensational trials and
convictions which led to a number of executions. Some of the acts
proved to be heinous, other innocuous and hardly deserving of
capital punishment. Ammianus' reports reveal, in any case, a dark
side to the old religion that bore little resemblance to the great
urban temple cults.

The most heinous act concerned a certain Numerius, who was
apparently the tribune of an imperial guards unit attached to the
palace in Constantinople. The historian refers to him as "a man of
surpassing wickedness." Numerius was pardoned after confessing
to an act of criminal divination:[226]

> This man was convicted at that same time on his own confession of
> having dared to cut open the womb of a living woman and take out
> her unripe offspring, in order to evoke the ghosts of the dead and
> consult them about a change of rulers; yet Valens, who looked on him
> with the eye of an intimate friend, in spite of the murmurs of the
> whole Senate gave orders that he should escape unpunished, and
> retain his life, enviable wealth, and his military rank unimpaired.

The incident provides the example of politics actually helping a
practitioner of magic. The woman must have been a slave of
Numerius, or one procured especially for the purpose. This particular form of sacrifice turns up again, with some modifications in
method and purpose, in the eighth century, when the Arab emir
Maslama was besieging Pergamum.[227] Important citizens of Constantinople and other cities underwent torture and execution for
lesser divinatory offenses, whether real or imagined. One man, who
resided in the province of Asia and was perhaps a senator (*quidem*

---

[226] Quoted from Amm. Marc., *Res Gestae* 29.2.17 (tr. Rolfe 3, 225).
[227] Trombley, "Paganism in the Greek World," 334.

municeps clarus), but certainly a wealthy decurion, having his personal papers examined on some business matter in 372, lost his life after a horoscope (*genitura*) naming a certain Valens turned up amidst the other documents. When asked why he had had a horoscope cast with the birth constellation of the emperor on it (*quam ob rem constellationem principis collegisset*), he indicated that he had had a brother named Valens, who apparently possessed a set of signs identical to those of the emperor, but had died years before.[228] Zealous officials could not exclude the possibility that, in the wake of the THEOD oracle trials, other ambitious men might be seeking foreknowledge of Valens' destiny in order to execute a *coup d'état* at the most favorable moment.

One did not have to be plotting against the life of the emperor to fall victim to the obsession with sorcery that prevailed during the 370's. Caution was dictated, for example, at the bath houses, particularly in the province of Asia, where Festus the proconsul was conducting a purge, for sorcerers and diviners met their clients in such places:[229]

> In the bath (*in balneis*) a young man was seen to touch alternately with the fingers of either hand first the marble [of the floor or wall] and then his breast, and to count the seven vowels, thinking it a helpful remedy for a stomach trouble. He was hauled into court, tortured and beheaded.

This behavior, evidently a ritual prescribed by a physician to help his patient distract himself from the periodic recurrence of stomach pains caused by an ulcer, closely resembled the recitation of Greek vowels recommended in certain magic texts.[230] The authorities sometimes mistook magic applied as a medicinal cure for the baser arts of sorcery and divination. At Caruntum, the metropolis of Pannonia Prima, a predominantly Latin-speaking area on the Danube, the nephew of the Praetorian Prefect of Illyricum, a certain Faustinus, was convicted of having killed a donkey (*asinus*) in 375. His accusers declared the act to have been a sacrifice connected with certain criminal "secret arts" (*ad usum artium secretarum*), although Faustinus professed that he had done it as part of a ritual to stop his hair from falling out (*ad imbecillitatem firmandam fluentium capillorum*).[231] A surer locus for investigating practitioners of the "secret arts" was the hippodrome. A favorite charioteer c. 372

---

[228] Amm. Marc., *Res Gestae* 29.2.27.
[229] Quoted from Amm. Marc., *Res Gestae* 29.2.28 (tr. Rolfe 2, 233).
[230] PGM 2, P.LXII (p. 195).
[231] Amm. Marc. 30.5.11. A minute examination of the magical papyri might yield information about such a sacrifice.

named Athanasius, a Greek who practiced his profession in the circus
at Rome, was suspected all along of a certain "vulgar levity" in his
life-style. He suffered capital punishment for having practiced poisoning (*veneficiis usus*) after he received a stern warning about his activities
from the Praefectus Urbi Romae.[232] We learn, finally, of a simple-
minded old woman who used to "cure intermittent fevers with a
harmless incantation" (*intervallatis febribus mederi leni carmine*). She was
executed despite the fact that she had, with the knowledge of the
provincial governor, treated his own daughter.[233]

The judge in this last case was Festus of Tridentum, at this time
(372 A.D.) proconsul of the province of Asia. Ammianus Marcellinus advises us that he had gotten it into his head to imitate the
relentless search for evidence about the different kinds of divination
and sorcery conducted by Maximinus, the erstwhile Praefectus
Urbi of Rome and later Praetorian Prefect of Italy.[234] It was this
Festus, as well, who had ordered the execution in 372 of the man
who had the Valens horoscope in his private papers and the young
man in the bathhouse who had recited the Greek vowels while
tapping on the marble panelling and then his own chest. In assessing the phenomena of cult revealed in these and other cases, one is
struck by Ammianus' tendency always to believe the alibi and to
exculpate the person executed, when the behavior or practices
involved bore a striking resemblance to sorcery or divination. The
critic is forced to choose between his own knowledge of the phenomena of divination and magic and the pronounced apologetic
tendency in Ammianus. For example, when the guilt of the offenders was unambiguous, as with Athanasius the charioteer, who
seems to have practiced poisoning after receiving a stern warning,
Ammianus complains that the man deserved indulgence because of
his profession as an artist in entertainments (*voluptatum artifex*) in
the circus,[235] a most surprising position for the historian to take to
judge from what he has to say about the poisoner's art elsewhere:[236]

> For if anyone wore on him an amulet against quartan ague or any
> other complaint, or was accused by the testimony of the evilly dis-
> posed of passing by a grave in the evening, on the ground that he was
> a dealer in poisons, or a gatherer of the horrors of tombs and the vain
> illusions of the ghosts that wander there, he was condemned to
> capital punishment and perished.

232 Amm. Marc., *Res Gestae* 29.3.5.
233 Amm. Marc., *Res Gestae* 29.2.26.
234 Amm. Marc., *Res Gestae* 29.2.22–23.
235 Amm. Marc., *Res Gestae* 29.3.5.
236 Adapted from Amm. Marc., *Res Gestae* 19.12.14–15 (tr. Rolfe 1, 541).

This datum derives from the reign of Constantius II in the year 359. On the other hand, our impartial historian (*pace* Gibbon) curses the system which allowed the tribune Numerius to go free after performing a sacrifice by cutting the fetus out of a living woman: a heinous crime, all will certainly agree, but one committed by a middle-ranking official among the palatines whom Ammianus may have had every reason to emulate, or hate secretly under the eyes of Valens and the court entourage. It would hardly be dangerous to suppose the prevalence of the cults described here in the late fourth century. If many of the executions were politically inspired and at times fell on the innocent, it is equally certain that Ammianus' account was inspired by a bitter loathing for a system which saw many good men, including friends of his, cashiered, and in which the historian perhaps failed to receive advancement commensurate with his own high opinion of himself. Bitter, talented men like Tacitus and Niccolo Machiavelli always write interesting history. The present-day historian must therefore question the alibis of the victims of Festus' executions as much as the motives of their apologist Ammianus. The close similarity of their behavior to known practices suggests that, if officials erred on the side of severity in rooting out "enemies of the Roman order", there were many other occasions when these criminal investigations landed right on the mark. These varieties of cultic behavior must therefore be taken as indirect evidence for the dark side of Hellenic religiosity in the 370's, on the eve of the anti-pagan legislation of Theodosius the Great, and possibly as something quite distinct which the "impartial historian" has obscured for his own purposes.[237]

IV. The Legislation against Sorcery

It remains to examine the status of sorcery and divination in the imperial edicts. The series of twelve statutes assembled in the Theodosian Code dates back to three laws promulgated c. 319 by Constantine the Great, whose *imperium* was still confined to the western parts of the empire at that time.[238] The most recent belongs to 409. These acts range widely over such questions as *haruspices* taking auspices from animal entrails, astrologers casting horo-

---

[237] This view of Ammianus Marcellinus' bias is, I find, generally shared. Cf. A.A. Barb, "Survival of Magic Arts," *The Conflict between Paganism and Christianity in the Fourth Century*, ed. A. Momigliano (Oxford 1963), 103. This view was originally stated by A. Alföldy, *A Conflict of Ideas in the Late Roman Empire*, tr. H. Mattingly (Oxford 1952), 3.

[238] On the legislation, see: Andreas Alföldi, *The Conversion of Constantine and Pagan Rome*, tr. H. Mattingly (Oxford 1948), 75–78.

scopes, and sorcerers practicing base magic to the detriment of their victims' health and virtue. Three of the edicts date from the early 370's, when the hysteria about magic had reached its zenith in the eastern provinces of the empire, and at Constantinople in particular.[239] As it turns out, more than a few of the laws seek remedies for phenomena closely related to those described by Ammianus Marcellinus and discussed in the previous section. The principles for judging such cases were firmly established during that time.

The three Constantinian laws reflect that emperor's anxiety about the activities of the *haruspices*, practitioners of the ancient Etruscan art of seeking omens in the entrails of sacrificial animals. Two laws on this question, given at Rome on 1 February and 15 May 319, did not seek to interdict the practice as such, but to confine it to the house of the *haruspex* himself. These folk were forbidden under any circumstances to approach the threshold (*limen*) of another, even under the pretext or fact of longstanding friendship (*sub praetextu amicitiae*).[240] Such friendship was, in fact, condemned implicitly.[241] The *haruspex* was subject to the penalty of being burned alive, the person who summoned him by persuasions or fees (*suasionibus vel premiis*) to exile.[242] Constantine perhaps felt threatened by a conspiracy of the largely pagan Senate of Rome and Licinius Augustus (ob. 324) in the East. He was therefore anxious to prevent secret consultations about omens, lest favorable signs trigger the audacity of some. The law of 1 February removes the odium of informers (*delatores*) from any who might divulge the identity of the offenders. The continuity of the *haruspices'* art into the early fourth century and down to the time of the Theodosian codification is thus evident, for a religious system requires a strong consensus for it to be used as a political tool. The law rejects secret combinations only. *Haruspices* were thus allowed to practice their rite publicly (*publice ritum proprium exercere*):[243]

> But those of you who think that this [practice] is profitable to you may go to the public altars and celebrate the sacrifices of your custom (*adite aras publicas adque delubra et consuetudinis vestrae celebrate sollemnia*).

---

[239] Alföldy, *Conflict of Ideas in the Late Roman Empire*, 69–72, 74f., 78f., etc. Alföldy rightly distrusts Ammianus' veracity in describing these cases of magic. Supra, Ch. I, Sect. 3. A.A. Barb's article even now remains the classic statement of the issue. Supra, n. 237. More recently, see: Richard Kieckhefer, *Magic in the Middle Ages* (Cambridge 1989), 1–42.

[240] *Cod. Theod.* 9.16.1.

[241] *Cod. Theod.* 9.16.1.

[242] Ibid.

[243] *Cod. Theod.* 9.16.2.

> For we do not forbid the ceremonies of the old observance to be
> carried out in the light of day (*libera luce*).

The subsequent history of these practices suggests their in-
eradicability.[244]

The laws of Constantine were considered good *ipso facto* by virtue
of their authorship and relative antiquity. Two laws of Constantius
II (337–361) make a new departure, putting the art of the *haruspex*
in the same crock of damnation as malevolent magic. The first of
these statutes (25 January 357) forbade *consultation* with *haruspices*
under the threat of capital punishment, but not the practice itself.
It adds: "The curiosity of all men about divination (*divinandi curiositas*) shall fall silent forever."[245] The second statute (5 July 358)
confuted *haruspices* with other diviners and sorcerers. It aimed not at
banning the practice as such, but only at eradicating it from the
imperial court circle (*comitatus*), which was constantly in movement
during the reign of Constantius II. More of this law will be seen in
connection with the problem of base magic.[246]

The periodic restatement of the original Constantinian law
against sacrifice implicitly bore on the *haruspex*'s art, since one could
hardly inspect animal entrails and divine the future without a
sacrificial victim to make the rite efficacious. These processes went
on all through the fourth and fifth centuries. They came to the fore,
for example, during the brief reign of Julian the Apostate. Justus,
his proconsul of Asia, "who depended upon every kind of divination" (καὶ μαντείας ἐξεκρέματο πάσης), performed public sacrifice during a visit to Sardis.[247] He was so addicted to ritual that,
when the victim collapsed after he applied the knife, he began the
divination by studying the meaning of the posture into which the
animal had fallen.[248]

---

[244] The anonymous *interpretatio* attached to this statute ridicules the idea that
the law actually invited persons to perform the *haruspicina* publicly. "Scholia
Vaticana: Similar to the [statute] above, but this one goes on to say that someone
might [actually] perform ceremonies. But it says this in a mocking tone, as though
one might actually attempt to perform sacrifices in the manner of ancient ceremonial (. . . *sed hoc inrisive dicit, ut templa conducta publica secundum ritum pristinum
sacrificare*)." The actual law is emphatic about the license given to sacrifice. The
interpretatio is in contrast the product of a later age, when all sacrifices were
forbidden. Constantine's complicity in such acts struck the commentator as impossible. Hence it appears that Constantine's forbearance during the early days of
his regime in Rome had been forgotten by the late fourth century. Cf. Barb, "The
Survival of Magic Arts," 105f.

[245] Or: "Let the curiosity of men about divination fall silent forever." *Cod.
Theod.* 9.16.4.

[246] *Cod. Theod.* 9.16.6.

[247] Eunapius, *Lives of the Philosophers* (Wright, 552f.).

[248] Ibid., 554–557.

A law of Valentinian I, given at Trier (29 May 371) and later ratified by the coemperors Valens and Gratian, clarified the relationship of the *haruspex*'s art (*haruspicina*) to other kinds of divination. Unlike the others, divination from animal entrails was vindicated by its origin deep in the Roman political and religious tradition. It was therefore legitimate so long as it was not practiced "harmfully", that is to predict the outcome of conspiracy and rebellion:[249]

> I do not judge the art of divination from entrails (*haruspicina*) to have connection with cases of sorcery (*ego nullum cum maleficiorum causis habere consortium iudico*), nor do I moreover consider this or any religious practice allowed by our ancestors to be a category of crime (. . . *neque ipsam aut aliquam praeterea concessam a maioribus religionem genus esse arbitror criminis*). The statutes given by myself at the beginning of my *imperium* are witnesses in which free opportunity (*libera facultas*) was granted to everyone individually (*unicuique*) of cultivating whatever he conceived in his mind. We do not censure the art of the *haruspex*, but we do forbid it to be practiced harmfully.

The Hellenes of Aphrodisias practiced *haruspicina* in its illegal form during the rebellion of Illus, the *magister militum per Orientem*, against the emperor Zeno c. 481–488,[250] an example that must be the tip of the proverbial iceberg. Valentinian I's clarification of the law given here was fully consistent with the Constantinian decrees of 319 and remained the rule until at least 484.[251] It provides a good example, as well, of the post-Julianic liberalization of the rules against *haruspicina* that Constantius II had imposed. This tendency of the Valentinian dynasty is a seldom appreciated feature of the period c. 363–378.[252]

Base magic, in the multifarious forms of sorcery (*maleficium*), poisoning (*veneficium*), and vulgar divination (the art of the *hariolus*), has a status completely divorced from that of *haruspicina* in the edicts collected in the Theodosian Code. Christian bishops, Hellenic philosophers, imperial officials, and a wide public of urban workers and agriculturalists believed in the efficacy of malevolent spells. Hellenic philosophers dignified such works with the term theurgy (θεουργία), which implied channeling the powers of an unseen divine world for the edification (mainly) or benefit of men.[253] If Damascius of Damascus is to be believed, the pagan

---

[249] *Cod. Theod.* 9.16.9.
[250] Infra, Ch. V, Sect. 4.
[251] Infra, Ch. I, Sect. 6.
[252] Infra, Ch. II, Sect. 2, n. 46.
[253] Cf. Garth Fowden's absorbing study: "The Pagan Holy Man in Late Antique Society," *Journal of Hellenic Studies* 102 (1982), 33–59.

"holy men" at times gave in to the perverse tendency to try to use their powers gratuitously and destructively.[254] Ordinary sorcerers by way of contrast summoned individual, and sometimes whole constellations of, *daimones* to effect their spells. Ammianus Marcellinus' histories provide a veritable rogues' gallery of base magicians and diviners along with other persons whom the "philosophic historian" seeks to exculpate from such charges posthumously.[255] The imperial edicts reflect the public opinion that the practitioners of these arts were "legally alien to nature" (*naturae peregrini sunt*).[256] "enemies of the human race in whatever part of the world they live" (*etsi omnes magi, in quacumque sint parte terrarum, humani generis inimici credidendi sunt*),[257] and undeserving of pardon in the periodic amnesties granted on the Christian Pasch.[258]

A man or woman who suddenly fell ill or gave way to an uncontrollable amorous passion often suspected the work of sorcerers right from the start, whether he was the simplest Christian catechumen or a Hellenic philosopher.[259] Eunapius of Sardis relates the intriguing story of the female philosopher Sosipatra (ante c. 361), who had landed estates in the vicinity of Pergamum. Something of a clairvoyant and theurgist herself,[260] Sosipatra was once troubled by a love charm, it was said, imposed on her by an admiring pupil named Philometor. When the young man left her presence, she would feel her heart "wounded and churning within her in such a manner as to burst from within her chest" (δάκνεταί μου καὶ στρέφεταί πως πρὸς τὴν ἔξοδον ἔνδον ἡ καρδία).[261] One can easily suppose with E.R. Dodds that a scarcely repressed subconscious eroticism lay behind her physical symptoms that was perhaps excited by Philometor's glances. A noble and sophisticated Hellenic woman could hardly admit such a craving, and so a *daimon* and spell had to be invented. Maximus of Ephesus, the inscrutable theurgist and crony of Julian the Apostate, generously stepped in and counteracted the spell with a stronger one, after discovering

---

[254] Supra, Ch. I, Sect. 3.
[255] Supra, Ch. I, Sect. 3.
[256] *Cod. Theod.* 9.16.5.
[257] *Cod. Theod.* 9.16.5.
[258] *Cod. Theod.* 9.38.3–5, 7, 8.
[259] This is the obvious interpretation in an age that saw an unseen world populated by *daimones* that affected the natural order and behavior of phenomena. See the comparative examples collected in Kieckhofer, *Magic*, 7, 19–20, and 81–83. In cases of life-threatening illness, too, suspicion of sorcery often preceded the search for material causes. Supra, n. 222.
[260] Eunapius, *Lives of the Philosophers* (Wright, 327).
[261] Ibid., 410–413.

the origin of the problem through his sacrificial lore (διὰ σοφίας μὲν θυτικῆς καταμαθὼν ᾧτινι κέχρηται, βιαιοτέρῳ τε καὶ δυνατωτέρῳ καταλῦσαι τὸ ἔλαττον).[262]

The opinion that Philometor had of these proceedings cannot be deduced from Eunapius' narrative. Maximus is said to have confronted him with the facts of the case: "'Colleague Philometor, by the gods, stop burning wood in vain.' He said this to him perhaps about the *maleficia* that he was practicing."[263] The "perhaps" (ἴσως) of this statement tells all. Sosipatra relieved herself of the anxiety about a potential liason with her pupil by a sublimated confession of libidinous desire to Maximus, whose "exorcism" of the *daimon* conferred a sort of symbolic absolution on the woman. It was easier for all the parties concerned to confront the "otherness" of the *daimon* than the "self-ness" of seemingly antisocial libido, especially as the Neoplatonic world-view of the participants despised such impulses.[264] The average law student, artisan, or farmer confronted these problems at a less philosophic level, but the emotional dynamics and rationalizations were essentially the same.[265]

The earliest statute on sorcery in the Theodosian Code dates from the reign of Constantine the Great in West (23 May 317–19; 321–24):[266]

> The science (*scientia*) of those who are discovered to be equipped with magic arts and to wield them against the safety of men or to deflect virtuous minds to lust is to be punished and deservedly avenged with the severest laws. But the remedies sought for human bodies shall not be involved in criminal accusations, nor those acts of assistance (*suffragia*) innocently applied in the rural districts, lest rains would threaten the ripening vintages or that they be shattered by the stones of a tumbling hailstorm, by which no one's safety or reputation is harmed, but whose performance might be beneficial, lest divine gifts or the labors of men be destroyed.
>
> *Interpretatio*: Sorcerers or enchanters or launchers of storms or those who through the invocation of *daimones* throw the minds of men into confusion shall be punished with every kind of penalty (*Malefici vel incantatores vel inmissores tempestatum vel hi, qui per invocationem daemonum mentes hominum turbant*, etc.).

---

[262] Ibid., 412f.

[263] Thus, by calling them *maleficia* (τὰ κακοῦργα), Eunapius or his source equates the rituals of concocting love charms in every respect with those designed to cause bodily harm. Supra, Ch. I, n. 259.

[264] Cf. E.R. Dodds' discussion, *Pagan and Christian in an Age of Anxiety* (Cambridge 1965), 29f.

[265] Cf. the case of Paralios' seemingly bad conscience after his baptism. Infra, Ch. V, Sect. 3.

[266] Remedia humanis quaesita corporibus aut in agrestibus locis, ne maturis vindemiis metuerentur imbres aut ruentis gradinis lapidatione quarterentur, innocenter adhibita suffragia. *Cod. Theod.* 9.16.3.

If Eunapius of Sardis can be trusted, even Constantine at times gave in to the persuasion that sorceries explained unusual deviations in the weather.[267] Ablabius, the great Praetorian Prefect, is supposed to have convinced the emperor that adverse north winds preventing the Black Sea grain fleet from reaching Constantinople had been induced by the pagan philosopher Sopater, who had supposedly "bound the winds through an excess of [theurgic] wisdom" (ἀλλὰ Σώπατρος γε . . . κατέδησε τοὺς ἀνέμους δι᾽ ὑπερβολὴν σοφίας).[268] Sopater was beheaded after this. If one accepts the notion that some men had the daimonic power to shift the winds, the act was seditious: civil rebellion could result if grain supplies ran low in the city. If Ablabius feared for his job, Constantine may have feared for his throne.[269]

A more interesting feature of the law of 17–23 May 317–19 is the special status accorded to the non-malevolent forms of magic (*innocenter adhibita suffragia*) designed to heal pagans and Christians from physical ailments (*remedia humanis quaesita corporibus*) and to prevent the destruction of harvests from immoderate rainstorms or the fall of hail (*in agrestibus locis, ne maturis vindemiis metuerentur imbres aut ruentis gradinis lapidatione quaterentur*). It would seem that the edict was a necessary response to the overzealousness of some officials who punished every kind of magic. Few examples of the pagan sacrifices and incantations survive.[270] The evidence for these rituals, including magic circles around tilled fields, the summoning of animate rain clouds, the averting of "wild" clouds full of hailstones, and healing the sick with oil and prayer, survives mainly in its modified and Christianized form.[271]

The systematic legislation against sorcery continued during c. 358–389, a time when the morose suspicions of emperors like Constantius II and Valens in particular floated to the political

---

[267] On Constantine's association with the theurgist Sopater, see Alföldi, *Conversion of Constantine*, 57 and 99.

[268] Eunapius, *Lives of the Philosophers* (Wright, 384f.).

[269] Even well-established emperors tested the murky depths of the political waters of Constantinople for sedition. That few emperors were ever overthrown in the city is more a testimonial to the logistic efficiency of their subordinates than the predictability of the urban crowds. In this instance, the demos is said to have been worn out by hunger. After observing that Sopater had bound the winds, it uttered a seditious shout: "But Sopater, he whom you honor, has bound the winds through an excess of [theurgic] wisdom that even you praise, and because of this he (you?) still sits on the imperial throne." Ibid.

[270] The anonymous *interpretatio* adds: "Sorcerers or enchanters or launchers of storms or those who through the invocation of *daimones* throw the minds of men into confusion shall be punished with every kind of penalty".

[271] Trombley, "Paganism in the Greek World," 337–341, 345.

surface in the form of emotional debris and anxiety about the
practitioners of malevolent magic (*malefici*), poisoners (*venefici*), versifiers about future events (*vates*), augurs (*augures*), Chaldaean
astrologers, Hellenic astrologers (*mathematici*), vulgar astrologers or
diviners (*harioli*), "Persian" astrologers (*magi*), and the rest. The
greater part of this catalogue derives from a law of Constantius II
(25 January 357) directed against "inquisitiveness about divination" (*divinandi curiositas*). Each one of these was a "depraved
science."[272] The first two (malevolent magic and poisoning) were in
the phrase of Constantine the Great a "science . . . of those who
are . . . equipped with magic arts and wield them against the safety
of men or to deflect virtuous minds to lust."[273] The law stipulates
capital punishment for these offenses.

All the sorcerers and diviners attested in the laws of Constantine
I and Constantius II turn up in later contexts: a sorcerer who
concocted a love charm in Berytus (late 5th century); poisoners
who robbed graves for organs of the dead to manufacture their
potions (Rome, c. 359–72);[274] versifiers of future events, that is
producers of hexametric oracles, in Aphrodisias in the time of Illus'
rebellion against the emperor Zeno (c. 481–484);[275] Persian magicians (*magi*) in Berytus (c. 490);[276] astrologers who cast the horoscope of Proclus, *diadochos* of the Neoplatonic school of Athens (5th
century);[277] vulgar mantics (*harioli*) like the man of Bithynia who
claimed that an "angel" helped him to see the future after
appropriate sacrifices had been made at idol temples (c. 443–46);[278]
and the cloud-drivers (νεφοδιῶκται) who were thought to direct
clouds bearing hailstones and immoderate rain from place to
place.[279] The list might be extended endlessly.[280]

Another edict, given at Milan probably on 4 December 356,[281]
reaffirmed the penalties against *malefici* and *venefici* in dramatic
form:[282]

---

[272] *Cod. Theod.* 9.16.4.
[273] *Cod. Theod.* 9.16.4.
[274] Supra, Ch. I, Sect. 3.
[275] Infra, Ch. V, Sect. 4.
[276] Infra, Ch. V, Sect. 5.
[277] Infra, Ch. IV, Sect. 3.
[278] Infra, Ch. VII, Sect. 1.
[279] Supra, Ch. I, Sect. 3. Trombley, "Paganism in the Greek World," 343.
[280] Examples may be found in Phaidon Koukoules, *Byzantinōn bios kai Politismos*
1/2 (Athens 1948), 226–265. Cf. "Magic," *Oxford Dictionary of Byzantium*, ed. A
Kazhdan *et al.* (Oxford 1991), 1265f.
[281] The date of the prescript to this law fails to conform to the known move-
ments of Constantius II and the *comitatus*. Pharr, *Theodosian Code*, 238.
[282] *Cod. Theod.* 9.16.5.

Many persons who dare to disturb the forces of nature (*elementa turbari*) and who dare to wave in the air after the spirits of the dead have been summoned do not hesitate to damage the lives of innocent persons, so that everyone might destroy his personal enemies by evil arts. Deadly ruin shall consume those persons, since they are alien to nature!

This statute only treated malevolent acts, but not the "innocent" magic mentioned in the Constantinian law mentioned above that was designed to benefit the health of men and their crops. This was manifestly the intention of the Theodosian codification as well.

It came to light around this time that members of the *comitatus* had engaged in sorcery, divination and astrology. Constantius II responded with a harsh edict designed to obliterate the persons in question (5 July 358). He evidently feared his *comites'* speculations about the "fated" end of his reign and perhaps attempts to poison him. Such acts suggest acrimonious relations among men bent on gaining personal dominance in the court hierarchy that could only be a bad thing for the execution of Constantius II's policies. The law is intransigent:[283]

> Although the bodies of those distinguished by offices of high rank are exempt from torture, except for those crimes which are stated in the statutes, and since all magicians, in whatsoever part of the world they live, should be trusted as though enemies of the human race (*humani generis inimici*), and since those who are in our *comitatus* have direct contact with our majesty: if any one of them is a *magus* or is trained in the contamination of the magic arts (*magicis contaminibus adsuetus*), who is called *maleficus* by the custom of the vulgar masses, or a *haruspex* or *hariolus* or at all events an augur, or even an astrologer, or someone concealing some skill at divining by interpreting dreams, or at any rate someone who practices *something like this* in my *comitatus* or that of the Caesar is caught by surprise, he shall not escape torture by his protected position of high rank. If he is convicted of his own crime and opposes those who discovered it by a denial, he shall be given to the wooden rack and to the claws that dig at his sides, and he shall endure penalties appropriate to his crime.

As *honestiores*, or men belonging to the higher grade of citizenship, counts of the imperial consistory, palatine guards such as protectors, and so forth were normally exempt from torture and summary execution.[284] This statute signifies an important exception to the rule of exorbitant privilege applied to membership in the *comitatus*. The men implicated in the THEOD- divination conspiracy at Antioch in 371–372 held various prefectural and notarial offices,

---

[283] *Cod. Theod.* 9.16.6.
[284] Jones, *Later Roman Empire*, 17f.

but did not at that time belong to the *comitatus*. Cruel tortures were
applied to them to extract confessions, just as the earlier law given
here provides. Two low-level officials, Patricius and Hilarius, who
gave a complete account of the Delphic ritual, were tortured with
hooks *after their confession* and then taken away unconscious from
pain and terror. Another conspirator, the young philosopher Simonides, had failed to divulge the conspiracy for reasons of honor
toward his friends' secrets. He was sentenced to be burned alive.
Ridiculing his fate, the man mounted the pyre unmoved.[285] All the
participants in the affair and some uninvolved persons were executed, including the famous theurgist Maximus of Ephesus (by
beheading). Alypius, the former vicar of the diocese of Britain, a
quiet man living in retirement, was denounced for a separate case
of sorcery, but was reprieved just before his execution. The only
evidence, according to Ammianus Marcellinus, came from a "low
fellow" (*vilus*) called Diogenes who was mangled until there was no
feasible torture left to be applied and then burnt to death.[286] Our
purpose is not to catalogue tortures, but only to identify the state of
danger that existed for *honestiores* after the edict of 358 became
law.[287] This regulation did not deter highly placed officials from
undertaking the proscribed rites. As with the pagan sacrifice, sorcery and divination certainly declined during the period being
investigated here, but could not be rooted out entirely.

An early law of Valens and Valentinian I (9 September 364)
reiterated the previous rulings on magic preparations along with
"nefarious prayers" and funerary practices (*Ne quis deinceps nocturnis
temporibus aut nefarios preces aut magicos apparatus aut sacrificia funesta
celebrare conetur*).[288] Funerary sacrifices existed in all the local cultures of the empire. Bishops like Gregory of Nazianzus in the borderlands of Cappadocia and the Armenias regarded them as a
form of backsliding into Hellenic religion.[289] The custom of funerary banquets at Christian tombs and their repetition on occasion is
evident in the *mensa* inscriptions of the North African provinces.
One in particular, dating from 299 A.D., emphasizes the transi-

---

[285] Amm. Marc., *Res Gestae* 29.1.37–39.
[286] Amm. Marc., *Res Gestae* 29.1.44.
[287] But see the case of Numerius, a tribune of the imperial guards at Constantinople, who completed the divinatory sacrifice of a human fetus and escaped
punishment thanks to the emperor Valens' favoritism. Supra, Ch. I, Sect. 3, n.
226.
[288] *Cod. Theod.* 9.16.7.
[289] Supra, Ch. I, Sect. 2.

tional character of these rites between the old and new religions.[290] Funerary rites themselves had been driven underground by a previous law of Julian the Apostate (12 February 363). Its validity remained unquestioned in the years after the Hellenic emperor's death. The law forbade the transit of funeral processions through crowds of people during the daylight hours because of the risk of ritual pollution to bystanders for the worship of the gods (*Qui enim dies est bene auspicatus a funere aut quomodo ad deos et templa venietur?*) and because of the unlucky aspect symbolized by such processions.[291] The statute is entirely consistent with a later regulation issued in the time of Gratian, Valentinian II and Theodosius I (30 July 381).[292] The Julianic law was incorporated into the Theodosian Code in its original wording, notwithstanding its clear reference to the gods of the old polytheism.[293] The few attested cases of pagan funerals suggest that this law was observed.[294]

To return to the law of 364, "nefarious prayers" and funerary banquets ("sacrifices") became theoretically illegal. To judge from the gloss or *interpretatio* attached to it at the time of the Theodosian codification, this rule had in view the nightly horror of poisoners' preparing their concoctions from the human debris inside tombs and the invocation of *daimones*.[295] It simplified the task of enforcement to ban all nocturnal rituals involving the spirits of the dead (*manes*). An overzealous proconsul of Achaea then apparently interdicted the mysteries of the underworld deities Demeter and Persephone being celebrated at Eleusis, as they were thought to enjoy a special relationship with the spirits of the dead. This interruption ran against the spirit of accommodation with the old religion that prevailed during the reign of the co-emperors Valentinian I and Valens. The error was belatedly recognized and the Eleusinian mysteries were reestablished and apparently continued

---

[290] The important pre-Christian *mensa* inscription of Satafis (299 A.D.) is conveniently found in *Inscriptiones Latinae Christianae Veteres*, ed. E. Diehl (Berlin 1961), no. 1570. On the pagan nature of the text: Antonio Ferrua, *Nuove correzioni alla silloge del Diehl Inscr. Lat. Chr. Vet.* (Vatican City 1981), 37. The dedication of a *mensa*, or altar table at tombs, passed over directly into Christian practice. The very many examples include ILCV 3710–3726, and others in Diehl's corpus.

[291] *Cod. Theod.* 9.17.5.

[292] *Cod. Theod.* 9.17.6. Cf. Frank R. Trombley, "Boeotia in Late Antiquity: Epigraphic Evidence on Society, Economy, and Christianization," *BOIOTIKA: Vorträge vom 5. Internationalen Böotien-Kolloquium zu Ehren von Dr. Siegfried Lauffer*, ed. Hartmut Beister and John Buckler (Munich 1989), 221f.

[293] *Cod. Theod.* 9.17.5.

[294] Supra, Ch. I, Sect. 3.

[295] *Cod. Theod.* 9.17.5, *Interpretatio*.

to function publicly until Alaric's Visigoths pillaged the *temenos* in 396.[296] The Hellenic historian Zosimus observes:[297]

> Once [Valentinian] had decided on the introduction of legislation, beginning as it were from his own hearth, he restricted nocturnal sacrifices from being performed, as he was desirous that the mysteries be impeded through this law. When Praetextatus, who had held the proconsulship of Greece (a man excelling in every virtue), told the emperor that this law had made life unliveable for the Hellenes, if the human race should be restricted from celebrating the most holy mysteries as usual according to customary law, the emperor ruled that all could be accomplished according to the ancestral custom of the earliest times, the [imperial] law being unenforced.

If pressed, Zosimus' text reveals the status of the law. It remained among the standing imperial edicts, but was simply not enforced in the case of the Eleusinian mysteries (ἀργοῦντος τοῦ νόμου).[298] Its passage was perhaps an oversight, a problem quickly corrected through the advice and protestation of Vettius Agorius Praetextatus, whose term as proconsul of Achaea had apparently expired not long before the publication of the new law, which was issued nine days after the beginning of the new indiction (9 September 364). It seems that his successor as proconsul interpreted the new statute as vitiating the Eleusinian mysteries. These were, however, ancestral customs from earliest times (τὰ ἐξ ἀρχῆς πάτρια), a body of cults and customs clearly unrelated to sorcery and whose legitimacy Valentinian I later recognized in principle in the edict of 371 on the *haruspicina*.[299] The public opinion of the urban Hellenes of Achaea still had the power to convince emperors of the legality of their cults in 364, and not in the least because they had a powerful patron in Praetextatus, a Hellene who rose to the Praetorian Prefecture of Illyricum and Italy in 384, and was named consul designate in that year as well.[300]

The co-emperors Valens and Valentinian I also tightened up the laws against casting horoscopes, making not only the purveyor, but

---

[296] Eunapius, *Lives of the Philosophers* (Wright, 436–439).
[297] Zosimus, *Historia Nova* 4.3.2–3 (Mendelsson, 160, lines 7–16).
[298] Zosimus' account here derives from the *Universal History* of Eunapius of Sardis, an author exceptionally well-informed about social, economic and religious conditions in Attica during the 360's. Cf. his discussion of the rise in the price of grain during the reign of emperor Constans I (337–350). Eunapius, *Lives of the Philosophers* (Wright, 508–511).
[299] *Cod. Theod.* 9.16.9. Supra, this section.
[300] Zosimus, *New History*, tr. Ronald T. Ridley (Canberra 1982), 185, n. 8.

also the receiver of the forbidden document, subject to the death penalty (12 December 370 or 373):[301]

> The practice of the astrologers shall cease. If anyone is caught publicly or privately at day or night entangled in this forbidden charlatanry, each of the two (*uterque*) shall be stricken with capital punishment. For the forbidden culpability of receiving the information is not dissimilar from making it known (*neque enim culpa dissimilis est prohibita discere quam docere*).

The statute sought to strangle the demand for horoscopes by terrorizing the market. Although reaffirmed by the Theodosian codification of 438, the law was unenforceable. Proclus, the *diadochos* or director of the Neoplatonist academy in Athens (ob. 485), might in theory have been liable to execution for possessing the horoscope that his successor Marinus published in his posthumous life of Proclus.[302] Proof of this might be found in the anecdote of Ammianus Marcellinus mentioned above about the wealthy decurion of the province of Asia executed in 372 for possessing the horoscope of a certain "Valens" whom he claimed was his brother.[303]

The law books were firmly closed on astrologers in the early fifth century by a decree of the co-emperors Arcadius and Honorius. Given at Ravenna (1 February 409), it aimed at the eradication of the *mathematici* from the cities of the empire, where the principal market for their services lay:[304]

> We decree that astrologers be driven from not only the city of Rome, but from all cities (*civitates*), unless they are prepared to surrender their faith to the worship of the catholic church and never return to their former error, after the books of their erroneous doctrine have been incinerated in a fire under the eyes of the bishops (. . . *codicibus erroris proprii sub oculis episcoporum incendio concrematis*). But if they fail to do this and, contrary to the saving disposition of our clemency, are caught in the cities or introduce the secrets of their error and profession, they shall receive the punishment of exile (*deportatio*).

Zachariah of Mytilene provides practically a textbook example of this system of enforcement c. 490. In this instance bishop John of Berytus supervised the burning of magic books in a public square with the defensor of the city and local corps of imperial notaries looking on.[305]

---

[301] *Cod. Theod.* 9.16.8. C. Pharr has, in my view, misunderstood the meaning of the Latin text here. *Theodosian Code*, 238.
[302] Infra, Ch. IV, Sect. 3.
[303] Supra, Ch. I, Sect. 3, n. 228.
[304] *Cod. Theod.* 9.16.12.
[305] Infra, Ch. V, Sect. 5.

A law of the co-emperors Valentinian II, Theodosius I and
Arcadius (given at Rome, 16 August 389) provided that sorcerers
be denounced publicly (*ilico ad publicum protrahat*) as an "enemy of
the public safety" (*communis hostis salutis*). Charioteers had in particular been the target of malevolent magic (*maleficia*). The edict
calls upon them to heed this rule of public denunciation and not to
avenge themselves on sorcerers or any other personal enemy (*inim-
icus*) on the pretext that they had imposed evil spells.[306] Charioteers
remained perpetual suspects of hiring sorcerers and poisoners to
destroy their enemies. Steering a team of horses in the hippodrome
could be extremely lucrative. One accepted the money and popularity of this trade not only at the risk of accident and poisoning,
but also of conviction in the courts for crime, as happened to the
Greek charioteer Athanasius in Rome.[307]

The edicts on magic remained in force throughout the era of the
Theodosian dynasty (379–457), and were, of course, reiterated in
the Theodosian Code in 438. The *quaestor* Tribonian's new codification of the edicts in 532, the so-called Justinian Code, repeated
most of the old edicts. Here the phrasing of the statutes received
certain minor alterations in response to the conditions then prevailing at Constantinople and in the other Greek cities. It causes no
surprise that, in 532, the law of 371 issued by Valentinian I,
Valens, and Gratian granting free practice (*libera facultas*) to the
ancestral cults (*concessa a maioribus religio*) was simply dropped from
the list of active statutes.[308] The empire of Justinian aimed at
nothing less than the complete eradication of the varieties of Hellenic religion and the assimilation of their practitioners into the
Christian social fabric.[309]

V. The Transformation of the Law after 438

The legislation against sacrifice and the other varieties of Hellenic
belief between 319–423 did not, in itself, envision the complete
obliteration of the old religion, but sought rather to regulate it in a
manner that fended off the perceived moral and social dangers
inherent in the ancestral cults. The men responsible for the framing
and publication of the Theodosian Code in the years before 438
held this opinion as well. One thinks, for example, of the law
against the propitiatory sacrifice of infants, or, presumably, mature

---

[306] *Cod. Theod.* 9.16.11.
[307] Supra, Ch. I, Sect. 3.
[308] Supra, this section.
[309] Infra, Ch. I, Sect. 6.

fetuses in the course of divination rituals (*piaculum*) (given by Valentian I, Valens, and Gratian, 7 February 374),[310] the restriction of funeral processions to the hours of the night, and the condemnation of the Maiuma.

The Maiuma was a water festival celebrated in specially designed sacred pools wherein women are thought to have bathed and, perhaps, to have frolicked naked.[311] The precise religious meaning of the Maiuma is unknown. It was possibly a fertility cult of some sort. At any rate, John Chrysostom, patriarch of Constantinople (398–404), condemned it, and two imperial laws attempted to control the behavior in question. The first of these, given at Constantinople in the name of the co-emperors Arcadius and Honorius to Caesarius, Praetorian Prefect of Oriens (25 April 396), was anxious to conserve the festival:[312]

> It has pleased our clemency that the joy of Maiuma be restored to the provincials, so long, that is, as decorum is maintained and modesty is preserved by morally unobjectionable practices.

A later law, issued by the same emperors to the same Praetorian Prefect, notes the continuing violation of the established rule on decorum and modesty at the festival (2 October 399):[313]

> We allow the sportive arts to be celebrated, lest dejection be caused by overzealous regulation. We flatly refuse that, however, which lays legal claim to the name of impudent license, the Maiuma, a foul and obscene spectacle (*Illud vero quod sibi procax licentia vindicavit, maiumam, foedum adque indecorum spectaculum*).

A mid-fifth century civil governor of Caria was given the civic titles of agonothete and Maiumarch.[314] It would seem, then, that the Maiuma festival survived despite imperial denunciation and ecclesiastical lament in a form uncoupled from its original religious and sexually interesting context. And so the co-emperors' policy succeeded in the long run, despite anything that Hellenes and Christians on the fringes of the catechumenate might have done privately or in small groups on that occasion, including invoking the relevant deities and making sacrifice.

The fourth- and fifth-century emperors continued to tighten the screws on Christian apostates in the area of civil law. An edict given at Constantinople by the three reigning Augusti (Gratian,

---

[310] *Cod. Theod.* 9.14.1.
[311] Ramsay MacMullen, *Paganism in the Roman Empire* (New Haven 1981), 19 and 21.
[312] *Cod. Theod.* 15.6.1.
[313] *Cod. Theod.* 15.6.2.

Valentinian II and Theodosius I) on 20 May 383 voided wills
made by catechumens or baptized Christians who "migrated to
pagan rituals and cults" (*qui ad paganos ritus cultusque migrarunt*)[315]
and once again approached Hellenic altars and temples "in such
great neglect of the venerable [Christian] religion" (*qui Christiani
et catechumeni tantum venerabili religione neglecta ad aras et templa
transierunt*).[316] A subsequent statute degraded Christian holders of
imperial titles who apostasized through sacrifices (*ac se sacrificiis
mancipassent*) to below the status of *humiliores*, or the lower category
of Roman citizenship. This technically reduced them to the status
of freedmen with Latin Rights:[317]

> If the splendor [of rank] is conferred upon persons or is inborn by
> reason of legal status, and they have deviated from the faith and
> practice of sacrosanct religion with the faith of a devious man and the
> mind of a blind man and they deliver themselves to sacrifices, they
> shall be degraded to the point of being evicted from their station and
> status (*de loco suo statuque deicti*) and be embarrassed with perpetual
> infamy. They shall not be numbered even among the lowest of the
> ignoble masses. For what can they have in common with those men
> who detest the grace of communion and retire from that of the [rest
> of] men?

The rule on wills was strengthened by another edict of Theodosius
II and Valentinian III (given at Ravenna, 7 April 426). If the
private papers or other testimonia about a man revealed that he
had performed sacrifices or had ordered them to be performed
"after assuming the name of Christianity" (*qui nomen Christianitatis
induti sacrificia vel fecerunt vel facienda mandaverint*), his bad faith, even
if proven posthumously (*etiam post mortem*), will have voided the
will. All other special bequests would be legally rescinded as
well.[318] The inclusion of these acts in the Theodosian Code demonstrates that Christian apostasy remained a problem of some dimension even towards the middle of the fifth century. The literature of
the Justinianic era and its sequel (c. 518–602) points to the periodic
occurrence of cryptopaganism, a concept implicit in the law of 426,
all through the sixth century.[319] Public and private behavior and

---

[314] Infra, Ch. VI, Sect. 1, n. 20.

[315] . . . qui ad paganos ritus cultusque migrarunt. *Cod. Theod.* 16.7.2. *prooem.*

[316] *Cod. Theod.* 16.7.2.1.

[317] *Cod. Theod.* 16.7.3.

[318] *Cod. Theod.* 16.7.3.

[319] There is ample evidence for the continuation of sacrifice, in fact, into the
mid-eighth century, as the *Ekloga* of the emperors Leo III and Constantine V
attests. Frank R. Trombley, *The Survival of Paganism in the Byzantine Empire during the
Pre-Iconoclastic Period* (Ann Arbor 1981), 213–227. This legal text has recently been
edited, but for some reason the Appendix is not included. *Ecloga: Das Gesetzbuch*

thought had therefore hardly crystallized along strictly Christian lines by the end of the period under consideration here. These three statutes are absolutely damning to the thesis of a "completely Christian society" emerging quickly in the wake of the legislation initiated by emperor Theodosius I.

The legislation of his grandson against the Hellenes of the Eastern Roman Empire came to an end in a law issued at Constantinople on 31 January 438, the Third Novel of Theodosius II, even as the new codification was being ratified by the Senate in elder Rome. It is a document of unparallelled rhetorical brilliance sustained with visually inspiring images of the beauty of the cosmos. It reflects the now established view that the supposed "peace of the gods" (*deorum pax*) in the old dispensation had been abrogated and transformed into a *nova pax unius dei solius Christianorum*. The new statute establishes a principle of monotheism, the only conceivable interpretation of the text *vis à vis* Hellenes, although it also addresses Jews, Samaritans, and various "heretical monsters":[320]

> For who is so demented, who is so condemned by the greatness of novel ferocity that, when he sees the sky with incredible swiftness set limits to the measure of the seasons within its spaces by the command of divine handiwork, the motion of the stars controlling the circumstances of life, the earth endowed with ripening harvests, the serene sea, the immensity of the great work confined within the bounds of the natural universe: who shall not inquire after the author of so great a handiwork, so great a mystery?

The divine power that harnessed and directed these regularized forces of nature (*divina ars*) belonged no longer to the Hellenic gods of the weather and harvest, the vault of the firmament, or the resolves of destiny, but to the Christian God, the originator of the great handiwork and mystery (*tanti secreti, tantae fabricae . . . auctor*). The verdict of the senses on this issue seemed obvious to Theodosius II and the Greek church of the period after the Oecumenical Council of Ephesus (431), but obvious in other ways to the more resistant Hellenes, from their senatorial estates in Bithynia to the libraries of Athens.

Leons III. und Konstantinos V., ed. Ludwig Burgmann (Frankfurt am Main 1983). For the Appendix cf. the early edition of Antonius G. Monferratus, *Ecloga Leonis et Constantini cum Appendice* (Athens 1889). Its importance is recognized by Edwin H. Freshfield (tr.), *A Manual of Roman Law: The Ecloga* (Cambridge 1926), 115–141. This evidence is absolutely *damning* for John Haldon's thesis that the Hellenic sacrifice is not attested in the law codes after the sixth century. *Byzantium in the Seventh Century* (Cambridge 1990), 336.

[320] *Nov. Theod.* 3.1. Although quite elegant, the Latin has been omitted for the sake of brevity.

The Novel of 438 authorized the confiscation and execution of all
who sacrificed, although it admitted the principle of leniency:[321]

> Hence our clemency perceives that we must allot surveillance over
> pagans and pagan excess (*paganorum quoque et gentilis inmanitatis vigi-*
> *lia*), who by some natural insanity and irreducible lawlessness depart
> from the path of true religion (*vera religio*) and do not disdain in any
> way to practice the nefarious rites of sacrifices and the deadly errors
> of superstition in hidden solitudes, unless their crimes are made
> public by nature of profession to the injury of our supernal majesty
> and to the contempt of our epoch. The thousand terrors of our
> published statutes do not deter them, not the threatened penalty of
> exile, so that, if they cannot amend [their behavior], they should at
> least defer to abstain from the mass of crimes and filth of sacrificial
> victims (*inluvie victimarum . . . abstinere*). Therefore, although love of
> religion can never be secure, although pagan madness demands the
> harshness of all punishments, nevertheless, being mindful of our
> innate leniency, we decree by our firm command that, if any person
> with polluted and contaminate mind is detected making sacrifice in
> any place whatsoever, our wrath shall rise against his fortune, against
> his blood! It were proper for us to give this better victim, with the
> altar of Christianity kept intact. (*oportet enim dare nos hanc victimam*
> *meliorem ara Christianitatis intacta servata*).

The statute adds in another context that anyone who "should lead
a slave or freedman, whether against his will or by punishable
persuasion, from the worship of the Christian religion to an impious sect or ritual" would suffer capital punishment (*quicumque*
servum seu ingenuum, invitum vel suasione plectenda, ex cultu Christianae
religionis in nefandam sectam ritumve transduxerit).[322] This provision
applied to pagans and "heretical monsters" like Manichaeans
more than to Jews. The Third Novel of Theodosius II embodies a
spirit of violence against seduction (*persuasio*) to entrap freemen
(*ingenui*) and free women (*ingenuae*) that many Christian bishops
shared, being anxious to prevent the apostasy of persons recently
baptized and of the catechumenate. This mentality drove bishop
Porphyrius of Gaza to destroy an Antiochene woman named Julia,
who had attracted newly baptized young men and women into a
syncretistic "Manichaean" cell (c. 408–415). These immature folk
had been led *ex cultu Christianae religionis in nefandam sectam ritumve*,
and so Mark the Deacon, our source for the episode, provides a
haunting demise for Julia, who lapses into a self-absorbed catatonic
state and descends to inexhorable damnation.[323] The Novel of 438

---

[321] *Nov. Theod.* 3.8.
[322] *Nov. Theod.* 3.4.
[323] Infra, Ch. III, Sect. 5.

provided a legally sanctioned and pragmatic solution to confrontations of this character instead of the poisoning (*veneficium*) or taboo death of Julia that seems to lie behind this piece of Christian "magic".

The Novel of 438 draws the inference that pagan sacrifices had upset the balance of nature, or rather the goodwill of the Christian God, because of the manifest impiety of the Hellenes:[324]

> Or shall we endure it any longer that the alterations of the seasons be changed, with the temperature of the sky growing angry, because the exasperating perfidy of the pagans knows not how to preserve the balance of nature? For why has spring denied us its usual charm? Why has summer abandoned the hard-working farmer with a meagre harvest, against his hope for ears of grain? Why has the immoderate ferocity of winter with its piercing cold cursed the fertility of the soil with the ruin of sterility? Why all this, unless nature has outstripped the decree of its own law to avenge an impiety? In order that we may not hereafter be compelled to sustain [these reversals], the revered majesty of the supernal deity must be appeased by a peaceful vengeance, as we have said.

The "peaceful vengeance" (*pacifica ultio*) would come in the form of confiscations and executions. The will of the Christian God, here designated as the supernal divinity (*supernum numen*), is embodied in the decree of nature against mankind for the impiety of sacrifice. If emperors and bishops held this view, rustic monks and their congregations had a different attitude toward forces of nature such as violent hail-bearing clouds and rivers surging above their banks into tilled fields: these phenomena became hostile, animate kratophanies, or epiphanies of daimonic power. The Christian cross could confine them to their allotted bounds in the terrestrial and meteorological zones of the cosmos.[325] Be this as it may, the religious attitude had come full circle since Pliny the Younger had served as governor of Bithynia during the reign of the emperor Trajan (99–117 A.D.): the polytheistic sacrifices that had once guaranteed the natural order now defiled and disrupted it. The God of erstwhile Christian atheists now guaranteed the toil of men in their tilled fields against the daimonic forces of nature that men had once thought to be divine.

The publication of the Theodosian Code and the Third Novel of Theodosius II in 438 did not in the end ensure the slow strangulation of Hellenic belief and ritual. Convincing evidence from cities

---

[324] *Nov. Theod.* 3.8.
[325] Cf. infra, Ch. II, passim. Trombley, "Paganism in the Greek World," 341 and 345.

like Athens, Aphrodisias and Alexandria, and from the rustic parts
of Bithynia, Syria, Egypt, Arabia, and elsewhere demonstrates the
survival of the old religiosity in forms entirely unaffected by Christianity. The later chapters of this book expound this thesis in
great detail.

The next attested statutes against sacrifice turn up in Book One
of the Justinian Code, whose first edition was brought out in 532 by
Tribonian, Justinian's *quaestor palatii sacri* and a Hellene. The edicts
given after 438 are four in number. The first of these, issued by the
coemperors Valentinian III and Marcian at Constantinople to
Palladius, Praetorian Prefect of Oriens (14 November 451), proves
that all the previous statutes were still being violated by polytheists
bent on practising their ancestral cults. Its purport is perfectly
consistent with known events in the Greek cities of the Roman
East:[326]

> No one with the mind of a person bent on reverencing and praying
> shall unbolt the shrines (*delubra*) which have aleady been closed. For
> it is unsuited to our era that pristine honor be restored to unspeak-
> able images, which should instead be execrated, that the impious
> doorposts of the temples (*templorum impios postes*) be crowned with
> wreaths, that fires be kindled on profane altars, that victims be
> slaughtered, that wines be poured from libation bowls (*pateris vina
> libari*), and that sacrilege be esteemed in place of religion. Whoever
> attempts to carry out sacrifices against this statute of our serenity and
> against the prohibitions of long-standing imperial constitutions shall
> be licitly accused as the guilty party of so great a crime in front of a
> criminal court, and upon being convicted he shall submit to the
> confiscation of all his property and to capital punishment. Even those
> who were merely cognizant of the sacrifices or servants (*conscii etiam ac
> ministri sacrificiorum*) shall endure the same penalty as that imposed on
> the principal party, in order that, terrified by the severity of our
> statute, they would cease to celebrate the forbidden sacrifices from
> fear of punishment.

The law provides for a fine of 500 lb. in gold (36,000 *solidi*) against
any provincial governor with the rank ordinary senator (*vir clarissimus*) who should connive at getting the case dismissed, and the
same penalty for his *officium*.

Marcian's edict of 451 corroborates the evidence of contemporary sources that the longstanding statutes in the Theodosian Code
and Novels were still being violated, a practice "unsuited to our
era" (*absit a saeculo nostro*) in view of the formal Christianization of

---

[326] *Codex Iustinianus* 1.11.7 in *Corpus Iuris Civilis*, ed. P. Krueger, 2 (Berlin 1929).
This text is hereinafter cited as *Cod. Iust.*

the empire enunciated in the Third Novel of Theodosius II, wherein the mastery of nature is attributed to the Christian God.[327] The
edict of 451 mentions that cult effigies (*simulacra*) still stood inside
some temples and that the clandestine use of their buildings for
prayer to the local divinity had survived as well. Near contemporary sources agree with this supposition. For example, the younger
Asklepiodotus, a rhetor of Alexandria, slept with his wife in front of
the image of Isis in her temple at Canopus c. 488–489.[328] In this
instance the shrine had been sealed with stone and mortar.[329] The
doorkeeper (θυρωρός) of the Parthenon in Athens secured the
place with his keys (τὰς κλεῖς) not only against theft, but also
against the risk of devotees' unbolting the gates, practicing rites,
and thereby incurring the wrath of the imperial government.[330]
Proclus the *diadochos* probably performed his devotions to Athena
outside the temenos even before the closure of the Parthenon c. 484,
as for example the many hymns he composed, whose significance
could hardly have been missed if recited in public.[331] Clandestine
sacrifices required the use of incense (*tur*), which is attested at
Athens,[332] Canopus,[333] and elsewhere. The Aphroditeion of Aphrodisias, dismantled and equipped as a Christian martyrion probably
c. 484, undoubtedly kept its cult image of the goddess past the time
of Marcian's law.[334] It was easy to sacrifice animals on the altars of
the surviving rural temples of Bithynia c. 443–446.[335] Finally, the
law contains an innovation of great import, declaring persons who
simply knew about the sacrifices (*conscii . . . sacrificiorum*) subject to
the same penalties of death and confiscation as applied to the
actual instigators. The *conscii* were regarded as sympathizers for
their failure to denounce the "sacrilege". Attendants (*ministeri*)
were held accountable in the same way, although they might be
slaves or dependents of the instigator. Such persons could hardly
resist the demands of their owner or patron without running legal
and financial risks. The previous statute on this question lies in
the Fourth Clause of the Theodosian Novel of 438.[336] It attaches

---

[327] *Nov. Theod.* 3.8.
[328] Infra, Ch. V, Sect. 2.
[329] Infra, Ch. IX, Sect. 2.
[330] Infra, Ch. IV, Sect. 2 and 3.
[331] Ibid.
[332] Ibid.
[333] Infra, Ch. IX, Sect. 2.
[334] Infra, Ch. VI, Sect. 1, n. 5.
[335] Infra, Ch. VII, Sect. 1.
[336] Supra, Ch. I, Sect. 5.

penalties only to the person using compulsion or persuasion against
his client, whether free or slave. It was perhaps incumbent upon a
new emperor (for Marcian was elected in 451) to reaffirm the laws
against paganism. In this instance he chose to confront the accessories to crimes against religion with a policy of terror and no
mincing of words.

The second post-Theodosian law, given by the co-emperors Leo
I and Anthemius at Constantinople (c. 472?), defines the position
of "sympathizers" (*conscii*) and "attendants" (*ministri*) at sacrifices
with greater clarity. Provincial governors seem to have applied too
broad a definition to the question of culpability:[337]

> Let no one dare to perpetrate those acts which have quite often
> (*saepius*) been forbidden to persons of the pagan superstition (*pagana
> superstitio*), knowing (*sciens*) how great a public crime he is commit-
> ting. So much do we desire crimes of this kind to be curtailed that his
> landed estate (*praedium*) or house (*domus*) shall be awarded to the
> holdings of the imperial treasury, even if the act in question was
> performed in the landed estate or house of another. Owners [shall be
> penalized] for this reason alone, that although cognizant they permit-
> ted their own grounds to be contaminated by such crimes.

The law prescribes the loss of title or military rank as the penalty
for persons holding imperial offices, but specifically excludes confiscation in such cases. Public disgrace was evidently considered a
sufficient penalty at the court of Leo I (456–474), a peculiar rever-
sion to the concept of leniency. In contrast, persons of private
condition were to be condemned to perpetual exile after the ap-
plication of torture. One could not therefore in theory witness a
sacrifice in the course of dining at another man's residence (*etiamsi
in alieno praedio vel domo*), nor could he escape penalties if his clients,
attendants, or slaves were observed contaminating the soil of his
own estate with sacrifices if he had done nothing to stop it (*domini
vero pro hoc solo, quod scientes consenserint sua loca talibus contaminari
sceleribus*). It thereby became incumbent on Christian citizens to
refuse the hospitality of religious Hellenes and at the same time to
have bailiffs police their estates for signs of sacrificial fires or
remnants of turf altars. If he became aware (*conscius*) of these acts,
the private citizen practically had to turn informer or suppress the
evidence on his own land in order to avoid indictment. The extension of the rule of culpability to witnesses and accessories to sacrificial rites did not prevent the forbidden acts, but simply widened
the legal net of entrapment for ambitious prosecutors and the

---

[337] *Cod. Iust.* 1.11.8.

personal enemies of imperial and civic magistrates. This law largely laid the groundwork for the numerous "pagan trials" of the sixth century under Justinian and his successors.[338]

VI. The Quasi-Justinianic Laws of Zeno c. 481–484

Two exceptionally comprehensive edicts of a later date (*inter* 472–529) designed to crush Hellenic belief and cult once and for all, appear in the *Codex Iustinianus*.[339] These statutes seem superficially to correspond to the jejune accounts of the Justinianic law of 529 found in the chronicles of John Malalas and Theophanes the Confessor,[340] but the supposed relationship is improbable. The two laws of the Justinian Code lack the customary prescript addressed to the Praetorian Prefect, with the date and place of issue, all of which Tribonian's staff of jurisconsults invariably incorporated with edicts of Justinianic authorship.[341] These two quasi-Justinianic laws—as I have designated them—almost certainly belong to a previous emperor, but which one? On the face of it, Justinian the Great seems to have gotten credit for acts which in fact belonged to a predecessor, as was the case with much of his building program.[342]

The most probable context for the statutes, which will be analysed forthwith, is the rebellion against the emperor Zeno by Illus, *magister militum per Orientem*, and his faction between 481–488. The insurgents attracted large numbers of followers from the aristocracies and intelligentsia of the East Roman cities. Among the Hellenes who rallied to Illus were the rhetor Pamprepius, who had held important imperial posts in Constantinople, and the circle that gravitated around the elder Asklepiodotus, a respected decurion of Aphrodisias in Caria who had many friends with similar views in Alexandria.[343] This circle performed divinatory sacrifices to discover the outcome of the rebellion with the specific hope of

---

[338] Rochow, "Oppositionellen Strömungen," 230ff. Eadem, "Die Heidenprozesse unter Kaisern Tiberios II. Konstantinos und Maurikios," *Studien zum 7. Jahrhundert in Byzanz: Probleme der Herausbildung des Feudalismus*, ed. F. Winkelmann *et al.* (Berlin 1976), 120–130. Cf. Frank R. Trombley, "Religious Transition in Sixth-Century Syria," Sect. 2 (publication data not yet available).

[339] *Cod. Iust.* 1.11.9 and 1.11.10.

[340] John Malalas, *Chronographia*, ed. L. Dindorf (Bonn 1831), 451 and 491. Theophanes the Confessor, *Chronographia*, ed. C. de Boor, 1 (Leipzig 1883), 180, lines 11–21.

[341] Cf. *Cod. Iust.* 1.4.21, a recent law of 528, and many other examples.

[342] C. Capizzi, *L'imperatore Anastasio I* (Orientalia Christiana Analecta 184, Rome 1969), 206ff. See infra, Appendices II and III.

[343] Infra, Ch. V, Sect. 2.

learning of emperor Zeno's overthrow.[344] This must have happened elsewhere as well.

Other synchronisms suggest a date c. 481–488 for the two laws. For example, to judge from the internal chronological evidence in Marinus of Neapolis' biography of Proclus, the closure of the Parthenon as a Hellenic *religious* shrine, along with the dismantling of Pheidias' chryselephantine Athena, took place near the end of Proclus' life (he died in 485), perhaps as late as 484, but easily within the terminal dates of the rebellion.[345] It was also around this time that Aphroditeion of Aphrodisias was dismantled and a martyrion constructed inside the temenos.[346] It is thought that the Hellenes of the East rallied to Illus' cause in the hope of having public sacrifices restored to the temple priesthoods.[347] Whatever the practicability of this design, Illus had a strong following at Aphrodisias, as we know from Zachariah of Mytilene. The civil war will have evoked a similar fervor in Athens, although Marinus of Neapolis scrupulously avoids reference to it in discussing Proclus' career. Illus' rebellion had been thoroughly crushed at the time Marinus wrote, so he could hardly raise the issue of sedition at Athens with impunity. The emperor Zeno may well have decreed the final cleansing of the temples in the two cities, and elsewhere as well, in reprisal for their bad faith during the civil war. As for the two statutes, Zeno probably aimed them at the now politicized Hellenes of those places, giving particular emphasis to destroying the economic underpinnings of the temples and philosophical schools. The laws are thus a product of the unpopular Zeno's struggle for political survival during the early stages of the civil war, when the issue was still in doubt. The laws perhaps had the effect of nullifying the bad impression made on the adherents of Chalcedonian theology by the Henotikon of 481, a decree ending the discussion of the human and divine natures of Christ, but it failed to conciliate the monophysites in the provinces controlled by the rebel Illus.[348] If so, the laws might be put more closely between the *termini* 482–484. The activities of the Hellenes during these years, coupled with the broad dates assigned to the archaeological

---

[344] Infra, Ch. V, Sect. 4.

[345] Alison Frantz, "From Paganism to Christianity in the Temples of Athens," *Dumbarton Oaks Papers* 19 (1965), 194–195 and 201–204. Cf. the discussion of Timothy E. Gregory, "The Survival of Paganism in Christian Greece: A Critical Essay," *American Journal of Philology* 107 (1986), 238f.

[346] Infra, Ch. VI, n. 5.

[347] Bury, LRE 1, 398f., n. 5.

[348] W.H.C. Frend, *The Rise of the Monophysite Movement* (Cambridge 1972), 177–181.

evidence, admit the working hypothesis that the two undated laws in the Justinian Code were an element in Zeno's propaganda war against Illus and the insurgents, either during the later stages of the war or shortly thereafter.

The first of the quasi-Justinianic edicts is directed against the endowments of schools and temples:[349]

> We command that our officials both in Constantinople and in the provinces go with all alacrity on their own initiative and on that of the bishops and search out, according to law, the teachers of all the impieties of Hellenic cult, that their acts would no longer occur and accordingly be punished. If their correction exceeds the competence of the provincial *officia*, let these matters be brought to us, lest accusation for misdeeds and prosecution be brought against the [officials].
>
> 1. It is unlawful for anyone to bequeath in a will or leave as a gift or for anything to be given to persons or places in support of the impiety of Hellenism, even if this is not comprehended specifically in the words of the will or testament or gift, but is otherwise truly bequeathed.
>
> 2. Let the things bequeathed or given in this manner be taken from those persons or places to whom or to which they were given, and be assigned instead to the cities in which such persons live or under whose jurisdiction such places lie, that they would be expended in the same way as public revenues.
>
> 3. All penalties, as many as were rescinded by previous emperors against Hellenic error or in behalf of the orthodox faith, are continuously valid and firm, and are affirmed through the present pious legislation.

If we place this decree c. 482–484, it constitutes a thinly disguised mandate to imperial counts, *agentes in rebus,* and provincial governors to apprehend the Hellenes of Illus' faction. The cooperation of these officials with the bishops was encouraged, the latter having envied the inner-city lots on which the pagan temples stood and wishing to raise the cross above their gables. The decree is directed against the sophists and philosophers of the Hellenic *paideia* and any who might still claim a priesthood.[350] The recommended inquiries would in theory have revealed the names of the malefactors and the identity of each crime. Yet, as it fell out, most of the suspects had in the past shown such discretion in their teachings and cultic acts that sufficient evidence seldom survived to secure convictions. Proclus remained the *diadochos* of the Neoplatonic

---

[349] *Cod. Iust.* 1.11.9.
[350] τὰ τοιαῦτα διδασκομένους πάντα τὰ τῆς Ἑλληνικῆς θρησκείας ἀσεβήματα νομίμως ἀναζητεῖν.

school in Athens until his death in 485.[351] His successors Marinus
and Isidore prospered in the years to come, as did the Alexandrian
Hellenes Horapollon the younger, Heraïskos, Asklepiodotus the
younger, and others whom the Christian *philoponoi* confronted during the late 480's.[352] The elder Asklepiodotus died a respected
citizen and philanthropist at Aphrodisias in the 490's, his divinatory sacrifices during the civil war with Illus never having been
detected.[353] To these must be added acts of theurgy. Religious
Hellenes talked much about this in their private circles all through
the fifth century, as Damascius' life of Isidore the *diadochos* reveals,
but no philosopher-theurgist is known to have been executed for his
arts since Maximus of Ephesus fell foul of the emperor Valens'
inquisitor Festus in 372.[354]

This statute also denied the legality of any testament (διαθήκη)
or gift (δωρέα) or "anything given to persons or places for the
support of the impiety of Hellenism" (διδόναι τι προσώποις ἢ
τόποις ἐπὶ συστάσει τῆς τοῦ Ἑλληνισμοῦ δυσσεβείας), where
the term *Hellenismos* refers both to culture and religious practice.[355]
The law takes aim, as well, at attempts to increase the endowments
that supported the late Hellenic sophistic and its religious institutions. It seems quite possible that some of the estates owned and
administered by the Athenian decurion Archiadas supported the
Parthenon and Asklepieion in Athens.[356] Under a ruling of the
jurisconsult Ulpian (3rd century A.D.) repeated in the *Digest* of
Justinian, the deities of five designated temples could inherit
property.[357] The Parthenon in Athens is not named in the list, but
this practice may have suffered less regulation than Ulpian's ruling
implies.[358] This principle of heritability does not seem to have
become otiose until the date of the quasi-Justinianic statute under
discussion here. Religious Hellenes like Proclus will thus have been
permitted to make bequests to Athena and Asklepios until c. 482–
484. It is not coincidental that a different law from the reign of Zeno
recognized the principle and established the procedure for making

---

[351] Infra, Ch. IV, Sect. 3.
[352] Infra, Ch. V, Sect. 2.
[353] Infra, Ch. VI, Sect. 2.
[354] Supra, Ch. I, Sect. 3. Eunapius, *Lives of the Philosophers* (Wright, 458f.).
[355] *Cod. Iust.* 1.11.9.1.
[356] Infra, Ch. IV, Sect. 3 and 4.
[357] Ulpian, *Liber Singularis Regulorum* 22.6 in *Collectio Librorum Iuris Anteiustiniani*,
ed. Paul Krueger, 2 (Berlin 1888), 24.
[358] The temples designated by Ulpian are those of Apollo at Didyma, Athena at
Ilion, Artemis at Ephesus, the Mother of the Gods at Sipylene, and Nemesis at
Smyrna.

a direct gift (δωρέα) to the person (εἰς πρόσωπον) of any apostle, martyr, prophet, or holy angel (who can hardly be considered fictive legal personalities in the cultural milieu of the late fifth century) in building a chapel (εὐκτήριον οἶκον οἰκοδομεῖν).[359] The principle derives directly from that enunciated by Ulpian. There is, for the rest, no convincing evidence that the imperial fisc (*res privata*) had confiscated all temple estates during the fourth century, as for example those of the temple at Eleusis, whose mysteries were still being celebrated c. 395. Nor is it to be doubted that monies deriving from landed estates directly owned by Athens paid in part for the routine maintenance of the temples and the huge outlays for the publicly secularized but privately religious celebration of the Panathenaia mentioned by Himerius.[360] Such properties may well have been owned by "Athena" in the local registers and have been open to heritable gifts.

So much, then, for one kind of legal person or place that the quasi-Justinianic law had in view. Another sort was certainly the Neoplatonic academy, whose endowment originated from donations by well-to-do founders and their successors. The Neoplatonic academy had appropriated the endowment of the Platonic school probably sometime after that philosophical system had become one and the same with "Platonism" under Ammonius (2nd century A.D.) and others in Late Antiquity. The endowment administered by the *diadochoi* in Athens survived the quasi-Justinianic law which we have assigned to c. 482–484, as Damascius reports in his life of Isidore:[361]

> Plato was poor and owned only the garden in the Academy, which was the least part of its endowment. For the garden straightaway yielded three *solidi* per annum, but the whole yield was later 1000 *solidi* or even a little more. It was augmented in more recent years when other holy and learned men died at various times and left to the philosophers a means of peace and leisure for the philosophic way of life in their wills (*kata diathēkas*).

Photius' summary of that lost work provides the date, putting the endowment at 1000 solidi in the time of Proclus.[362] The legacies and gifts to this fund seem to have grown rapidly in the middle decades of the fifth century, the years of Proclus' greatest fame as an interpreter of Plato. The emperor Zeno may perhaps be forgiven for

---

[359] *Cod. Iust.* 1.2.15.
[360] Supra, Ch. I, Sect. 2.
[361] Damascius, *V. Isidori*, Fr. 265 (Zintzen, 213).
[362] Damascius, *V. Isidori*, Epit. Phot. 158 (Zintzen, 212).

supposing that this hypertrophic munificence was fuelling rebellion as well as philosophy. A careful reading of the law under discussion here suggests that *it did not confiscate the endowment*, but rather outlawed all *future* legacies and gifts, as Clause 2 makes explicit. Thus, the income of the Academy remained the same. One thousand *solidi* could support ten or more sophists in an enviable state of luxury, the annual income of the typical artisan being about 20 *solidi* at best. The Athenian decurion Theagenes added monies to these out of his own pocket:[363]

> For he was fond of giving and gave to excess, and paid much money [to Marinus] for teachers and physicians and the other management of the fatherland.

These private acts of generosity (Damascius calls Theagenes φιλόδωρος τε καί μεγαλόδωρος) came during Marinus' tenure as *diadochos*. While technically gifts, the monies given as salaries were perhaps laundered under the rubric of "administrative funds", but, as will be seen, Zeno seems to have allowed the force of the law to lapse after the successful suppression of Illus' insurgency, for with the military threat to his regime gone, the emperor will have regarded the crowd of Hellenic sophists as so much chaff in the wind.

The precedent for such *de facto* abrogations of imperial edicts is seen in Valentinian I's failure to enforce the law of 364 against nocturnal sacrifices after Vettius Agorius Praetextatus complained of the grief this measure had caused for the Hellenes of Attica.[364] Like the law of 364, Zeno's statute of c. 482–484 will have remained on the books unenforced, only to be revived from dormancy in the Justinianic codification of 532 and later mistaken for a new act of the sixth-century emperor.[365] The force of the imperial hand was felt elsewhere, in the closure of the Parthenon and Asklepieion, with the confiscation of the precious metals built into the cult images therein.[366] This display of imperial power was effected quickly (by 484) and easily. It proved to be a sufficient warning. This was the "persecution" of Hellenes that Damascius later noted, writing in the 520's or later.[367]

---

[363] Damascius, *V. Isidori*, Fr. 264 (Zintzen, 213).

[364] Supra, Ch. I, Sect. 4.

[365] It must be remembered that Tribonian came up with many rare and forgotten legal documents in the course of the researches that went into the new codification.

[366] Infra, Ch. IV, Sect. 3.

[367] Damascius, *Das Leben des Isidoros* (Asmus, 115). Infra, n. 394.

The quasi-Justinianic law ruled, finally, that the estates and gifts *unlawfully* bequeathed to the temples and schools be remanded to the cities under whose jurisdiction they lay to defray public administrative costs.[368] It would not be suprising if local bishops profited from this, as they had in the late fifth century increasingly to expend church funds on the repair of fortifications, food for the poor, and so forth.[369] In the instance of Aphrodisias, the local church acquired the temple of Aphrodite. At Athens, the Parthenon perhaps became a Christian shrine at an early date, but the earliest inscription cut on the temple proving this dates from 693.[370] The Asklepieion of Athens became the healing shrine of St. Andrew in the years immediately after the closure of the temples, as we suppose in 482–484.[371] Finally, the decrees of the Theodosian Code and all later edicts against "pagan error" (κατὰ τῆς Ἑλληνικῆς . . . πλάνης) were reaffirmed.

The second of the quasi-Justinianic laws is probably contemporaneous with the first one. It sets forth several rather simplistic formulas for the final and absolute Christianization of the Eastern Roman Empire, thus speaking for the sense of crisis that the emperor Zeno associated with the Hellenic opposition to his rule. This statute provided, first, for the execution of Christians who had lapsed, performed Hellenic sacrifices, and celebrated festivals, on the ground that the goodwill of the Christian God toward the Roman state might be compromised:[372]

> Since certain persons have been found to be gripped by the error of the unholy and defiled Hellenes and to be performing those acts which move philanthropic God to just anger, we cannot bear to leave matters concerning them unsettled. But since we know that there are

[368] τὰ δὲ οὕτω καταλιμπανόμενα ἢ δωρούμενα ἀφαιρείσθω μὲν ἐκείνων τῶν προσώπων ἢ τόπων, οἷς δέδοται ἢ καταλέλειπται, προσκυρούσθω δὲ ταῖς πόλεσι. *Cod. Iust.* 1.11.9.2.

[369] This problem merits fuller study. Under one law the bishop was required to select the purchaser of public grain in the cities in cooperation with the *curiales*. *Cod. Iust.* 1.4.17 and 10.27.4. A law dated 503/4 and published in an inscription at Korykos in Cilia Trachea specified that the bishop select the defensor of the city. *Monumenta Asiae Minoris Antiqua III: Denkmäler aus Rauhen Kilikien*, ed. J. Keil and A. Wilhelm (Manchester 1931), no. 197. It is of interest that a law of emperor Anastasius barred Hellenes from holding the office of defensor (505 A.D.) *Cod. Iust.* 1.4.19. Bishops acquired all sorts of municipal responsibilities under a law of 530, including inspecting such public works as bath-houses, aqueducts, harbors, fortifications, bridges and roads. They also became responsible for supervising the accounts and revenues assigned to these facilities. *Cod. Iust.* 1.4.26.

[370] A.K. Orlandos and A. Vranousē, *Ta Charagmata tou Parthenōnos* (Athens 1973), no. 34.

[371] Gregory, "Survival of Paganism in Christian Greece," 238.

[372] *Cod. Iust.* 1.11.10. *prooem.*

those who leave the worship of the one and true God and offer sacrifices to idols in irrational error and celebrate festivals sated with all unholiness, we impose on those who sinfully perform these acts after being deemed worthy of holy baptism that their offenses be reproved by suitable legal vengeance, and this in a rather humanitarian manner.

A rhetorical *tour de force*, it echoes earlier statutes. It was the first imperial law to invoke the "One God" formula (τοῦ ἀληθινοῦ καὶ μόνου θεοῦ), which in other contexts was the literary companion of the "conquer" (νικᾷ) inscriptions and symbols of Christianization like the crosses incised on temples, martyr relics, Chi-Rho monograms, and the raising of the cross (σταυροπήγιον).[373] To cite one example from the time of the rebellion against Zeno, Christians were present when Asklepiodotus the elder conducted divinatory sacrifices outside the walls of Aphrodisias.[374] These Christians were liable to suffer severe punishment as accessories to sacrifice and the *haruspicina* under the laws of Marcian (451) and of Leo I (472?) mentioned above.[375] The new law implicitly condemned sorcerers' sacrifices as well, like the human sacrifice plotted by the Christian John Foulon at Berytus in the 490's.[376]

Three sections of the new statute required the baptism of all citizens and residents of the empire and their systematic instruction in the Christian scriptures and canon law, with particular emphasis on procuring the "genuine conversion" (γνησία μετάνοια) of small children:[377]

It is necessary for as many persons as have not been deemed worthy of baptism to make themselves manifest, whether living in this imperial city or in the provinces, and proceed to the most holy churches with their wives and children and entire household and be taught the true Christian faith. After being taught in this manner and having cast off their former error with all purity, they shall be deemed worthy of saving baptism. Or, if it seems that they are contemptuous of these things, they shall not partake of our way of life nor be permitted to be owners of moveable or real property. But, being deprived of everything of consequence, they shall be left in want, in addition also to being subjected to the appropriate penalties.

If there is such a person, whether someone here or in the countryside, and he does not run to our most holy churches with his own women and children, as was said, he shall be subject to the previously

---

[373] Infra, Ch. II, passim.
[374] Infra, Ch. V, Sect. 4.
[375] Infra, Ch. I, Sect. 5.
[376] Infra, Ch. V, Sect. 5.
[377] *Cod. Iust.* 1.11.10.1, 3, and 5.

stated penalties: the fisc shall confiscate their property and they shall
be given over to exile.

We enact this so that children who are at an early age will at once
and without delay partake of saving baptism in such a manner that,
after they have advanced in maturity sufficiently to sit in the most
holy churches and be taught the sacred scriptures and canons and
thus partake of genuine conversion, they shall receive reverend baptism only after shaking ancient error from themselves. For they ought
to receive this way of life firmly and keep the true faith of the
orthodox and not convert again back into the ancient error.

This measure was unrealistic in its purport and claim on the
resources of the church, not to mention the increased work load its
enforcement would have imposed on the *officia* of the provincial
governors. As A.H.M. Jones has stressed, the ability of the Late
Roman administration to carry out sweeping reforms of any kind
was restricted.[378] The entire business seems to have been laid aside
after the end of Illus' insurgency in 488, to be revived only in 532
along with the other clauses of the quasi-Justinianic laws. There is
no evidence for the confiscation of rural lands on the charge of
sacrifice either in the 480's or 530's, except for one perhaps aberrant case.[379] As the task of denouncing the unbaptized will have lain
mainly in the hands of the urban churches, little progress was
made. The first initiatives for converting villages in the *territoria* of
the cities did not always lie in the hands of the bishops. The literary
record of the period c. 365–c. 550 suggests that the task often fell to
the monks, as for example in Bithynia, northern Syria, the Nile
basin, and western Asia Minor.[380] Such a manpower shortage
existed for the task that the emperor Justinian had to mobilize
numerous monophysite bishops and monks of Syrian and Armenian extraction in western Asia Minor, all under the leadership of

---

[378] Supra, n. 11.

[379] Procopius' *Anekdota*, tr. H.B. Dewing (London-Cambridge, Mass. 1935)
provides some interesting cases of prosecution for Hellenic cults. In the first
instance there was a fellow named Theodotus the "Pumpkin", who after serving as
praefectus urbi of Constantinople was indicted for poisoning and sorcery. The
quaestor Proclus exonerated him, but Theodotus was hounded out of the city and
forced to go into hiding from assassins. The fate of his properties is unknown.
Procop., *Anekdota* 9.37–42. Elsewhere Procopius makes a general statement, to the
effect that estates were confiscated on various grounds, including polytheism
(πολυθεία), heresy, sodomy, sexual relations with ascetic women, and so forth.
Procop., *Anek.* 19.11–12 (Dewing, 230f.). It is difficult to make anything out of this,
as the cases in question are undated and the names of the victims not given. The
incidents in question perhaps belong to the 540's and 550's, when pagan trials
again occurred. Trombley, "Religious Transition in Sixth-century Syria," Sect. 2.

[380] Infra, Ch. VII, Sect. 1, and Ch. VIII, Sect. 2. This thesis is presented in
Trombley, "Paganism in the Greek World," passim.

John, the monophysite archbishop of Ephesus.[381] The speed with which this enterprise was executed required a great deal of Christianizing the local pagan rites in order to make a strong case for the new religion.[382] If much "genuine conversion" took place, the opposite occurred as well, as for example the semi-Christianization of many Iranian-speaking fire-worshippers or Mazdaeans living in Cappadocia and the Taurus mountain areas, whose incomplete catechization became a fertile ground for the dualistic Paulician heresy which fully emerged only in the ninth century.[383]

The catechization of the rural folk had definite procedures that existed before the law in question, many of which are discussed in the later chapters of this work. It is necessary to consider some few examples in order to understand the practicability of enforcing the second quasi-Justinianic law. The career of Euthymius, who converted the pro-Iranian Arabs who had defected to the empire in the early fifth century under the leadership of Aspebetos-Peter, provides a case in point. Euthymius, a solitary monk, provided brief instruction in the Arabic tongue for his co-workers, supervised the construction of rural churches as central shrines for these pastoral folk, and requested a presbyter to celebrate the Christian liturgy.[384] One could hardly confiscate lands from pastoralists, but it seems quite clear from the literary record that voluntary conversion was invariably the principle followed. The Christian elites, whether bishops, *philoponoi*, monks, or rustic presbyters, seem only to have used compulsion with sorcerers and other seemingly dangerous characters, as in the case of John Foulon at Berytus or Theodotus Kourappos in rural Galatia.[385] Persuasion and a spirit of accommodation seem otherwise to have prevailed even after the revival of militant Christianization by the emperor Justinian in the decades after 529.[386] One could avoid this in the countryside by simply not "making oneself manifest" (τούτους . . . καταδήλους ἑαυτοὺς ποιεῖν) and by not "proceeding to the most holy churches" (προσιέναι ταῖς ἁγιωτάταις ἐκκλησίαις). It should not be surprising in light of this that monks actually had to go *hunting* for new rural congregations all through the sixth century. Nor was it considered expedient where the countryside was thinly settled to confiscate the lands of pagan families, as the decurions will have had to

---

[381] Trombley, "Paganism in the Greek World," 330–334.
[382] Ibid., 337.
[383] Infra, Ch. VII, Sect. 5.
[384] Infra, Ch. VIII, Sect. 2.
[385] Trombley, "Paganism in the Greek World," 340. Infra, Ch. V, Sect. 5.
[386] Ibid.

make good the taxes disrupted by the confiscations. The prospect existed that poorly-off smallholders might simply have rented the same lands after their confiscation. The law therefore excluded this possibility by providing for the exile of the unbaptized (αὐτοὶ δὲ ἐξορίᾳ παραδοθήσονται).

The articles on compulsory Christianization enunciate one original principle, that of producing "genuine conversion" (γνησία μετάνοια) by making small children sit in church to receive instruction, thus preventing them from "converting back again into the ancient error" (καὶ οὐ πάλιν ἐπὶ τὴν παλαιὰν μεταβάλοιεν πλάνην) amidst an ethos of semi-Christianization.[387] Little is known about the conversion of small children at this time. There was the case of little Salaphtha-Irene, to whose family bishop Porphyrius of Gaza paid out four silver *millaresia* daily (for Irene and her grandmother) and a *solidus*, apparently a one-time gift, to her aunt. We do not know the fate of the older generation, apart from their baptism, but little Irene reflected a more "genuine conversion" by becoming a deaconess of the Gazan see and an ascetic.[388] In the instance of Euthymius' catechization of the Arabs at his church in the Judaean desert, all we know is that entire extended families came in from the so-called Encampments for brief instruction prior to baptism. It was continued for sometime afterwards as well.[389] The tribal chieftain Aspebetos-Peter had the authority and prestige to enforce these journeys on his relatives and dependents. Even so, the "genuine conversion" of children will have more often occurred in the anomia of the cities than amidst the ethos of village custom and the ties of kinship in pastoral society. One best learned the Christian scriptures and canons in the social flux and vacuum of the cities, lost in the crowd and buried in poverty.

Another clause of the second quasi-Justinianic law denied pagan professors of the Greek *paideia* the right to teach their particular academic disciplines (μάθημα παιδεύειν) lest they destroy the souls of their students (τὰς τῶν δῆθεν παιδευομένων διαφθείρειν ψυχάς).[390] This expression already had a certain currency at Alexandria in the late 480's, where Christian students mocked the younger Horapollon, a Hellene and teacher of rhetoric, as Psychapollon or "Soul-destroyer" in an invidious pun on his name.[391]

---

[387] *Cod. Iust.* 1.11.10.5.
[388] Infra, Ch. III, Sect. 6.
[389] Infra, Ch. VIII, Sect. 2.
[390] *Cod. Iust.* 1.11.10.2.
[391] Infra, Ch. V, Sect. 2.

Under the new law these persons lost certain rights of citizenship, both urban and Roman:[392]

> We forbid every science to be taught by those who are sick with the madness of the Hellenes, that they might not according to this rule teach those who miserably approach them and destroy the souls of the persons supposedly studying truths with them. But they shall not draw grain from the public dole since they do not have freedom of speech, nor shall any such person have freedom to bring suit in his own behalf by reason of imperial writs and pragmatic sanctions.

The sophists and philosophers of Athens, Alexandria, Aphrodisias, and other cities continued to practice their professions after c. 484, as overwhelming evidence proves.[393] Nor did the Justinianic law of 529 have much effect in the long run.[394] This section of the law applies strictly only to *imperial* grain doles and writs. A Hellene would thus suffer privation only if he lived in Constantinople or other important cities where imperial officials dominated the local patronage network. The greater number of pagan rhetors and philosophers had little need of public grain in any case because their estates supported them.[395] The endowment of the Neoplatonic academy in Athens survived the crises of 484 and 529 for the reasons explained above, namely that the law did not provide for its confiscation, but only that of newly and illegally acquired gifts and legacies. Salaries could thus be paid out of existing rents.

It is almost unthinkable that civil magistrates would have accepted the letter of the law and not have allowed pagan professors or their patrons to defend their interests in the local courts. The law probably came into play when the provincial governor sought to eliminate personal or political enemies. A likely author of such litigation may have been a certain Albinus who, as civil governor of Caria in the reign of the emperor Anastasius (491–518), had to contend with the "envy" of certain unnamed local enemies. We cannot say whether they were pagan sophists or philosophers, although such existed in Aphrodisias at this time, but the acclamations accorded to him and to the emperor in the inscriptions taunt the local pagans in the rhetoric of the ongoing religious conflict: "The faith of the Christians conquers!" and "One God for the

---

[392] *Cod. Iust.* 1.11.10.2.

[393] Cf. Ch. I, Sect. 3; Ch. IV, Sect. 3–4; Ch. V, Sect. 1–4; and Ch. VI.

[394] Alan Cameron, "The Last Days of the Academy of Athens," *Proceedings of the Cambridge Philological Society* 145 (1969), 7–29.

[395] Cf. the case of Proclus of Athens, who seems to have owned extensive estates in and around Xanthos in Lycia, the home of his family. Infra, Ch. IV, Sect. 3.

whole world!"[396] It seems probable that the Aphrodisian Hellenes were the enemies in question.

The test of "true conversion" for military officers and imperial civil officials was the baptism of their households. Otherwise they fell under suspicion of *pro forma* Christianization (ἐσχηματισμένως, "in the manner of posturing, keeping up appearances") to advance their careers and of cryptopaganism:[397]

> Those persons who have come forward or shall come forward to saving baptism fraudulently with the motive of keeping military rank or a title of honor or property, but leave their wives or children or others in their household in a state of Hellenic error: we command that they not only suffer confiscation and have absolutely no share in our government, but that they also be subjected to suitable penalties, as they plainly and of their own accord do not partake of the pure faith of holy baptism.

During the emperor Zeno's civil war, public officials civil and military alike will have fallen under the natural suspicion of sympathizing with Illus' promise to rehabilitate the Hellenic cults. In the uncertainty of the public emergency, rough and ready tests of loyalty like this prevailed. The existence of whole households in a state of "Hellenic error" c. 482–484 is reflected in the inscriptions of the decurion class and historical sources (τοὺς κατὰ τὸν αὐτῶν ὄντας οἶκον ἐπὶ Ἑλληνικῆς . . . πλάνης).[398] The culpability of the offenders for "utterly leaving" (καταλείψαιεν) their families and slaves pagan reflects the position of the householder as *paterfamilias* under Roman law. This position now carried the obligation of forcing one's dependents to accept baptism. The demand seems unwarranted in view of the demographic realities of Christianization, as the female members and slaves of the typical household invariably accepted the new religion before the *paterfamilias*, as the striking example of a certain Aelia's family at Gaza suggests c. 400.[399] This corroborates the hypothesis that the second quasi-Justinianic law sought to achieve the short-term political aim of crushing religious dissent in the palatine army commands and in the *officia* of the provincial governors.

Two other clauses of the second quasi-Justinianic law equate the behavior of Hellenes with that of the Manichaeans, who fell under the penalty of capital punishment. This sentence is laid against

---

[396] Infra, Ch. VI, Sect. 1.
[397] *Cod. Iust.* 1.11.10.6.
[398] Infra, Ch. V, Sect. 4, and Ch. VI, Sect. 2.
[399] Infra, Ch. III, Sect. 2.

pagans who performed sacrifices and acts of idolatry *secretly* (ἐμφωλεύων). This point of emphasis links the law once again with fear of the treasonable designs against Zeno during Illus' insurgency. The elder Asklepiodotus of Aphrodisias might, for example, have been executed under this statute. The news of his activities had gotten into the hands of the *philoponoi* at Alexandria through the testimony of a young student of rhetoric c. 488–89 while Asklepiodotus was still alive. Peter Mongus, the patriarch of Alexandria, denounced the man to his archiepiscopal colleague at Aphrodisias, but nothing came of it.[400] With the civil war ended, it evidently seemed pointless to pursue charges such as these against an influential man, whose friends in the provincial aristocracy and *officium* of the governor probably protected him. This reflects how quickly Zeno's laws will have fallen into disuse once the civil war had ended.

The tendency to equate Hellenes with Manichaeans goes back to the early fifth century, being a logical consequence of the closure of the temples.[401] Hellenes who continued to sacrifice secretly—and very many did—belonged to an increasingly "underground" religion, a status held by the Manichaeans since the edict of Diocletian against them in 297.[402] Like some Manichaeans, Hellenes could be found among respectable decurions, sophists, and civil servants.[403] Even so, it was less palatable to treat pagans like religious outlaws down to 529, and so the equation of the two religious systems remained a practical fiction during the period under discussion here.

VII. Conclusion

It has been necessary to treat the legal status of the Hellenic cults at length because of the badly grounded skepticism that surfaces at times in the minds and statements of scholars that the old cults did not survive the legislation of the late fourth-century emperors.[404] The imperial edicts could not address imaginary religious phenomena without making the regime look ridiculous. By the same token, the state apparatus could not expeditiously suppress every

---

[400] Infra, Ch. V, Sect. 4.
[401] Cf. the case of Julia in early fifth-century Gaza. Infra, Ch. III, Sect. 5.
[402] *Mosaicarum et Romanorum Legum Collatio* 15.3.4. ed. Theodor Mommsen in *Collectio Librorum Iuris Anteiustiniani in Usum Scholarum*, ed. Paul Krueger, 3 (Berlin 1890), 187f.
[403] Infra, Ch. II, Sect. 5.
[404] Cf. Ramsay MacMullen's comment on Adolf Harnack's work in *Paganism in the Roman Empire* (New Haven 1981), 137 and 206, n. 16.

activity that it condemned, as A.H.M. Jones has shown.[405] If some
of the laws had aims that were partly political, one can hardly deny
the existence of urban Hellenes and rustic pagans between c.
370–529, as the later chapters of this work will demonstrate conclu-
sively. Prosecution of sacrifice, divination, and sorcery, even if
politically inspired at times, would not have been a plausible course
of action unless these cultic acts existed as real social and cultural
phenomena. The consideration is often overlooked that, while divination, *haruspicina*, and poisoning had the direct political effect of
rallying conspirators, they nevertheless corresponded to the religious
suppositions and superstitions of many pagans and Christians alike,
including philosophers and Christian bishops. The prevailing rage for
Hellenic theurgy decisively proves this. The degree of Christian belief
in the efficacy of these practices varied considerably by locality and
with the attitude of each individual monk or bishop and his congregation. Hypatius, the hegumen of Rufinianae in Bithynia, is said to have
actually seen an ephiphany of Artemis and to have perceived a
magical belt dedicated to her on the person of a visitor to the
monastery.[406] On the other hand, the rationalistic Zachariah of
Mytilene doubted the ontological reality of pagan miracles and magic,
ascribing them instead to fraud. Yet even he believed that the old gods
in the recategorized form of *daimones* appeared in visions to men asleep
and sometimes even in the waking state.[407] Christian writers like
Theodoret of Cyrrhus agreed in general that sacrifices attracted
daimones and violated the newly established peace of the Christian
God.[408] This new covenant guaranteed the terrestrial, marine, and
meteorological elements to the benefit of men so long as the Christian
victory was conserved by the eradication of sacrifice and the erection
of the cross. This is the thrust of both the imperial edicts and of much
fifth-century Christian literature, including hagiography, apologetical
treatises, canon law, and even the inscriptions. These texts corroborate the imperial laws about the survival of Hellenic cult and practically never contradict them.

A clear watershed was reached in the relations between the
Christian empire and the priesthoods of the Greek cities with the
comprehensive law of Theodosius the Great (8 November 392)
from the standpoint of public worship. A generation earlier, the

---

[405] Supra, Ch. I, n. 11.
[406] Infra, Ch. VII, Sect. 1.
[407] Infra, Ch. V, Sect. 2.
[408] Theodoret of Cyrrhus, *Graecarum Affectionum Curatio VII: De Sacrificiis*, PG 83,
992–1060. Cf. idem, *Thérapeutique des maladies helléniques*, ed. tr. P. Canivet, 2 (Paris
1958), 296–309.

agents of Julian the Apostate had rededicated the temples of the old
faith everywhere, as an altar inscription of Thessalonike attests in
362. Julian is here celebrated as the "restorer of the temples"
(ἀνανεωτοῦ τῶν ἱερῶν).[409] His demise gave way to an uneasy
tolerance during the first decade of Valens' reign in the Roman
East. Christians criticized Valens for permitting public festivals
like the Diasia, the Dionysia, and the "frenzies" of Demeter at
Antioch during his residence there.[410] As late as 392 a local official
at Antinoopolis in Aegyptus felt able to erect a pagan altar in the
name of the Christian emperors. He consecrated it "with the customary dedication" (τῇ συνήθει καθοσιώσει) at the instigation of
Flavius Eutolmius Tatianus, a sincere Hellene and the great
Praetorian Prefect of the elder Theodosius.[411] It was not long before
this time that a frieze was erected at the temple of the imperial cult
in Ephesus. Its sculpture depicted Theodosius the Great standing
to the right of Artemis Ephesia. His father Theodosius the elder
stands half-naked in heroized form along with the Augusta and the
co-emperor Arcadius. They stand enclosed by figures of Pallas
Athena at the extremities of the frieze, which also incorporates the
goddess Selene.[412] It is as though Theodosius the Great and his
immediate family mingled freely with the Hellenic gods.

All this began to change quickly. Tatian fell from power between
September–November 392, and the comprehensive edict against
pagan cult came out on 8 November of the same year. This decree
marked an important transition in imperial policy that was never
thereafter reversed. Public sacrifice and other religious rituals were
permanently banned. From this time onward Hellenic rites could
only be performed in the greatest secrecy or with the connivance of
civil officials who took bribes or looked the other way.[413] The poet
Palladas of Alexandria could thus justly lament: "We Hellenes are
reduced to ashes, having buried the hopes of the dead. For now all
affairs have been turned upside down."[414] The dictum of Heraclitus
the Obscure criticizing sacrifice spoken some 900 years before now
gained the force of law:[415]

---

[409] SEG 31.641.
[410] Theodoret, HE 4.24.2 (Parmentier, 262f.).
[411] Orientis Graecae Inscriptiones Selectae, no. 723.
[412] Franz Miltner, Ephesos: Stadt der Artemis und des Johannes (Vienna 1958), 105f.
[413] See Jones' comments, Later Roman Empire, 395, 407, 409, 792, etc. Temple
lands remained under the administration of the imperial res privata under the
rubric of fundi iuris templorum. Ibid. 415f., etc. On their confiscation, ibid., 732.
[414] Greek Anthology 10. 90. Cf. 9.89 and 10.94.
[415] Heraclitus, Fr. 5 in Early Greek Philosophy, tr. J. Barnes (New York 1987),
118.

They vainly purify themselves with blood when they are defiled: as though one were to step in the mud and try to wash it off with mud. Any man who saw him doing that would think he was mad. And they pray to these statues as though one were to gossip to the houses, not knowing who the gods and who the spirits were.

The law nevertheless respected the consciences of pagans, and so prominent Hellenes had direct access to the "most Christian" emperors in the conduct of state business. Among these was Athenais-Eudokia, the daughter of the Athenian philosopher Leontios who married Theodosius II in 421 and accepted baptism.[416] Her great friend and another Hellene, Cyrus of Panopolis, served as Praetorian Prefect and Praefectus Urbi at Constantinople c. 439–440.[417] And in the time of Leo I (457–474) the *quaestor sacri palatii*, a certain Isokakios, was discovered to be a Hellene.[418] This state of affairs continued straight through to the time of Justinian.[419]

These few examples bespeak the existence of many other Hellenes whose names and frustrations no historian saw fit to record. The Hellenes' demographic and cultural bases declined steadily through the fifth century. After the shock of the rebel Illus' defeat between 481–488, those bases began to erode more rapidly.[420] This was partly the result of emperor Zeno's harsh laws, but was also a product of the historical moment, which had seen the Greek *paideia* merge with the Christian sophistic and rural pagan religion merge with Christianity through the devices of *Ritenchristianisierung*.[421] A Hellene could thus accept baptism and retain his cultural roots comfortably in the new monotheistic scheme of things. Some perhaps remembered the dictum of Xenophanes of Colophon cited in Clement of Alexandria's *Miscellanies* that: "There is one God, greatest of gods and men, similar to mortals neither in shape nor in thought."[422] It echoes the words of the psalmist who calls the God of the Jews the "God of gods."

---

[416] Bury, LRE 1, 200f.

[417] Bury, LRE 1, 227f.

[418] John Malalas, *Chronographia*, ed. L. Dindorf (Bonn 1831), 369–71.

[419] Supra, Ch. I, Sect. 6. In the time of Justinian, Tribonian the *quaestor* and John Lydus, a subordinate of the Praetorian Prefect of Oriens, were Hellenes. See now the work of Michael Maas, *John Lydus and the Roman Past* (London 1992).

[420] The inscriptions of Aphrodisias are of critical importance in this connection. Infra, Ch. VI.

[421] Infra, Chs. II and V.

[422] Heraclitus, Fr. 23 (Barnes 95).

CHAPTER TWO

CHRISTIANIZATION

The exact processes by which the ecclesiastical authorities degraded local deities to the status of *daimones* and grafted their
identitic aretalogies and iconographies onto Christian martyrs and
angels is little understood.[1] Nor has the monks' and bishops' habit
of modifying pagan ritual by the adducement of Christian cult
formulae (Ernst Kirsten's *Ritenchristianisierung*, the "Christianization of rite") been traced with any success.[2] John Cuthebert
Lawson attempted something like this long ago in his *Modern Greek
Folklore and Ancient Greek Religion*, a pioneering work which greatly
contributed to understanding certain aspects of the origins of
Byzantine and Neohellenic folk religion and belief, but which contains only fragmentary and unsystematic analysis of the sources of
the Late Antique period.[3] He not only missed many obvious lines of
transformation apparent from any exhaustive survey of the literary
sources of this period—which proved to be the crucible of the
religious transformation—but also drew many implausible and
even comical lines of correspondence between the old and new
religions.[4] Lawson's book was something of a seminal work and will

---

[1] For the links between the cult of Michael the Archangel and the earlier
typologies of Attis, the Anatolian cult of angels, and so forth, see infra, Ch. II,
Sect. 4.

[2] Ernst Kirsten, "Artemis von Ephesus und Eleuthera von Myra mit Seitblick
auf St. Nicolaus und auf Commagene," *Studien zur Religion und Kulten Kleinasiens:
Festschrift für Karl Dörner*, ed. S. Sahin et al., 2 (Leiden 1978), 465.

[3] John C. Lawson, *Modern Greek Folklore and Ancient Greek Religion* (1910; repr.
New York 1964).

[4] Lawson, "The Survival of Pagan Tradition," *Greek Folklore and Religion*, 36–64.
For example: "It became the hope [of the church] to supplant paganism by
substituting for the old gods Christian saints *of similar names and functions*" (my
italics) (p. 43). Lawson associates St. Demetrius, the protector of Thessalonike,
with the cereal goddess Demeter solely on the basis of similar nomenclature. Here
there is neither similarity of function nor do their festivals coincide. (p. 43f.) I am
unable to discover any plausible connection between the cults of the hero Theseus
and St. George, nor is continuity of cult at the Theseum in Athens assured in
ancient times. (p. 45) The parallelism that Lawson sees between a church of the
Theotokos and Poseidon's *hagiasma* ("holy spring") on the island of Tenos has no
discernible justification. (p. 45f.) Lawson's explanation for the rationale of temple
conversions is inadequate: "The adoption of the old places of worship made it

require detailed and exhaustive criticism before the final verdict
can be laid on it. Two methodological weaknesses underlie the
book, the first being its restriction to the religious phenomena of the
classical Greek deities and their supposed evolution, at the expense
of the local cults of the Greek-influenced, but not always Greek-
speaking, *oikoumene*—I am thinking here of central Asia Minor,
Syria, Armenia, Arabia, and Coptic Egypt—and secondly, the fact
that Lawson produced his book in 1910, well before the extensive
archaeological and epigraphic discoveries of later decades, and the
edition of many early Christian texts which provide new and important data.

No definitive answers to these questions will emerge without the
reconciliation of texts and archaeology, of which the present survey
will constitute a beginning. Three issues—the transformation of local
gods, the Christianization of rite, and temple conversions—have an
integral relationship and are three aspects of a single problem.

I. Christianization and the Transformation of Local Gods[5]

Psalm 95.4–5 provided the scriptural justification for reducing
pagan gods to the status of *daimones*: "Wherefore all the gods of the

---

inevitable that the old associations should survive and blend themselves with the
new ideas, and that the churches should more often acquire prestige from their
heathen sites than themselves shed a new lustre of sanctity upon them." (46) My
own analysis suggests that the real prestige of the old temple sites' being Christianized derived from the bishop or monk's success in eradicating the former local
"great god" through the power of Christian invocations, the cross, the Chi-Rho
symbol, and the importation of martyr relics, which proved the impotence of the
old god in the face of the ritual pollution of his temenos. The pagan awe associated
with the temple buildings, statues, and architectural fragments arose only
amongst groups who resisted Christianization or were later forcibly Christianized
under the Justinianic law of 529. Lawson's approach amounts to the crass sim-
plification both chronologically and functionally of a complex social and cultural
process. The supposed connection between Michael the Archangel and Dionysus
as patrons of a winepress on Rhodes is impossible according to Lawson's criteria
in terms of either nomenclature, function, or festival time (p. 55). Lawson misses
the connection between the holy physicians Sts. Kosmas and Damian (p. 55) and
the Hellenic Dioskouroi, discussed infra, Ch. II, Sect. 4. Some saints listed by
Lawson with cognate deities do not belong to the earliest period of Christianization (4th–6th c.), lack martyr status and identifiable relics, and thus have little
relevance to his thesis, as for example Sts. Therapon and Eleutherios (p. 56).
Other examples abound. This is not to say that Lawson's pioneering work lacks
constructive features, but only that the problem is more complex than he envisioned. For an equally confused, but considerably more complacently framed set
of supposed "survivals", see: John Ferguson, *The Religions of the Roman Empire*
(Ithaca 1970), 238–242.
    [5] The following section was initially discussed at the Philadelphia Seminar on
Christian Origins, Department of Religion, University of Pennsylvania, 7 April
1988.

pagans are lesser *daimones*," in the Septuagint: ὅτι πάντες οἱ θεοὶ τῶν ἐθνῶν δαιμόνια. An extensive and seemingly endless demonology already existed in the Hellenic writers of the third through fifth centuries A.D., among them Plotinus, Porphyry, Iamblichus, and Proclus.[6] Porphyry laid particular emphasis on both the beneficent and troublesome nature of *daimones* in his tractate on abstaining from animal meat. Johannes Geffcken powerfully sums up the philosopher's views:[7]

> There are good and evil demons. Both are derived from the soul of the all. The good ones care for the well-being of man; they bring good weather and beneficial activity among men; it is impossible that both good and ill should come from them but rather, they effect what is good only in terrestrial existence; moreover, according to Plato, they are the mediators between gods and men. The evil demons on the other hand, although, like good ones, they are invisible and in every way imperceptible, have many forms and are longaeval, though not eternal, do not have the noble aspect of the good demons but are disharmonious in appearance; they cause us to regard the anger of the gods as the origin of pestilence, earthquakes and drought, and even cause us to regard the anger of the gods as the origin of these sufferings and cause us to address ourselves to them for relief from these afflictions.
>
> Wild passion, greed, desire for domination, ambition and their consequences, among them war: such are their works. And all these things, so they try to convince us, are the fault of highest god.
>
> Even philosophers have been deceived by them, and hence the masses were confirmed in their unreason. It is true that good demons seek to modify these veiled works by dreams and other signs, but not everyone is able to withstand them.
>
> Magicians on the other hand are informed about the nature of evil demons whose chief they worship, and by their love potions inspire base passions. Greed for wealth and fame, and every deceit, originate from those demons, who feed off libations and the smoke of sacrifices, so as to fatten their aerial and yet corporeal being. Hence such sacrifices must be omitted; they attract demons. But demons cannot touch the pure soul. It is only where material goods are valued, in the cities of men, that the cult of demons is practised. But we who, removed from everything that is connected with matter, only seek to be like God, have no need for them.

The philosopher maintains with Apollonius of Tyana that "the true sacrifice was to be like god."[8] Except the concept of good *daimones*, Porphyry's notions did not differ widely from the Christian view:

---

[6] Johannes Geffcken, *The Last Days of Greco-Roman Paganism*, tr. Sabine MacCormack (New York 1978), 53f., 58, 61, 67–70, 134, and 245f.

[7] Ibid., 69.

[8] Ibid.

libations and the scent of burning fat in sacrifices, on which the *daimones* were thought to feed, attracted them; the criminality of magic lay precisely in the harnessing of the spirits' daimonic, that is to say evil, powers. Writers of the late Christian sophistic like Theodoret of Cyrrhus did, in fact, formulate their demonologies from Porphyry's theories.[9] The Christian view differed from the Hellenic, however, in two respects. First of all, martyrs and angels stepped forward as the helpers of mankind, even the unbaptized, in place of Porphyry's good *daimones*.[10] Secondly, Christians grouped locally prominent deities with *daimones*. These included Artemis of Ephesus, the Aphrodite of Gaza, Sarapis of Alexandria, and many others whose names the temple-bashers of the new religion would have concealed from us without the luck of fortuitous epigraphic finds, such as the inscription on an olive-oil factory naming the divine triad worshipped at the north Syrian village of Kefr Nabo, "the ancestral gods Seimios and Symbaitylos and Leon."[11] Inscriptions describe the unambiguously new status of the old deities under the Christian regime. The first example derives from

---

[9] Theodoret quotes a long section directly from Porphyrius' *Letter to Anebo the Egyptian Priest* in the *Therapeutic for Hellenic Maladies*, PG 83, 881D–884C. Theodoret refers a bit later to "those who currently practice Hellenic religion" (τῶν νῦν Ἑλληνιζόντων). Ibid. 888D. He is thus not inventing antiquarian arguments but combating the extant Hellenic beliefs and devotions with all the arguments at his disposal. Iamblichos of Chalkis (ob. 325–330 A.D.), the Neoplatonist theologian, found Porphyrius' attack on sacrifice and divination as nothing more than the invocation of evil *daimones* so troubling that he wrote the lengthy *De Mysteriis* in reply, quoting the *Letter to Anebo* at the beginning and then developing a systematic reply that owes much to Plotinus' ontology of immaterial and spiritual beings, the gods, archangels, angels, *daimones*, archons, heroes, and ordinary souls. He argues with considerable force that both gods and *daimones*, being spiritual and therefore impassible, are unaffected by the vapors that arise from sacrifices. *De Mysteriis* 5.10–12. For text and translations, see: Jamblique, *Les Mystères d'Égypte*, ed. tr. Edouard des Places (Paris 1966). Iamblichus, *On the Mysteries of the Egyptians, Chaldeans, and Assyrians*, tr. Thomas Taylor, 3rd ed. (London 1821).

[10] This is the thrust of Peter Brown's chapter, "The Invisible Companion," in *The Cult of the Saints: Its Rise and Function in Latin Christianity*, 50–68. Theodoret of Cyrrhus sums up the fifth-century view of the Greek episcopate succinctly: "The philosophers and rhetors have been delivered to oblivion, and few know the names of emperors and generals, but all know the names of the martyrs better than their best friends. And they are eager to give their names to their children, thereby devising security and protection for their [little ones]." *Therapeutic for Hellenic Maladies*, PG 83, 1033A. The martyrs along with the angels thus became the tutelary friends of the next Christian generation that arose in the first half of the fifth century. This tendency explains, for example, the disappearance of pagan theophoric names from personal nomenclature at Athens and Aphrodisias. Infra, Ch. IV and VI.

[11] *Publications of the Princeton University Archaeological Expeditions to Syria in 1904–5 and 1909, Division III: Greek and Latin Inscriptions, Section B: Northern Syria*, ed. W.K. Prentice (Leiden 1922), no. 1170. This series hereinafter cited as Prentice, PAES III B. Cf. infra, Ch. X, Sect. 1.

Ephesus, where the temple of Artemis, considered one of the wonders of the ancient world and having a Mediterranean-wide body of
patrons, suffered closure. Margherita Guarducci dates the inscription of the basis of letter forms to the fifth century, and perhaps
even after 435:[12]

> Having torn down the beguiling image of the *daimon* Artemis, Demeas
> set up this marker of the truth in honor of God, the expeller of idols,
> and the cross, the deathless victory-bearing symbol of Christ.

Many examples of the Ephesian goddess' "beguiling image"
(ἀπατήλιον εἶδος) have turned up in excavations and to the
Christian mind had a distinctly "daimonic" appearance. Beneath
Artemis' mural crown and brooch some twenty breasts protrude in
representation of her role as fertility goddess, and acorns often hang
from the brooch, which bears the crescent moon or other symbols.
Her ankle-length tunic often displays rows of panels which contain
in descending order animals of various kinds, including griffins.[13]
The Christian God became the expeller of idols (εἰδώλων ἐλατὴρ
Θεός) through his *locum tenens* Demeas, who supervised the erection
of the inscription and who was either an imperial official or, more
likely, a member of the city council. The cross was the symbol of
victory over the *daimon* Artemis (νικοφόρος Χριστοῦ σύμβολος
ἀθάνατος), a phrase which seems to echo the imperial law of 14
November 435, given at Constantinople, which called for the
magistrates to cleanse their temples by the erection of the sign of
the revered Christian religion (*conlocationeque venerandae Christianae
religionis signi*).[14] Statuary of the Ephesian style differed considerably from popular notions of Artemis' epiphany in the countryside.
In rural Bithynia she was thought to appear as a tall woman with
the stature of ten men who went about spinning and grazing flocks
of swine,[15] and her hostility to passers-by earned her the epithet
"hater of strangers" (μισόξενος),[16] so that the Christian was
advised to make the sign of the cross in front of himself should he

---

[12] *Recueil des inscriptions grecques-chrétiennes d'Asie Mineure*, ed. Henri Grégoire
(Paris 1922; repr. 1968), no. 104. For the date and a drawing of the block, see:
Margherita Guarducci, *Epigrafia Greca IV: Epigrafi sacre pagane e cristiane* (Rome
1978), 400f.

[13] Cf. the many examples collected by Hermann Thiersch, *Artemis Ephesia: Eine
archäologische Untersuchung*, I (Berlin 1935).

[14] *Cod. Theod.* 16.10.25. Guarducci seems to infer the date of the inscription from
this law. On stylistic grounds the letters may be even later, perhaps c. 484, when
Illus' rebellion was brought under control. Bury, LRE 1, 398. Cf. supra, Ch. I,
Sect. 5, and infra, Chapter V, Sect. 4.

[15] Infra, Ch. VII, Sect. 1.

[16] Infra, Ch. V, Sect. 2.

meet the *daimon* on the road, much as Demeas had formally erected that symbol in Ephesus.[17]

Christian victory inscriptions marked a sharp divergence from the older views which saw feminine deities as the givers of all good things. A remarkable group of hexametric inscriptions from Lindos on Rhodes commemorates the planting of olive trees in honor of Athena—whom many Athenians, including the Neoplatonist Proclus, still worshipped in the late fifth century—by Aglochartos, her local priest. The longest of the inscriptions dates from c. 300 A.D.:[18]

> Broad is the repute of ancient Lindos, which received the Unwearied [Pallas Athena] on the skyward hills of the akropolis. But her great, delightful reputation goes far upon the earth, filled as it is with the bright grey blessings of the virgin goddess. For now a flourishing "house" of Athena resounds, to be a place for those who gaze upon fruit-bearing promontories. For the priest Aglochartos gave a rich votive offering to Athena, by alloting properties (κτεανῶν) better than those of Keleos and Ikarios, so that the sacred olive tree (ἡ ἱερὴ ἐλέη) might grow on the land.

The patient work of Aglochartos appears elsewhere around the akropolis in the form of an aretalogy of Athena:[19]

> I, the Unwearied, the Undefiled (ἀμωμ[ή]τη), daughter of great Zeus, am a tiller of the soil (γιο[πόν]ος) and husbandman (ἐργοπό[νος]). Aglochartos, renowned son of Moiōnis.

This theme is repeated in two other inscriptions which attest the strength of agrarian deities in the popular imagination and in Aglochartos' priestly consciousness:[20]

> Keleos was a husbandman of chaste Demeter, and Ikarios of Bacchus, and Aglochartos of the offspring of Tritonis [Athena].

And finally:[21]

> Ikarios reached to Bacchus for the grape-fruit and Keleos delighted in the friendly grain-sheaves of Demeter, and the priest Aglochartos crowned Athena with the olive and adorned a sacred precinct (τέμε[νος]) on the akropolis with the young shoot.

The rich imagery of verdure in Aglochartos' verses signifies the strength of a religious ethos which had turned to Athena in good times and bad. The erection of the "victory-bearing and immortal

---

[17] Infra, Ch. VII, Sect. 1.
[18] Guarducci, *Epigrafi sacre*, 213f. IG 12/1 783.
[19] IG 12/1 779.
[20] IG 12/1 780.
[21] IG 12/1 781.

cross" and other tokens of Christianization must have struck the old believers as little more than polemic and fraud. That victory eclipsed, as well, the reputations of past generations of city councillors who had taken on the burden of the expense of erecting and refurbishing the temples. With the ongoing conversions of the fourth and fifth centuries, men like Aglochartos became a dying breed. The emulation which goaded some public figures appears in another of Aglochartos' inscriptions which asserts that he crowned the akropolis with olive-trees at his own expense (ʼΑγλωχάρτου ἑαῖς στρεψαμέ[νου δαπ]ά[ν]αις), if the reading is accurate, a typical claim of those who competed for honour in their cities.[22] These were, then, the female *daimones* which the catechists of the new religion rejected.

The recategorization of local gods into *daimones* appears strikingly in a Syrian inscriptions at the martyrion of St. George at Zorava, a site west of Djebel Hauran. The octagonal building supplanted a pagan temple. The parataxis of antitheses is remarkable:[23]

> The abode of *daimones* has become the house of God. The light of salvation shines where darkness caused concealment. Where sacrifices to idols occurred, there are now choirs of angels. Where God was provoked, now He is propitiated. A certain Christ-loving man, the town-councillor (πρωτεύων) John, son of Diomedes, offered a gift to God from his own property, a beautiful building, after having installed within it the worthy body of the martyr George, who appeared to this John not in a dream, but manifestly (τοῦ φανέντος αὐτῷ Ἰωάννῃ (καὶ) οὐ καθ' ὕπνον, ἀλλὰ φανερῶς).

The inscription dates from 515 A.D. No proof exists for continuity of cult at the site down to that year, but the old religion survived widely elsewhere in sixth-century Syria, even in the *territorium* of Antioch, as the life of Symeon Stylites the Younger attests, and in particular at Ḥarrān-Carrhae.[24] The religious experience of the martyr's apparition closely resembles one averred in another inscription of 324 A.D., some 190 years earlier, which would doubtless have been classed as "daimonic", had Christian clergy or monks been on hand to provide suitable guidance. It is a funerary

---

[22] IG 12/1 782.

[23] *Publications of an American Archaeological Expedition to Syria in 1899–1900, Part III: Greek and Latin Inscriptions*, ed. W.K. Prentice (New York 1908), no. 437a. This collection is hereinafter cited as Prentice, AAES III. For fuller discussion of this inscription, see infra, Ch. XI, Sect. 3.

[24] Frank R. Trombley, "Paganism in the Greek World at the End of Antiquity: The Case of Rural Anatolia and Greece," *Harvard Theological Review* 78 (1985), 328, n. 3.

inscription from Frîkyā in the Djebel Rîhā district in northern Syria on a tomb that is incontestibly pagan:[25]

> These things Abedrapsas states in giving thanks. When I came of age, my ancestral god, the god of Arkesilaos, appeared to me visibly and conferred many benefits on me. For when [I reached the age of] twenty-five, I was given over to the study of an artisan trade, and I received the same trade in a very short time, and furthermore, through my own provision, I purchased a plot of land for myself, with no one knowing it, and freed myself from having to go down to the city. And I was just, and was justly guided.

Abedrapsas lays emphasis, like George the son of Diomedes, on the wakeful reality of the epiphany or vision (δήλως μοι φ[ε]νόμενος). The *daimon*—that is, the pagan god unnamed except as the object of veneration of Arkesilaos, owner of the slave Abedrapsas, who seems to have purchased his freedom from the *peculium* earned from his trade, also unstated—guided his adherent in the ways of justice (κὲ ἐ(γ)ὼ δίκεος ἤμην κὲ δικέως ὁδηγήθη). Abedrapsas' name was, in fact, a pagan theophoric, "slave of Rabb", that is the Master.[26]

Christian clerics and monks subjected the old gods to anonymity wherever possible. Theodoret of Cyrrhus (ob. 458) rises to unsurpassable hyperbole in the *Historia Philotheos* or "Lives of the Monks", a typical product of the late Christian sophistic, when relating the career of the monk Thalaleios, who invaded a rural temenos some 20 *stadia* from Gabala, "a small yet splendid city" (πόλις δὲ αὕτη σμικρὰ καὶ χαριεστάτη) that had evidently become Christian.[27] The violence of Theodoret's rhetoric suggests that the new religion had made few inroads into parts of its *territorium* at that time, probably around 400–420 A.D. The temenos lay on a hill (λόφος), "on which there was a temple reserved for *daimones* and formerly honored by the impious with many sacrifices."[28] Thalaleios built a hut in the precinct and, as Theodoret had it, discovered the daimonic powers of the previously beneficent deities of the site, who presumably resembled the previously mentioned triad found at Kefr Nabo, Seimios, Symbaitylos, and Leon. The monk attributed his problems to them, the same

---

[25] Prentice, AAES III 242. For fuller discussion of this inscription, see infra, Ch. X, Sect. 6.

[26] Frank R. Trombley, *The Survival of Paganism in the Byzantine Empire during the Pre-Iconoclastic Period (540–727)* (Ann Arbor, University Microfilms, 1981), 193. Cf. infra, Ch. XI, Sect. 2.

[27] Theodoret of Cyrrhus, *Historia Philotheos*, PG 82, 1488A-B.

[28] Ibid.

problems which the pagans of the place sought to avoid by soothing
their deities with sacrifices: "For they destroy many persons, both
those nearby and their neighbors, not only men but also mules,
asses, cattle and sheep. [The *daimones*] make war not on animals,
but plot against men through them."[29]

The ultimate reversal of the peace of the gods began when
Christian monks penetrated the temple precincts and provoked the
wrath of the erstwhile deities. It will be recalled that Aglochartos,
priest of Athena the Unwearied at Lindos, had planted the akropolis of her temple with olive trees. The temple at Gabala which the
monk Thalaleios penetrated also had a grove, which, presumably
because the rustics no longer performed propitiatory sacrifices, the
old gods in daimonic form destroyed:[30]

> Then, upon seeing this man Thalaleios arriving, [the *daimones*] at-
> tempted to strike him, but could not because his faith fortified him
> and grace protected him. Being struck with rage and madness, they
> rushed against the trees growing there, and many olive and fig trees
> on that hill were weakened. They say that, of these, more than 500
> were suddenly torn down. This I heard from the neighboring farm-
> ers, who tell the story. They formerly embraced the gloom of impiety,
> but received the light of knowledge of God through the teaching and
> miracle-working of that man.

Theodoret leaves the historian with too inexact a set of data to
permit positing a natural cause for all this, although hailstorms or
human agency provide the likeliest explanation. The *daimones* are
said thereafter to have made screaming sounds at night and to have
shown lights in order to terrify Thalaleios and confuse his reasoning power. Here human agency seems most probable. The monk
replied with laughter. Thalaleios thereafter built a cage for himself.
Theodoret observes with some irony: "Since he had a large body,
he was not able to sit with his neck straight. He always sat bent
forward, having his feet nailed to his face"! Theodoret himself
spoke to Thalaleios, who as a Cilician conversed in Greek and
seems not to have spoken the local Aramaic dialect at first.[31]

Thalaleios' ascetic acts led to the conversion of the rustics dwelling around the temenos (περίοικοι). Taking the analogue of the
pagan and Christian visions witnessed in the already mentioned
inscriptions of Zorava and Kefr Nabo, the martyrs here too re-

---

[29] Ibid.
[30] Ibid.
[31] Ibid., 1488C-D.

placed the local gods who became *daimones*. Theodoret formulates a succinct descriptive paradigm:[32]

> The inhabitants say many miracles are done through his prayer, not only on men, but also on camels, mules, and donkeys, which enjoy cures. The entire populace of that place was formerly gripped by impiety, but learned to despise *ancestral folly* and received the radiance of divine light. By making use of these services he abolished the temenos of *daimones* and raised a great precinct to the splendidly victorious martyrs, substituting the divine dead for the falsely named gods.

To wit, the *daimones* were none other than "falsely named gods". The hagiographer neither admits the names of the local deities nor those of the martyrs whose relics were interred in the church which arose over the ruins of the temple. The *daimones* ceased to have the beneficent qualities that the tiller of the soil required, but did "daimonic" things, as it were, of the sort that the Hellenic philosopher Porphyrius and Christian catechists of every stamp attributed to the evil demons thought to be at the disposal of magicians, sorcerers, and poisoners. The personality and rhetoric of the catechists played a vital role in this transformation, as did the material presence of the symbols of Christianization: martyr relics, the cross, and other tokens of Christian victory. Theodoret of Cyrrhus writes in an Atticist cant that obscures many details. One can hardly doubt that the temenos had carvings on it bearing the accepted formula: Χριστὸς νικᾷ, the Chi-Rho Christogram, and so forth, as appear on the pagan tombs of Athens and northern Syria, and on the great Isis temple at Philae, which underwent Christianization only in the sixth century.[33]

The *Problematik* of daimonization thus becomes clear by means of a few richly illustrative examples. The paradigm is consistent throughout the literature of the period. On the one hand the local deities fall to the status of *daimones* because truly divine or—to risk coining a new term—*theic* powers exist only in the Christian God. At the same time, the recategorized deities reveal "daimonic" powers, that is, they allegedly attack their former adherents who trespass in the vicinity of the sites of the age-old sacrifices and direct their vengeance against the rustics and their animals, and particularly against Christian clerics and monks, but unsuccess-

---

[32] Ibid., 1489A-B.
[33] Charles M. Bayet, *De Titulis Atticae Christianis Antiquissimis Commentatio Historica et Epigraphica* (Paris 1878), no. 92. Infra, Ch. IX, Sect. 3.

fully where the symbols of Christian victory, including the holy man himself, stand.

The merging of old deities with Christian angels and martyrs reflects another and more complex variation in this process of transformation, but, for this, extant evidence is intractable and susceptible to bizarre misinterpretation. One thinks, for example, of the entirely superficial and specious notions that St. Phokas as the protector of mariners descended from the Earthshaker Poseidon, or that St. Demetrius, with an entirely opposed typology, might derive from the underworld fertility deity Demeter—a resemblance based on name only.[34] The solution to the question lies more in the *identity* and its *localization* to a pre-Christian site of religious awe which underwent Christianization as a matter of necessity because the cult practiced there lay too deep in the local ethos simply to be eradicated. It will be necessary to turn from Syria to Asia Minor in this connection, where the evidence speaks clearly.[35]

II. The Social Context of Temple Conversions

The term "temple conversion"—the demolition or partial dismantling of a sacred edifice and its modification into a church or martyrion—was the logical consequence of the theological tendency to recategorize pagan deities into destructive *daimones*. The expression has been applied not only to the transformation of a temple building into a church, but also to the construction of a church within a temenos or sacred precinct such that the entrance of the temple facing east (an architectural feature designed to ensure that the rays of the rising sun touched the cult effigy) directly confronted the entrance of the new Christian basilica, which at times lay in the temple courtyard, and had its own main entrance of the west end of the building.[36] The space between the entrances of the temple and church might serve as the *atrium* of the Christian basilica. As one walked into this space, he might pass

---

[34] Supra, Ch. II, n. 4.
[35] Cf. the striking example of a mountain peak near Miletus. Trombley, "Paganism in the Greek World," 345. Cf. also the case of Djebel Sheikh Berekat in the Limestone Massif east of Antioch in Syria. Infra, Ch. X., Sect. 1. Iamblichos of Chalkis did not find the gods' presiding over certain localities inconsistent with his own Neoplatonist interpretation of sacrifice. *De Mysteriis* 5.24.
[36] The standard survey is still that of Friedrich W. Deichmann, "Frühchristliche Kirchen in antiken Heiligtümern," *Jahrbuch des Deutschen Archäologischen Instituts* 54 (1939), 105–136. It is supplemented in some particulars by Jean-Michel Spieser, "La Christianisation des sanctuaires païens en Grèce," *Neue Forschungen in griechischen Heiligtümern*, ed. Ulf Jantzen (Tübingen 1976), 309–320.

from there through the narthex and *tribelon* of the basilica into the main aisle of the church, or instead enter the *pronaos* of the pagan temple which led to the cella where the cult effigy had stood and sometimes to the *adyton* beyond, a secret chamber where initiatory rites were performed or oracles given.[37] Whichever way one turned from the *atrium*, the symbols of the new religion confronted him. The temple to the west, if it were a structure of imposing beauty and of high quality in its interior sculpture and panelling, might be preserved intact, without the incision of crosses and Christian victory formulae,[38] but the cult effigies which had received sacrifices would probably have been removed by the early fifth century.[39] In less urbanized areas, where fewer concessions were made to the old culture, the interior of the temple might reveal crosses and Christian graffiti hacked everywhere into the stone, or even a martyrion or depository for martyr-relics where a Christian monk or cleric would recite the psalmody or even conduct the eucharistic liturgy. A hybridized church-temple complex invariably had a sacristan (παραμονάριος or προσμονάριος), often a monk with the clerical rank of deacon, who observed and supervised the behavior of all who entered the buildings.[40] If small offerings or gratuities fell into his hands from Christian visitors,[41] his eye invariably fell on those who approached the *pronaos* of the temple. Clandestine sacrifices in the form of small incense fires and the scattering of whey were quite possible in these circumstances and by the law of 8 November 392 had a mandatory death penalty attached to them.

The term "temple conversion" is used as well to describe the demolition of the old buildings to make way for Christian basilicas. Such actions became a particular necessity when local bishops desired to erect churches within the city walls, where large lots were seldom available amidst the public buildings and areas such as the council-chamber and agora (a social and economic neces-

---

[37] Thus the temple of Zeus Heliopolitanus at Baalbek-Heliopolis in Phoenicia Libanensis. Deichmann, "Kirchen in Heiligtümern," 115–117, with plans.

[38] A certain exception to this proposition is the Isis temple of Philae in the upper Nile basin. Cf. infra, Ch. IX, Sects. 3 and 4.

[39] Supra, Ch. I, Sect. 2.

[40] Cf. the small chapel of Michael the Archistrategos of the heavenly army at Colossos-Chonae. "Le Miracle de Saint Michel à Colosses," ed. tr. F. Nau, *Patrologia Orientalis* 4 (1907), 650, lines 11ff. and the so-called Second Martyrion at Berytus in Phoenicia, infra, Ch. V, Sect. 5.

[41] We learn that in the time of the emperor Heraclius (610–641) the *hebdomarioi* of the martyrion of St. Artemius in Constantinople were inclined to deny a wealthy man access to the shrine without being offered a sum of money (*logarin*). *Diēgēsis tōn thaumatōn tou hagiou megalomartyros kai thaumatourgou Artemiou* (BHG 173), *Varia Graeca Sacra*, ed. A. Papadopoulos-Kerameus (St. Petersburg 1909), 17f.

sity), the large town houses of the decurion class, and the tenements which housed the folk of the absolutely essential artisan and food-handling classes.[42] The temples of the Greek and Semitic deities thus attracted the interest of the bishops, who might claim with justification that the demolition of these buildings posed the fewest economic risks to the community out of all other possibilities.[43]

This tendency corresponded to the demographic reality that the cities of the eastern Mediterranean lands had by the time of Julian the Apostate (361–363 in East) achieved equal pagan and Christian populations, as in the case of Bostra, the metropolis of the Provincia Arabia.[44] Julian's fate shattered any hope for the revival of Hellenic religion, despite many enduring measures, such as the reincorporation of Christian Maiuma with pagan Gaza into a single *polis*.[45] It seems undisputable that his death increased the prestige of the local churches and led to increasing numbers of conversions in the cities and their suburbs after about 365, all this despite the moderate and tolerant policy conducted toward the old temple cults by the eastern emperor Valens.[46] This supposition is based in part on John Chrysostom's *Homilia in Ignatium*, a product of his early career at Antioch. This city, the earliest Hellenistic site to have a large Christian congregation, had a population of circa 200,000, excluding slaves and children, when the homily was writ-

---

[42] This motivation is implicit in Porphyrius' demolition of the Marneion in Gaza. Infra, Ch. III, Sect. 4. On the concentration of different categories of essential trades in the inner city, see: Frank R. Trombley, "Korykos in Cilicia Trachis (sic): The Economy of a Small Coastal City in Late Antiquity," *Ancient History Bulletin* 1 (1987), 16–23.

[43] This was perhaps one of the most important factors left unstated in the sources that lay behind the demolition of the great temples in Apamea, Gaza, and Aphrodisias. Cf. infra, Ch. II, Sect. 3 passim, and Ch. VI. See the comment of Robert Markus, *The End of Ancient Christianity* (Cambridge 1990), 147.

[44] καίτοι Χριστιανῶν ὄντων ἐμφαμίλλων τῷ πλήθει τῶν Ἑλλήνων. Julian the Apostate, *Epistle XLI* in *The Works of the Emperor Julian*, tr. W.C. Wright, 3 (London-New York 1923), 132f.

[45] Infra, Ch. III, Sect. 2.

[46] Theodoret of Cyrrhus observes: "Valens encouraged all others [including Hellenes] to worship as they pleased and to celebrate their rites (τὰ θρησκευό-μενα θεραπεύειν). . . . All through his reign the altar fire was kindled (ἐπιβώμιον πῦρ). [The Hellenes furthermore] poured libations and made sacrifices (σπονδαὶ καὶ θυσίαι) to idols and celebrated public festivals in the agora (καὶ τὰς δημοθοινίας κατὰ τὴν ἀγορὰν ἐπετέλουν). Those who celebrated the mysteries of Dionysus ran about wearing goatskins, tearing dogs asunder and raging, roused to Bacchic frenzy, and doing other things that made clear the evil of their teacher." HE 5.21, 1–5 in *Kirchengeschichte*, ed. Léon Parmentier (Leipzig 1911), 317f. Theodoret's obvious bias against Valens, who tolerated the semi-Arian theology in the Roman East, is offset by the fact of this emperor's explicit permission for the nocturnal sacrifices celebrated in connection with the Eleusinian Mysteries to go on. Supra, Ch. I, Sect. 4.

ten in the 370's. Its principal church alone had a congregation of 100,000, a figure which certainly included Christian slaves, but this does not speak for the Christians affiliated with the other local churches, who must have been quite numerous.[47] Thus, when Christian bishops called for the demolition of temples and reuse of their urban lots for new churches, they often had a majority of public opinion behind them. Where such an initiative lacked the full backing of the public, bishops seem at times to have played upon the superstition of the recently converted, but not necessarily baptized, folk, that is to say the catechumens, who in some instances believed that the old deities had retained a *residuum* of their powers which endangered the community, whether from the clandestine sacrifices reputed to attract *daimones* or from the very stones of the buildings which had been the scene of these acts. Episcopal propaganda in such cases fed on the fact that cult effigies were often thought, as was seen in the previous chapter, to harbor *daimones*, although not necessarily the actual *persona* of the deity. The former gave them a certain power to receive votive offerings and answer the petitions of suppliants, and even at times to become animate (ἔμψυχος). The latter belief, found in high-cultural and everyday Greek theologies alike, resulted from the priesthoods' cynical but nevertheless effective use of automated statues and other devices.[48] Where bishops lacked the local political power to acquire inner city temple lots, they relied on imperial decrees and troops to carry out their programs, as did Porphyrius, bishop of Gaza.[49]

Archaeologists have generated a great deal of research on the mechanics of demolishing temples or adapting them to Christian liturgical purposes, but less is known about the social and economic context of these acts. After reviewing certain material phenomena of temple conversions, which serve to illustrate data usually accessible only in archaeological reports, the social context of three incidents will be examined: the destruction of the Zeus temple at Apamea in Second Syria by the metropolitan Marcellus c. 388; the closure of the Serapeum in Alexandria in 391; and the smashing of the statuary of the temple of Allat-Athena at Palmyra in the Provincia Arabia circa 385–388. Emphasis will be laid on the behavioral and economic significance of these events, which, although

---

[47] Adolph Harnack, *The Mission and Expansion of Christianity in the First Three Centuries*, 2nd ed., 2 (London-New York 1908), 133.

[48] Supra, Ch. I, Sect. 3. Cf. Edwyn Bevan, *Holy Images* (London 1940), 25, 31–39, with examples from the Hellenistic and Late Antique periods. Cf. the case of the effigy of Sarapis in Alexandria. Infra, Ch. II, Sect. 3.

[49] Infra, Ch. III, Sect. 4.

of late fourth-century vintage, provide the essential background for understanding how the social apparatus of cult evolved during the fifth century.

A comprehensive theory, if not a theology, on temple conversion began to emerge in the early fourth century, if the statements of Eusebius of Caesarea be taken as the reflection of a Graeco-Palestinian consensus. Its fullest expression comes in the section of his *Life of Constantine* dealing with the supposed discovery of the Holy Sepulchre.[50] The site in question was evidently a cave-temple dedicated to Aphrodite or some Semitic equivalent from the time of the emperor Hadrian (117–138 A.D.), when he refounded Jerusalem as Aelia Capitolina in the wake of the Bar Kochba rebellion (132–135).[51] Eusebius has it that impious men (ἄνδρες δυσσεβεῖς), or "the entire race of *daimones*" (πᾶν τὸ δαιμόνων διὰ τούτων γένος), that is the pagan gods, acting through the former, conspired to hide from men the sacred cave where Christ was buried, a peculiar admission that those deities actually had the capability of perpetuating their own cult at the expense of the Christian God! This contrived explanation, a fourth-century polemic against Hellenic and Semitic polytheism, relied on the notion that men had fallen into "forgetfulness" about true religion. Palestine was full of shrines which had double or triple associations amidst Hellenism, Judaism, and Christianity, as for example the Oak of Mambre, which Christians (and possibly Jews as well) associated with Abraham, but which in the fourth century lay inside a pagan temenos with an altar set up next to the tree for sacrifices.[52] As with the cave-temple in Jerusalem, the shrine was converted back to its pristine Judaic-Christian associations, or so it was thought. Eusebius fails to explain how a Christian holy place with quasi-magical powers to defeat the influence of the pagan gods or *daimones* could have fallen into such a state. The reality seems to be, quite to the contrary, that these sites, as with caves and trees in many cultures, had always had sacred associations in more than one local religion and evoked awe in all who visited them.[53] The

---

[50] Eusebius of Caesarea, *De Vita Constantini* 3.26–29 in Eusebius, *Werke*, ed. Ivan A. Heikel, 1 (Leipzig 1902), 89–91. Cf. Deichmann, "Kirchen in Heiligtümern," 107.

[51] Albino Garzetti, *From Tiberius to the Antonines: A History of the Roman Empire AD 14–192*, tr. J.R. Foster (London 1974), 398f., 422–424.

[52] Eusebius, *De Vita Constantini* 3.51–52. Deichmann, "Kirchen in Heiligtümern," 107f. and 120.

[53] Tree and bethel stone shrines were common among the Canaanites. Cf. the survival of the tree and altar in the cult of Indian fertility deities, the Yaksas, through all stages of religious transformation (pre-Indic, Hindu, and Buddhist).

discovery of the Holy Sepulchre had more of a symbolical function than archaeological reality about it, but served all the same as one more proof of the triumph of the Christian God.

The procedure used to convert the sacred cave into a Christian shrine, the earliest example of a temple conversion, set the precedent for all such acts in the future, and owed not a little to Constantine the Great's own notions of liturgical formalism and superstition. Sacrifices had been performed in the Holy Cave, after the Hellenes had "remodelled a dark cavern for *the unchaste daimon of Aphrodite* and had performed defiled sacrifices and libations upon the impure and accursed altars there".[54] The "*daimon* of Aphrodite" (Ἀφροδίτης ἀκολάστῳ δαίμονι), evidently a *daimon* of the type thought to dwell in sacred precincts and in idols, was not considered to be Aphrodite herself, whom the cultists worshipped, but her *locum-tenens*. The emperor Constantine, having ascertained to his own satisfaction the true identity of the cave, ordered it cleansed "after calling upon his own God to be his collaborator" (θεὸν τὸν αὐτοῦ συνεργὸν ἐπικαλεσάμενος), presumably to overcome the power of the *daimon* of the cave.[55] The systematic demolition of the pagan site followed, as "the buildings of error belonging to those idols and *daimones*" were razed (αὐτοῖς ξοάνοις καὶ δαίμοσι τὰ τῆς πλάνης οἰκοδομήματα).[56] Eusebius goes into great detail about the precautions taken to cleanse the site:[57]

> Out of zeal [Constantine] did not allow [the buildings] to stand in those places, but ordered the stone and wooden materials of the defiled [places] to be taken and cast away. He attended closely to the idea with action. The emperor saw fit not only to proceed with this, but, having ascribed that piece of ground to God, and having excavated a great depth of soil, he commanded that the earth be carried off, inasmuch as it was defiled by the daimonic gore [of sacrifices], somewhere far away and as far off as possible.

The Christian, or rather Constantinian, idea of ritual pollution from pagan sacrifices, including the vapors of incense and burnt animal flesh, animal blood, and combusted wine sediment, extended, not only to the altars, but the building materials of the temple, and even the soil which lay beneath the paving stones, a concatenation so extreme as to lack parallels even in other

---

Mircea Eliade, *Patterns in Comparative Religion*, tr. Rosemary Sheed (New York 1958), 269f.

[54] Eusebius, *Vita Constantini* 3.26.
[55] Eusebius, *Vita Constantini* 3.26.6.
[56] Eusebius, *Vita Constantini* 3.26.7.
[57] Eusebius, *Vita Constantini* 3.27–28.

monotheistic religions.[58] Under these conditions, reusing the spolia
of razed temples might theoretically pose the danger to a pious
Christian of pollution by the *daimones* inhering in the spolia after
being drawn there by the vapors of burnt offerings.

Not all local bishops and monks who destroyed temples with
their altars in the late fourth and fifth centuries had time for such
bizarre speculations, which belong partly to the realm of propaganda and partly to that of superstition. The surviving accounts
suggest that these suppositions varied with the degree of rationalism possessed by the catechist idol-breaker and his own opinion
about what approach to use with his congregation, but it seems
unlikely that such ideas of ritual contamination were ever completely excluded from the ethos of temple conversions. Superstition
more than anything else would explain the complete incineration of
valuable building materials from the impressively constructed temples of Zeus at Apamea and that of Zeus Marnas at Gaza,[59] unless
the episcopal propagandist had some real certainty that unlimited

---

[58] Eliade, *Patterns in Comparative Religion*, passim. Temple conversions as such
did not take place in the Roman East before Constantine the Great established his
power there with the defeat of Licinius in 324, although some local Christian
communities may have established shrines through synoikism or manifest squat-
ting in temple precincts, as two examples given below suggest, one from Phrygian
Laodikea, the other from Colossae. Infra, Ch. II, Sect. 4. No theory of Christian
ritual purification seems to have lain at the disposal of the agents of Constantine
who supervised the cleansing of the Aphrodite temple in Jerusalem. It is possible
that they derived the idea of the soil's being ritually contaminated from locally
prevalent Jewish ideas, as a section of the *'Aboda Zara* or Mishna on Idolatry
suggests. The most recent of the sages to be cited is rabbi Yehuda ha-Nasi (ob. 210
A.D.). The redaction seems to have come out not long afterward. Chapter 3.6
holds: "The occupant of a house adjoining an idol's shrine is forbidden to rebuild
it if it has fallen down. How is he to act? He must withdraw into his own ground
four cubits, and then rebuild. If the wall belonged jointly to him and to the idol, it
is adjudged to belong half to each; *its stones, wood, and débris cause defilement* like a
creeping thing, as it is written 'Thou shalt utterly detest it'." Chapter 3.7 indicates
that a structure originally designed and built as a pagan temple is prohibited for
use, but that one renovated with panelling and plaster for pagan cult might
legitimately be used if the materials related to the pagan cult be removed. A
structure into which an idol was brought for worship after its construction for a
different purpose is considered cleansed merely by the removal of the cult effigy.
The Mishna on Idolatry 'Aboda Zara, ed. tr. W.A. Elmslie (Cambridge 1911), 53.
Temple conversions followed principles similar to these. The reattribution of the
Oak of Mambre to the patriarch Abraham and its sanctification within a Christian
shrine is in accordance once again with the rulings in *'Aboda Zara* 3.7: "There are
three sorts of Askeras. A tree, which a man has first planted for the purpose of
idolatry, behold! this tree is forbidden. . . . If he has merely erected an idol
beneath a tree, and has desecrated the idol, behold! this tree is permitted." Ibid.,
55. On the recommended methods of desecrating an idol (*'Aboda Zara* 4.5), see
infra, Ch. II, n. 212.
[59] Infra, Ch. II, Sect. 3, and Ch. III, Sect. 4.

monies from the imperial till and other donors were on hand for his
own use. This proved to be the case at Gaza.[60] Yet many temples
became churches through the simple erection of the cross and some
architectural modifications required for the Christian liturgy: the
addition of an apse at the east end and knocking through an
entrance at the previously walled western end. The erection of the
cross served as an apotropaic as well as propagandistic device,
followed by the addition of apses and erection of Christian sculptures. Of this more will be said later.

In the instance of the Holy Cave in Jerusalem, Constantine
erected an awe-inspiring multi-shelled rotunda around the site and
fused it with a basilica of complex design. Eusebius calls the place
"a chapel building suitable for God [built] round about the cave of
salvation" (οἶκον εὐκτήριον θεοπρεπῆ ἀμφὶ τὸ σωτήριον
ἄντρον). The emperor ornamented it splendidly and provided an
endowment, that it would seem magnificent (ὑπερφυές) by comparison to the pagan temples of the Roman East.[61] The splendor of
such imperial structures aimed not only at showing up the
Hellenes' traditional cultic architecture, but also at getting
prospective converts to tour the buildings and thereby to learn the
humane character of the new religion. The play of streaming sun-
light amidst the marble columns and grilles created just the right
emotional atmosphere for the catechumen and tourist alike to
peruse and believe the stories told by the mosaic program.[62] Gone
were the expressionless or idealized figures of the recategorized
gods, all of them now replaced by the wide-eyed, humane figures of
Christ, the martyrs, and the prophets, often depicted amidst an
Elysian pastoral or apocalyptic-celestial backdrop.[63]

---

[60] Infra, Ch. III, Sect. 4.
[61] Eusebius, *Vita Constantini* 3.29.
[62] Infra, Ch. V, Sect. 5. The *acheiropoietos* image of Christ of Camuliana ("made
without human hands") is said to have appeared after a woman contemplating
conversion whose name was Hypatia asked her catechist: "How can I worship
him when he is not visible and I do not know him?" Zachariah of Mytilene, *The
Syriac Chronicle Known as That of Zachariah of Mitylene*, tr. F.J. Hamilton and E.W.
Brooks (London 1899), 320. The Sassanid cavalryman and fire-worshipper
Magoudat-Anastasius convinced a Persian silversmith of his sincere desire to
accept Christianity only after he accompanied the latter to the churches of
Hierapolis in Euphratensis "and prayed and *saw the hitories of the martyrs*" (τὰς
ἱστορίας τῶν ἁγίων μαρτύρων ἑώρα). *Acta M. Anastasii Persae*, ed. Hermann
Usener (Bonn 1894), 2.
[63] Cf. the highly individualized portraits of martyrs depicted in the mosaics of
the Rotunda of Thessalonike and the spiritualized paradise in the apse mosaic at
St. Apollinare in Classe, Ravenna. Theocharis Pazaras, *The Rotunda of Saint George
in Thessaloniki* (Thessalonike 1985), 32–44. Clive Foss and Paul Magdalino, *Rome
and Byzantium* (Oxford 1977), 58 (for convenient reference).

It is but a short step from Eusebius of Caesarea's description, which quickly developed a theoretical cant, to the practical considerations of converting temples. Freidrich Deichmann and Jean Michel Spieser have discussed the archaeological side of this question in great detail, and their findings need not be treated here except certain points relevant in this context.[64]

Spolia taken from the temples were put to different uses, depending on local attitudes. Porphyrius of Gaza used the partly incinerated stones of the Marneion to pave the courtyard in front of the planned Eudoxiana basilica, although the materials were thought to be ritually contaminated (*dem Dämon gehörige Materie*).[65] On the other hand, the Aphaka temple of Aphrodite, a rural shrine in the mountains of Lebanon where ritual prostitution continued until Constantine closed the place,[66] saw its spolia reused to build a Christian church. The temple was razed to its foundations and a new building constructed all over again, with the same stones, on the same spot, and with identically sited exterior walls.[67] In contrast to this, the legendary St. Nicholas of Myra was said to have torn up even the foundations of the Aphrodite temple at Myra, the metropolis of Lycia in southern Asia Minor, lest the *daimon* of the place continue to dwell there.[68] If the story be apocryphal, examples of this kind of behavior certainly lie behind the legend. At Baalbek-Heliopolis in Phoenicia Libanensis the unknown catechists left the splendidly sculptured temple building of Zeus Heliopolitanus alone, but erected a three-aisled basilica to the east of it in the middle of the old courtyard, so that the respective entrances faced each other. The positioning of the central aisle of the Christian basilica directly on top of the pagan altar made the continuance of sacrifice impossible.[69] Alternatively, a small martyrion staffed by a monastic caretaker (παραμονάριος or προσμονάριος) with the rank of deacon might be erected within the circuit wall of the temenos off to the side, to serve merely as the symbol of the new religion at a large urban temple, such as the small martyrion of St. John supposed to have been built inside the enclosure of the Zeus temple at Damascus.[70] On the other hand, a small church might be put up at a rural temenos through the ambition of a local

---

[64] Supra, Ch. II, n. 36.
[65] Deichmann, "Kirchen in Heiligtümern," 109.
[66] Eusebius, *Vita Constantini* 3.55.
[67] Deichmann, "Kirchen in Heiligtümern," 108, 115, 117.
[68] Ibid., 111.
[69] Ibid., 109, 115f., 117.
[70] Ibid., 116.

monk and martyr relics placed there to serve the purpose of disrupting cult, as sacrifices were thought to be inefficacious if the shrine were polluted. The introduction of the Christian dead served this purpose admirably. Such is certainly the explanation of the Syrian martyr chapels whose construction Theodoret of Cyrrhus reports in his *Historia Philotheos*,[71] and perhaps also that erected within the temenos of Despoina at Lykosoura in the mountains of the Arcadian Peloponnese.[72]

The question of temple conversions in Greece, touched upon initially by Friedrich Deichmann, was updated by Jean Michel Spieser, who maintains that no continuity of cult existed at the temples there between the Hellenic and Christian religions, that is, that a long interval of time elapsed before temples like the Parthenon, Theseion, and Asklepieion in Athens were remodelled into Christian churches, an interval of anywhere between one to two hundred years, between c. 485 and as late as the last decades of the seventh century, when dated Christian inscriptions first appear on the Parthenon.[73] Spieser sums up his thesis in these terms after discussing the fate of the Asklepieion on Kos and the Christian basilica in the temenos of Hebraiokastro on Thasos:[74]

> Here too, it cannot be excluded that the pagan sanctuary had been abandoned well before the triumph of Christianity. It follows that, if in certain of the examples cited clear conclusions do not impose themselves, it is certain for the rest that the transformation of a temple or the reuse of its site is linked to causes proper to each site (*liés à des causes propre à chaque site*) and do not appear as manifestations of the triumph of Christianity, which sought to mark its victory over paganism in this manner.

This conclusion relies upon the long chronological intervals, at sites of temple conversions, between the last dateable votive offerings or attested priesthoods on the one hand (most often falling in the third century A.D.), and evidence of Christian architectural modifications or new basilicas.[75] The absence of secure literary *testimonia* about temple conversions makes such a thesis tenable when the evidence from the Greek mainland and Aegean islands is considered in hermetic isolation from the rest of the Eastern Roman Empire. This view can hardly be maintained in a comparative

---

[71] Infra, Ch. VIII, Sect. 2.
[72] Trombley, "Paganism in the Greek World," 346f.
[73] Spieser, "Christianisation des sanctuaires," 310.
[74] Ibid., 311f.
[75] This view of the evidence goes back to Geffcken, *Last Days of Paganism*, 25–34.

context, however, particularly in light of behavioral evidence
gleaned from other parts of the eastern Mediterranean world, unless
one posits the existence of entirely unique religious patterns in local
Greek society and culture, the demonstration of which constitutes a
desideratum for the present, but which nevertheless seems feasible.
Spieser himself hints at such a distinctive paradigm:[76]

> It is clear that the end of Delos as a great sanctuary is well anterior to
> triumphant Christianity. For the rest, the pagan cults, or at least
> certain of them, survived much longer than the written sources tell.
> Without doubt small cults addressing local needs (*petits cultes pour les
> besoins locaux*), which disappeared little by little, brought the decline
> of the great temples in their ruin and a support too costly for com-
> munities that were quite impoverished and, in any case, reduced in
> size. Equally modest Christian sanctuaries were born beside them in
> the image of the [social and cultural] milieu for which they provided
> expression, and which had neither the cause nor the means to refur-
> bish or reuse the splendid buildings of the past.

As not one of the early Christian basilicas built next to great shrines
such as those at Eleusis and Epidauros survives, it is difficult to
speculate about local means for basilica construction, and so these
arguments hang in mid-air. Another consideration elucidated by
the laws found in the Theodosian Code is that Hellenic buildings
were often kept intact by reason of local civic patriotism, a powerful
factor in the cities of mainland Greece.[77] Furthermore, Timothy E.
Gregory has plausibly argued in the instance of the Asklepieion in
Athens that a Christian healing cult of St. Andrew entailed incubation and made use of the dormitories attached to the temple.
Significantly, the Christian cult postdated the similar worship of
Asklepios immediately, probably in the 480's.[78] Nor does the violent destruction of Pheidias' chryselephantine statue of Athena in
the Parthenon, perhaps also in the 480's, tie in with notions of the
auto-extinction of the Hellenic cults.[79]

We come next, as regards Greece, to the daimonic powers which
some early Christian bishops with their urban communities attributed to the recategorized deities thought still to dwell in their
shrines. Spieser argues sensibly that this sort of thinking explains
the usual practice in Greece of constructing Christian churches
outside the entrances of the pagan sacred enclosures. One can

---

[76] Spieser, "Christianisation des sanctuaires," 315.
[77] *Cod. Theod.* 16.10.8. Infra, Ch. IV, Sect. 2.
[78] Timothy E. Gregory, "The Survival of Paganism in Christian Greece: A
Critical Essay," *American Journal of Philology* 107 (1986), 237f.
[79] Infra, Ch. IV, Sect. 3.

hardly contest this thesis in light of the abundant evidence that Christians feared daimonic kratophanies in the absence of the symbols of the new religion and the cross in particular. The question remains why Spieser should doubt that the cross was erected on the temples of Greece. Some few cases, which hardly exhaust the data, indicate that it was. The incision of the cross on the gorgoneion of the breastplate of Marcus Aurelius on the clipeus sculpture at Eleusis is well-known.[80] Another example is found on an altar discovered at Epidauros which bears the inscription: "To Asklepios. Antipatros a suppliant".[81] On the next side of the block to the right, a cross with the tiny loop of a Rho on its upper arm, which thus combines two sacred Christian symbols, is incised within a circle.[82] The votive inscription of Antipatros is partially erased, particularly the name of the *"daimon"* Asklepios, and the wreath below it has been largely chipped off.[83] The epigraphy indicates the survival of cult at Epidauros in the form of a dedication to the Asklepios of Aigai in Cilicia until 355. The Christian basilica outside the temenos belongs to the late fourth century.[84] Christians of the sixth or seventh century who had forgotten the daimonic powers of the old gods can hardly have been responsible for these effacements, which belong to an earlier era of Christianization, the late fourth and fifth centuries. Hellenism did in fact remain a powerful force in mainland Greece all through the fifth century, and produced a rather unique style of conversion, to judge from the Christian funerary inscriptions of Attica.[85]

A view expressed by Timothy E. Gregory has force here, namely that the Christian basilicas erected on the perimeters of temple enclosures served the function of catechetical "competing shows" orchestrated by the local Christian bishops.[86] The architecture and ornamentation should have been anything but modest to secure this aim, but the archaeological record does not fully bear this out. There is the consideration as well that even Christian Hellenists of the city councils, who enjoyed education in the Greek *paideia* and possessed more than a little civic pride, found themselves in the quandary of admiring the old buildings no less than the literature,

---

[80] Trombley,"Paganism in the Greek World," 345, n. 108. Cf. Otfried Deubner, "Zu grossen Propyläen von Eleusis," *Deutsches Archäologisches Institut, Athenische Abteilung, Mitteilungen* 62 (1937), 75 and Plate 39.

[81] Werner Peek, *Neue Inschriften aus Epidauros* (Berlin 1972), no. 44.

[82] Ibid., Tafel XII, Abb. 26 and 27.

[83] Ibid., 30.

[84] Spieser, "Christianisation des sanctuaires," 318f.

[85] Infra, Ch. IV, Sect. 1.

[86] Oral communication.

yet being unable to restore them, whether for reasons of conscience, the bishops' prodding, or even fear of "daimonic rage". Hence the temples fell down from neglect and seismic activity. It seems safest to put the defacement of inscriptions and statues in the late fourth and fifth centuries, when the local adherents of the old cults had diminished sufficiently for such acts to be carried out with impunity. Even then, the clandestine sacrifices repeatedly proscribed by the Theodosian Code and reported, for example, in Marinus of Neapolis' biography of Proclus went on in the precincts when the watchful eyes of the Christian clergy were averted. The final conversion of buildings like the Erechtheion, Parthenon and Theseion in Athens, the Thesmophoreion on Delos, and the site closed by the bishop Jovian on Corfu, which Spieser puts in the sixth century,[87] belongs to the terminal stage of Christianization, when the buildings around which civic tradition were centred became churches.

There remains one theoretical question to be considered before the detailed analysis of some specific temple conversions, and that is the adoption of the "One God" (Εἷς Θεός) formulae, which are in fact acclamations, as one ideological feature of the Christianization of the empire, and of temple conversions in particular. The "One God" formula goes back unquestionably to pre-Christian usage, as Erik Peterson demonstrates in *EIC ΘEOC*.[88] This study cites or quotes most of the extant texts in the original Greek, the greater number of them epigraphic, in a liturgical analysis which, in the interest of thematic unity, abstracts them from their original social and archaeological contexts. It is argued in great detail below in connection with the Christianization of rural Syria that the "One God" formula lent itself to adaptation by recent converts, and that such an interpretation is incontestable in the unique archaeological context of the villages of the Limestone Massif that lies east of Antioch on the Roman road running due east to Aleppo-Beroia, where at many sites dated examples of these texts ornamented with crosses and sometimes naming Christ represent the earliest series of identifiably Christian inscriptions.[89] This rule stands quite firmly, whether one argues that the social origin of the phenomenon lies in the outright conversion of the rustic population, or whether the persons who erected the "One God" inscriptions were Christian migrants to this district from Antioch, who as

---

[87] Spieser, "Christianisation des sanctuaires," 312.
[88] Erik Peterson, *EIC ΘEOC, Epigraphischen, formgeschichtliche und religionsgeschichtliche Untersuchungen* (Göttingen 1926), passim.
[89] Infra, Ch. X.

capitalistic producers of an olive oil crop were the progenitors of the urban style of masonry in the houses, churches, and public buildings of the district.[90]

At any rate, the specific role of the "One God" formula in temple conversions, a topic never really worked out in detail, requires brief mention in a non-Syrian context. One turns in this connection to the temple of pharaoh Hatshepsut at Deir al-Bahari in Nilotic Egypt, which dates from the XXIII or XXIV dynasty. Here, under the Hellenizing influence of the Ptolemaic kings, a new cult, that of the god Amenothes son of Hapou, is first mentioned in 261/260 B.C.[91] It essentially became the sanctuary of the divine triad Imhotep-Asklepios, his daughter Hygeia, and Amenothes son of Hapou. Imhotep was of course assimilated to the Greek physician deity Asklepios, whose incubation cult, replete with healing visions and miracles, existed as well at Oxyrhynchus and Ptolemais until at least the time of the emperor Trajan (c. 99–117 A.D.).[92] The temple at Deir al-Bahari attracted cure-seekers thereafter, through the third century A.D., who filled the walls of the temple rooms with inscriptions and graffiti, very many of which refer to a sacrifice or act of obeisance (*proskynēma*) with the formula: τὸ προσκύνημα τοῦ δεῖνος.[93]

Nothing survives in the way of later evidence at the temple of Deir al-Bahari except a Christian inscription and three crosses grouped around an early votive text. The pagan inscription reads:[94]

> The *proskynēma* of Eugraphios before the lord god Asklepios and Amenothes and Hygeia. Remember us and grant us a cure.

The invocation of the divine triad with the plea for a healing miracle received a Christian reply, probably sometime in the fifth century: "There is [in reality] one God who helps you!" (Εἷς Θεὸς ὁ βοηθῶν ὑμῶν).[95] Around the pagan *proskynēma* the same or another Christian incised three crosses, one of them a sort of rounded

---

[90] Oral communication from Zvi Maʿoz. The distribution of olive-growing zones in the Limestone Massif is discussed analytically by Georges Tchalenko, *Villages antiques de la Syrie du Nord* 3 vols. (Paris 1953–58). Cf. vol. 2, Plate XXXI (zones of olive and olive-vine cultivation), Plates CXVIII-CXX (olive presses of the village of Beḥyo on Djebel il-ʿAlā), and the impressive examples of ashlar block architecture used in the churches, houses, towers, and other buildings.

[91] André Bataille, *Les insctiptions grecques du temple de Hatshepsout à Deir el-Bahari* (Cairo 1951), vii.

[92] Bataille, ix.

[93] Bataille, xxvii.

[94] Bataille, no. 86.

[95] Bataille, no. 89 (Note itacism).

swastika, the other two being examples of the Egyptian *ankh* (*deux croix ansées*) trefoil or Maltese crosses with their top petals in the shape of loops. This Egyptian symbol of Life (Ζωή) was adopted as a Christian sign in the wake of the demolition of the Serapeum at Alexandria in 391,[96] and passed into the Christian *koinē* thereafter.[97] A Christian "One God" inscription with a trefoil cross appears in one other location in the temple, next to another *proskynēma* text.[98] The conclusion to be drawn in the first case is obvious: the "One God who helps" formula used in connexion with crosses belongs to the local Christian resistance to the dying cult of the daimonic triad.

The temple conversions at the end of the fourth century gave final shape to the closure of the sacred precincts which imperial officials of sundry ranks and jurisdictions had carried out with varying degrees of thoroughness since the early 380's. These events marked the end of the public celebration of the old gods, except in the context of civic processions shorn of cultic associations, from then onward. Such acts preceded the next stage of Christianization that came to prevail in the fifth century, that is the gradual conversion of the urban elites through argumentation and cajolery, and the penetration of the countryside by monks and sometimes even fanatical bishops, who smashed altars and shrines of every kind and disrupted sacrifices. Friedrich Deichmann, writing in 1939, lists eighty-nine temple conversions in what is by no means an exhaustive survey.[99] Jean Michel Spieser greatly expands Deichmann's list of only five for Greece.[100] It is beyond the scope of the present study to analyse in detail the archaeological minutiae of all known instances of this phenomenon. The intent is rather to examine those which illustrate most clearly the social, economic, and administrative mechanisms which contributed to the Christianization of the Eastern Roman Empire. Three select examples have therefore been chosen for this task: 1) The closure c. 388 of the Zeus temple at Apamea, the metropolis of Second Syria, by its archbishop Marcellus; 2) The destruction of the Serapeum and other temples of Alexandria at the instigation of the Christian patriarch Theophilus in 391; and 3) The smashing of the image of Allat in a small temple at Palmyra in the Provincia Arabia between 25 May 385 and 19 March 388.[101]

---

[96] Infra, Ch. II, Sect. 3.
[97] Cf. Françoise Thelamon, *Païens et chrétiens au IVe siècle* (Paris 1981), 481 and Plate 38.
[98] Bataille, nos. 141 and 142.
[99] Supra, Ch. II, n. 36.

III. The Temple Conversions at Apamea, Alexandria, and Palmyra

Marcellus, archbishop of Apamea, the metropolis of Second Syria, took in hand the Christianization of the city and its *territorium* with fanatical zeal. The detailed account given by Theodoret of Cyrrhus[102] of the social and administrative consequences of the bishop's actions have consistent parallels in the later narrative of Mark the Deacon about bishop Porphyrius' destruction of the temples of Gaza.[103] Marcellus' first ambition was the demolition of the temple of Zeus inside the city, but he found it impossible to accomplish this without imperial help, because the place still had a large pagan population (πλῆθος) that would riot.[104] He therefore procured an imperial rescript for the task he had in mind (ὅπλῳ τῷ νόμῳ χρησάμενος).[105] The actual work was to have been carried out initially by about 1000 imperial troops commanded probably by the Praetorian Prefect of Oriens Maternus Cynegius, who was a fanatical Christian, and two tribunes who would keep order during the proceedings as well.[106] The temple itself had impressive architectural features. The blocks were apparently closely fitted together, with no apertures for the insertion of breaking-rods. The clamps which held the rows of blocks together made the task of pulling out individual blocks extremely difficult:[107]

> An attempt was made to dismantle the temenos of Zeus, which is very large and decorated with magnificent works of ornamentation. Upon seeing that the structure was solid and strongly built, the Prefect surmised that it would be impossible for [him] to break the joining of the stones. For they were quite large and well-fastened to each other, and bound together with iron and lead [clamps]. The divine Marcellus, seeing his loss of courage, sent him to other cities, and prayed to God that means would be given for the destruction of the [temenos].

---

[100] Ibid.

[101] There is an interesting parallel in the destruction of the temple of Vahevanean the Dragon-Handler in the district of Taron west of Lake Van in Armenia. Gregory the Illuminator accomplished this and other temple conversions after winning over the princely houses of the land. He seems to have gotten some initial experience in catechetical technique in Christian Cappadocia. Agathangelos, *History of the Armenians*, tr. R.W. Thomson (Albany 1976), 347–351, 489f.

[102] Theodoret of Cyrrhus, HE 5.21.

[103] Infra, Ch. III.

[104] Theodoret, HE 5.21 (Parmentier, 318, line 13).

[105] Theodoret, HE 5.21 (Parmentier, 318, line 6). Marcellus' act predates the very restrictive legislation of the 390's against paganism by several years.

[106] Ibid., line 12.

[107] Ibid., lines 14–21.

The troops evidently resented the backbreaking nature of a task
more suitable for day-laborers. Bishop Marcellus dismissed the
Prefect, whose "loss of courage" (δειλία) may reflect the attitude of
the troops used to skulking about the *officium*. This circumstance
allowed Marcellus to carry out the work of destruction in a dramatic fashion symbolic of the victory of the new religion. The failure of
the troops to work vigorously at the demolition may reflect as well
their religious attitudes.

Bishop Marcellus effected the destruction of the Zeus temple
with the assistance of "a certain self-employed man who came from
the East, and who was neither a house-builder nor learned in any
other craft, being accustomed rather to carry stone and lumber
upon his shoulders".[108] This day-laborer, perhaps a Syrian from
Persia, knew a great deal about practical building techniques, and
engaged to receive double the pay of an artisan.[109] His method of
pulling down the temple consisted of inserting wooden beams as
props under the upper parts of the columns of the colonnade that
surrounded the cella on all four sides, then removing the lower
column drums, and finally setting fire to the props.[110] The columns
had a circumference of sixteen cubits or about ten feet, and the
stone was exceptionally hard (στερροτάτη). Good timber did not
apparently abound in the *territorium* of Apamea, for beams of olive
trees (ξύλοις ἐλαΐνοις) had to be used. It would seem that the
timber had been freshly cut, for it refused to burn when the time
came to apply the torch. Bishop Marcellus evidently circulated the
story later told by Theodoret of Cyrrhus:[111]

> But a certain black *daimon* appeared and the wood did not according
> to its nature begin to be consumed by the fire because of the black
> *daimon* hindering the action of the flame. After they tried this often,
> and seeing that the device was without profit, they informed the
> shepherd [Marcellus] of this while he lay asleep after midday.

The "black *daimon*" which appeared (δαίμων τις μέλας φαινόμενος),
evidently embodied in the moist smoke of the flagging fires, seems
not to have been in the minds of the superstitious the same *daimon*
as the Zeus-Baal of the temple, but the sort of "gremlin" thought to
affect all forms of mechanical devices and building operations.[112]

---

[108] Ibid., line 23f.
[109] Ibid., 319. line 1.
[110] Ibid., lines 7–10.
[111] Ibid., lines 10–14.
[112] Ibid., line 11. Cf. the incident reported in the *Acta of St. Demetrius* (7th–8th
c.), wherein the failure of the mechanical apparatus of the city gate to operate is
blamed on a *daimon* thought to be active inside the machinery. The spell is said to

Archbishop Marcellus is then said to have applied some Christian ecclesiastical magic that induced the flight of the resisting *daimon* (τοῦ ἀντιπάλου δαίμονος):[113]

> He immediately ran to the church of God, and having ordered water to be put in a container, he set the water upon the altar. Having bowed his head down on the floor, he begged the Philanthropic Master not to yield to the tyranny of the *daimon*, but to expose its wickedness and manifest His own power, that there would be no pretext for greater harm being caused by the unbelievers there [in Apamea]. Having said these things and the like, and making the sign of the cross over the water, he ordered Equitius the deacon, [a man] well-fenced by faith and zeal, to take the water and run quickly, to pour with faith and apply [the water] to the flame. When he did this, the *daimon*, unable to bear the pouring of the water, absconded. The fire, as if making use of water against the wood, ignited it and consumed it in a moment. When their support vanished, the columns fell down, and so the men pulled down twelve other columns. The wing [of the temple] attached to the columns was pulled down by their force. The crash resounded throughout the entire city (for the sound was very great) and roused everyone to go and see. When they learned of the flight of the resisting *daimon*, they set the tongue in motion in a hymnody to the God of all things. It was in this manner that that God-like archbishop destroyed many other temples.

The story is scientifically implausible unless we suppose that the water which had received the sign of the cross (ἐπιθεὶς τοῦ σταυροῦ τὸν τύπον τῷ ὕδατι) was actually applied to a solution of sulphur, pitch, and quicklime that had been smeared onto the timber, which burned furiously when the workmen applied the water to it. Such an interpretation is consistent with the chemicals used to incinerate the Marneion in Gaza a decade and a half later.[114] The social and religious consequences of this act must have been similar to what Mark the Deacon reports about Gaza: many initial conversions resulting from the shock of the temple's destruction, followed by a trickle of converts thereafter, when the impact of the event had worn off.[115] The burning of the temple rather than the tale of the sanctified water was the critical causative factor.

Archbishop Marcellus was a real fanatic, for after cleansing Apamea of its temples he carried these depredations into the *territorium* of the city. This seems to be the meaning of Theodoret's

---

have been broken when a workman cried out: "Christ with us!" *Les plus anciens recueils des miracles de Saint Démétrius et la pénétration des Slaves dans les Balkans*, ed. P. Lemerle, 1 (Paris 1979), 153.
  [113] Theodoret, HE 5.21 (Parmentier, 319, line 12 – 320, line 9).
  [114] Infra, Ch. III, note 146.
  [115] Infra, Ch. III, Sect. 5.

comment that "that divine man destroyed the other temples"
(τἄλλα τεμένη).[116] Pierre Canivet believes that one of these shrines
lay at Nikertai, where a monastery with Christian architectural
carvings typical of the "Theodosian renaissance" arose circa 400.[117]
One of these missions of destruction cost Marcellus his life, but
Theodoret finds it expedient not to describe the circumstances of
his "martyrdom":[118]

> Having at my disposal many other rather admirable accounts about
> that man (for he sent for [the relics of] the victorious martyrs, and
> even wrote against [the Hellenes] and finally earned the crown of
> martyrs), I nevertheless hesitate to write the history of these things
> now, lest by lengthening [my account] rather much I deny attention
> to [other] persons met with in my narrative. I shall now turn to
> another story.

This convenient pretext for avoiding a difficult issue may reflect
Theodoret's categorical rejection of Marcellus' violent and irreg-
ular methods of destroying rural temples, against which practice
one of the post-Theodosian laws, dated 10 July 399, seems to be
directed.[119] The temple conversions which Theodoret describes in
his *Historia Philotheos* or *Lives of the Monks* all came about by acts of
persuasion in which the monks at times endured physical injury
and risked death at the hands of the rustics by raising the cross over
their temples.[120] Marcellus did not fall into this category.

It was left to another ecclesiastical historian, Salaminias Hermias
Sozomenos, to relate the consequences of archbishop Marcellus' bellicose tactics:[121]

> There were still pagans in many cities, who contended zealously in
> behalf of their temples; as, for instance, the inhabitants of Petraea
> and Areopolis in Arabia; of Raphi and Gaza in Palestine; of Hiera-
> polis in Phoenicia; and of Apamea on the river Axius in Syria. I
> have been informed that the inhabitants of the last-named city often
> armed the men of Galilee and the peasants of Lebanon in defense of
> their temples; and that at last, they carried their audacity to such a
> height as to slay a bishop named Marcellus. The bishop had com-
> manded the demolition of all the temples in the city *and villages*, under

---

[116] Theodoret, HE 5.21 (Parmentier, 320, lines 8f).
[117] Maria-Theresa and Pierre Canivet, "Sites chrétiens d'Apamène," *Syria* 48
(1971), 295–314.
[118] Theodoret, HE 5.21 (Parmentier, 320, lines 10–15).
[119] *Cod. Theod.* 16.10.16.
[120] This body of evidence is fully analysed in Ch. VIII.
[121] Sozomen, HE 7.15. Translation adapted from *A Select Library of Nicene and
Post-Nicene Fathers of the Christian Church*, Ser. 2, vol. 2 (Grand Rapids 1983), 386.
All citations in Greek below derive from: *Sozomeni Ecclesiastica Historia*, ed. Robert
Hussey, 2 (Oxford 1861). This passage 722, line 22 – 723, line 4.

the supposition that it would not be easy otherwise for them to be converted from their former religion. Having heard that there was a very spacious temple at Aulon, a district of Apamea, he repaired thither with a body of soldiers and gladiators. He stationed himself at a distance from the scene of conflict, *beyond the reach of arrows*; for he was afflicted with gout, and was unable to fight, to pursue, or to flee. Whilst the soldiers and gladiators were engaged in the assault against the temple, some pagans, discovering that he was alone, hastened to the place where he was separated from combat; they arose suddenly and seized him, and burnt him alive.

Sozomen had a great personal interest in questions of Christianization, having come of a wealthy rural family from the *territorium* of Gaza that accepted the new religion under the impress of St. Hilarion's teaching. His rather dry account of Marcellus' death suggests a certain ironic detachment from the event and a dislike of these tactics, which seem to indicate a fanatical private and illegal war.[122] The bishop had an army of soldiers, perhaps retired, and gladiators (στρατιώτας τινὰς καὶ μονομάχους παραλαβών), and retreated a safe distance, lest he be caught in *the clouds of arrows fired against his troops* (ἔξω βελῶν περιέμενεν), being unable to maneuver with them (καὶ οὔτε μάχεσθαι, οὔτε διώκειν ἢ φεύγειν ἠδύνατο), because of his physical condition (ποδαλγός).[123] The pagans of the district (τινες τῶν Ἑλληνιστῶν) executed a flanking maneuver, it seems, and thereby destroyed the enemy leader.

An official inquiry was subsequently held under the auspices of the provincial council of Second Syria. Sozomen continues:[124]

> The perpetrators of this deed were not then known, but, in the course of time, they were detected, and the sons of Marcellus determined upon avenging his death. The council of the province, however, prohibited them from executing this design, and declared that it was not just that the relatives or friends of Marcellus should seek to avenge his death; when they should rather return thanks to God for having accounted him worthy to die in such a cause.

Two circumstances suggest that the landed magnates of the Aulon district led their retainers, composed of bailiffs and agricultural laborers, out against archbishop Marcellus. The first is Sozomen's peculiar reference to the enemy militia as the "Hellenists", a term usually reserved for sophists, philosophers, and generally Hellenes educated in the *paideia*.[125] The second is the lawsuit which Marcellus'

---

[122] Sozomen, HE 5.15 (Hussey, 487f.).
[123] Sozomen, HE 7.15 (Hussey, 723, lines 37–39).
[124] Cf. Ch. II, footnote 121 for translator. Sozomen, HE 7.15 (Hussey, pp. 723, lines 4 – 724, line 2).
[125] Julian the Apostate seems first to have coined the expression with this

sons (παῖδες) registered at the provincial council (σύνοδος),
which certainly conducted its business in close touch with the
governor, who resided at Apamea, the metropolis of Second Syria.
If the perpetrators of the act—one hesitates to call it a crime—had
been a rabble of smallholders or tenant farmers without political
connections, they would easily have been prosecuted, fined, or
executed, for Marcellus and his sons had a strong voice in the
council and evidently came from a family of curial or decurion
rank. Other landed magnates, evidently pagan Hellenes whose
clients carried out the execution of Marcellus, also sat on the
provincial council and successfully blocked the prosecution. The
Hellenists may well have had the support of their Christian peers in
all this, which was seen as a defense of privilege and property rights
in the countryside, where wealthy pagans and Christians alike
found refuge from the rapacity of the civil and ecclesiastical officials
at Apamea, among whom archbishop Marcellus was counted,
being perceived as a social and economic rival with a desire to
aggrandize his family's interests and having a private army of
bucellarii at his disposal.[126]

The decree of the provincial council betrays an evident cynicism
in its response, paying lip service to the idea of martyrdom, that
Marcellus' family and friends (but not the church of Apamea)
should give thanks to God, as the man had been deemed worthy of
dying on His behalf (ὡς ὑπὲρ Θεοῦ ἀποθανεῖν ἠξιωμένου).[127]
Sozomen, who concludes with the observation "and thus it turned
out" (καὶ τὰ μὲν οὕτως ἔσχεν), took care to put the pious sentiments about martyrdom into the mouths of the provincial councillors, the status group to which his own family belonged, but not the
local church or imperial officials. It all sounds like latent hostility to
archbishop Marcellus and his like. Behind the exoneration of the
murderers probably lay the hand of the Praetorian Prefect of
Oriens, Tatian (16 June 388-ante 10 September 392), who as a
Hellene had reversed Maternus Cynegius' policy of systematically
destroying temples.[128] Two imperial laws eventually issued from

cultural-religious significance in his letter to Arsacius, archpriest of the province of
Galatia. Julian, *Epistle 22* (Wright, 3, 70, line 9).
    [126] The province of Achaea had a provincial council that met at Corinth from
time to time to discuss such questions as the allocation of the *annona* or grain tax in
kind, as IG 7.24 demonstrates. Cf. Julian's *Epistle 28* (Wright, 3, 85ff.), and
Frank R. Trombley, "Boeotia in Later Antiquity," *BOIOTIKA*, ed. H. Beister and
J. Buckler (Munich 1989), 217.
    [127] Sozomen, HE 7.15 (Hussey, 724, lines 1-2).
    [128] Barbara Gassowska, "Maternus Cynegius, Praefectus Praetorio Orientis,

this flap about archbishop Marcellus, one of them the comprehensive law of 8 November 392 on sacrifice,[129] the other given 10 July 399 requiring that rural temples be razed "without disturbance or tumult" (*sine turba ac tumultu*), the idea being that so long as bishops did not invade the countryside with private armies, the local Hellenes should pacifically acquiesce to the destruction of their temples: "For when they are torn down and removed, the material basis for all superstition will be destroyed" (*His enim deiectis atque sublatis omnis superstitioni materia consumetur*).[130]

The second example of temple conversions belongs to Alexandria in Egypt in 391, when the Christian *demos* under the leadership of patriarch Theophilus (385–412) attacked and destroyed the Serapeum and other temples of the city. The event had a profound impact on Egyptian and Mediterranean religion, leading to many conversions, as often happened when the old gods proved powerless in the face of the Christian God and His symbols.[131] The event was commemorated, for example, in the *Alexandrine Chronicle* with a series of miniatures which depict patriarch Theophilus standing with gospel book in hand atop a small shrine housing the effigy of Sarapis with the Basket on his head.[132] The corresponding passage in the text indicates: "In this year [109 in the era of Diocletian or 392 A.D.] the temples of the Hellenes were destroyed" (καὶ αὐτῷ τῷ [ἔτει οἱ ναοὶ τῶ]ν Ἑ[λ]λή[ν]ω(ν) ΕΛΗ).[133] The producer of the miniature implicitly invested this event, along with the birth and accession of Honorius, the destruction of the pagan usurper Eugenius, and the consecration of Theophilus, with the same significance as events in the lives of Christ, John the Baptist, and prophets, not to mention the Roman, Macedonian, and other kings.[134] The destruction of the Serapeum proved to be of immense interest throughout the Greek-speaking parts of the Mediterranean, as for example in Palestine, where Rufinus of Aquileia (ob. 410) appended the longest extant account of that event to his Latin translation and continuation of the *Ecclesiastical History* of Eusebius

---

and the Destruction of the Allat Temple in Palmyra," *Archeologia* 33 (1982), 121f. Cf. Charlotte Roueché, *Aphrodisias in Late Antiquity* (London 1989), 47–52.

[129] *Cod. Theod.* 16.10.12, discussed supra, Ch. I, Sect. 2.

[130] *Cod. Theod.* 16.10.16.

[131] This was the case at Gaza. Infra, Ch. III, Sect. 5. Cf. Peter Brown's statement of method in *The Cult of the Saints*, 17–22.

[132] A. Bauer and J. Strzygowski, *Eine Alexandrinische Weltchronik* (Denkschriften der Kaiserlichen Akademie der Wissenschaften, Wien 5/2, Vienna 1906), 1–204.

[133] Ibid., 74, lines 23–25.

[134] Ibid., 204, for a list of the miniatures.

of Caesarea.[135] The learned writer viewed the seemingly final destruction of the Hellenic cults as the sign of a culminating epoch.
The subsequent history of the fifth century proves the closure of the
Alexandrian temples to have been a mere froth of bubbles on the
heaving seas of ancient Greek religiosity, but the incident reveals
many features of the transition going on all over the Greek east.
Rufinus gives, as well, the fullest description of the engineering
mechanisms inside the Serapeum which lent superstitious awe to
the material objects and forces seemingly controlled by the *numen*
of the deity.

A pagan riot preceded the destruction of the Serapeum and
provided patriarch Theophilus with a suitable pretext for deman-
ding this act of demolition. The uprising began with the consign-
ment of a roofless and neglected public basilica to the patriarch for
the use of the city's steadily growing Christian congregation. A
crypt (literally "caves", *antra*) was discovered in the process of
inspecting the foundations, wherein ancient mysteries had been
celebrated. The place was evidently the *adyton* of a Mithraeum of
the sort discovered during the earlier patriarchate of George (357–
361).[136] The Christian profanation of the site triggered a riot of the
urban Hellenes, who exploded "as if a cup of snakes had been
drunk from" (*velut draconum calice potato*).[137] Rufinus' informant was
undoubtedly right in asserting that the Christians of the city were
in the majority, but lacked aggressiveness (*modestia religionis*) in the
initial stages of the ensuing fighting. The Hellenes apparently
fortified themselves in the Serapeum and tortured certain of the
Christian captives they had taken, in some instances using yokes
(*patibula*). A certain Olympus, a teacher of philosophy whom
Rufinus' source criticized as having been "a philosopher in name
and garb only" (*Olympus quidam nomine et habitu solo filosofus*),[138]
thereafter commanded the desperadoes, who raided the adjoining
quarters of the city as opportunity permitted. Neither Olympus nor
his colleagues had clear aims, for when the magistrates, perhaps at
the behest of the Augustal Prefect, stood before the barricades and
asked for an explanation, they received back only shouts. This
irrationalism finds a close parallel in the resistance of the rustic

---

[135] Rufinus of Aquileia, *Historiae Ecclesiasticae*, ed. tr. Theodor Mommsen in
Eusebius Werke, 2, ed. Eduard Schwartz (Leipzig 1908).
[136] For the fullest account, see: Socrates Scholasticus, *Historia Ecclesiastica* 3.3.
PG 67, 381C–384A. Cf. the reference to the *adyton* of the Mithraeum as one of the
buildings destroyed in 391. Ibid., HE 5.16. PG 67, 604B–C.
[137] Rufinus, HE 11.22 (Mommsen, 1025, line 18f.).
[138] Ibid., 1026, line 3.

pagans of the Aulon district to the "search and destroy" tactics of
Marcellus of Apamea, but more particularly to the riots that broke
out in Gaza some years after the demolition of the Marneion and
erection of the Eudoxiana basilica.[139] This irrationalism became
fully apparent when the matter was referred to the emperor (*res
gesta ad imperatorem refertur*).[140] The inquiry went directly from the
Augustal Prefect to Theodosius I, but the influence of Tatian, the
Praetorian Prefect of Oriens, came into play. The latter, as a
Hellene, stood behind the moderation of the imperial response:[141]

> [The emperor] preferred to emend rather than lose the erring be-
> cause of his inborn clemency of mind, and replied (*rescribit*) that the
> punishment of those whom [Olympus] had caused to create martyrs
> by shedding their blood in front of the [pagan] altars was not to be
> demanded, for among them [the martyrs] the glory of merit had
> overcome the grief of being killed. Litigation (*caussa*) about the rest of
> the evils and roots of the discord, whatever had come forth in behalf
> of the defense of images, was not to be pressed. After these issues had
> been removed, the cause of the war would be removed.

The imperial gaze simply overlooked the nasty and convoluted
business of litigation (*caussa*) over the deaths of the Christians by
simply granting them the title of martyrs. This solution has an
exact parallel in the Aulon affair, after which the provincial council
denied Marcellus of Apamea's sons compensation from the instigators of his assassination. All this suggests that Tatian exerted a
powerful moderating influence on the "most Christian" Theodosius by pointing out the real economic and local political power of
the Hellenes of Syria and Egypt.

The promise of imperial clemency in the letter (*epistola*) contained in its exordium, however, the accusation that "the vain
superstition of the pagans" (*vana gentilium superstitio*) had caused the
rioting. This charge induced many of the Hellenes to hide by
mixing with the Christian crowds that had begun to form. As
Rufinus puts it: "The rage of the *daimon* [Sarapis] that had previously roused frenzy in the crowds had fled" (*furorem daemonis qui*

---

[139] Infra, Ch. III, Sect. 2.
[140] Rufinus, HE 11.22 (Mommsen, 1026, line 13).
[141] Ibid., 1026, lines 13–19. The last decree issued to Tatian as Praetorian
Prefect of Oriens is dated 10 September 392. The anti-Christian riot and subsequent destruction of the Serapeum thus occurred well within his period of administration. The riot seems to have taken place well before the rising of the Nile
waters in June. The expeditious reply indicated by Rufinus' survey of events
suggests that the season for ships sailing from Constantinople to Alexandria had
not yet ended. The events thus belong to the early spring of 391. Cf. Venance
Grumel, *Traité d'Études byzantines I: La chronologie* (Paris 1958), 367.

in illis prius debacchatus fuerat effugatum).[142] The resultant dispersions
permitted the Christian part of the *demos* to undertake the demolition of the Serapeum and other temples.

The historian Rufinus of Aquileia provides what is by far the
most detailed description by any Christian writer about the destruction of the Serapeum, and expatiates also upon its architectural scheme and the mechanical devises designed to simulate the
action of the *numen* of Sarapis within the cella of the temple building. Rufinus observes: "I think the temple of Sarapis at Alexandria
has been heard of by all, and is even known firsthand to many"
(. . . *plerisque vero etiam notum*).[143] The historian's description of the
temenos has been studied at length and reconciled with the data
from excavations.[144] Our primary concern here lies with the cultic
apparatus. It suffices to note that the enclosure wall of the temenos
measured 173.70 by 77 meters. The Roman temple proper lay at
the north end of this rectangular enclosure along with the shrines of
Isis and Harpocrates. The enclosure wall itself was riddled with
many small priests' lodges (*exedrae et pastoforia domusque*).[145] The site
was, furthermore, built on an extensive land-fill. In consequence,
the subterranean parts were full of vaulted passageways and *adyta*
(rooms for the celebration of mysteries). The temples had a staff of
wardens (*aeditui* or νεωκόροι) even in 391.

The Serapeum had an interior ornamentation designed to be-
dazzle the pilgrim. Rufinus describes its impact on the viewer:[146]

> In the middle of the entire space was the temple building (*aedes*),
> constructed splendidly and richly on the outside with stone, and
> furnished with columns and marble plaques. Inside this temple the
> image of Sarapis was enormous and frightful, as it grazed one wall on
> the left and the other on the right. This prodigy (*monstrum*) was said to
> be composed of all kinds of metals and woods. The interior walls of
> the shrine (*delubrum*) were dressed with plates of gold, above them with
> plates of silver, and at the upper extremity with plates of copper,
> which bear precious metals. There were also some devices made with
> cunning skill to arouse the amazement and admiration of the onlook-
> ers. On the east side of the temple there was a very narrow aperture
> which was made in such a way that on the day established to bring in
> the image of the Sun to salute Sarapis, when the time had been
> carefully observed and the image came in, a beam of the Sun directed
> through that aperture illuminated the mouth and lips of Sarapis so

---

[142] Rufinus, HE 11.22 (Mommsen, 1026, line 26f.).
[143] Rufinus, HE 11.23 (Mommsen, 1026, line 28f.).
[144] Thelamon, *Païens et chrétiens au IVe siècle*, 165–173, with two plans.
[145] Rufinus, HE 11.23 (Mommsen, 1027, line 4f.).
[146] Ibid., 1027, lines 8–21.

that it seemed to the onlooking people that Sarapis was being greeted with a kiss by the Sun.

An orb which passed for the image of the Sun (*signum solis*) seemed to levitate amidst the upper parts of the cella and provoked the wonder of the viewer:[147]

> There was another fraud of this kind. The nature of the magnetic stone is said to be of such virtue as to snatch and draw iron to itself. The image of the Sun had been fashioned from that stone by the hand of an artisan out of a very fine grade of iron, whose nature as we said draws iron to itself. It was fixed within the ceiling panels above. When the image of the sun had been properly positioned under the light-beam in relation to a balance (*ad libram*) and drew the iron toward itself, the orb rose up before the people and seemed to hang in the air. Lest this trick be given away by the quick motion (*lapsu propero*), the ministers of deception (*ministri fallaciae*) would say: "Sol has risen up, so that saying farewell to Sarapis he would go back to his own abodes."

Patriarch Theophilus and the Christian leadership exposed these and other devices (μηχανήματα) when they overran the temples in the aftermath of the riot of 391.[148] They discovered, for example, that the images, composed of bronze and wood, backed into walls from which secret passageways issued, permitting the temple wardens and priests to climb inside the effigies and issue commands through their mouths, apparently with a sort of trumpet that augmented and distorted the speaker's voice.[149] When the head of the image of Sarapis was torn off during the demolition of the Serapeum, masses of mice scampered out from the interior. Theodoret of Cyrrhus observes with irony: "For the god of the Egyptians was the dwelling place of mice" (μυῶν γὰρ οἰκτήριον ἦν ὁ Αἰγυπτίων θεός),[150] and "the Sarapis received the blow and did not feel the pain (for he was made of wood), nor did he give forth a cry, being inanimate" (ξύλινος . . . ἄψυχος).[151] The priests of Sarapis seem to have maintained sundry levers, balances, and possibly hydraulic systems until this time, and so Hellenic religion looked to Hellenistic engineering science for its survival. Rufinus adds: "But many devices were constructed by the ancients in this place for the cause of deceiving which it is now tedious to enumerate in individual cases (*sed et multa alia decipiendi causa a veteribus in*

---

[147] Ibid., 1027f.
[148] Theodoret, HE 5.22 (Parmentier, 320, line 21).
[149] For an example of how this worked, see: Robin Lane Fox, *Pagans and Christians* (New York 1986), 135.
[150] Ibid., 321, line 12.
[151] Ibid., 321, lines 9–11.

loco fuerant constructa, quae nunc longum est enumerare per singula).[152]

The historian of Hellenistic science regrets this omission. It is conceivable that one of these devices was a subterranean, steam-driven hydraulic system used to simulate earthquakes like the one later invented by Anthemius of Tralles in the early sixth century.[153] Theodoret hints at the existence of such a contrivance with the observation: "In addition to great size of Sarapis' image, there was the generally believed false report that, if someone were to approach it, the earth would tremble (κλονηθήσεται μὲν ἡ γῆ) and total destruction would seize everyone."[154] Such a system evidently lay behind the popular view of the Alexandrians that, when Theophilus approached the statue to dismantle it, a seismic release would occur, and destroy the entire world. As Rufinus of Aquileia puts it:[155]

> Nevertheless a certain *convincing* story (*persuasio*) had been disseminated by those pagans that if human hand should touch that image, the earth splitting open would then and there be reduced to chaos, and the firmament would rush down headlong.

When a soldier applied the axe to the wooden image and no earthquake occurred, the Christian *demos* chanted: "The heavens did not rush down, nor did the earth sink."[156] One can, at any rate, imagine how much the descriptions of such a mechanical system would have taxed Rufinus' well-honed rhetorical skills. It seems that this aspect of Hellenistic engineering remained unforgotten by Anthemius of Tralles a century later, despite its associations with the fraud of the ancient cults.

The consequence of the raid on the Serapeum was the demolition of the image of Sarapis. After the removal of the head and limbs, the torso was burned in the amphitheatre as a public demonstration of the Christian victory. Patriarch Theophilus' propaganda had it that these acts had abolished the cult of Sarapis and with it the entire structure of ancient religion in Egypt. So Rufinus: "And here was the end of the vain superstition and ancient error of Sarapis."[157] Theodoret of Cyrrhus, writing a quarter of a century later and with the benefit of hindsight, puts the affair in more emphatic terms: "Thus the temple precincts everywhere on land

---

[152] Rufinus, HE 11.23 (Mommsen, 1028, line 7f.).
[153] Agathias of Myrina, *Historiarum Libri Quinque* 5.6.3 to 5.7.5 (ed. Rudolf Keydell, Berlin 1977, 171f.).
[154] Theodoret, HE 5.22 (Parmentier, 321, line 5).
[155] Rufinus, HE 11.23 (Mommsen, 1028, lines 10–13).
[156] Ibid., 1028, line 16f.
[157] Ibid., 1028f.

and sea were released from the *daimones*."[158] The Alexandrian
Christians with their usual capacity for inventing epithets ridiculed
the fallen deity (κωμῳδοῦντες),[159] who had become the "trickster"
(*veterator*), the smoke-filled *daimon* of rotten wood (*putris ligni fumosus
genius*), and the ancient lethargic deity (*senex veternosus*).[160]

The immense prestige of the cult of Sarapis did, however, outlive
the destruction of the Serapeum. Theodoret's sophistries attest to
that cultural fact, as does the survival of the Nile river cults in
certain localities for another century and beyond.[161] Christian
ecclesiastics fended off these deeply embedded habits of thought by
identifying Sarapis with the prophet Joseph, who had by his pru-
dence averted famine. This idea originated in a Hellenistic Alexandrian syncretism that owed something to the allegorical method of
interpreting religious texts, Jewish, Christian and Hellenic, and
was rooted in the Euhemerist tradition of assigning heroic origins
to the gods:[162]

> The opinion of the pagans (*paganorum*) about his origin is diverse.
> Some think him Jove, upon whose head a *modius* is superimposed,
> either because he fixes how all things are to be governed with the
> measure (*mensura*), or because he supplies life to mortals by an
> abundance of produce (*frugum largitate*). Others think Sarapis to be
> the virtue of the Nile (*virtutem Nili fluminis*), whose Egypt is fed by its
> abundance and fertility. Certain others say that his image was
> shaped in honor of Joseph because of the rationing of grain by which
> he assisted the Egyptians in time of famine. Others refer to Sarapis as
> being found in the ancient histories of the Greeks as Apis, a certain
> *paterfamilias* or king settled at Memphis in Egypt when the grain gave
> out at Alexandria in time of famine. He provided maintenance
> (*alimenta*) out of his own property, enough for the citizens; they say
> that after his death a temple was erected at Memphis in his honor in
> which a bull with some characteristic colorings was tended as a
> representation, so to speak, of that excellent farmer, which was called
> Apis after him. In truth, the *soron*, that is the sepulchre in which his
> body lay, they brought to Alexandria and called him Sarapis later
> through a corruption of *Soron Apis*, from the composite *Sorapin*. Whether
> this be the truth or nothing at all, God sees concerning these things.

The "virtue of the Nile river" (*virtus Nili fluminis*) was none other
than the ἔργον ἀρετῆς of the deity, a "wonder" (θαῦμα) at the
point of conjuncture between the divine and material worlds.[163] It

---

[158] Theodoret, HE 5.22 (Parmentier, 321, line 15f.).
[159] Ibid.
[160] Rufinus, HE 11.23 (Mommsen, 1028, lines 15, 18, 22).
[161] Infra, Ch. IX passim.
[162] Rufinus, HE 11.23 (Mommsen, 1029f.).
[163] Yves Grandjean, *Une nouvelle arétalogie d'Isis à Maronée* (Leiden 1975), 1–8.

was a simple case for the Christians to argue that, as with the Holy
Sepulchre in Jerusalem and the nearby Oak of Marbre, "ignorant
men", that is the Hellenes, had corrupted the cult of the prophet
Joseph into that of a hero who had undergone apotheosis.

Many scandals emerged in the wake of the cleansing of the
Serapeum, not the least of which derived from the opening of the
adyta where the mysteries were celebrated. The more fanatical
Christians produced the skulls of decapitated infants allegedly
found in gilt basins. Such demonstrations led to some conversions,
as did revelations about priestly corruption. Rufinus of Aquileia
singles out only one example of criminality for the sake of brevity.[164]
It concerns a priest of Saturn named Tyrannos, who used to seduce
the wives of the Alexandrian city councillors and men of senatorial
rank (*nobilibus quibusque et primariis viris*) on the pretext of bogus
oracles (*quasi ex responso numinis*).[165] Rufinus relates the story with
great relish:[166]

> As their wives were pleasing to his libido, he said that Saturn had
> commanded him that someone's wife incubate in the temple (*ut uxor
> sua pernoctaret in templo*). The man who heard this, rejoicing that his
> wife was summoned by the reputation of the divinity, sent his wife to
> the temple greatly adorned, even burdened with gifts, lest she be
> repudiated. When the matron was enclosed within in the sight of all,
> Tyrannos went away after the gates were closed and the keys surren-
> dered. Silence being made, he was creeping through hidden and
> subterranean *adyta* and into the image of Saturn itself, the hollows of
> which were open (*per occultos et subterraneos adytus, intra ipsum Saturni
> simulachrum patulis erepebat cavernis*). For that image was gnawed away
> at the back (*a tergo exesum*) and closely connected to the wall (*et parieti
> diligenter annexum*). With lamps burning bright inside the temple, he
> suddenly brought forth a voice through the image of ribbed bronze
> (*per simulachrum aeris concavi*) to the attentive and prayerful woman, so
> that the unfortunate woman shook with fear and joy because she
> thought herself worthy of the exhortation (*alloquium*) of so great a
> divinity (*numen*). All the lamps were suddenly extinguished by some
> device, small linen cloths being drawn over them, after the unclean
> divinity (*numen impurum*) had spoken what it pleased, whether for the
> incitement of sexual desire or to create greater consternation. He then
> came down and imposed the deceit of an adulterer with profane
> rhetorical tricks upon the bewildered woman. After these doings had
> been brought upon the wives of the wretched [pagans] for a long
> time, it happened that a certain woman of modest mind shuddered at
> the deed (*facinus*), and carefully marking it, recognized the voice of

---

[164] Rufinus, HE 11.24.
[165] Ibid., 1031, line 11f.
[166] Rufinus, HE 11.24 (Mommsen, 1031f.).

Tyrannos, and after returning home indicated the fraud to her husband. Ardently inflamed by the insult to his wife, he led away the accused Tyrannos to torture (*ad tormenta deducit*).

After Tyrannos confessed and was convicted, with his unknown frauds being revealed, all shame and disgrace invaded the households of the pagans (*paganorum*), with the women made into adultresses, fathers impious, spurious children surprised. When this was divulged and publicized, the crimes suffered violent destruction along with the images and temples.

Rufinus' informant certainly had particular individuals in mind, but perhaps omitted their names to prevent ridicule of those who had embraced Christianity (*fidem Christi et cultum verae religionis amplexi sunt*) after the fake *numen* had driven them to atheism.[167] The *adyta* of the temples concealed not only heinous sacrifices but acts of rank seduction. The floating orb of the sun, the earth-shaking Sarapis, and *daimones* thought to dwell within the images of the gods and issue commands fell as much before rational inquiry as the cross.

A considerable temple complex, with shrines dedicated to Isis and other deities, lay at Canopus some 14 miles down the main road northeast of Alexandria. The beginnings of the Christianization of those sites came at the same time as the destruction of the Serapeum in 391. The Isis temple's gates were blocked up with masonry and its images stored in a treasury within. The Tabennesiote monks established a convent there which presumably received the local priestly estates as its endownment. It will be seen in a later chapter that these monks did not pursue the Christianization of their villages vigorously, and that in consequence a clandestine priesthood of Isis survived there into the 480's.[168] Furthermore, the rustics lived in terrible fear of Isis' daimonic powers, although they were at least superficially Christianized and had a regular clergy sent out by the Alexandrian church. The chthonic female deity thought to cooperate in raising the Nile flood dominated local belief the more because her temple was left standing and sealed up, although covered with intricate reliefs and hieroglyphic writings. Its survival substantiated the local perception of unseen forces, the "virtues" or "wonders" of Isis in the rising waters. The "daimonic" character of the goddess in Christian demonology corresponds to the image of the angry goddess after her believers' apostasy.[169]

[167] Ibid., Mommsen, 1031, line 4f.
[168] Infra, Ch. IX, Sect. 2.
[169] Cf. Frank R. Trombley, "Prolegomena to the Systemic Analysis of Late Hellenic Religion: The Case of the Aretalogy of Isis at Kyme," *Religious Writing and Religious Systems*, ed. Jacob Neusner *et alii* (Atlanta 1989), 96f.

At any rate, patriarch Theophilus' suppression of the Canopic cults concentrated first on the externals.

Canopus had close ties to Alexandria not only because of the festivals of the Nilotic gods, but also because of a group of the so-called Chaldaeans, who resided there regularly and offered bogus interpretations of the hieroglyphic texts. The priesthood of Isis at Philae on the upper Nile could still read and incise hieroglyphics as late as 394, but the competence of the Chaldaeans in the art is much less certain.[170] Rufinus of Aquileia attributes the continuing production of the Canopic jars exclusively to this group, a supposition that is certainly erroneous. These stout vessels, riddled with many holes and surmounted by the head of the god Osiris-Canopus, symbolized the fertility resulting from the Nile flood. On the other hand, the Chaldaeans may have used these objects in their cult. The learned ecclesiastic observes:[171]

> Who can number the superstitious crimes of Canopus? There, on the pretext of priestly writings (*praetextu sacerdotalium litterarum*) (for so they call the ancient Egyptian writings), there was a public school of magic arts (*magicae artis erat pene publica schola*). The pagans (*pagani*) revered this place so much as though it were the source and origin of the *daimones* that there was a great festival there that was held at Alexandria. But concerning the error of this monstrosity it would not be unreasonable to set forth the origin in a few words, in which [the pagans] tell it. They relate that this god was believed in by all when the Chaldaeans, disseminating their fire-god, had it joined with the gods of all their provinces, which is to say that he conquered.
>
> The gods of the remaining provinces were made of bronze or gold, silver or wood, or stone, or of whatever material, which was corrupted without doubt by fire. Because of this the Fire cult prevailed everywhere. When the priest of Canopus (*Canopi sacerdos*) heard this, he devised a ruse. Clay water-jars (*hydriae fictiles*) are customarily made in Egypt, everywhere wide-open with many tiny apertures, in which disturbed water labors and is restored to a state of higher purity without dregs. The priest set up one of these vases with its holes stopped up with wax and painted with colors, and he carefully adapted the head of an ancient image set on top, which was said to be that of Menelaus the shipmaster. The Chaldaeans were thereafter present, and a conflict came about. A fire was kindled around the vase. The wax with which the apertures were sealed was melted. When the vase dripped, the fire was extinguished. By the fraud of the priest, Canopus was shown to be victor over the Chaldaeans.
>
> Wherefrom the image of Canopus himself, with his feet small, his neck drawn in, and his stomach swollen as if bruised, was formed in the shape of a vase, with its back equally polished, and from this

---

[170] Infra, Ch. IX, Sect. 3.
[171] Rufinus, HE 11.26 (Mommsen, 1032f.).

persuasion the conqueror of all things was worshipped as a god. [The priest of Canopus] perhaps did these things at times for the Chaldaeans, but now with the advent of the priest of God Theophilus no dripping comes forth, nor does any concealed fraud of wax help.

This stream of rhetoric suggests that one tangible effect of Theophilus' raid against Canopus, apart from the bricking-up of the temples, was a curtailment of the production of Canopic jars and the cult associated with them. The veracity of Rufinus' description is confirmed by archaeological examples of these objects.[172] On the other hand, their cultic use seems to predate the advent of the fire-worshipping Chaldaeans, and Canopic-style jars continued to be produced thereafter, as one example from Karanis suggests (4th-mid-5th century), a wine-jar with faces and grape vines in relief.[173]

The final stage of purging Alexandria of its cults came with the construction of martyr shrines. Two Christian buildings arose within the Serapeum, "the tomb of Sarapis" (in Serapis sepulchro), a martyrion and a basilica, one on either side of the razed temple, which Rufinus calls "the taverns of shameful crimes and ancient tombs" (flagitionum tabernae ac veternosa busta).[174] The relics available for the superimposition of the Christian dead over the Euhemeristically dead god were said to be those of John the Baptist. The bones, whatever their original provenance, had come from Sebaste in Palestine. The monks of the monastery of Philip in Jerusalem collected the relics after the martyrion housing them had been plundered and the bones scattered and burned by a crowd of unstated religious allegiance during the reign of Julian the Apostate (361–363), a common occurrence at that time. Philip, proprietor of the monastery in Jerusalem, sent the objects to Athanasius, patriarch of Alexandria, for safekeeping. The latter stored them under the wall of a chapel (sacrarium) in the presence of a few witnesses.[175] The translation of the relics in 391 from the chapel to the Serapeum thus celebrated a double victory, the destruction of the temple to be sure, but also that of the pagan emperor whose meteoric rise and acts still lived in the memories of the bishops, pagan priests, and city councillors alike.

Patriarch Theophilus' propaganda, the basis for all Rufinus'

[172] Thelamon, Païens et chrétiens au IVe siècle, Plates 16 and 19.
[173] Florence B. Friedman, Beyond the Pharaohs: Egypt and the Copts in the 2nd to 7th Centuries A.D. (Providence 1989), no. 2.
[174] Rufinus, HE 11.27 (Mommsen, 1033, line 14f.).
[175] Rufinus, HE 11.29 (Mommsen, 1033f.).

statements, laid claim to the conversion of the whole of Egypt in the immediate wake of the victory over the *daimon* Sarapis, his priesthood and "sepulchres of dead gods", that is when the urban and rural temples were pulled down in many localities. As in the case of Gaza, Apamea, and other places, the impact of the closure of the temple of a great god (μέγας θεός) generated cultural and institutional shock waves that resulted in a sudden and temporary rise in the number of conversions to Christianity and in the demolition of temples in the surrounding countryside.[176] The effect was more apparent than real in Alexandria, on the Nile delta, and in the upper reaches of the river basin,[177] notwithstanding Rufinus' paean:[178]

> [The relics of John the Baptist translated to the Serapeum were thus] on hand for the next generation. Over them golden rooves now rise in the formerly profane temples, now that the traces of idolatry have been cast down and laid low.
> But after the fall of Sarapis, who had in fact never lived, what shrines of any other *daimon* could remain standing? I would have said too little if all the neglected temples of Alexandria of whatever *daimon* had been destroyed down to their individual columns. But through all the cities of Egypt, and in the fortresses (*castella*), in the villages (*vici*), on every farm (*rus*), along the banks of the River (*per ripas fluminis*), and in the desert (*heremum*) too, wherever precincts, or rather the sepulchres [of the pagan gods] could be found (*si qua fana vel potius busta repperiri potuerunt*), they were undermined and dragged down to the earth at the instance of some bishop, so that the countryside (*rus*) was restored to [righteous] worship (*cultura*) once again, which had been unjustly pruned away by the *daimones* (*quod iniuste fuerat daemonibus deputatum*).

Fifth-century evidence, particularly that in the life of Shenute of Atripe, contradicts this claim.[179]

All Rufinus' claims do not, however, lie in the imaginary. The golden roofs (*aurea tecta*) of the *kibotia* or reliquaries probably came from the bullion extracted from the plundered statues and ornaments of the temples. Patriarch Theophilus strictly controlled the disposition of metals, the statues being melted down and poured into sundry kettles and other vessels owned by the Alexandrian church (τὰ δὲ ἀγάλματα τῶν θεῶν μετεχωνεύετο εἰς λεβήτια, καὶ εἰς ἑτέρας χρείας τῆς Ἀλεξανδρέων ἐκκλησίας).[180] The emperor

---

[176] Infra, Ch. III, Sect. 5.
[177] Infra, Ch. IX.
[178] Rufinus, HE 11.28 Mommsen, 1034, lines 15–26).
[179] Infra, Ch. IX.
[180] Socrates, HE 5.16 (PG 67, 605A-B).

Theodosius I ordered that "the gods"—an ironic reference to their bullion content—be given as a gift to support the church's dole for the poor of the city (τοῦ βασιλέως χαρισαμένου τοὺς θεοὺς εἰς δαπανήματα τῶν πτωχῶν).[181] It is inconceivable that Theophilus should not have put some of the captured metals to use in order to gain spiritual *charismata* for the city by ornamenting the martyr chapel with it. In the parallel instance of Gaza less than a decade later, bishop Porphyrius received the metals taken from the Marneion after carefully monitoring their collection.[182] Discrepancies exist in Rufinus' account, however, as to the disposition of the statues. The historian Socrates had it on the eyewitness testimony of the grammarians Helladius and Ammonius, both of them priests of the Hellenic religion in Alexandria in 391, that Theophilus had left the statue of an unnamed god standing in a public place (δημοσίᾳ) "that the Hellenes might not deny in future time that they had worshipped such gods" (ἵνα, φησί, χρόνου προϊόντος μὴ ἀρνήσωνται οἱ Ἕλληνες τοιούτους προσκεκυνηκέναι (θεούς)).[183]

All historians of the closure of the Serapeum mention the Christianization of the use of the Ankh cross (*crux ansata*), a trifoil cross whose top petal had the shape of a loop (♀). The symbol, a hieroglyphic letter, turns up in pre-Christian Egyptian iconography as the sign of "life", whether "happy" or "eternal". It thus belonged to the very extensive Egyptian theology about the afterlife, in the sense of "the life to come" (τοῦτο γὰρ εἶναι τὴν ἐπερχομένην ζωήν or *vita ventura*).[184] Patriarch Theophilus gave the order that the Alexandrians should scrape the so-called *thoraces* of Sarapis from the walls, doorposts, and windows of every house, "lest there be any trace whatsoever of [Sarapis] or any other *daimon*, to the extent of even speaking its name" (*ut ne vestigium quidem usquam vel nominis appellatio aut ipsius aut cuiuslibet alterius daemonis*).[185] The populace of Alexandria was then ordered to paint the Christian cross, perhaps in the common red dye of Coptic epigraphy, in the erased

---

[181] Ibid., 605B.
[182] Infra, Ch. III, Sect. 4. The imperial mint took its share of the bronze from the pagan statuary in 391 as well, turning the bullion into *folles*, as the Hellenic poet Palladas of Alexandria relates: "Those having houses on Olympus, who have become Christians (i.e. the gods), dwell here without molestation. For the melting pot shall put them on the fire and turn them into life-preserving *folles*." *Greek Anthology* 9.528. In general, see: C.M. Bowra, "Palladas and Christianity," *Proceedings of the British Academy* 45 (1959), 255–267.
[183] Socrates, HE 5.16 (PG 67, 605B).
[184] Socrates, HE 5.17 (PG 67, 608B). Rufinus, HE 11.29 (Mommsen, 1035, line 9).
[185] Rufinus, HE 11.29 (Mommsen, 1034f.).

spaces and on columns throughout the city. This done, some of
those who accepted Christianity seem to have begun using the
Ankh cross because of its emotional association with the dead cults
of the Egyptian gods. Socrates, once again relying on his pagan
professors and mentors Helladius and Ammonius, gives the fullest
account of this act of liturgical Christianization:[186]

> When the temple of Sarapis was torn down and laid bare, there were
> found in it, engraven on stones, certain characters which they call
> hieroglyphs, having the forms of crosses. Both the Christians and
> pagans, on seeing them, appropriated and applied them to their
> respective religions: for the Christians, who affirm that the cross is the
> sign of Christ's saving passion, claimed this character as peculiarly
> theirs; but the pagans alleged that it might appertain to Christ and
> Sarapis in common; "for," said they, "it symbolizes one thing to
> Christians and another to the pagans." Whilst this point was con-
> troverted amongst them, some of the pagan converts to Christianity,
> who were conversant with these hieroglyphic characters, interpreted
> the form of a cross and said it signifies "Life to come." This the
> Christians exultingly laid hold of as decidedly favorable to their
> religion. But after other hieroglyphics had been deciphered contain-
> ing a prediction that "When the cross should appear,"—for this was
> the "life to come"—"the temple of Sarapis would be destroyed," a
> very great number of pagans embraced Christianity, and confessing
> their sins, was baptized. Such are the reports I have heard respecting
> the discovery of this symbol in the form of a cross. But I cannot
> imagine that the Egyptian priests foreknew the things concerning
> Christ, when they engraved the figure of a cross.

Socrates omits the vitally important fact that many who accepted
the plausibility of this hidden revelation in their hieroglyphic texts
came from the pagan priests and temple officials whose task was
certainly to interpret the writings (*unde accidit, ut magis hi, qui erant ex
sacerdotibus vel ministris templorum, ad fidem converterentur*).[187] The knowledge of reading hieroglyphics had evidently died out in Hellenized
Alexandria by this time, although it was still known at Philae until
at least 394; otherwise this bogus case of *Ritenchristianisierung*, based
on the accidental coincidence of shape between the Ankh cross and
cross of Christ, but with no clear correspondence of symbolic
meaning at all, would have been exposed. The religiously sincere
and possibly naive priests of Sarapis, as well as the more pragmati-
cally minded, accepted the new religion according to these arguments, whatever their secret beliefs. It was said that the others,

---

[186] Socrates, HE 5.17 (PG 67, 608A-609A): Quoted from *Nicene and Post-Nicene
Fathers*, Ser. 2, v. 2, 126f. Cf. supra, n. 121, for full citation.
[187] Rufinus, HE 11.29 (Mommsen, 1035, line 12f.).

"whom the devices of deception and illusions of error delighted," refused conversion, an apparent reference to priests like the infamous Tyrannos who had faked oracles and imitated the voice of Saturn inside the god's effigy.[188]

The historian Socrates' teachers, the grammarians Helladius and Ammonius, had held respectively the priesthoods of Zeus and the "Ape-god" (Ἀμμώνιος δὲ πιθήκου). Neither accepted Christianity, but migrated to Constantinople to continue their careers as teachers of rhetoric. Their good conduct guaranteed free professional practice and great freedom of speech. Both publicly criticized the closure of the Serapeum. Ammonius opined that "the cult of the Hellenes has suffered terrible things" (δεινὰ πεπονθέναι τὴν Ἑλλήνων θρησκείαν), and complained that the single cult effigy left standing in a public place in Alexandria was kept there as a mockery (ἐπὶ γέλωτι) of the old religion.[189] Helladius boasted, on the other hand, that he had himself killed nine men during the initial melee against the Christians.[190] He was free to speak of the homicides publicly because, it will be recalled, the rescript of Theodosius the Great sent to the defenders of the Serapeum had decreed amnesty for the perpetrators of these crimes and raised the dead to the rank of martyrs. Socrates heard all this as a student in early fifth-century Constantinople. The lawyers who migrated to the monastery of St. Hypatius at Rufinianae had doubtless moved in this milieu as well before their conversion.[191] It is unknown if Ammonius and Helladius performed sacrifices at Constantinople, but the freedom with which the sophists of Alexandria performed such acts in the 480's suggests the plausibility of this.[192]

One last act marked the closing of the Serapeum, to wit, the handing over of the Nilometer to patriarch Theophilus. It was reported after the event that Sarapis would refuse to let the waters

---

[188] Ibid., line 13f.

[189] Socrates, HE 5.16 (PG 67, 695B).

[190] Ibid. The statue in question was perhaps that of Herakles mentioned by Palladas of Alexandria in one of his epigrams: "I was amazed to see Zeus' bronze son, once [called upon] in prayers (ἐν εὐχωλαῖς) but now cast aside. In anger I said: 'Averter of evils, offspring of three moons, you were never defeated but are today prostrated" (Ἀλεξίκακε τρισέληνε, μηδέποθ' ἡττηθείς, σήμερον ἐξετάθης). But the god stood beside me in the night and said: 'Even though a god, I have learned to serve the times'." Greek Anthology 9.441. Proclus, the Neoplatonist of Athens (5th c.), is said in a similar vein to have had a vision of Athena not long before her chryselephantine image was removed from the Parthenon. Infra, Ch. IV, Sect. 3, n. 139.

[191] Infra, Ch. VII, Sect. 1.

[192] Infra, Ch. V, Sect. 2.

of the Nile rise for the flood of 391, but the inundation when it came proved to be deeper than usual. From then onward, the Christian patriarch rather than a priest of Sarapis made the public announcement when the water level of the river began to increase. The Christian God became Lord of the Waters (*aquarum dominus*), probably taking over some of the titulature of the Nile, which had consisted of such names as *daimon* (δαίμων), god (θεός), lord (κύριος), and "equal of the gods" (ἰσόθεος).[193] Christian prayers and processions for the Nile flood preexisted the transfer of the Nilometer to the church.[194] It was now said that the Christian God commanded the waters to rise at times suited to his own purposes (*suis temporibus*) and the Euhemerist idea was enunciated that "Sarapis was much later in time than the Nile" (*Serapin qui multo erat Nilo posterior*).[195] This, with the recategorization of Sarapis into a corrupted variant of the Hebrew Joseph, son of Jacob, completed the Christian polemic.[196] It should be added that the Ankh cross permanently penetrated Christian Egyptian iconography, perhaps being initially used by the converts of the 390's and appearing with other Christian symbols on a basis of equality from then onward. One pre-Christian Ankh cross appears on the funerary portrait of a dead woman, who holds the symbol in her left hand while making an orant gesture of prayer with her right.[197] Examples of Christian use of the Ankh abound. On the sixth-century funerary stele of a certain Rodia, it dominates the Alpha-Omega.[198] Its top loop at times encloses the trefoil Christian cross (6th-7th century).[199] On the funerary stele of a certain Plenios the lector, Ankh crosses stand on either side of the Christian cross, but are dominated in turn by a wreathed Chi-Rho Christogram (5th-6th century).[200] Ankh crosses

---

[193] Danielle Bonneau, *La Crue du Nil: Divinité égyptienne à travers mille ans d'histoire (332 av.–641 ap. J.–C.)* (Paris 1964), 357f.

[194] Ibid., 421–439.

[195] Rufinus, HE 11.30 (Mommsen, 1035, lines 19–21).

[196] Firmus Maternus, a fourth-century Christian writer, had already tampered with Sarapis' name to make him "son of Sarah" (Σαρρα παῖς), thus making an etymological connection between the deity and the offspring of the marriage of Abraham and Sarah. Bonneau, *La Crue du Nil*, 427f.

[197] A pre-Christian Ankh cross appears in the funerary portrait of a dead woman, who holds this symbol in her left hand while making gesture of prayer with the right (Fayum, 3rd c. A.D.). Benaki Museum, Athens, no. 6877. Cf. Maria Cramer, *Das altägyptische Lebenzeichen in christlichen (koptischen) Ägypten* (Wiesbaden 1955).

[198] Alexander Badawy, *Coptic Art and Archaeology* (Cambridge, Mass. 1978), no. 3.198.

[199] Ibid., no. 3.192. Friedman, *Beyond the Pharaohs*, no. 177.

[200] Badawy, *Coptic Art and Archaeology*, no. 3.207.

enclose various Christian symbols on Coptic tapestries,[201] and appear on tapestry panels that depict birds along with crosses (5th century).[202]

There remains a third temple conversion to be considered, that of the shrine of Allat-Athena at Palmyra in the Provincia Arabia, which the Polish scholar Barbara Gassowska has dated to the campaign of Maternus Cynegius, the Praetorian Prefect of Oriens, against the temples of the East between 25 May 385 and 19 March 388.[203] The temple, dedicated by a certain Taimarsū, a citizen of Palmyra, probably between c. 123–164 A.D., has the shape of a rectangle with a colonnaded porch.[204] The pronaos leads down to an *adyton*, where both the cult effigy *and altar* stood. The ritual conducted in the temple varied considerably from the stereotypical, for the positioning of the altar, which was taken from the previous temple on the site, required *indoor sacrifice*, the meat from which will have been distributed to and consumed by persons sitting on the benches placed around the pronaos. The statue of the goddess Allat, reassembled from the fragments, corresponds to a type of Athena found in Athens in the fifth century B.C.,[205] although Allat turns up occasionally as the equivalent of the Greek Artemis.[206] The feet of a baldaschino which stood over the effigy of Allat are still *in situ*.[207] This interior architectural device was later used in Christian churches to cover the altar table or depository of martyr relics. The temenos of Allat is surrounded by an enclosure wall which fronts on the main street near the tetrapylon of the city. It thus occupied an expensive plot of inner-urban real estate.

The cult of Allat-Athena retained its vitality in Palmyra until the 380's, to judge from the objects discovered in the *adyton* put there before the destruction of the temple. Two deposits of clay votive lamps of local, fourth-century manufacture have turned up, as has a hoard of forty-four bronze Roman coins, hidden intentionally before the demolition of the statue.[208] Twenty-six of the coins belong to the reign of Valentinian I with his co-emperor Valens (364–375), and

---

[201] Friedman, *Beyond the Pharaohs*, no. 129.
[202] Ibid., no. 204.
[203] Barbara Gassowska, "Maternus Cynegius, Praefectus Praetorio Orientis and the Destruction of the Allat Temple in Palmyra," *Archeologia* 33 (1982), 121f.
[204] Ibid., 110.
[205] Ibid., 111.
[206] Ibid., 110, n. 8.
[207] The open air shrine of the Gazan Aphrodite reported by Mark the Deacon was covered by a sort of canopy. Infra, Ch. III, Sect. 1, n. 21.
[208] Gassowska, "The Allat Temple in Palmyra," 112 and Fig. 8.

two of them to Valens alone.[209] A later loose coin found in the destruction debris bears the effigy of Aelia Flavia Flacilla Augusta, wife of Theodosius I between 376–386.[210] On the basis of this data, the excavators have put the temple conversion some years after 386, in the suitable context of Maternus Cynegius' actions against the temples of Oriens.

The ruin of the temple of Allat-Athena has two striking features. The first of these, the architectural proof that the cult ritual was celebrated *inside the temple*, has already been mentioned. This will have permitted the offering of clandestine sacrifice, away from the public gaze, during the 380's, after the initial laws on that subject given by Theodosius I. The second feature is the abandonment of the fragments of the statue within the *adyton*. From the available pieces it proved possible for the excavators to demonstrate the sequence of blows which the image received as Cynegius' agents ransacked the interior of the building. The statue was first decapitated with a blow behind the head. The face was then smashed into several pieces so dextrously that no fragments survive of the nose, upper lip, and chink between the eyes of Allat-Athena. The partly mutilated torso was then deposited behind the baldaschino.[211] The decapitation and obliteration of the goddess' facial features constituted a sort of "symbolic annihilation of personality" in order to drive out the *daimon* inhabiting the image, somewhat like the expulsion of the genius of the emperor thought to reside in imperial statues in a formal *damnatio memoriae*.[212] Superstitious pagans and Christians had both theological and artifice-induced reasons for such suppositions, as has been demonstrated in this and the previous chapter. The top of the impressive altar was cut off, dumped behind the cella, and later covered with debris, undoubtedly to

---

[209] Ibid. The dates of minting are not given.

[210] Ibid.

[211] Ibid., 113–115. Fig.'s 7 and 10a–c.

[212] Quoted from: Ibid., 117. It is worth noting here the method prescribed for desecrating an idol in the *Mishna on Idolatry* (3rd c. A.D.): "In what manner can one desecrate an idol? By cutting off the tip of its ear or *nose* or finger, by *battering it*—even although (sic) its bulk be not diminished—it is desecrated. But by spitting in its face, making water before it, dragging it about, or casting dirt upon it, behold! the idol is not desecrated. If one sells or pawns it, Rabbi holds that it is desecrated, but the Wise are of the contrary opinion. *'Aboda Zara* 4.5 (Elmslie, 67). W.A. Elmslie remarks: " . . . a hollow-cast idol might be battered in without lessening its bulk. Maimonides says that in such cases profanation is *only* effected *when the face is damaged*." Ibid., 66, n. (5). An obvious connection exists, once again, between Jewish methods of dealing with pagan cult effigies and the devices invented by Christian civil officials in the fourth-century temple conversions. Cf. supra, Ch. II, n. 58.

prevent the celebration of the clandestine sacrifices frequently mentioned in the Theodosian Code.[213] The *missing element* in these various acts of destruction, insofar as the remnants permit us to judge, is the incision of Christian crosses and other symbols on the statuary, altar, and walls of the building, a circumstance suggesting that officials acting under orders performed the despoliation rather than fanatical laymen, monks, or a bishop like Marcellus of Apamea.[214]

Palmyra certainly had a Christian community before 388–392, its bishop Marinus having participated in the Council of Nicaea. Two three-aisled early Christian basilicas, constructed from reused building materials and not yet excavated, date from no earlier than the fourth century.[215] Neither the bishop nor the civil government had any further use for the temple of Allat-Athena, but in the latter half of the fifth century converted two other temples of Palmyra, the small temenos of Baal-Shamin and the old and splendid shrine of Bel into churches.[216]

The case of the temple of Allat-Athena is instructive on several counts. It demonstrates that generalizations about the character of Semitic-Hellenic liturgical practices will remain subject to revision as more such buildings are excavated. It also reveals that a theologically thought-out system lay behind the dismantling of cult-effigies. For all the rhetoric spilled by fifth-century writers on the destruction of Sarapis' image at Alexandria, an epigraphically mute site with no literary *testimonia* like that of Allat-Athena in Palmyra gives new and important data about the religious thought processes that accompanied such acts.

IV. Christianization of Rite and Christianization of Culture

The recategorization of the old deities as *daimones* and the destruction of temples proved to be only the beginning of a process of Christianizing many features of the pre-Christian Hellenic, Semitic, and Egyptian religious ethos. Fanatics like Marcellus of Apamea stood in fundamental agreement with the moderates who avoided violence in their aim of generating a new Christian ethos in town and countryside. It was quickly discovered, however, that the ancient traditions connected with the Greek *paideia*, the peace of the

---

[213] Gassowska, "The Allat Temple in Palmyra," 114.
[214] Gassowska suggests the action of the bishop, with the help of soldiers from the local legionary camp.
[215] Ibid., 122 and n. 66.
[216] Ibid., 123. Deichmann, "Kirchen in Heiligtümern," 122.

gods, and fertility rites of agriculture lay deep in the popular psychology. As more persons accepted the new religion, often for reasons of social, political and economic advancement, it proved impossible to refuse their protestations of good will, and many brought their cultural baggage with them into the mind-shaping process of their catechization. Episcopal and monastic polemicists discovered as well that powerfully rooted ritual and myth could be adapted to Christian cult and theology. By demonstrating the supposed Christian, or at any rate Judaic, origin of a given cultural formation, the catechist framed effective arguments to induce conversions to the one real or original God, the Christian one. The example of revaluing Sarapis as Joseph the provider, son of Jacob, the citation of no longer understood hieroglyphic texts to prove a prophecy about the destruction of the Serapeum, and the adoption of the Ankh cross as a Christian symbol, have already made this process apparent. Where polytheistic myth and ritual lay too deeply entrenched in the local ethos for plausible conversions even to take place, "administrative conversions" occurred instead. A village might be formally catechized by a resident monk, followed by a presbyter who recited the Christian liturgy at a local chapel. Some baptisms might occur, but the populace would summon the aid of the traditional deities in their daily concerns, whether to induce rainfall, fend off hailstorms, achieve successful childbirth,[217] or other things, often through the aid of a local priest, shaman, or magician.

The typical anxieties of the agriculturalist are succinctly summed up in a poem of the *Greek Anthology* that dates, surprisingly, from the sixth century A.D.:[218]

> Calligenes the husbandman, after he had cast seed into his land, went to the house of Aristophanes the astrologer and begged him to say if he would have a favorable harvest and a good surplus of grain.

---

[217] See, for example, the many dedications composed to Artemis for successful childbirth, most of them perhaps literary exercises but nevertheless reflecting real attitudes. *Greek Anthology* 6.59, 203, 242, 271, and 273. In the composition of Marcus Argentarius (6th c. A.D.), a good example of the Late Sophistic, the fictive female dedicant Euphrante offers to Artemis her sandals, headband, a scented lock of hair, her belt, undervest, and waistband in thanksgiving for successful childbirth. The offering is made at a temple of Artemis (Εὐφράντη νηῷ θῆκεν ὑπ' Ἀρτέμιδος). Marcus Argentarius relied on earlier dedications as exemplars for this piece, perhaps an actual inscription taken from one of the now closed temples (6.203). Another of these epigrams refers to Artemis as the "soother of child-bed pangs" (6.242). For the use of diviners and magicians to aid the pagan matron Aelia of Gaza in a difficult childbirth, cf. infra, Ch. III, Sect. 2, n. 51.
[218] Adapted from *Greek Anthology*, 11.365 (tr. Paton 4, 243f.).

Taking his counters and spreading them out on a tray, and then extending his fingers, the latter said to Calligenes: "If your plot of land receives enough rain and produces no crop of wildflowers, if frost does not break the furrows, if hail does not nip off the tops of sprouting ears, if no goat browses on the corn, and if it meet no other injury by air or earth, I prophesy that your harvest will be excellent and you will cut the ears with success. Keep watch only for locusts.

Whatever the fees charged by such an astrologer, the farmer can hardly have found much comfort in his pronouncement. The usual propitiatory and apotropaic rites thought to ward off such phenomena did not always lend themselves to Christianization readily, but a sort of pragmatic pact seems to have been made between the catechist and rustic pagan during the prehistory of Christianization at individual villages, which emerge as fully Christian only later in the hagiographic texts, inscriptions, and other narratives. This theoretically binding and irreversible pact required adherence to Christian monotheism in the formal ritual of the village chapel, but gave grudging public recognition to all other religious forms and formulae as acceptable, seeking all the time to recontextualize them in the embrace of the new religion. Christian archangels might suddenly guard the sacred water of springs in Asia Minor where the chthonic Attis had previously resided, and with the same iconography.[219] Sacrifices might go on, but what Bronislaw Malinowski calls the "collective effervescence" of village religiosity would be channeled wherever possible to Christianized sacrifices in front of the chapels, all celebrated on the purported example of King David, as happened in sixth-century Lycia under the guidance of Nicholas, hegumen of the Hagia Sion monastery.[220]

But what did the average catechumen think of such transpositions? It seems probable that on the intuitive level of understanding the manifestation of divine powers, he saw the old deity but repeated the name of the Christian martyr, prophet or archangel out of respect or fear of the representative of the elite, the Christian monk or presbyter. As Mircea Eliade has put it: " . . . a given hierophany may be lived and interpreted quite differently by the religious elite and the rest of the community."[221] Or later: "Where . . . Jacob saw

---

[219] On the cult of Attis as found in the Neo-Phrygian inscriptions (3rd c. A.D.), cf. infra, Ch. VII, Sect. 2. See also Cyril Mango's discussion of the possibility that Attis was the Anatolian predecessor of Michael the Archangel, whose iconography resembles that of the deity, in: "St. Michael and Attis," *Deltion tēs Christianikēs Archaiologikēs Etaireias* 12 (1984), 39–62.

[220] Trombley, "Paganism in the Greek World," 339.

[221] Eliade, *Patterns in Comparative Religion*, 7.

the angels' ladder and the house of God, Palestinian peasants saw
the god Bethel.''[222] Eliade continues:[223]

> But we must remember that, whatever god the local population
> may have seen in Bethel, no *stone* ever represented more than a *sign*, a
> dwelling, a theophany. The divinity was *manifest* by means of the
> stone, or—in other rituals—*witnessed* and sanctified a covenant made
> near it. This witness consisted, in the minds of simple folk, in the
> divinity's being embodied in the stone, and to the elite, in the stone's
> being transfigured by the divine presence.

This paradigm is perfectly applicable to Christianized sacrifices,
cults of stones, magic circles, and much else.[224]

Only the remnants of this process survive in the extant evidence.
Some scholars have argued that it is sufficient to regard the society
as "Christian" and forgo this pre-history of cultural transformation
wherein nothing is "pagan".[225] This is a descriptive rather than
analytical methodology, and although anthropological in its outward form, it ignores many of the data and mechanisms which the
study of comparative religion has revealed. It is thus necessary to
disagree with Mircea Eliade's assessment that only the ritual and
theological disposition of the Christian village priest matters in the
local context because of its "purity," as a principle of analysis not
useful to understanding the process of Christianization:[226]

> The modalities of the sacred revealed by Christianity are in fact
> more truly preserved in the tradition represented by the priest
> (however strongly coloured by history and theology) than in the
> beliefs of the villagers. What the observer is interested in is not the
> one moment in the history of Christianity, or one part of Christen-
> dom, but the Christian religion as such. The fact that only one man,
> in a whole village, may have a proper knowledge of Christian ritual,
> dogma and mysticism, while the rest of the community are ill-
> informed about them and practise an elemental cult tinctured with
> superstition (with, that is, the remains of outworn hierophanies) does
> not, for his purpose at least, matter at all. What does matter is to
> realize that this single man has kept more completely, if not the
> original experience of Christianity, at least its basic elements and its
> mystical, theological and ritual values.

To take up Eliades's stone of Bethel once again in the context of
Christianization in the fifth century, it was the task of the catechist

---

[222] Ibid., 229.
[223] Ibid., 229f.
[224] For general discussion, see: Trombley, "Paganism in the Greek World,"
337–345.
[225] Rochow, "Zu einigen oppositionellen Strömungen", passim.
[226] Eliade, *Patterns in Comparative Religion*, 6.

to direct the attention of his congregation to the "real" source of the power, that is Christ, the martyrs and archangels, and reembody it in the material reality of everyday life. Mosaic religion had abolished the "sign" to avoid its confusion with the "Divinity" himself. In the era of Christianization, however, the catechists would *tolerate* or even *encourage* such a confusion, so long as it led to *conversions* and guaranteed *correct practice*. Eliade's analysis is elsewhere penetrating and highly illuminating as regards conceptualizing phenomena. For example, the "daimonic rage" which Christian catechists saw in the powers of the recategorized, that is devalued or revalued, gods, Eliade would have defined (had he addressed the issue) as negative hierophanies ("manifestations of the sacred") or kratophanies (manifestations of power that are feared and venerated).[227]

The phenomena of *Ritenchristianisierung* ("Christianization of rite") exist in an endless array over a period of many centuries. It is best to begin analysis with the topic of the previous section, temple conversions.[228]

The countryside of Asia Minor is littered with the remains of temples at pre-Christian sites of religious awe such as hot springs or *hagiasmata* (ἁγιάσματα), unusual rock formations, and mountain peaks. William Mitchell Ramsay called attention nearly a century ago to the continuation of cult at these sites through all stages of religious transformation, that is the Lydian-Phrygian, Hellenic, Greek Christian, and Muslim epochs.[229] His arguments have been largely forgotten or ignored. Among the *hagiasmata* were sacred springs in which according to popular credence curative and even magical powers inhered, all of them attributable to the subterranean deities thought to reside there. One thinks here, for example, of the Ploutoneion and its hot springs near Laodicea-Hierapolis,[230] the Seleucian grotto and its torrent in Cilicia Tracheia where the healing cult of St. Thecla eventually prevailed over that of the local

---

[227] Ibid., 14, 18, and 25.
[228] The following section derives from the communication: "Greek Paganism and Christianity in Late Antiquity: Some Continuities in Cultural Forms," *Seventeenth International Byzantine Congress*, Washington, D.C., 3–8 August 1986.
[229] William M. Ramsay, "The Orthodox Church in the Byzantine Empire," and "Asia Minor: Country and Religion," in *Luke the Physician and Other Studies* (London 1908), 158ff. Idem, "The Permanence of Religion at Holy Places in Western Asia Minor," and "St. Paul's Road from Cilicia to Iconium," in *Pauline and Other Studies* (London 1906), 163ff. and 273ff., respectively. Ramsay's suppositions have been successfully criticized in their more extravagant form by F.W. Hasluck, *Christianity and Islam under the Sultans*, 2 vols. (Oxford 1929), 3–118 and 175–225.
[230] Strabo, *Geography*, 13.4.14.

deity Sarpedonius,[231] and the Charoneion in Caria which emitted
deadly vapors.[232] The cults practiced at these sites underwent
Christianization. Two examples will be considered, one of them
conjectural, the other certain.

The first site appears to be attested in the early fourth-century
epitaph of Eugenius, bishop of Laodicea in Phrygia Combusta.[233]
W.M. Calder connects the inscription with the considerable ruins
of an ancient temple of an unknown deity which stood several miles
south of the city. Within the temenos was a rectangular tank cut in
the ground, nine feet by six, which was fed by a fresh water spring,
a typical *hagiasma*.[234] The Eugenius inscription mentions its protagonist's reconstruction of a church with its auxiliary buildings
(ἀνοκοδο[μ]ήσας ἀπὸ θεμελίων), including porticoes, tetrastoas,
paintings, mosaics, a propylon, Christian sculptures, and, interestingly, a reservoir.[235] Calder inspected the site, and was inclined to
identify this church with the fragments of "engaged columns" of a
"Byzantine" church found near the temple spring, and the spring
itself with the Christian reservoir mentioned in the inscription.
Although Calder's hypothesis is speculative, it may be correct and
has important implications, particularly as literary evidence to be
discussed shortly indicates the Christian occupation of pagan
hagiasmata.

If the argument is accepted that the Christian reservoir of the
inscription and temple reservoir are one and the same, one begins
to see how the resident deities of sacred sites were transformed into
Christian martyrs or archangels with similar typologies. Bishop
Eugenius was a survivor of the Great Persecution conducted by
Diocletian and Galerius, who ordered the destruction of many
churches. Eugenius *rebuilt* (ἀνοκοδο[μ]ήσας) the church and its
auxiliary buildings. The inscription clearly affirms the existence of
an earlier church at the site of the reservoir, dating probably from
the second half of the third century. Barring the death of the pagan
god and his cult (the countryside around Laodicea contains inscriptions dedicated to Zeus Eukarpios and Eukarpos),[236] it is conceiv-

---

[231] Basil of Seleucia, *Vie et miracles de Sainte Thècle*, ed. tr. G. Dagron (Brussels 1978), 59–63 and 85–90.
[232] Strabo, *Geography* 14.1.11.
[233] *Ed. princ.* W.M. Calder, "A Journey around the Proseilemmene," *Klio* 10 (1910), 233. Guarducci, *Epigrafi sacre pagane e cristiane*, 394–398. I have followed Calder's edition (reprinted as MAMA 1, no. 170).
[234] Calder, "Proseilemmene," 234.
[235] Ibid., 233, lines 13–17.
[236] MAMA 7, nos. 453 and 476. The former is Calder's inscr. no. 8 in "Proseilemmene."

able that the late third century saw the temporary synoikism of competing cults at the spring, with the adherents of the new religion occupying the site and absorbing the remnant of the local Hellenes along with their rituals and typologies of the divine. Such an argument is consistent with the decline in the numbers of votive inscriptions found at pagan temples from the mid-third century onward.[237] It depends, however, on the secure identification of the reservoir of the Eugenius inscription with the building seen by Calder.

There is some literary corroboration for such a process of transformation at a site near Laodicea. This example of a synoikism occurs in the eighth-century text called *The Miracle of the Archistrategos Michael*, which repeats an earlier, probably fifth-century tradition.[238] The story concerns a sacred spring (ἅγιον ὕδωρ) at Colossae in Phrygia, near the geologically formed tunnel into which the Lykos river was said to have plunged and vanished by way of a subterranean channel.[239] It is related that a pagan (εἰδωλόθυτης) from Laodicea, which lay some 17 kilometers away, frequented the spring to pray for the cure of his daughter, who was affected with dumbness. He had been directed there by the vision of an angel whom the man seems to have identified with Michael the archangel *after* his conversion to Christianity.[240] It is most probable that the sacred spring at Colossae had been the site of the cult of a chthonic deity since the earliest pre-Hellenic epoch, to follow William Mitchell Ramsay's arguments. In thanksgiving for the cure of his daughter, the man from Laodicea accepted baptism with his entire household, and erected a small chapel (εὐκτήριον) at his own expense to shelter the spring.[241] The *Miracle of the Archistrategos* suggests the existence of an inscription erected by the donor to commemorate these events that included a date.[242] The chapel lay

---

[237] Geffcken, *Last Days of Greco-Roman Paganism*, 25–34.

[238] "Le Miracle de Saint Michel à Colosses," ed. F. Nau, *Patrologia Orientalis* 4 (Paris 1907), 542–562 (BHG 1282). This text is hereinafter cited as *Miraculum Michaelis*.

[239] *Miraculum Michaelis*, 542f.

[240] Cf. the semi-divine status assigned to angels and archangels by Iamblichos of Chalkis, *De Mysteriis* 2.3ff., where these beings constitute an order of the divine hierarchy directly below the gods, but above *daimones*, archons, heroes, and human souls. Iamblichos' view reflects the synthesis of Hellenic and Neoplatonic ideas of the celestials orders independent of Jewish syncretism, as A.A.R. Sheppard demonstrates. Cf. Ch. II, n. 246.

[241] *Miraculum Michaelis*, 549f.

[242] The anonymous hagiographer observes that the *prosmonarios* who later occupied the chapel arrived "after the ninetieth year from when the chapel was built above the spring (καὶ μετὰ ἐνενηκοστὸν ἔτος ἀφ᾿ οὗ τὸ εὐκτήριον ᾠκοδομήθη ἐπάνω τοῦ ὕδατος). *Miraculum Michaelis*, 550. This observation ultimately derives

vacant for many decades, until a *prosmonarios* or monastic caretaker occupied the site.[243] At that time, both Hellenes and Christians had continued to frequent the sacred spring, but it was said that only those who invoked the Christian Trinity through the archangel Michael actually received cures.[244] The Hellenes had evidently continued to invoke the unnamed chthonic deity whose cult survived in a synoikism with that of the Christians.

The *Miracle of the Archistrategos* contains many correspondences which corroborate the *behavioral* side of Calder's hypothesis about the Eugenius inscription. In each case the spring was quite small, the former nine feet by six, the latter capable of being enclosed beneath the roof of a small building. In each case Hellenes and Christians alike recognized the curative properties of the waters through the spirits thought to reside in them. The question arises as to why a Hellene from Laodicea should have had a dream vision of the archangel Michael instead of a martyr or an epiphany of the Christian God. The best explanation lies in the pre-Christian cult of angels in Phrygia and other parts of Asia Minor. The Thirty-fifth Canon of the Council of Laodicea (4th century) observes:[245]

> Christians are forbidden to abide in the church of God, and depart, and summon angels, and make assemblies. If anyone is detected spending time in this secret idolatry, let him be anathema.

The framers of this Canon clearly had pagan cult in mind in using the term "idolatry". The rule was not, as is often supposed, simply a reaction to Jewish-Hellenic syncretism. A recent study of the epigraphy of Caria by A.A.R. Sheppard indicates that angels (ἄγγελοι) were, in fact, special supernatural beings and deities, and not simply messengers of the gods.[246] An inscription of third-century A.D. date from the upper Tembris reads: "Aurelius . . . the association of the friends of angels [made] a vow to the Holy Just One" (Αὐρ . . .φιλαγέλων συμβίωσις Ὁσίῳ Δικέῳ εὐχήν).[247]

---

from the earliest recension of the miracle story, whose author knew a building inscription commemorating the dedication of the shrine. The story, which has the essential elements of a florid ex-voto, may ultimately go back to a detailed text like that erected by bishop Eugenius (supra, Ch. II, n. 233). For that matter, it cannot be entirely excluded that the Christian story did not originate in the careless misinterpretation of a *pagan* ex-voto dedicated to a locally worshipped chthonic deity called the "archangel".

[243] *Miraculum Michaelis*, 550.

[244] Ibid., 552f.

[245] *Canones Laodicenae, Quae Est Urbs Phrygiae Capatianae ex Diversis Asiae Provinciis Congregatae*, PG 137, 1384C–1385A.

[246] A.A.R. Sheppard, "Pagan Cults of Angels in Roman Asia Minor." *Talanta* 12–13 (1980–81), 77–101.

[247] Ibid., 87–90.

Such an association (συμβίωσις) seems to correspond to the assemblies (συνάξεις) and idolatries anathematized by the Council of Laodicea about a century later. One discovers as well that in Bithynia, according to Callinicus of Rufinianae's *Life of St. Hypatius* (5th century), angels are variously qualified, as for example "angel of God" and, significantly, as simply "angel".[248] The latter was a pagan deity and the object of cult. A rustic diviner with whom Hypatius once conversed claimed to be able to predict future events and find lost objects. The man asserted that revelations came to him at night, after he told the person seeking his guidance to sacrifice a cow, a sheep, or a bird at the idol temple. "Angels", he claimed, sometimes made the revelations to him.[249] The status of this angel as a divinity or *daimon* is to be supposed by the use of the local *hieron* as the place of supplication.

To return to the sacred spring at Colossae, it will have made perfect sense for pagan suppliants to call upon the angels of their own cult, and then to turn to Christian angels if their own disappointed them, particularly if a chthonic angel cult existed at the *hagiasma*. The local Christian church perhaps encouraged such transfers of allegiance to typologically similar beings of the new dispensation. This interpretation is consistent with the behavioral realities of conversion. Once the process was completed, however, the archangel had an exaggerated status in the Christianized cult. The *Miracle of the Archistrategos*, probably following local usage, juxtaposes the angel with the persons of the Trinity, referring to cures being given with the formula: "Having called in fear upon the Father and Son and Holy Spirit and archistrategos Michael" (καὶ φόβῳ ἐπικαλούμενος Πατέρα καὶ Υἱὸν καὶ ἅγιον Πνεῦμα καὶ Μιχαὴλ τὸν ἀρχιστράτηγον) thus seemingly adding a fourth person to the Divine Triad.[250] This usage corresponds, interestingly, to that found in two second-century inscriptions which invoke Zeus the Most High and the Angel in parataxis (Διὶ ὑψίστῳ καὶ θείῳ ἀγγέλῳ and Διὶ ὑψίστῳ καὶ ἀγαθῷ ἀγγέλῳ).[251] A.A.R. Sheppard rejects any substantive borrowing from Judaism or actual syncretism in these instances.[252]

---

[248] The "angel of God" hinders the *daimones* employed by sorcerers to effect spells of illness upon their victims. Callinicus of Rufinianae, *De Vita S. Hypatii Liber*, ed. Seminarii Philologorum Bonnensis Sodales (Leipzig 1895), 58. This text is fully analysed in Ch. VII, Sect. 1.

[249] Ibid., 90f.

[250] *Miraculum Michaelis*, 561.

[251] Sheppard, "Pagan Cult of Angels," nos. 1 and 2.

[252] For conclusions, ibid., 86f. Cf. SEG 32.1539 (Gerasa, 2nd–3rd c. A.D.), a dedication to Zeus in his messenger form (Διὶ Ἀγγέλωι).

The Eugenius inscription cited by Calder and the *Miracle of the Archistrategos* offer, in any case, unmistakable proof for the continuity of cult at temples, an important corrective to some of the arguments formulated by Alison Frantz who suggests that cultic edifices could not have been converted into Christian churches within the living memory of the cults practiced there because of the former gods' daimonic powers.[253] These arguments are based, as was indicated above, on ambiguous and fragmentary evidence largely confined to Greece.

Some pagan hierophanies and typologies did not lend themselves to Christianization. The cult of trees falls into this category, although the Oak of Mambre in Palestine, thought to have been the oak of Abraham, provides a single exception to this rule. It was the paradigmatic Indo-European practice to set up an enclosure around a sacred tree and emplace an altar beside it, which thereby became a medium for worshippers of fertility deities. Pre-Indian sanctuaries of this type existed at the time of Buddha's teaching, but neither Buddhism nor Hinduism could weaken the grip of these sacred places in popular religiosity and eventually absorbed and incorporated such cults. Similarly, Semitic shrines in many places consisted of a tree and bethel-stone.[254] The Oak of Mambre, whatever its Judaic and Christian associations in the manner of a Hellenic *heroeion* of Abraham, derived its typology, if not origin, from the Semitic tree and bethel sanctuary.

Trees were thought to be the hierophany of Greek deities as well, particularly that of Artemis,[255] whose cult survived until the sixth century at a large oak tree in Lycia that was thought to control the fertility of the surrounding fields. This tree, like many others, fell to the axe of the Christian monk.[256] The monks of Asia Minor such as Hypatius of Rufinianae were anxious to break the residual powers of the female deity, and destroyed sacred trees and groves wherever the rumor of "daimonic error" at such sites reached them.[257] In performing these acts of mutilation and burning, the monks imitated a common form of impiety in the ancient world, just as during temple conversions when they deliberately effected the ritual pollution of the temenos by depositing the relics of Christian dead within the enclosures. The direct nature of the affront is illustrated in the earlier literature. The balance of nature, a mate-

---

[253] Supra, Ch. II, Sect. 2.
[254] Eliade, *Patterns in Comparative Religion*, 270.
[255] Ibid., 279.
[256] Trombley, "Paganism in the Greek World," 338.
[257] Infra, Ch. VII, Sect. 1.

rial reflection of the state of the peace of the gods, was always a precarious issue in the Mediterranean ecospace. The *Geoponika*, a tenth-century compilation of texts on agriculture and its lore mostly from the Roman period, lists the traits desirable in a farm-gang supervisor. After enumerating the typical work virtues, it adds:[258]

> And, above all, he must resist lying and swearing falsely, be pious to God, keep the traditional rites of worship, and not be an insulter of sacred trees or anything else holy.

This set of qualifications reflects the perceived need for pious men to till the soil, lest the peace of the gods be violated. Yet the abuse of sacred trees was common in Hellenic antiquity. One epigrammist, Antipater (of Thessalonike?) (1st century B.C.) recapitulates the words of a sacred tree (δένδρον ἱερόν) bidding the passer-by (παρερχόμενος) not to mutilate it (πημαίνειν) by stripping off its bark (φλόος).[259] Such acts of gratuitous sacrilege became the means of monastic attacks on the chthonic deities of the fertility cults. Unlike their Hindu and Buddhist counterparts, the Christian monks waged a ruthless warfare of "search and destroy" raids that seems to have been partially successful in eradicating the memory of tree cults.

The cult of Artemis proved exceptionally difficult to eradicate, whether it was observed at temple enclosures, trees, or groves. The great festival (μεγάλη ἁγιστεία) of the Basket (κάλαθος), whose ritual entailed worshippers making baskets "dance" (χορεύειν),[260] perhaps on their heads in imitation of the effigies of the goddess, whose *polos* sometimes served as a mural crown, survived in virulent form in Bithynia until at least the 440's.[261] The groves sacred to Artemis were thought to be dangerous at the hour of noon in First Galatia a century later.[262] Artemis' statues represent her with numerous breasts. She was the archetypal fertility deity. Women were particularly devoted to Artemis, it appears, even in the sixth century, wherever Hellenic religion survived. The poetry mentions their making dedications at temples in thanksgiving for successful childbirth.[263] An epigram of Marcus Argentarius (6th century A.D.) describes such an offering by a certain Euphrante of her sandals, headband, a scented lock of hair, belt, undervest, and

---

[258] *Geoponica* 2.44.1–2 (ed. H. Beckh, Leipzig 1895, 79f.).
[259] *Greek Anthology* 9.706.
[260] Strabo, *Geography* 13.4.5.
[261] Infra, Ch. VII, Sect. 1.
[262] Trombley, "Paganism in the Greek World," 335.
[263] *Greek Anthology* 6.59, 240, 242, 271, and 273.

CHAPTER TWO

waistband to Artemis at a temple (Εὐφράντη νηῷ θῆκεν ὑπ᾽ ᾿Αρτέμιδος).[264] The episcopal and monastic catechists sought to tap into such devotion and redirect it to the Christian Mother of God, the Theotokos, and other suitable cults. Artemis' and other female deities' appellations survive in Christian nomenclature, as for example in a graffiti on the Athenian Parthenon:[265]

> Mistress, all-holy, virgin, undefiled, all-hymned: importune your son to save your suppliants in the kingdom.

"Mistress" (δέσποινα), "all-holy" (παναγία), and "virgin" (παρθένος) all turn up in the inscriptions of Artemis at Ephesus, and "undefiled" (ἁγνή) at Sardis in a petition to Iaso, divine daughter of Asklepios, the physician god.[266] These epithets are some of them repeated or amplified in the sermon of Proclus, patriarch of Constantinople, on the Theotokos.[267] The transcendence of such nomenclature for the many female deities required this *Namenchristianisierung*. It marked an important, and possibly initial, stage in transferring religious allegiances to the Christian. Other Christian epithets have early analogues in Hellenic terminology, and only a preliminary list can be given. For example, Isis was called "begetter of fruits" (καρποτόκος) and "mother of grain" (σταχυμήτηρ), corresponding exactly to two Christian terms for "Mother of God" (θεοτόκος and θεομήτηρ).[268] On the other hand, Isis was also said to be "thousand-shaped" (μυριόμορφος), a conception hardly adaptable to the new religion.

Popular religiosity associated Artemis with acts of healing at her

---

[264] *Greek Anthology* 6.203.
[265] A.K. Orlandos and A. Vranousē, *Ta Charagmata tou Parthenōnos* (Athens 1973), no. 130.
[266] Infra, Ch. II, n. 273.
[267] Proclus refers to the virgin as the "pure one" (ἁγνεία) and "maiden" (ἡ παρθένος), at a time (c. 434–447) when it was common simply to call her the Mother of God or Theotokos. She is called the "all holy" (παναγία) in the title of the *enkomion*, which was composed to celebrate the "festival of the maiden" (παρθενικὴ πανήγυρις). Elsewhere Proclus observes that "land and sea bring gifts to the maiden" (γῆ καὶ θάλαττα δωροφορεῖ τῇ παρθένῳ). To reduce the Hellenic color of his remarks, he resorts to the juxtaposition of Christian terminology (ἡ ἁγία θεοτόκος Παρθένος Μαρία). Proclus of Constantinople. *Enkōmion eis tēn panagian Theotokon Marian*, PG 65, 680C–681B. In a later section of the oration, he criticizes the Hellenes who ridicule the incarnation (κἂν Ἕλληνες κωμῳδῶσι τὸ θαῦμα). Ibid., 684B. It must be borne in mind that, while this piece uses rhetoric highly suited to devotion to Isis or Artemis, its context is Christian. We should not go far wrong, however, in supposing that many recent converts from Hellenic religion made up Proclus' congregation. Cf. Infra, Ch. VII, Sect. 1. One of their requirements will have been hearing the theology of the new religion conceptualized in the terminology of the old.
[268] *Greek Anthology* 16.264.

temples and also at hot springs that were thought to have curative properties. Thus, a temple and cult dedicated to Artemis Sebaste by a freedman of Augustus grew up at Buyuk Tepe Keui in Bithynia.[269] The Neohellenic cult of St. Constantine in existence at the *hagiasma* c. 1929 may well date from the Christianization of the site in Late Antiquity,[270] perhaps deriving from the demolition of the temple and erection of a basilica by that emperor. The previously cited example of the cult of Michael the archistrategos at Colossae-Khonai reflects the initial synthesis of Christian and Hellenic cults that occurred at such sites of religious awe. The goddess might perform cures for her suppliants at temples as well. A marble stele of Roman Imperial date, with an inscription and two human eyes carved in relief, was found at Sardis. It reads: "To Artemis Anaitis: Ammias daughter of Matris erected [this] because of being chastized [in the eyes—]."[271] The editors observe:[272]

> Ammias had some eye complaint which she regarded as a chastisement for sin; in the hope of being cured or in gratitude for a cure she made a propitiatory confession, i.e. publicly acknowledged her sin and the goddess' power.

Another stele, dated by the Sullan era to 172/3 A.D., has a pair of human eyes incised amidst the inscription and is dedicated to Iaso, the divine daughter of the physician god Asklepios:[273]

---

[269] CIG 4.3695c.

[270] "It may be noted that the collocation of natural hot baths and mosques . . . does not necessarily imply a sacred site, . . . but a mosque at a hot spring may also be regarded as a *precaution against unorthodox superstition*." (my italics) Hasluck, *Christianity and Islam*, 108f. The same rationale was attached to providing a *prosmonarios* at springs after the Christianization of the site, as the *Miraculum Michaelis* makes clear. Hasluck indicates elsewhere that the continuities between Hellenic religion and Christianity in Anatolia were much more pervasive and direct than those between Christianity and Islam in the later middle ages. Ibid., 4. Cf. the Pythia Therma, the "Pythian hot springs" noted by Procopius, which later became those of Michael the Archangel at Kuri Yalova in Bithynia (*Buildings* 5.3.16–20). Hasluck, *Christianity and Islam*, 107. The Christian archangel was here quite obviously the successor of the chthonic divinity identified by Hellenes as the local Apollo, who was worshipped as the owner of the subterranean waters. The sick of Constantinople frequented the place until the time of Justinian the Great, who established a palace and bath-house. The church of the archangel, peculiarly referred to as his *temenos* (τοῦ ἀρχαγγέλου τέμενος), with its dormitory, guaranteed the suppression of publicly "unorthodox superstition", that is, the open invocation of the chthonic deity, in line with Justinian's policy of suppressing Hellenic belief and practice.

[271] *Sardis VII: Greek and Latin Inscriptions Part I*, ed. W.H. Buckler and David M. Robinson (Leiden 1932), no. 95, with photo.

[272] Ibid.

[273] Ibid., no. 97.

To the undefiled goddess Iaso.
(θεᾷ ἁγνῇ' Ἰα[σοῖ])
(Eyes)
In the 257th year (of the Sullan era)
Apphion daughter of Apollonios
set up this votive offering.

The practice of reproducing the part of the body which required
healing on a votive stele or other object passed into Christian
euchology during the period of Christianization in the form of less
expensive metal foil reproductions of the organs with prayers incised on them.[274]

Nor did the practice of worshipping female deities in cults parallel to, and apart from, that of the Theotokos entirely die out. John
Cuthbert Lawson notes the evidence for various cults of the Despoina, "Mistress of the World" (ἡ δέσποινα τοῦ κόσμου) and
"Mistress of earth and sea" (ἡ κυρὰ τσῆ γῆς καὶ τσῆ θάλασσας) in
late nineteenth-century Arcadia, Messenia, and Zakynthos, all of
which conform to the character of the chthonic Demeter.[275] The
formula "Mistress of land and sea" also has something in common
with Hellenistic typologies of Isis,[276] just as a molded terracotta
figure of Isis Lactans of fourth-fifth century date from Palestine
does with later representations of the Christian Virgin and Child.[277]
Another set of terracotta figurines discovered at Ephesus around
the turn of the century depicts Artemis with bulging breasts and
holding a small child. One of the images dates from the fourth
century B.C.[278] They bear a striking resemblance to representations
of the Theotokos with Christ. William M. Ramsay refers to this
object as "the Mother-Goddess of Ephesus anthropomorphized."[279]

It will be recalled that with the destruction of the Serapeum in
391 the pre-Christian Ankh cross, a letter of the Egyptian hieroglyphic script, was cited as an oracle from pharaonic sacred texts to
prove that Christ would displace Sarapis as the God of the Nile. A

---

[274] Lawson, *Greek Folklore and Religion*, 58ff.

[275] Ibid., 89–91.

[276] See the various categories listed in the Isis aretalogy of Kyme. Trombley,
"Systemic Analysis of Late Hellenic Religion," 98f.

[277] *Age of Spirituality: Late Antique and Early Christian Art, Third to Seventh Century*,
ed. Kurt Weitzmann (New York 1979), no. 167.

[278] D.G. Hogarth, "Small Objects from the Croesus Temple," in *British
Museum. Excavations at Ephesus: The Archaic Artemisia*, ed. D.G. Hogarth (London
1908), 313–315.

[279] William M. Ramsay, "The Worship of the Virgin Mary at Ephesus,"
Pauline and Other Studies in Early Christian History (London 1906), 139. Cf. Plate II,
Fig. 2. All this is problematical.

bogus Judaic-Christian derivation for the name of Sarapis was circulated at this time as well. Much additional "evidence" of this kind existed amidst the epigraphy and rock-cut reliefs of Egypt to abet such schemes of proselytization even further. How much archaeological material the patriarch Theophilus put to use is hard to say because the literary sources are silent on this point. A likely candidate for such employment was a series of rock-cut reliefs of the pharaohs Ramses IV and Sethos I receiving ritual purification at the hands of two gods pouring water over their heads from large ladles, a veritable "baptism of pharaoh". The flow of water is depicted by many Ankh crosses tumbling down over the kings' bodies.[280] If a Christian interpretation had been given to such iconography—and perhaps it was—it would have been that the pharaohs were baptized into the "life to come", the literal meaning of the Ankh cross in both its hieratic and Christian context. The rite might have been construed as a species of "Christian" baptism, another prophecy of the Christian victory and an inducement for the pagan population of town and countryside to collaborate in the scheme and complete it by becoming Christian.

Other schemes of *Ritenchristianisierung* emerge from the archaeological materials. In the construction of the church of the Evangelists at Alahan in the Isaurian mountains of southeastern Asia Minor, the stonemasons produced an altar of design and workmanship almost identical to pagan altars of Roman Imperial date. The pagan altar of this type was an orthostatic structure hewn out of stone. Its facade imitated a small gabled or arched shrine supported by columns or pillars, with an apse carved into the stone. This recess left a shallow platform whereupon incense, wine, cakes, whey, or other sacrificial substances might be offered to the deity. The Christian altar at Alahan has all these features, but one in addition: a Christian cross stands in high relief at the back of the shallow apse. No reliquary was cut into the stone, thereby making the altar identical to a pagan one in every other respect except for the new symbol and the implicitly new sacrificial ritual. The altar dates from c. 425.[281] The church and altar undoubtedly date from the time when the rugged uplands around Alahan were Christianized. The new catechumenate came down from its abodes to open-air services around the orthostatic Christian altar. The

[280] Alan Gardiner, "The Baptism of Pharaoh," *Journal of Egyptian Archaeology* 36 (1950), 3–12 and Plate I.
[281] Michael Gough, "The Church of the Evangelists at Alahan," *Anatolian Studies* 12 (1962), 75f. and Plate XXX.

missionary activities of John Chrysostom during his exile in Isauria
(after 20 June 404) corroborate the existence of many rural pagans
at this time.[282]

Another element of the pagan koinē of local, non-Hellenic culture crept into Christian ascetic practice, that of stylitism.[283] A
well-known passage in Lucian of Samosata's *Syrian Goddess* (c. 160
A.D.) mentions the existence of two stylite pillars (οἱ φαλλοί) in
the propylaia of the great temple at Hierapolis in Euphratensis.
Here pagan holy men called "phallus-walkers" (οἱ φαλλοβάται)
stood atop tall pillars for long periods of time, behaving like animate statues and praying to the local Baals in their high places
amidst the clouds:[284]

> In these propylaia also stand two phalluses having a height of 300
> feet which Dionysus erected. A man goes up one of these twice each
> year and dwells on the peak for the time of seven days. And the
> reason for the ascent is this: the people think that he converses with
> the gods on high and asks blessings for all Syria, and that the gods give
> ear to the prayers from near at hand. . . . Many persons arrive and
> put gold and silver, or in some cases bronze [coin], whatever they see
> fit, into a basket lying in front, each speaking his own name. Another
> man standing nearby announces it upward. And [the stylite] receives
> it and makes a prayer for each [contributor], and while praying
> strikes a bronze thing that makes a loud and harsh sound when
> shaken. [The stylite] never sleeps. For if sleep should ever take him, a
> scorpion goes up and rouses him and injures him. This is the penalty
> laid upon him for sleeping.

The connection between this style of prayer and that of the Christian stylites is generally ridiculed, although the argument of continuity seems obvious. The routine resembles that of the Christian
cult in several respects, including the making of offerings in specie,
the use of intermediaries to convey the petitions of pilgrims, the
avoidance of sleep, and the siting of steles in sacred enclosures. The
Christian monks went a step further by residing permanently atop

---

[282] Infra, Ch. VII, Sect. 5.
[283] On the subject of *Christian* stylitism, see: Hippolyte Delehaye, *Les Saints
stylites* (Subsidia Hagiographica 14, Brussels 1923). On the acts of Symeon Styli-
ties the Elder, see infra, Ch. VIII, Sect. 2 and 4. On Thalaleios the Stylite, Ch.
VIII, Sect. 2. This subject has attracted less scholarship that it deserves. One
exception to this is the detailed commentary given to the life of Daniel the Stylite
in *Three Byzantine Saints*, tr. Norman H. Baynes and Elizabeth Dawes (1948; repr.
Crestwood, N.Y. 1977), 72–84.
[284] Lucian of Samosata, *De Syria Dea* 28–29 in *Lucian*, tr. A.M. Harmon, 4
(London-Cambridge, Mass.: 1925) 278–383. In general see: H. Stocks, "Studien
zu Lukians 'De Syria Dea'," *Berytus* 4 (1937), 1–40.

their pillars to demonstrate the unique power of their new God and by reciting the psalmody.[285]

A midrash whose tradition ultimately goes back to rabbi Phinehas bar Hama (c. 350–400) mentions a pagan priest of Damascus called Abba Gulish who converted to Judaism. As a Jew he spent a day standing on a pillar in front of a pagan temple at Damascus as part of a penitential ritual to make amends for having embezzled money from the sacred funds kept for the poor in the synagogue at Tiberias. The midrash corroborates the existence of stylite pillars at the Syrian temples and provides a good example of adapting stylitism to a monotheistic religion. Finally, it brings the continuity of Syrian polytheistic stylitism down to the later fourth century A.D., when the temples were being occupied by monotheists for various purposes. Abba Gulish had been guilty of similar offenses before this as a pagan priest, having converted to Judaism after "the idol", that is the deity whose *numen* was thought to reside in the cult image, had blinded him and the God of Abraham cured him of this incapacity. Now blinded again, this time by the Jewish God for his acts of larceny, Abba Gulish is said to have recovered his eyesight after confessing his offenses to both deities on a pillar erected for such purposes in front of the temple in Damascus, which was perhaps that of the local Baal known to us as Zeus Damascenus.[286] To the surprise of Hellene and Jew, he gave testimony to the Holy One. Abbas Gulish's monotheistic confession is said to have gotten him back his eyesight, and also to have converted many pagans:[287]

> When they reached the hamlets in the vicinity of Damascus, people gathered about him and said: "Lo, it is Abba Gulish." And they further said: "The idol was right to blind your eyes". Said he to them: "I, too, have come only to entreat him and to make my peace with him; perchance he will restore my sight. Go and gather together all the people of the state." They went and multitudes upon multitudes assembled in the idol-house and (even) went up on the roofs. When the place was full, he asked his wife to stand him upon a pillar that he knew there. He went and stood upon it and said to the assembly: "My brethren, citizens of Damascus, when I was a priest and ministered to the idol, people used to leave deposits with me, and I subsequently denied receiving them, because the image has neither eyes to see nor ears to hear, so that he might punish me. Now I went to a God whose eyes roam the whole world, and no plot is hidden

[285] Supra, Ch. II, n. 283.

[286] Deichmann, "Kirchen in Heilligtümern," 116, no. 11 (bibliography).

[287] Quoted from Ephraim E. Urbach, *The Sages: Their Concepts and Beliefs*, tr. I. Abrahams (Jerusalem 1975), 105f.

from Him . . . hence He blinded my eyes [again]." . . . Before ever he descended from the pillar the Holy One, blessed be He, gave him better sight than he had enjoyed before, so that His name might be sanctified in the world: and thousands and tens of thousands of Gentiles were converted through him.

Abba Gulish's deviousness in feigning a desire to beg the pardon of the pagan god enabled him to assemble a large crowd of onlookers. This, in turn, enabled him to make a monotheistic statement of great impact. Unlike the apostle Paul's proclamation of the "Unknown God" before the Areopagus assembly in Athens, Abba Gulish is said to have used not ambiguity but words that amounted to apostasy to set the stage for the confession and "miracle" that followed.

The story of Abba Gulish reflects the common belief that pagan gods at times inflicted "chastisement" or "correction" (κόλασις) on their adherents for sin. It will be recalled that a certain Ammia of Sardis erected a stele of Artemis Anaitis after becoming convinced that the goddess had blinded her.[288] A Sardian man also erected such a stele to Men Axiottenos, a local variant of Attis. The man publicly confessed an unstated sin (ὁμολογῶ τ[ὸ ἁμάρτημ]α) to the divinity after it had shown him mercy ([ἐλεη]θείς) when he fell into a state of ill-health ([κα]ταπίπτω εἰς ἀ[σθένειαν]).[289] Those who recovered from sickness not caused by some sin might set up a shrine or image of Asklepios ('Ασκληπῖον) in thanksgiving for their restored health (αὐτοῦ ὁλοκληρία).[290] This terminology was passed on to Christianity, especially when it was necessary to demonstrate the superiority of the "magic" of the new religion. The ritual often differed, however, consisting of Christian prayers and making the sign of the cross over the sick person with oil.[291] The afflicted person and his family might then exclaim a "One God" formula and accept the blessing of the cross which introduced them to the catechumenate.[292]

The sense of personal crisis in an illness and the cure in the name of the Christian God (the so-called "miracle", but actually and simply a work of his virtue, a property of his power over nature, an ἀρετῆς ἔργον), at times led through two stages of "atheism" prior

---

[288] Supra, this section. Cf. Hasan Malay, "New Confession-Inscriptions in the Manisa and Bergama Museums," *Epigraphica Anatolica* 12 (1988), 147–152 and Tafeln 10–12, for an exceptionally important collection of texts.
[289] *Sardis: Inscriptions* (1932), no. 96.
[290] *Sardis: Inscriptions* (1932), no. 94.
[291] Infra, Ch. VII, Sect. 1.
[292] Supra, Ch. III, Sect. 2.

to conversion to Christianity. The first stage was the Hellene's initial despair in the healing power of the old deity. This led in turn to the use of base sorceries to reverse the illness. The second stage of atheism came with the failure of this magic. With nowhere else to turn, the sick person might do the unthinkable and call upon the Christian God, apostasizing from the old multiplicity of divinities in a radical "leap of faith", or rather change of allegiance. This process was pragmatic and operated in both directions between the old and new religions. An example of this "second stage of atheism", that is the turn to Christian healing, turns up in the anonymous and undated *Miracles of Saint Kosmas and Damian*.[293] As with the Hellenic cult of Asklepios, persons seeking cures (τὰ χαρίσματα τῶν ἰαμάτων αὐτῶν) would incubate in the church of Kosmas and Damian, the holy physicians "who took no fee" (οἱ ἀνάργυροι). It had a special area designated for that purpose beside the small baptistry (ἐν τῷ μικρῷ τῶν ἐνταῦθα φωτιστηρίῳ), a site full of significance for pagans seeking cures.[294] The sick person would spend the night, or as many nights as needed to bring about the healing dream-vision in which the two martyrs confirmed the cure and faith of the sick person.[295]

Apart from the Christianization of rite no serious typological differences existed between this and Hellenic incubation, as for example that practiced at the Asklepieion of Athens through c. 484.[296] Both systems of belief relied on the impact of the new surroundings in the shrine to provoke vivid dreams in which the deity or martyrs performed physiological or spiritual surgery on the afflicted believer.[297] Christian mosaics and Hellenic cult images, along with autosuggestion and priestly encouragement, caused the divine figures to emerge in lifelike, material form in the dream-sequence. Modern psychoanalytic research has shown that dreams are invariably creative reconstructions of the previous day's experiences synthesized with earlier, often deeply buried recollections in the unconscious mind.[298] The catharitic effect of admitting the dream experience to the priest in the protective atmosphere of the

---

[293] *Kosmas und Damian. Texte und Einleitung*, ed. Ludwig Deubner (Leipzig-Berlin 1907).

[294] *Kosmas und Damian*, 118, line 26.

[295] For bibliography on Hellenic incubation, see infra, Ch. V, Sect. 2, n. 36.

[296] Infra, Ch. IV, Sect. 3.

[297] Cf. the dramatic dreams recorded in the *Acta S. Artemii* in *Varia Graeca Sacra*, ed. A. Papadopoulos-Kerameus (Petersburg 1909), 1–79.

[298] Stanley Palombo, *Dreaming and Memory* (New York 1978), 219, quoted in Anthony Storr, *Solitude: A Return to the Self* (New York 1988), 25.

shrine often resulted in the improvement of the patient's physiological and spiritual disposition.

It should be evident even to the least skeptical person that the "cures" found in Hellenic and Christian incubation narratives comprise only a very small number of the cases. One could not expect a shrine to prosper if the priesthood published documents about failed cures. It seems probable, therefore, that a strong kernel of historicity exists in reports about social phenomena in the miracle collections, despite the inexplicability of the cures, whose publication lay in the hands of priestly redactors skilled in the rudiments of medicine. In an age without the techniques of microbiology, there was much about disease that mystified even the adherents of Galen and Hippocrates.

The first case of relevance reported in the Acta of Kosmas and Damian concerns a Hellene who went to the martyrs' shrine, but invoked the divine pair Castor and Polydeukes instead.[299] He was a lawyer whose friends had encouraged him to do this. They are said to have gotten the idea from books on mythology (ἐν τοῖς ματαίοις καὶ ἐπιβλαβέσιν ἀναγνώσμασιν ἐμφερομένων μύθων Κάστορος καὶ Πολυδεύκους).[300] The typologies of the local Hellenic and Christian cults evidently converged so closely that one could see the common pagan origin of the ritual. It is also possible that a Christian basilica had been erected over a pagan temple of the Dioskouroi.[301] Whatever the truth was, the Hellene is said to have been denied any dream-vision of the Dioskouroi, but to have received one of Kosmas and Damian instead, which is not improbable in view of the psychological mechanisms in play. The Christian wardens of the shrine accepted all comers, including Hellenes who had ulterior cultic motives, much as they distributed bread to pagan and Christian alike at their basilicas,[302] as this procedure brought about at least a marginal increase in the number of conversions. With the perceived cure accomplished, the barrister accepted Christianity and cursed the names of the Dioskouroi (βδελυξάμενος τὰ ὀνόματα καὶ τὰ σεβάσματα Κάστορος καὶ Πολυδεύκους). He dressed his remarks in the terminology of Roman customary law:

---

[299] *Kosmas und Damian*, 113–117.

[300] *Kosmas und Damian*, 114, line 21f.

[301] One thinks here of the Aphaka temple converted into a church in the reign of Constantine the Great (*post* 324): the old temple was pulled down, then rebuilt into a Christian basilica using the same stones. Deichmann, "Kirchen in Heiligtümern" 108. The blocks of the Marneion at Gaza are said to have been revered by the Hellenes after being used to pave a courtyard outside the temenos, wherein the Eudoxiana cathedral had been erected. Infra, Ch. III, Sect. 4.

[302] Infra, Ch. III, Sect. 6.

the martyrs became his benefactors (εὐεργέται) and patrons (πρόξενοι).³⁰³ It is said that many other Hellenes became Christians upon his testimony of the cure, after learning to "hate the impious worship, or rather perdition, of the Hellenes" (μισῆσαι τὴν ἀσεβῆ τῶν Ἑλλήνων θρησκείαν μᾶλλον δὲ ἀπώλειαν).³⁰⁴

This affair, which possibly belongs to the first half of the fifth century, suggests that at least some Hellenes were hesitating between the old and new religions, waiting for some convincing sign or testimony. Pagans and Christians mixed freely at all levels of society, as for example a Christian (πιστός) businessman mentioned in a second miracle of Kosmas and Damian who had a contract (συνάλλαγμα) with a pagan colleague. Apart from issues like sacrifice, animate idols, credence in Hellenic oracles and so forth, few pragmatic values separated the men. The Christian, who paid regular Friday visits to the matryrion, invited his friend to accompany him and "to apostasize from Hellenic error as it was soul-destroying and opposed to God because of sacrifice to inanimate idols, but instead to offer himself as a bloodless sacrifice to the only immortal God".³⁰⁵ This statement, which owes more to the authorship of the miracle collection than any actual conversation, combines three aspects of the ongoing polemic: the "soul-destroying" (ψυχοβλαβής) nature of sacrifice (an expression found in one of the quasi-Justinianic laws issued in fact by the emperor Zeno c. 484),³⁰⁶ the "inanimate" character of cult images (a question of fact that few Christians or Hellenes disputed),³⁰⁷ and the singleness of the Christian God as a point of differentiation between him and the Semitic-Hellenic pantheon (a point emphasized by the "One God" inscriptions of Syria),³⁰⁸ who is here "the only immortal God" (ὁ μόνος ἀθάνατος θεός). These rather common slogans convinced the Hellenic businessman to visit the shrine of Kosmas and Damian. Its emotional impact is difficult but not impossible to reconstruct. In this instance it was sufficient to lure the Hellene into the martyrion. He was already close to accepting the Christian

---

³⁰³ *Kosmas und Damian* 116, lines 58–60 and 66f. This Hellene went from despair of the old cults almost at once to confidence in Christianity while in the church, but we cannot exclude the possibility that there was an intermediate stage, when he tried sorceries and mantic rites. The hagiographer has perhaps telescoped the "first and second stages of atheism" because Christians considered the gods of healing and the *daimones* of medical magic to be one and the same.
³⁰⁴ *Kosmas und Damian*, 116f., lines 68–73.
³⁰⁵ *Kosmas und Damian*, 117, lines 6–11.
³⁰⁶ Supra, Ch. I, Sect. 6.
³⁰⁷ Supra, Ch. I, Sect. 3.
³⁰⁸ Infra, Ch. X passim, and Appendix V.

revaluation of ethics on such questions as the need to practice a
sober life-style (σώφρονα βίον) and to give to the poor.[309] Openly
entering the building, he capitulated and asked how he might
believe and be saved (ὅπως πιστεύσας σωθήσεται), providing that
a "vision and divine illumination" (ὀπτασία τὶς καὶ θεία
ἔλλαμψις) could be provoked. The method proved quite simple.
The Hellene toured the narthex and small baptistry of the church
until he reached the spot where his friend prayed on Fridays, and
was filled with religious awe (ἔμφοβος) as the evening progressed.

It was here that the Hellene incubated and experienced the
hoped-for dream-vision. It consisted of two phases: first, the
apparition of three boys eating bread dipped in wine (βουκάκρατον),
followed by the coming of the martyrs who gave him "common" or
eucharistic bread to eat (ἄρτους κοινοὺς . . . ἐσθίειν) with the
cup.[310] This nocturnal religious experience tipped the scales and
brought the man to accept baptism. Something as small as a
liberation of his unconscious mind in sleep sufficed. The apparition
of the martyrs belonged to the experience of the past day, probably
through the viewing of mosaics, but that of the boys seems to derive
from an earlier experience modified by a eucharistic symbolism
which the redactor probably exaggerates. Perhaps the small boys
were siblings, childhood friends, or deceased children of his own. If
so, the hagiographer leaves the reader in ambiguity. It remains
evident that such trifling "wonder" as this caused some of the
conversions that the "One God" inscriptions attest.

V. The Christianization of the Decurion Classes

The decurion class, composed of the households of men who sat in
the city councils of the Greek towns, felt the cultural impact of the
phenomena described in previous sections in varying degrees.
Apart from their fiscal and administrative duties connected with
the repair of public buildings and raising the *annona* and *capitatio*,
not to mention the running of their own estates, these folk set the
tone for cultural life in the cities between 370–529. Their grasp of
the Greek *paideia*, however mediocre, guaranteed the survival of
Hellenic religion, which was closely linked to a certain literary
fastidiousness gained in the grammar schools of metropoleis like
Constantinople, Antioch, Athens, and Alexandria.[311] If anyone

---

[309] *Kosmas und Damian*, 117f., lines 15–17.
[310] *Kosmas und Damian*, 118f.
[311] For extensive discussion, see: Jones, *Later Roman Empire*, 737–757 and pas-

wanted clear instructions for the performance of sacrifice, he needed only to recall certain sections of the Homeric poems that gave practically a clinical description of how to cut the animal open and what sections to lay onto the altar.[312] This fastidiousness was reflected, as well, in the ornamentation of urban townhouses and rural residences with the best mosaic work that one could buy and local talent could produce. This decorative art, with appropriate inscriptions, often reveals local religious preoccupations.[313] Many young men returned to their provincial homes to enjoy their estates and play some role in local politics.[314] This reintroduction of talent is attested in the funerary inscriptions.[315]

The clustering and comparison of inscriptions from many different provinces without due attention to the local context of each text can hardly be expected to yield a clear picture of the transformation of Hellenic religious ideas into Christianity. The remainder of this work does examine this process in a variety of local contexts, both urban and rural, including Gaza, Athens, Alexandria, Aphrodisias, rural Bithynia, the Limestone Massif east of Antioch in Syria, and the Hauran in Arabia. It will nevertheless be necessary to analyse certain texts whose singular importance requires independent comment, even though the site and epigraphic environment provide no additional evidence about the local context, among them Hierapolis in Phrygia, Antioch in Pisidia, Kourion in Cyprus, and Caesarea in Cappadocia, with some reference to other areas as well.

The first of these, an honorific inscription for a certain Magnus, comes from Hierapolis, the "Holy City" of Phrygia Pactiana. This man, who was probably Flavius Magnus, held the office of *vicarius* of Asia in 352–354. An inscription was erected to commemorate his services to the city in the theatre of Hierapolis. The frank expression of Hellenic belief reflects the religious mentality of the city councillors. It is rendered in a mixture of Epic and Hellenistic koinē. The inscription is unfortunately damaged:[316]

---

sim. There is also a valuable discussion in J.H. Liebeschuetz, *Antioch* (Oxford 1972), 41–51, 167–186, and esp. 224–255.

[312] Walter Burkert, *Homo Necans: The Anthropology of Ancient Greek Sacrificial Ritual and Myth*, tr. P. Bing (Berkeley 1983), 3ff.

[313] See the discussion of the Eustolius Complex at Kourion in Cyprus. Infra, this section.

[314] Infra, Ch. V, Sect. 3–4.

[315] Infra, Ch. VII, Sect. 2. Trombley, "Boeotia in Late Antiquity," 225f. A study of this question in connection with the funerary texts reproduced in the *Greek Anthology* remains a desideratum.

[316] SEG 36 (1986), no. 1198.

For Good Luck. This marvellous work would not as yet have such
great splendor but that the wise Magnus now set up. . . . For he
devised it joined with stones and . . . matter, and by oracular writings . . . [large gap in text] . . . beautiful all . . . as a lover of wisdom
he completed a temple of the nymphs (?) . . . and set up . . . [god-
dess?] honored with lovely festivities, . . . after the residents made
recompense with a statue and inscriptions inside the holy city. Be
mindful of Magnus the judge, offspring of child-rearing (and) fair-
minded Dike, a man who gave right judgement, savior, preserver of
traditional law, ritually pure *vicarius*. For the Phrygian Mother knows
how to keep her graces for good works.

I am unable with Pleket to detect a solely "political motive" for this
inscription. Flavius Magnus appears, rather, to have protected the
local cults of Hierapolis in some fashion, for he is called "preserver
of traditional law" (θεμισσόον) and "ritually pure" (ἀγνόν) prefect, a peculiar juxtaposition suggesting that previous *vicarii Asianae*
(vicars of the diocese of Asiana) had had different sets of priorities.
His services perhaps consisted only in preserving the temples and
defending Hellenes from overzealous inquiries into their cultic
activities. It has been argued, as well, that Delphi kept its title
"holy city" (given here as ἱερῆς . . . πόληος) until the majority of
its city councillors became Christian,[317] but this came only during
the reign of the co-emperors Valens and Valentinian I c. 364–375.
To judge from the evidence of other sites, there is no compelling
reason to suppose that Hierapolis was not still largely pagan at
such an early date as 352–354. The sponsors of the inscription
tossed in Dike, a divine personification of a virtue that had no
cult.[317a] The reference to Kybele or the Phrygian Mother is a
different matter (ἡ Φρυγίης γὰρ Μήτηρ το[ῖς] ἀγαθοῖς οἶδεν
ἔχειν χάριτας). The cults of female deities, like Artemis, Kybele
and Ge, persisted throughout the fifth and sixth centuries, and are
still occasionally attested in the eighth and ninth.[318] Kosmas of
Jerusalem (8th century) mentions a story he had heard about
conditions in rural Caria until his own times:[319]

---

[317] Trombley has argued thus in "Boeotia in Late Antiquity," 222. Lebadeia in
Boeotia, where the priesthood of Zeus Trophonius is attested in the third century
(*post* 213 A.D.) (SEG 32.475), still claimed to be his "holy city" (ἱερὰ Λεβαδέων
πόλις) during the reign of Constantius I Chlorus (ob. 306). Claude Vatin, "Quel-
ques inscriptions d'époch impériale," *Bulletin de Correspondence Hellénique* 90 (1966)
246f. Cf. Julian the Apostate's repeated reference to Alexandria as a "holy city"
some three decades before the destruction of the Serapeum in 391 (τὴν ἱερὰν
αὖθις ἐμιάνατε πόλιν). *Ep.* 21 ("To the Demos of Alexandria") (Wright 3, 60ff.).
[317a] But cf. Georg Kaibel, *Epigrammata Graeca ex Lapidibus Conlecta* (Berlin 1878),
no. 909, mentioning figuratively a temenos of Dike (Megara, 5th c. A.D.).
[318] Trombley, "Paganism in the Greek World," 334f., 344, and 349–351. For
Artemis in the fifth century, see infra, Ch. VII, Sect. 1.
[319] Cosmas of Jerusalem, *Scholia in Gregorii Carmina*, PG 38, 502.

Certain irrational pagans in the mountains of Caria practice self-castration even until the present day, as the story goes, gripped by this ancient custom.

There is no particular reason to doubt that the Hellenes of Hierapolis c. 352 still sought Kybele's blessings, so long as their estates in the Maeander valley continued to yield a considerable surplus. There is other relevant evidence on this point.

Julian the Apostate attempted to revitalize that same cult at Pessinus in Galatia Salutaris only a decade later, c. June 362, where a high-priest (ἀρχιερεύς) named Arsakios presided over the local cults.[320] Julian sent a letter adding such duties to Arsakios' tasks as showing hospitality to foreigners (ἡ περὶ τοὺς ξένους φιλανθρωπία), maintaining the pagan nekropoleis (ἡ περὶ τὰς ταφὰς τῶν νεκρῶν προμήθεια), and supervising the personal piety of the priests under his jurisdiction (ἡ . . . σεμνότης κατὰ τὸν βίον).[321] Any number of pagan priests existed in the towns of Galatia at this time.[322] The sacred rites of sacrifice were once again practiced (ἱερατικῆς λειτουργίας) with the aid of temple servants (θεραπόντων).[323] Christianity was making inroads into the priestly families, for Julian warns them against atheism (ἀθεότης), a Hellenic term for the new religion.[324] Some priests had been practicing skilled and unskilled trades that cast discredit on their religious office (τέχνης . . . ἐργασίας).[325] Julian therefore assigned revenues in kind from the imperial estates to the temples of Galatia Salutaris, an annual donation of 30,000 *modii* of grain and 60,000 *sextarii* of wine. Constantine the Great or Constantius II had evidently confiscated the estates of the Pessiniote temples, for the fifth part of this allocation was to go to "the poor who served the priests" (ὧν τὸ μὲν πέμπτον εἰς τοὺς πένητας τοὺς τοῖς ἱερεῦσιν ὑπηρετουμένους ἀναλίσκεσθαι).[326] The lack of temple lands had thus impoverished the wardens, deacons, and doorkeepers. Pagan villages still existed round about Pessinus, but during the Constantinian epoch (c. 324–362) had ceased to make first-fruit offerings to the gods (τὰς Ἑλληνικὰς κώμας ἀπάρχεσθαι τοῖς θεοῖς τῶν καρπῶν).[327] In deference to priestly authority, Julian

---

[320] Julian, *Ep.* 22 (Wright 3, 66–73).
[321] Julian, *Ep.* 22 (Wright 3, 68, lines 4–7).
[322] ὅσοι περὶ τὴν Γαλατίαν εἰσὶν ἱερεῖς. Julian, *Ep.* 22 (Wright 3, 68, line 9f.).
[323] Julian, *Ep.* 22 (Wright 3, 68, lines 11–13).
[324] Julian, *Ep.* 22 (Wright 3, 68, line 15).
[325] Julian, *Ep.* 22 (Wright 3, 68, line 18).
[326] Julian, *Ep.* 22 (Wright 3, 68f.).
[327] Julian, *Ep.* 22 (Wright 3, 70, line 9f.).

now reduced imperial officials to private citizens when entering a
temenos. Julian closes the letter by offering further financial help to
Arsakios "if the entire people should become suppliants of the
Mother of the Gods" (πανδημεὶ τῆς μητρὸς τῶν θεῶν ἱκέτας
γενέσθαι).[328] It should be obvious that the cult of Kybele at Pessinus had fallen into decline, but that its *territorium* still contained a
noticeable number of pagan villages. The local epigraphy suggests
that the rustics began entering the Christian church in large numbers only after these measures collapsed with the untimely death of
Julian in 363, a paradigm borne out by the epigraphic evidence in
some parts of Phrygia[329] and in the Limestone Massif east of Antioch
in Syria.[330] It is thus quite difficult to accept the notion that the
reference to Kybele in the Hierapolis inscription should be considered "a political rather than a religious metaphor (sic)".[331]

The obscure phrasing of some inscriptions makes it extremely
difficult to ascertain the religious belief of those who erected it.[332]
Nor are the canons of interpretation always in agreement. Such are
the problems connected with two funerary inscriptions erected by
the family of Gaius Calpurnius Collega Macedon, a city councillor
(βουλευτής) of Antioch in Pisidia. The phraseology of the texts is
Hellenic, but is susceptible to both pagan and Christian interpretations. The ambiguity is heightened by the badly damaged right-hand
side of the stone, which reveals no crosses or other symbols of Christian cult. Both William M. Ramsay and C.P. Jones have attempted
to resolve the enigma. They have also come to opposite conclusions:[333]

> Gaius Calpurnius Collega Macedon, city councillor, a man worthy of
> honor who was accomplished in every virtue, as the ancient . . .
> says. . . . A rhetor among the first ten of Athens. A philosopher in the
> [school?] of Plato and Aristotle. A master-physician in the books and
> works of Hippocrates who lived among men thirty years and . . .
> days. By the providence of God and in the company of sacred angels
> [he . . .] to the sky more quickly than is necessary . . ., leaving behind
> the clay chiton hither . . . having fitted out the tomb for his most
> sweet and beloved. . . . And . . . G. Calpurnius Makedon.
>
> Collega, young child of immortal virtue, scion of sacred Collega
> and of blessed Makedon, the young immortal. Remembrance has
> joined him with the ancients. His mother Magna, mother of noble
> sons, deposited his sweet limb (?), he a wise physician who lived
> twenty years.

[328] Julian, *Ep.* 22 (Wright 3, 72, line 14f.).
[329] Infra, Ch. VII, Sect. 2 and 4.
[330] Infra, Ch. X, passim.
[331] SEG 36 (1986), no. 1198, p. 366.
[332] See the problems of interpretation connected with some ambiguous inscriptions at Aphrodisias. Infra, Ch. VI, Sect. 2.
[333] C.P. Jones, "A Family of Pisidian Antioch," *Phoenix* 36 (1982), 264–271.

These inscriptions probably belong to the second half of the fourth century.

In this instance, one can do little more than indicate the hermeneutic reasons that permit one to regard Gaius Makedon as either a Hellene or Christian. Christian iatrosophists, that is philosophers schooled in medicine as their specialty, are exceedingly rare, if attested at all during the fourth century.[334] While belief in the "providence of God" (θεοῦ προνοίᾳ) has a certain Christian cachet, it is in essence a Stoic formulation that turns up, for example, in a letters of Julian the Apostate, "by the providence of him who oversees all things [Apollo]" (τοῦ πάντα ἐφορῶντος προνοίᾳ), and also Pronoia as an epithet of Athena.[335] A pagan cult of angels existed in rural Phrygia, in fact in the vicinity of Hierapolis, at Laodikea, where a synoikism of Hellenic and Christian cults subsisted until the latter religion prevailed.[336] The expression in the Makedon inscription is peculiar, calling the angels "sacred" rather than "holy" (ἱερῶν ἀγγέλων συνοδίᾳ). Here the preponderance of evidence falls on the side of identifying them as Hellenic angels because their function closely approximates that of the spirits thought to accompany the souls of men through the different heavens to the arch of the firmament (εἰς [ο]ὐρανὸν ἐξ ἀνθρώπων).[337] In Iamblichus of Chalkis' theology, souls associating

---

[334] Cf. two Christian physicians named in the funerary inscriptions of Korykos in Cilicia Trachea, whose qualifications seem to have been negligible. Frank R. Trombley, "Korykos in Cilicia Trachis (sic): The Economy of a Small Coastal City in Late Antiquity (Saec. V–VI)–A Précis," *Ancient History Bulletin* 1 (1987), 23.

[335] Julian, *Or.* 4 ("Hymn to King Helios Dedicated to Sallust") (Wright 1, 406, line 22f. and 408, line 7). *Imp. Caesaris Flavii Claudii Iuliani Epistulae Leges Poematia Fragmenta Varia*, ed. J. Bidez and F. Cumont (Paris-London 1922), *Ep.* 44 ("To Priscus") 14, line 10.

[336] Supra, Ch. II, Sect. 4.

[337] The ascent of the soul towards God in the firmament seems, as a concept, to go back to Plato's *Phaedrus*. See Origen's critique of Hellenic ideas in *Contra Celsum* 6.19–23, tr. Henry Chadwick (Cambridge 1965), 331–337. The spheres of the upper air occupied by gods, archangels, angels, archons, and *daimones* are treated in some depth by Iamblichus, *De Mysteriis*, Book 2. The lack of materiality found in the cultivated lives of philosophers will have enabled their souls to ascend most easily through the lower spheres occupied by *daimones*. Theurgic devices directed against the *daimones* will have assisted the process. For ordinary men, magic incantations seem to have been the principal remedy, until the advent of Christianity, which degraded the power of the *daimones* forever. The angels that accompanied G. Calpurnius Makedon were no doubt thought to be the angels occupying the heavenly sphere above that of the *daimones*. The angels will then have sent Makedon's soul on the sphere of the lesser gods according to this line of reasoning. Such notions belong to the realm of Neoplatonism rather than the Stoicism that elsewhere typifies the inscription of Makedon.

with angels would necessarily attain the abode of the gods.[338] The "clay chiton" or "garment" seems plausibly to be a Christian reference to the corruptibility of the body in the tomb, but obvious Stoic-polytheistic parallels exist to this expression.[339] The monument is literally called a "hero's tomb" (τὸ ἡρῷον), a Hellenic term having an occasional Christian currency, although "place of sleep" (κοιμητήριον) and other terms are more commonly Christian.[340] The family of a Christian educated in the Greek *paideia* would probably not have objected to calling the tomb a *herōon*, but nothing about the inscription compels such an interpretation.[341] G. Calpurnius Macedon seems thus to have been a Hellene, a supposition that is perfectly consistent with the known distribution of pagans and Christians down to the end of the fourth century. There is no reason to suppose that Macedon's wife was a Christian either.[342]

---

[338] Iamblichus, *De Mysteriis* 1.7 (Des Places 50f.).

[339] In Marcus Aurelius' *Ta eis heauton*, the references to the human body resemble those in Makedon's inscription quite closely. It is a "vessel" or "pitcher" (ἀγγεῖον) (an object most often made of clay) (3.3). Man is called "a little soul carrying a body" (ψυχάριον εἶ βαστάζον νεκρόν). (4.41). The body is elsewhere the "sheath" of the soul (τὸ ἔλυτρον) (9.3), and an "overlying vessel" (τὸ περικείμενον ἀγγειῶδες) (10.38). Other analogies are given for the body, such as "husks and sloughs" (φλοιῶν καὶ καθαρμάτων) (12.2), and especially "garment" (περιβολή), a perfect correspondence with the *chiton* of the Makedon inscription (12.2). The body is, in fact, "the baser and mortal part" (τῇ ἀτιμοτέρᾳ καὶ θνητῇ μοίρᾳ) of man (11.19). I have dwelt on these similes at length to demonstrate that this notion is fundamentally Stoic and not, C.P. Jones supposes, a Neoplatonic construction. The text is that of Marcus Aurelius Antoninus, *The Communings with Himself*, ed. tr. C.R. Haines (Cambridge, Mass.-London 1930). It would seem, therefore, that the rather old-fashioned Stoic notions were still in circulation amongst the conservative decurion classes of Asia Minor well after they had begun to pass out of favor with the professional Hellenic philosophers.

[340] Each city and district had its own characteristic Christian term for tomb. In Attica, it was *koimētērion*. Infra, Ch. IV, Sect. 1. At Korykos in Cilicia Trachea, it was *sōmatothēkē* (literally, "body box"). For references, see: Trombley, "Korykos." A term enjoying currency in both religions was *mnēmorion* ("memorial place"). For a Christian example, see: J. Laurent, "Delphes chrétien," *Bulletin de Correspondence Hellénique* 23 (1899), 273–275. The list might be extended considerably. For the funerary terminology of northern Syria in the Antiochene and Apamene, see infra, Ch. X passim. For the Hauran district of Arabia, infra, Ch. XI.

[341] In a locality where persons affixed crosses to *koimētērion* inscriptions, but not to *herōion* texts, the latter should usually be regarded as pagan. Cf. infra, Ch. X, Sect. 5.

[342] C.P. Jones argues that "the ancients" (τοῖς παλαιοῖς) in Calpurnius' wife's inscription should be taken to mean "the gods". In my view, it should be taken more probably to mean "the ancient dead" who lie in ancient tombs. The life of Theodore of Sykeon, although late, illustrates this point, referring to a marble sarkophagos "having in it the corpses of ancient pagans protected by *daimones*" (ἐχούσης σκηνώματα ἀρχαίων ἀνθρώπων Ἑλλήνων). George the Monk, *Vie de Théodore*, Cap. 118 (Festugière, 1, 94f.). Lampe in *Patristic Greek Lexicon* provides many references to "the ancient", such as pre-Christian men, beliefs and prac-

Basil of Caesarea, who presided over that city c. 370–379 as archbishop of First Cappadocia, had urban and rural Hellenes in the areas under his jurisdiction. His letters mention them only in passing, probably because of his greater preoccupation with resolving the theological debate with the semi-Arians and with the pastoral care of Christians.[343] Thus, in writing to Vitus, bishop of Carrhae-Ḥarrān in 376, Basil makes no reference to the prevailing astral and planetary cults there but advises the bishop to greet "all the brotherhood in Christ" (πᾶσαν τὴν ἐν Χριστῷ ἀδελφότητα) as though Ḥarrān were no more pagan than most places. Basil had made the personal acquaintance of some Hellenes as an inevitable consequence of his position. For example, he kept in contact with a pagan philosopher named Eustathius through 357, as is evident from Basil's references to the latter's "opinions".[344] Late in life Basil addressed a letter to the elder Harmatios, a Hellene evidently of decurion rank whose son had converted to Christianity. The locale seems to have been Caesarea itself. The son was still subject to his father under the Roman law of *patriapotestas* (τῷ νόμῳ τῆς φύσεως καὶ τῷ πολιτικῷ). Basil pleads with Harmatios not to interfere:[345]

> Since he has preferred the God of us Christians, that is true God, before the gods of your people, which are numerous and are worshipped through material symbols, do not be angry at him but admire instead his nobility of soul.

To assuage the parental fury, which perhaps consisted of disinheriting the son, Basil assures old Harmatios that through their prayers the Christian congregation had accepted him as a Christian along with his son. There was an obvious conflict between the two generations, with the younger favoring the new religion because of the dynamism of Basil's teaching.[346] The outcome of the family squabble is unknown, but time was on the side of the new religion. Basil had sufficient personal respect for Harmatios not to accuse him of worshipping inanimate idols. Instead, he refers to a polytheism that made use of "material symbols" to elucidate ideas

---

tices. It is also used adjectivally of the Logos and substantively of the Father, the latter being a peculiar usage deriving from the Septuagint. This is admittedly a tentative list, but I find it difficult to think of "the ancients" as the gods.

[343] Basil of Caesarea, *Ep.* 255 in *Saint Basil: The Letters*, tr. R. Deferrari *et al.*, 4 (London-Cambridge, Mass. 1934), 24f.

[344] Basil of Caesarea, *Ep.* 1 (Deferrari 1, 1f.).

[345] Basil of Caesarea, *Ep.* 276 (Deferrari 4, 156–159).

[346] Cf. the use of Basil's *Hexaemeron* in preference to Hellenic cosmogonies. Infra, Ch. V, Sect. 5.

of the divine (δὶ ὑλικῶν συμβόλων). Christian catechists were seldom so fair.[347]

Basil of Caesarea wrote to Amphilochius, bishop of Iconium, on the subject of Christians who had continued to practice the old cults and included a list of canons. These documents reflect the free association of Christians with Hellenes and some backsliding by the latter. Christian idol-worshippers (εἰδωλολάτραι) and sorcerer-poisoners (φαρμακοί) are condemned along with homosexuals, practitioners of bestiality, murderers, and adulterers in a letter of 374.[348] Christian deaconesses were known to fornicate with Hellenes.[349] We learn that Christians hired "dream-vendors" and "dream-hucksters" (ὀνειροπῶλαι καὶ ὀνειροκάπηλοι), whose art Basil calls hemlock (κώνειον).[350] Another letter addressed "to the well-educated" (τοῖς λογιωτάτοις) of Neocaesarea suggests the reason for Basil's annoyance. Those who hired dream-interpreters (ὀνειροσκόπους) made Basil the subject of stories, and perhaps banter, over their cups of wine at banquets.[351] These and other select epithets are also used for adherents of the Sabellian heresy,[352] but apart from that one reference invariably designate Hellenic practices. For example, the canons of Basil make provision for the practice of magic and poisoning (No. 65), consulting with mantics (No. 72), and much else.[353] There were Christians "who consult seers and follow the customs of the pagans, or bring them into their houses for the discovery of sorceries and for purification from them" (Canon 83).[354] Persons fearful of sorcery were still using Hellenic rituals to ward off the *daimones* of spells even after their conversion, evidently trusting "proven" Hellenic techniques rather than the "magic" of Christian apotropaic rites. Basil considered this to be a relatively lesser offense, the stipulated penance being of six years' duration.

Lest it be supposed that the Christian house was in too good an order, one must consider Basil's Canon 73. For apostasy it provided lifelong penance and reception of the sacrament (τὸ ἁγίασμα) only on one's deathbed. Basil defines the apostate as "one who has

---

[347] Humanity of this sort probably explains more conversions than the bellicose tactics of Marcellus of Apamea and of Porphyrius of Gaza. Supra, Ch. II, Sect. 3, and infra, Ch. III, Sect. 5.

[348] Basil of Caesarea, *Ep.* 188 (Deferrari 3, 28f.).

[349] Basil of Caesarea, *Ep.* 199 (Deferrari 3, 130f.).

[350] Basil of Caesarea, *Ep.* 211 (Deferrari 3, 216f.).

[351] Basil of Caesarea, *Ep.* 210 (Deferrari 3, 196–199).

[352] Basil of Caesarea, *Ep.* 210 (Deferrari 3, 200f.).

[353] Basil of Caesarea, *Ep.* 217 (Deferrari 3, 252f.).

[354] Basil of Caesarea, *Ep.* 217 (Deferrari 3, 262–265).

despised Christ and transgressed the mystery of salvation".[355] This can only refer to sacrifice. It must be borne in mind that the time of Basil's episcopate corresponds to the reign of emperor Valens in the East (364–378), which saw the pragmatic toleration of sacrifice so long as it was not practiced with opulence.[356]

The mentality of bishops like Basil of Caesarea tells us a great deal about the offical view of Christianization, but very little about the outlook of the typical decurion family. For this we must turn to the nearly contemporaneous archaeological evidence about a certain Eustolius, whose conversion to the new religion is attested in the mosaics of a splendid townhouse at Kourion near Paphos in western Cyprus.[357]

The decline of the Hellenic cults of Kourion is obscure. The temenos of Apollo at Hyle suffered severe damage in one or more early fourth-century earthquakes. The temple was never rebuilt, a symptom more of economic decline than the abandonment of polytheism, for the theatre suffered a similar fate. The damage to this part of the island seems to have caused the transfer of the provincial capital from nearby Paphos to Salamis, now renamed Constantia in honor of emperor Constantius II (337–361). Kourion's first Christian basilica was erected in the Akropolis only in the early fifth century.[358] Christianity had, however, taken root some decades earlier.

Eustolius, who was probably one of the few decurions still having his legal residence, or *origo*, at Kourion, began ornamenting the house called the Eustolius Annex sometime after 364. He and his household had accepted Christianity before this time, the date being consistent with the progress of the new religion elsewhere. The welcome inscription advises the visitor: "Enter this house fortunately, for the good."[359] This greeting may well have a concealed Christian meaning.[360] Elsewhere the religious mood is more

[355] ὁ τὸν Χριστὸν ἀρνησάμενος καὶ παραβὰς τὸ τῆς σωτηρίας μυστήριον. Basil of Caesarea, *Ep.* 217 (Deferrari 3, 256f.).
[356] Supra, Ch. II, n. 46.
[357] T.B. Mitford, *The Inscriptions of Kourion* (Philadelphia 1971), 351–364.
[358] Mitford, *Kourion*, 351 and n. 3.
[359] Mitford, *Kourion*, no. 201.
[360] This expression has the peculiar ring of some Christian Syrian door-lintel inscriptions that bid the just man to enter. *Inscriptions grecques et latines de la Syrie*, ed. L. Jalabert *et al.* (Paris 1929–   ), no. 1682 (558 A.D.) If Eustolius were proven to be a Syrian of Antioch, these words might reflect an attempt to atticize the psalm in question. Apart from the known Syrian maritime and cultural connections with Cyprus, there are only two ambiguous hints of Eustolius' possible Syrian ancestry. One is his seeming preference for the square uncial script common in Syria between c. 380–420 (that is, before it was revived again in the sixth century, with

emphatic:[361]

> Instead of by large stones, instead of by hard iron, instead of by
> yellow bronze and steel, these buildings are girded with the much-
> venerated markers of Christ.

The excavator T.B. Mitford observes: "The absence of Christian
symbolism is, however, conspicuous in these mosaics; and this,
with the tone of no. 203, hints that the conversion of Kourion was a
matter of convenience."[362] This supposition is obviated by the
emphatic assertion that "these buildings are girded with the much-
venerated markers of Christ" ((ο)ἴδε δόμοι ζώσαντο πολύλλιτα
σήματα Χριστοῦ). The use of the Old Ionian dialect in the inscription and the lack of Christian symbols is, on the other hand,
perfectly consistent with the attitudes toward the Greek *paideia*
found elsewhere in the Christian sophistic.[363] Christ is here referred
to by name rather than by symbol, and that sufficed. The other
inscription in question has it that:[364]

> Reverence, temperance, and obedience to law, [all] sisters, attend
> this hall and incense-scented room.

The prosaic virtues here personified have something in common
with Stoicism, Neoplatonism, and Christianity all alike. They were
more than anything "bourgeois" values, the virtues of the decurion
class, and entirely unrelated to late Hellenic religious life. It is most
questionable that even the stuffiest Roman traditionalist would
have burnt incense to the abstract personalifications of virtues like
Reverence and Temperance in the late fourth century.[365] Nor is one
last building inscription inconsistent with Christian opinion:[366]

> Seeing unfortunate men coming on foot to all bliss in the presence of
> Koureia, Eustolius himself did not come to his fatherland. But bles-

---

certain stylistic features that distinguish it from the earlier period of its use). The
other point is the synchronism between Eustolius' acceptance of Christianity and
that going on in the *territoria* of Antioch and Apamea in the years after Julian the
Apostate's death. Eustolius' reference to Kourion as his fatherland in Mitford,
Kourion no. 204, even if sound, is purely the editor's conjectural reconstruction of a
hopelessly damaged portion of the mosaic. Even if Eustolius resided in Antioch, he
might still have regarded Kourion as his legal *origo* or "fatherland".

[361] Mitford, *Kourion*, no. 202.
[362] Mitford, *Kourion*, p. 354.
[363] As in Trombley, "Boeotia in Late Antiquity," 225f.
[364] Mitford, *Kourion*, no. 203.
[365] The ridicule that Augustine of Hippo heaps on such deities in *De Civitate Dei*
4.20–21 is aimed at a western literary audience schooled in traditional Latin
rhetoric and religious ideas, and mostly residing in Carthage and the municipalities of Africa.
[366] Mitford, *Kourion*, no. 204.

sing our city with bath houses, he did on one occasion seek out
Kourion, just as Phoebus came and established a cool wind.

The analogy drawn between Eustolius and Phoebus Apollo is a
literary simile and not a cultic one. None of this is particularly
daring compared to the fact that the nearly contemporary Christian
sophist Prohaeresius is said to have consulted the hierophants at
Eleusis for an oracle about the destiny of Julian the Apostate, and
to have drawn confidence from the fact that he as a Christian could
soon practice his profession again after the death of that pagan
emperor.[367] Eustolius might easily have been regarded as one of the
many Hellenes that populated the city councils of the Greek East,
had one crucial phrase been omitted from his inscriptions, "the
much-venerated markers of Christ." These words, chosen with
deliberation, remove all ambiguity about the religious allegiance of
the householder. The house was fitted out tastefully by the standards of the time, but no real doubt was left to the visitor about the
Christian monotheism of its owner. Eustolius, like many contemporaries, held a diverse set of personal allegiances, but all were
subsumed under the standards of the Christian sophistic.

A final episode about the Christianization of the decurion class
reflects the role often played by slaves (οἰκέται) in this process.
Appearing in the *Lausiac History* of Palladius (ob. ante 431), the
narrative concerns a monk called Sarapion the "Linen-Wrapt"
(συνδόνιος), who devised a unique style of *askesis* to convert urban
Hellenes.[368] Sarapion, who had studied grammar (εὐγράμματος)
and could recite the scriptures and other texts from memory
(ἀπεστήθιζε πάσας τὰς γραφάς), got into the habit of letting
himself be sold as a household slave to pagans in order to turn them
away from the old cults. He was legally a free Roman citizen and
thus took care to keep on hand the retail value of a slave, 20 *solidi*,
should the need arise to buy his way out. The high price suggests
that he was bought for his literacy.[369]

Palladius mentions two occasions on which such transactions
took place. In the first instance Sarapion was sold to a family of
pagan mimes (μίμοις Ἕλλησι), whom he got to accept Christianity
and then to abandon their career in the theatre. By eating only
bread and water and by reciting the scriptures, he succeeded in first

---

[367] Eunapius, *Lives of the Philosophers* (Wright, 512f.).
[368] Palladius, *The Lausiac History*, ed. Cuthbert Butler (Hildesheim 1967), 109–
116.
[369] This important datum on the price has gone unnoticed. Jones, *Later Roman
Empire* 996f.

converting the head of the household, then his wife, who was also a
mime, and finally the rest of the household, which evidently contained other slaves. Upon their baptism, Sarapion was offered
manumission in recompense for having manumitted them from the
slavery of Hellenic religion and their trade (αἰσχρᾶς ἡμᾶς
δουλείας ἠλευθέρωσας αὐτός). At this juncture the monk is said
to have revealed his true status and to have departed a free man.[370]

Sarapion is then said to have sailed for Athens, where he visited
the Areopagus, "the hill in the city where the magistrates custo-
marily assembled," and confronted the local Cynic philosophers,
the "wearers of threadbare cloaks" (τριβωνοφόροι), a group that
Julian the Apostate had abominated in his Seventh Oration,[371] and
other sophists who are called simply "cloak-wearers" (βιρρο-
φόροι). Sarapion evidently failed to make any inroads into the
Hellenic ethos of Athens. Nor did even the Christians give him
bread. Sarapion's rough manner eventually earned him a *solidus*
from certain of these philosophers, who suspected him of an ethical
ruse. He is said to have gone to a bakery, put down the *solidus*, and
walked away with a mere loaf of bread. Palladius observes: "Then
the philosophers recognized that he was truly virtuous (ἀληθῶς
ἐνάρετος), and giving the price of a loaf to the baker they kept the
solidus for themselves." It would seem that Sarapion had outdone
even the Cynics in disregarding the full value of the gold coin. Even
so he made no conversions.[372] The Athenian elites' intractability to
Christianization is well known.[373] The probable historicity of Palladius' account, which certain of the ascetic fathers had transmitted
to him, lies in its admission that Sarapion had failed to gain the
conversion of the Hellenes, but merely their respect.

Sarapion is then said to have pressed southward into the parts of
Lacedaemon and to have gained the conversion of a Manichaean
decurion, his wife, and their household (τινα τὸν πρῶτον τῆς
πόλεως Μανιχαῖον εἶναι ἅμα παντὶ τῷ οἴκῳ αὐτοῦ) by letting
himself be sold as a domestic slave (ὡς οἰκέτην) once again.[374]
Manichaeans occupied a grey area somewhere between Christianity and Hellenism, as the case of Augustine of Hippo suggests, and
were equally abominated with pagans.[375] Like Augustine, the Spar-

---

[370] Palladius, *Lausiac History* 109f.
[371] Julian, *Or.* 6 ("To the Uneducated Cynics") (Wright 2, 4–65) and *Or.* 7
("To Herakleios the Cynic") (Wright 2, 72–161).
[372] Palladius, *Lausiac History*, 110–112.
[373] Infra, Ch. IV, passim.
[374] Palladius, *Lausiac History*, 112.
[375] Brown, *Augustine of Hippo*, 44–60.

tan was "virtuous in other respects" (ἐνάρετον ὄντα τὰ ἄλλα).[376] Sarapion accomplished his conversion in two years' time, along with that of his wife. In this instance, the new Christians are said to have revered the monk "as a legitimate brother or father."[377]

Palladius' tales about Sarapion's exploits in the eastern Mediterranean reflect the role of domestic slaves in Christianizing the decurion class. Here, however, the influence of the new religion is said to have affected the *paterfamilias* first rather than the women-folk. Palladius puts it this way out of an ascetic dislike for women. This version of events truthfully reflects the fact that only the Roman *patriapotestas* could sanction and enforce the final Christianization of a household. Elsewhere we learn that a decurion family of Gaza in First Palestine had Christianity introduced into the house through a female domestic slave. It was only after the prayers of bishop Porphyrius and the successful birth of a child to the mother Aelia after a difficult pregnancy that the family raised a "One God" acclamation to Christ.[378] This was done at the bishop's behest, but only *patriapotestas* could sanction it within the household. It is worth noting that one proconsular governor of Achaea who was a Hellene had a Christian household slave. The latter was buried in the *territorium* of Athens with a Christian funerary marker.[379] These varied examples demonstrate the continuous tendency of Christianity to make inroads into noble families by way of their domestic slaves. If we accept the veracity of Palladius' story about Sarapion, which admittedly relies on hearsay evidence, it would seem that at least one monk used the existing structure of social relations to impose his own religious program on the upper classes of the eastern Mediterranean cities. Conscious manipulation of this and other kinds is certainly an underrated factor in the process of Christianization.

VI. Conclusion

Much that was Hellenic began to change in the fifth century. The novel Christian imprint affected both nomenclature and things unspoken. Damascius of Damascus, writing in the early sixth century, sums up the drift of events in the outlook of his subject, Isidore the Hellene:[380]

---

[376] Palladius, *Lausiac History*, 112, line 8.
[377] Palladius, *Lausiac History*, 112, line 11f.
[378] Infra, Ch. III, Sect. 2.
[379] Infra, Ch. IV, n. 51.
[380] Damascius, Fr. 38 (Zintzen, 64=Asmus, 26).

He was clearly no lover of present events (i.e. the Christianization of the empire), nor did he wish to make *proskynesis* to the idols, but was quite eager after the gods themselves hidden within, not those within the *adyta* but rather those inside the ineffable thing that once was of absolute unknowing.

The superficial observer might have taken this as a form of quietism and resignation to the Christianization of the empire and its religious practice, but it was not that in fact.

A deep sense of insecurity toiled beneath the public facade of Christianization, a feeling that would prevail well into the early medieval period.[381] This was perhaps felt by Basil of Caesarea (ob. 379) when he made the observation: "If anyone receives the name of Christianity (χριστιανισμός) and insults Christ, he shall not profit from the title."[382] Or as Callinicus of Rufinianae put it: "Christianity is not a chance thing" (οὐκ ἔστι τὸ τυχὸν χριστιανισμός).[383] A man of learning like Domestikos, a physician of the island of Gaulus off Sicily, was afraid of being taken for a Hellene or even a lax Christian Hellenist, and so signed himself as "the *pious* Christian and physician" on his gravestone (ὁ εὐ[σεβ]ὴς χριστιανὸς καὶ ἰ[α]τρός).[384] Monotheism remained an issue at the oasis of Kargeh in upper Egypt. While the latest pagan inscriptions there belong to the third century, they still troubled Christians in the sixth, as with the records of hieratic sacrifices: "The act of obeisance (τὸ προσκύνημα) of Psennēsis, son of Pelebios the priest, priest of the great gods Isis and Sarapis" (. . . ἱερεὺς Ἴσιδι καὶ Σάραπις θεῶν μεγίστων).[385] In the sixth century we still discover the strident assertion of Christian monotheism with the "One God" formula grafted onto a previously pagan votive prayer: "One God the helper. May his Christ preserve and guard the Latopolitans with their animals."[386] The inscription comes from a church and its annexes. The people must have been recently Christianized. In the end, it was the popular prayer and not the hieratic one that passed

---

[381] This is illustrated by the canons of the Council in Trullo of 691–92 pertaining to the survival of Hellenic cult practices. The earlier bibliography is assembled in Trombley, "Council in Trullo." See the recent discussion of John Haldon, *Byzantium in the Seventh Century* (Cambridge 1990), 327–337. It is difficult to understand why Haldon does not address the issue simply as the *Nachleben* of Hellenic religious practice in a Christian cultural and religious context, hence the endless discussion of what is "pagan" and what is a "survival".

[382] Basil of Caesarea, *Ep. 199* (Deferrari 3, 130f.).

[383] Callinicus of Rufinianae, *De Vitae S. Hypatii Liber*, ed. Seminarii Philologorum Bonnesis Sodales (Leipzig 1895), 99. Cf. infra, Ch. VII, Sect. 1.

[384] CIG 4.9451.

[385] SEG (1976–77), 1792.

[386] SEG 26.1784. For similar pagan examples, see infra, Ch. VII, Sect. 2.

into Christian usage. All memory of the local priesthood thus ceased as the new religion fused its liturgies with those of local provenance.[387]

Liturgy and ritual of other kinds passed into Christianity as well. Magic circles were employed against natural forces like hailstorms and overflowing rivers that were thought to be animate and driven by daimonic spirits. In pre-Christian times, however, these forces owned the names of respectable divinities and were welcomed onto sacred lands, as an inscription of Termessos in Phrygia reveals (2nd–3rd century A.D.):[388]

> Orthagoras, having made a beginning of peace, set up altars to Phoebus and the maiden Artemis because of a vow, having marked out the breadth of the Mēnē stream with stakes accompanied by the Nymphs, in order that the river would cover both (the altars) with the torrents of its banks.

The inscription describes the celebration of a sort of cosmic marriage between the sun and soil through the river waters in spate. Put mythologically, the Nymphs aided the copulation (ὀχεύω, translated here as "to cover", also has the sense of "mount" or "copulate") of Phoebus and his young bride (κούρη) Artemis. These divinities had become *daimones* by the time of Theodore of Sykeon (6th century Galatia) to be resisted by cross-shaped stakes or cairns with crosses cut on the individual stones.[389] Christians might summon rainfall through Christ and his angels, the latter being thought by the rustics to propel clouds through the lower air. A barely literate inscription of Kamarina, Sicily seems to record such an intention:[390]

> Amēl. Ga(briel). . . . Christ, you who multiplied the stars in the sky and increased the water in the sea, increase too the fruits in the vineyard of Paul! (Two lines of magical signs.)

Christ had in a sense become the new Dionysus.[391]

At times rites were Christianized by simply adding a cross to an

---

[387] See infra, Ch. IX, Sect. 3, for numerous inscriptions of this sort at Philae in upper Egypt.

[388] Cf. the translation of W. Peek, SEG 30 (1980), 1511.

[389] Cf. the numerous examples attested in the Syriac life of Symeon Stylites the Elder. Infra, Ch. VIII, Sect. 4.

[390] SEG 34 (1984), 944.

[391] According to the Sixty-second Canon of the Council in Trullo, (691–692), Dionysus was still being invoked during the grape-crushing phase of the wine cycle: τοῦ βδελυκτοῦ Διονύσου ὄνομα τὴν σταφυλὴν ἐκθλίβοντας ἐν ταῖς ληνοῖς ἐπιβοᾶν. Périklès-Pierre Joannou, *Discipline générale antique (IIe–IXe s)*. (Rome 1962), 199.

otherwise pagan formula. One thinks here of the "fair-sailing" (εὔπλοια) inscriptions found at Aliki on the southeastern tip of the island of Thasos in the northern Aegean. It was customary to name ships after Hellenic deities even in Late Antiquity, when the greater part of the merchant marine had become Christian. Take, for example, this pagan text:[392]

> For good luck. Fair sailing to the fortunate Herakles, (a ship) of Thessalonike, owned by Epiktetos and Zoilos, to Zoilos fortunately the president of the merchants' guild . . . to Kaisarianos, to Trophimos the shipmaster, and to those sailing together. One cargo (or "payment").

One could Christianize the wish by simply adding the appropriate symbol: "(Cross) Fair sailing to the Poseidon and Asklepios . . ." (+εὔπλοια τῷ Ποσειδ[ῶνι κ]αὶ τῷ Ἀσκληπιῷ).[393] The latter inscription belongs to the fourth or fifth century. The two ships were certainly manned by Christian sailors, but perhaps had a pagan owner or backer.[394] The peril of sea voyages explains the increased reliance that Christian sailors placed in holy men like St. Nikolaos, as they quite obviously no longer felt able to pray to Poseidon, who even in Neohellenic times was called "the *daimon* of the sea" (ὁ δαίμονας τῆς θάλασσας).[395] St. Nikolaos of Hagia Sion Christianized the *territorium* of Myra in Lycia during the middle years of the sixth century.[396] He became popular with seafarers who invoked his protection when rounding the Celidonian promontory to enter Andriake, Phoinike, and the other Lycian ports because of his reputed ability to get the winds to change at that spot in a semi-legendary account that most probably reflects his knowledge of certain predictable local wind currents.[397] The cult spread into the Aegean because the Lycian coast lay on the main shipping route from Egypt and Syria to Constantinople.[398] A vast number of Christianizations of rite were developed in the sixth century in connection with the Justinianic program of eradicating rural paganism.

A vivid memory of the great temple conversions in the 380's and 390's

---

[392] IG 12/8. 581.
[393] IG 12/8 582.
[394] Cf. IG 12/8 584, 585, 586 for examples without crosses.
[395] Lawson, *Modern Greek Folklore and Ancient Greek Religion*, 75f.
[396] Frank R. Trombley, "Monastic Foundations in Sixth-century Anatolia and their Role in the Social and Economic Life of the Countryside," *Greek Orthodox Theological Review* 30 (1985), 55f., 58.
[397] *Hagios Nikolaos: Der heilige Nikolaos in der griechischen Kirche*, ed. Gustav Anrich, I (Leipzig 1913), 9, 31f.
[398] For maps, see: R.M. Harrison, "Churches and Chapels of Central Lycia," *Anatolian Studies* 13 (1963), 117, 123.

persisted through the mid-fifth century. Ammonius of Alexandria (fl. c. 458) recalled the closure of the temple of Artemis Ephesia in the relevant section of his commentary on the Acts of the Apostles:[399]

> So Demetrius knew that he deceived men by making silver temples and gods for them. He feared lest his deceit and lack of principle would be proven through Paul's teaching. It is indicated that the true faith dawned on him, although at that time it had not yet prevailed in the *oikoumene*, because Demetrius feared lest the temple of Artemis in Ephesus be destroyed. And he predicted the destruction of that temple, which has also happened.

The last phrase indicates that it happened within Ammonius' living memory (ὃ καὶ γέγονεν). He and many others saw an eschatological significance in the closure of temples. John Chrysostom gives by way of contrast a strangely detached commentary on the same passage.[400] It was certainly written before the deposition of Artemis Ephesia, which some scholars put as early as 407.[401] Artemis' name was erased from some of the inscriptions of Ephesus.[402] Soon traces of the vanished cult could be discovered only in the city's *territorium* where the *horoi* marking the properties of the ex-temple lands were left in place for purely legal reasons.[403]

As for the closure of the Serapeum of Alexandria, a Greek named Sophronius wrote a work on the event with the provocative title: "On the Overthrow of Sarapis." It does not survive, but perhaps went into Rufinus of Aquileia's treatment of the subject in his ecclesiastical history.[404] The euhemerism that reduced Sarapis to the biblical figure of Joseph the provider offered useful grist for the mills of writers like Ammonius of Alexandria.[405] By the later sixth century the event hardly seemed worthy of mention, as John Malalas dismisses it in a single sentence.[406] Yet the theophoric personal name was still around. We learn of a certain Sarapis who commanded troops loyal to Justinian in Numidia (c. 534).[407] The man was perhaps of Thracian origin.[408] He or his family had converted to

[399] *Fragmenta in Acta Apostolorum*, PG 85, 1577A–B.
[400] *Homiliae in Acta*, PG 60, 297f.
[401] *Recueil des inscriptions grecques-chrétiennes d'Asie Mineure*, ed. Henri Grégoire (Paris 1922), no. 104.
[402] *Die Inschriften von Ephesus*, ed. H. Wankel *et al.*, 8 v. in 10 (Bonn 1979–84), nos. 422, 508, 509, 517.
[403] SEG 29 (1979), 1099–1102. On the separate status of temple lands, see *supra*, Ch. I, Sect. 7.
[404] Hieronymus, *Liber de Inlustribus Viris*, Cap. 134.
[405] *Fragmenta in Acta Apostolorum*, PG 85, 1545.
[406] John Malalas, *Chronographia* 349.
[407] Procopius, *Wars* 4.15.50.
[408] Procopius, *Wars* 3.11.7.

Christianity in the early sixth century. As with Artemis and Dusares, belief in the blessings of Sarapis remained a cultural fact long
after the closure of their temples.

The idea of "temple conversions" is inherent in any religious
culture that seeks to achieve the transformation of a preexisting one
by rapid and aggressive means. The agents of the Terror in the
French Revolution took measures of this kind in behalf of the
"religion" of Reason at the village of Puy-de-Dome:[409]

> Chateauneuf-Randon remained at Clermont as representative on
> mission in the locality. His most stubborn problem was the religious
> one. During his tenure church bells were removed and steeples
> demolished. There were many protests. Citizens in various com-
> munes betrayed sudden concern for the beautiful, petitioning that
> their church towers be spared as masterpieces of architecture. A few
> of these requests were granted, usually on condition that in towers
> left standing the doors should be blocked up, and placards posted
> announcing "the triumph of reason over the vestiges of error and
> fanaticism." In some places caps of liberty were hung upon spires,
> and statues of liberty placed ostentatiously on the roofs. A church,
> though standing, was thus signified as belonging to the Republic.

There is much in this campaign that echoes the edicts of the
Christian Roman emperors between 381–438.

The manipulation of the mechanisms designed to Christianize
late Hellenic belief and practice went hand in hand with actual
conversions. The foregoing discussion leaves all the questions relevant to this in a necessary, but nevertheless unstructured, limbo,
a generalized reference frame that can have no meaning for the
evolution of religious thought or behavior without the painstaking
examination of those phenomena inside their varied local contexts.
The following chapters attempt such a reconstruction for urban
and rural sites that have left coherent bodies of evidence either in
the form of detailed hagiographic texts or inscriptions. Only by this
process will it be possible to lay the foundation for broader generalizations about the religious transformation of Hellenic Antiquity
into Christian Late Antiquity. I mean by this the minute delineation of the micro-institutional structures of family, village, urban
quarter, trade, profession, and education. We shall go on to identify
the phenomena of these local contexts and arrive at some conclusions about the points of conjuncture between the old new religions,
and about the Christianization of everyday life, in the chapters that
follow.

---

[409] Quoted from R.R. Palmer, *Twelve Who Ruled: The Year of the Terror in the
French Revolution* (Princeton 1989), 151.

CHAPTER THREE

GAZA

The biography of Porphyrius, bishop of Gaza (395–420), composed by Mark the Deacon, provides the fullest extant account of the forcible demolition of urban temples and lapse of the Hellenic cults.[1] Raymond Van Dam has analysed the administrative side of this question in a recent article, which defines the issue largely in terms of shifting allegiances inside the urban community and the pursuit of prestige by status groups ("paradigms of prestige and authority"), which evolved into the "new Christian consensus."[2] He largely avoids the demographic analysis which is the object of the present study, and fails to treat the phenomena described in Porphyrius' life extensively, perhaps because a considerable controversy enshrouds Mark's work. Paul Peeters regarded it as an almost entirely fraudulent piece of myth-making. This question is left to an appendix at the end of this chapter.[3] The appendix demonstrates that Peeters' arguments against the authenticity of the life of Porphyrius are deeply flawed on the twin grounds of logical reasoning and of irrefutable historical evidence. Mark's work should be considered almost completely vindicated as a near contemporary document of the episcopate of Porphyrius, and as an eyewitness account of the administrative realities of temple conversions and of Christianizing urban populations. The following analysis has a twofold aspect: first, a delienation of the pagan cults of Gaza, and the social, economic, and political structures which supported them; and thereafter the means employed by Porphyrius, with the help of the imperial administration, to bring those structures down.

---

[1] Marc le Diacre, *Vie de Porphyre, Évêque de Gaza*, ed. tr. Henri Grégoire and M.-A. Kugener (Paris 1930). *Marci Diaconi Vita Porphyrii Episcopi Gazensis*, ed. Societatis Philologae Bonnensis Sodales (Leipzig 1895). There is, in addition to the Greek text, a Georgian version. For the Latin translation and an analytical introduction, see: Paul Peeters, "La Vie géorgienne de Saint Porphyre de Gaza," *Analecta Bollandiana* 59 (1941), 65–216. The introduction to the 1930 edition is cited as Grégoire-Kugener (1930).

[2] Raymond Van Dam, "From Paganism to Christianity at Late Antique Gaza," *Viator* 16 (1985), 1–20.

[3] Supra, n. 1 for the relevant editions.

I. The Hellenic Cults of Gaza in 395

Gaza, a city in the southwestern part of First Palestine, was the center of a considerable traffic in luxury goods that came up the Red Sea coast and proceeded thence to the Mediterranean by way of Trajan's road westward from 'Aqaba and the towns of the Negev desert.[4] Gaza was still largely pagan when Porphyrius became bishop of the place in 395. The Christian elements of the city were concentrated in the once separately incorporated, but now no longer independent, seaport town of Constantia Maiuma, to which emperor Constantine the Great had granted separate urban status because of its general adherence to Christianity sometime after 324.[5] The Christians seem to have avoided the upper city, that is old Gaza, where the cults of the Hellenic and Semitic deities flourished and where the population remained almost completely pagan.

The principal god of Gaza was Marnas, the local Baal, the sky-god thought to move the clouds about and control the annual rainfall. The population had, since the Hellenization of the Semitic East, worshipped this divinity in the form of Zeus Marnas, an assimilation of the local cult to that of the Cretan-born Zeus.[6] This form of the cult was of no great antiquity.[7] Mark the Deacon sums up the religion of pagan Gaza in these terms:[8]

> There were eight public temples in the city, those of Helios, Aphrodite, Apollo, Kore, Hekate, the so-called Heroeion, that of the Tyche of the city, which they called the Tychaion, and the Marneion, which they say is that of the Cretan-born Zeus and reckon to be the most splendid of all temples everywhere. There were very many idols in the townhouses and villages whose numbers no one could count. For the pagan gods, having taken hold of the Gazans' preference, as the people were easily moved, filled the entire city and also its *territorium* (*perioikis*) with error. The Gazans persisted in this attitude out of great simplicity of mind. Wherefore the Christians, altered by the holy faith, became zealots. So much, then, for the Gazans.

---

[4] On Late Antique Gaza, see: Martin A. Meyer, *History of the City of Gaza* (New York 1907), 55–72. Also worth consideration is: M. Avi-Yonah, "The Economics of Byzantine Palestine," *Israel Exploration Journal* 8 (1958), 39ff. On Gaza's connections with the 'Aqaba-Bostra trading route, see: Glen Bowersock, *Roman Arabia* (Oxford 1983), 64f., 143, etc.

[5] On Gaza and certain other examples of this, see: Jones, *Later Roman Empire*, 91.

[6] Grégoire-Kugener (1930), xlvii–liv. On the cults of Gaza, see also: Meyer, *History of Gaza*, 114–124.

[7] Javier Texidor, *The Pagan God: Popular Religion in the Greco-Roman Near East* (Princeton 1977), 97f.

[8] *V. Porphyrii*, Cap. 64.

This strange admixture of cults reflects the historically diverse ethnic background of Gaza, which had had Latin settlers when it became a Roman colony, where Greek and Aramaic had previously prevailed as the *linguae francae*.[9] Most Greek cities and many Syrian villages had a local Tyche and Tychaion for her worship.[10] The other gods enumerated bear the Greek names often conveniently applied to Semitic deities with similar typologies, whose Aramaic names varied widely from place to place. There is no epigraphic corroboration for the Semitic name of the local Aphrodite. Equivalents to Aphrodite among the Semitic female fertility deities perhaps included Symbaitylos, who is honored in an inscription of 224 A.D. at Djebel Sim'ān in the *territorium* of Antioch in First Syria.[11] The fourth-century A.D. Aramaic equivalents for the other Hellenic deities attested in Mark the Deacon's list of temples are difficult to come by. It is possible that the Gazan Helios represents Zeus Heliopolitanus, the principal deity of Baalbek-Heliopolis in Phoenicia Libanensis.[12] Thus, behind the Greek names provided by Mark the Deacon, one discovers two Baals (Zeus Marnas and Heliopolitanus) as sky-gods, and another two sun gods (Helios and the Hellenic Apollo). There appear to be no Semitic equivalents to the female Kore and Hekate.[13] The cult temples, built at different dates in the Hellenistic and Roman imperial periods, reflect a gradual syncretism and accretion of functionally overlapping cults. The fact of this diversity is, strictly speaking, of subordinate importance to the cultural and demographic reality of the city's almost complete adherence to the old cults as late as 395.

Zeus Marnas held a preeminent position among the deities of Gaza and received worship at his temple, the so-called Marneion. Mark the Deacon's biography of Porphyrius documents the characteristics of the cult in some detail. Zeus Marnas was thought to control the rains which fell in January and February, and bore the

---

[9] Gaza became a colony during the reign of the emperor Hadrian (117–138), perhaps when he visited the city in 129. The place still seems to have borne the title Colonia Gaza Aelia in Late Antiquity. This explains the survival of the Roman *gens* Aelius in the late fourth century as the *nomen* of the decurion family that parented Aelia. Infra, Ch. III, Sect. 2. Cf. Henri Leclercq, "Gaza," DACL 6/1 (Paris 1924), 707f. The daughter of a family, of course, always took the *nomen*, or middle name of her father, as her own *praenomen*.

[10] Infra, Ch. XI, Sect. 2.

[11] *Publications of the American Archaeological Expeditions to Syria in 1904–5 and 1909 Division III: Greek and Latin Inscriptions Section B: Northern Syria*, ed. W.K. Prentice (Leiden 1922), no. 1170. Grégoire glibly identifies the Gazan Aphrodite as Astarte without epigraphic corroboration. Grégoire-Kugener (1930), lvi.

[12] Earlier names include Balmarqod and Iarebol. See previous note.

[13] Grégoire-Kugener (1930) and Texidor, *Pagan God* omit comment.

title "Master of the Rains" (κύριος τῶν ὄμβρων).[14] The priesthood still performed public sacrifices as late as 395/6, this undoubtedly a vestige of the tolerance of pubic sacrifice under the
regime of the co-emperors Valens (364–378) and Valentinian I
(364–375), and a certain streak of political realism in Theodosius
the Great (379–395). The ritual at the shrine included a hymnography (ὕμνοι) which was repeated for seven days running during the
drought that occurred in the winter of 395/6. Processions frequented another site outside the city called a "place of prayer" or
"sanctuary" (ἔξω τῆς πόλεως εἰς τόπον καλούμενον προσευχῆς)
of Marnas.[15] It seems to have been nothing more than an open-air
altar within a sacred precinct.

The priests of the Marneion proferred oracles from time to time.
This task required no more skill than the ability to compose the
alleged utterances of the deity in the form of dactylic hexameters, a
talent widely shared among the adherents of the Greek *paideia*, as
the Gazan priesthoods and its decurion colleagues must have been.
The oracles of the fourth and fifth centuries often served the political aim of discrediting the Christian government of the empire.[16] It
was also said that human sacrifices occurred at the Marneion (αἱ
ἀνθρώπων θυσίαι).[17] On the occasion of the drought of 395/6, the
priests of Zeus-Marnas circulated an oracle in which the god
ascribed the lack of rainfall to the presence of Porphyrius, the new
Christian bishop, in their city:[18]

> [It said that] Porphyrius is a bringer of bad luck to the city. Since the
> god withheld the rains in the first month [of the year], which is called
> Dios, and even in the second month Apellaion, everyone has suffered.

This oracle, which Mark the Deacon summarizes briefly in prose,
must have been read to the populace when it assembled at the
Marneion as suppliants for rain (ἐχρηματίσθη ἡμῖν ὑπὸ τοῦ
Μαρνᾶ, ὅτι κακοποδινός ἐστιν ὁ Πορφύριος τῇ πόλει). The
priests, decurions, and pagan populace justifiably suspected the
intrusive new bishop of the Christians, whose monastic credentials
and alien origin immediately suggested an end to the policy of
accommodation adhered to by the previous bishop, whose name
was Aeneas.[19] Political necessity thus dictated the circulation of the

[14] *V. Porphyrii*, Cap. 19.
[15] *V. Porphyrii*, Cap. 19.
[16] For the fifth-century purveyance of Hellenic oracles, see infra, Ch. V, Sect. 4.
[17] *V. Porphyrii*, Cap. 66.
[18] *V. Porphyrii*, Cap. 19.
[19] *V. Porphyrii*, Cap. 11.

oracle, lest the aggressive Porphyrius increase his small congregation with recruits from the Gazan *demos*.

Although there were seven other temples standing in Gaza at this time, Mark the Deacon omits all other reference to them. He does describe a fertility cult of Aphrodite at the Maiuma gate of the city. The marble statue of a naked woman regarded as the deity herself stood under a sort of tetrapylon or canopy, in front of which lay a stone altar (περὶ τὸ καλούμενον τετράμφοδον, στήλη ἵστατο ἀπὸ μαρμάρου ἥν ἔλεγον εἶναι 'Αφροδίτης · ἦν δὲ ἐπάνω βωμοῦ λιθίνου, ὑπῆρχεν δὲ τὸ ἐκτύπωμα τῆς στήλης, γυναικὸς γυμνῆς).[20] It is impossible to judge from this reference whether the statue was of Hellenistic or strictly Syrian style.[21] The cult practices associated with the cult were predictable:[22]

> All the citizens honored the statue, but most of all the women, who attached lamps and burned incense [in front of it]. They asserted that it gave oracles in dreams to those who wished to have intercourse in lawful marriage (χρηματίζε κατ' ὄναρ ταῖς βουλομέναις προσομιλῆσαι γάμῳ), but they deceived each other by relating this falsehood. After entrusting themselves often to the *daimon* to get its help in marriage, they failed so badly that their menfolk got divorces or cohabited [with other women] illicitly.

Such was the not improbable account of the cult which Mark got from a number of recent converts to Christianity, whom the services of the deity had disappointed. This shrine, like the Marneion and other temples of Gaza, underwent demolition during Porphyrius' tenure as bishop of Gaza.

II. The Urban Pagan Establishment

Mark the Deacon asserts that in 395 the population of old Gaza was entirely pagan except for a small congregation of Christians, who numbered 280 men, women, and children.[23] There is no reason to doubt this claim. Elsewhere he observes that when bishop Porphyrius led a very large crowd of Christians in procession up from Maiuma to demolish the temples, these folk mixed with and, not surprisingly, outnumbered the Christian residents of Gaza.[24] It

---

[20] *V. Porphyrii*, Cap. 59.

[21] The Georgian text is corrupt at this point, referring to the statue of Aphrodite as being "supported by four columns" (*simulacrum quoddam, columnis quattuor innixum*), a statement that makes no sense. Peeters (1941), 173 and notes.

[22] *V. Porphyrii*, Cap. 59.

[23] *V. Porphyrii*, Cap. 19.

[24] *V. Porphyrii*, Cap. 58.

would seem, then, that the Christian seaport had a considerably larger Christian population than the old city of Gaza. The reasons were partly economic: "The people of the coast were more numerous because it had many Egyptian wine merchants" (πλείους γὰρ ἦσαν οἱ ἀπὸ τῆς παραλίου διὰ τὸ πολλοὺς ἔχειν Αἰγυπτίους ἐμπόρους οἴνων).[25] Maiuma was thus the mercantile zone of the local economy, and many Christians, who dominated the maritime trades, augmented by an influx of Egyptian merchants, had concentrated their businesses there. By way of contrast, conservative agricultural interests dominated old Gaza. This would explain the predominance of the pagan priesthoods and the largely unconverted *territorium* of the city.[26] This phenomenon is fully consistent with known paradigms: coastal towns were Christianized earlier, whereas inland towns and villages resisted the new religion because of their reliance upon the peace of the gods and the ancient rituals connected with the agricultural cycle. Constantine the Great (324–337 *in oriente*) recognized that fact in granting Christian Maiuma a separate urban charter from old Gaza, just as he had done for Christian Orkistos in Phrygia when its citizens requested permission to secede from pagan Nakolea.[27] Julian the Apostate (361–363 *in oriente*), however, deprived Maiuma permanently of its separate status. The reason for this was fiscal: Julian's pagan constituents in old Gaza had lost the income from the markets, harbor tolls, and tariffs of the extensive caravan and maritime trade. Later Christian emperors did not see fit to alter Julian's arrangement. Thus, in the life of Porphyrius, the residents of Maiuma are called the "people of the coast" (οἱ τοῦ παραλίου) and those of old Gaza "the people of the city" (οἱ τῆς πόλεως).[28] The bishop of Gaza maintained the episkopeion, his residence, in the hostile territory of the old city. It should be added that, although Gaza and Maiuma were reintegrated into a single urban unit, Maiuma nevertheless retained its own bishop.[29]

The resultant segregation of cults and prejudice isolated late fourth-century Gaza from the cultural and political trends that were driving the populations of the towns to Christianity, and thereby slowed the process locally. The harassment which bishop

---

[25] *V. Porphyrii*, Cap. 58.
[26] Infra, Ch. III, Sect. 3, and Sect. 4, n. 134.
[27] Jones, *Later Roman Empire*, 91, 877, and 1363f., n. 7. Antarados, the mainland suburb of Arados proper, which was an island over against the Syrian coast in Phoenicia, achieved independent status on this ground as well.
[28] *V. Porphyrii*, Cap. 58.
[29] Michael Le Quien, *Oriens Christianus* 3 (Paris 1740), 621–626.

Porphyrius encountered upon his entry into Gaza was symptomatic
of this condition, as was the small size of the Christian congregation
there, which seems to have kept a low profile amidst the unfriendly
atmosphere. The datum about the wine merchants suggests,
however, that throughout the Maiuma-Gaza urban zone, but excluding the countryside, the Christians sufficiently outnumbered
the pagan Gazans that a mass procession up from the coast could
put the latter in the minority. Thus, pagan Gaza was not so much a
pagan city as one element in a larger urban demographic con-
glomerate that had considerable numbers of Christians in it.
Although the *territorium* right around old Gaza had not been Christianized, the areas closer to the coast had begun the feel the impact
of the preaching of the monk St. Hilarion in the mid-fourth
century.[30]

The real political power in the city lay in the hands of the landed
magnates of the decurion class who owned extensive estates in the
territorium of Gaza and elsewhere. These folk were pagan to a man
in 395/6, and found themselves in conflict with the Christian trading interest groups at Maiuma, over whom a law of Julian the
Apostate had extended their control, as previously noted. This
constitutes one more example of how far-reaching and popular the
reforms of that Hellenic emperor remained even thirty years after
his death, an important corrective to the patriarch of Alexandria
Athanasius' characterization of his reign as a "passing cloud". The
city council of Gaza refused to admit Christians as members or to
let them participate in any other civil office (μετελθεῖν πολιτικῶν
ὀφφίκιων).[31] Bishop Porphyrius later brought up this charge in an
audience before the Augusta Eudoxia and the *cubicularius* Amantius: "They told her about the idol-maniacs, in what manner they
performed unholy acts (τὰ ἀνόσια) without fear, and how they
tyrannized (καταδυναστεύουσιν) the Christians, not allowing
them to participate in civil office or to farm their fields (τὰ χωρία
αὐτῶν γεωργηθῆναι), from which they assess public taxes to your
majesty" (ἐξ ὧν τὰ δημόσια τελοῦσιν τῷ ὑμετέρῳ κράτει).[32] The
conflict was thus not only one of differing cults, but also between
opposing economic interests. The decurions of old Gaza probably
saw themselves as the cultural superiors of the multi-ethnic huck-
sters of Maiuma. Although late, the date of 395/6 for an entirely
pagan city council is not entirely improbable. For example, it was

[30] Infra, Ch. III, Sect. 3.
[31] *V. Porphyrii*, Cap. 32.
[32] *V. Porphyrii*, Cap. 40.

only c. 364–375 that the Boule of Delphi in Achaea fell under the control of a Christian majority.[33] Other examples include Carrhae-Ḥarrān and Ascalon in First Palestine.[34]

The Christians of old Gaza not surprisingly felt themselves persecuted by the magistrates. Mark the Deacon sums up the position of the Gazan church in these terms:[35]

> The idol-maniacs did not cease to plot against the blessed [Porphyrius] and the other Christians. For since they were presided over by a pagan magistrate (ἄρχων Ἕλλην), [the Hellenes] went to him either with bribes or their atheistic sacrifice and wronged the Christians.

For example, when bishop Porphyrius led a procession outside the west gate of the city to a rural martyrion to pray for rain during the winter drought of 395/6, his small party found the gates locked upon its return "at the ninth hour," which must have fallen around sunset during the winter season.[36] The prefect of the watch had apparently ordered the gates closed on schedule, and perhaps derived a certain sense of satisfaction from prohibiting reentry to the Christian bishop with his suppliants. As Mark the Deacon relates the story, the pagans suborned the populace at large (λαός) to keep them out of the city for two hours, until a miraculous thunderstorm burst which caused them to give way.[37] The imposition of such administrative technicalities on the movement of Christian processions provided a useful argument to Porphyrius when he petitioned for the closure of the Gazan temples. Nor can the hypothesis be ruled out that the bishop synchronized the procession in order to provoke such an incident.

Mark the Deacon elsewhere specifically identifies the magistracies dominated by pagan officeholders, this in connection with another altercation concerning a subdeacon or lector of the Gazan church named Baruch.[38] The man had gone out to a village not far from the city (εἰς κώμην οὐκ μήκοθεν τῆς πόλεως) to recite the

---

[33] Trombley, "Boeotia in Late Antiquity," 222.

[34] Supra, Ch. II, Sect. 3, n. 121. Jones, *Later Roman Empire*, 93 and 943. Harnack, *Mission and Expansion of Christianity*, 2 (1908) 112. Raphia in First Palestine had a strong polytheistic population c. 388 (Sozomen, HE 7.15). It is of interest that its first attested bishop Romanus flourished at a relatively late date, c. 431. Le Quien, *Oriens Christianus* 3, 629f. Areopolis, another hotbed of Semitic paganism, had its first known bishop only c. 449. Le Quien, 3, 733–736. Strong local anti-Christian sentiment may have kept these sees temporarily vacant in the fourth century, that is, if they had bishops at all.

[35] *V. Porphyrii*, Cap. 21.

[36] *V. Porphyrii*, Cap. 20.

[37] *V. Porphyrii*, Cap. 20.

[38] On Baruch, see Appendix I.

ecclesiastical canon when a pagan (ἀνόσιος) called in his fellow
villagers, who like him were farmers (γεωργοί τινες ὁμοίοι αὐτοῦ
συγκωμῆται), and gave the isolated Christian a sound beating.[39]
When Cornelius the deacon and two other Christians found Baruch
and carried him into the city the next day in an unconscious state,
certain citizens raised the issue with the magistrates, inasmuch as
they supposed the man to be dead. Both Hellenic and Christian
funerary custom forbade the interment of the dead inside city walls,
the former regarding it as a form of ritual pollution (διὰ τὸ
νομίζειν μύσος εἶναι νεκρὸν ἐπιφέρειν εἰς τὴν πόλιν),[40] the latter
as a threat to public health. The pagans may also have feared the
creation of a new martyr cult in their midst, with a consequent
increase in Porphyrius' political leverage. A recent imperial law of
Gratian, Valentinian II, and Theodosius the Great (30 July 381)
had emphatically forbidden the importation and burial of bodies in
churches on the specious ground that the presence of martyr relics
in Christian buildings justified such acts:[41]

> All bodies that are contained in urns or sarcophagi and are kept
> above the ground shall be carried and placed outside the city, that
> they may present an example of humanity (i.e. the common lot of
> mortals) and leave the homes of the citizens their sanctity (i.e. fear of
> the pollution of the dead) . . . [Let] no person evade the purpose of
> this regulation by false and cunning shrewdness and suppose that the
> shrines (sedes) of apostles and martyrs are granted for the burial of
> bodies.

The pagan bystanders attacked Cornelius and his men, whereupon
Porphyrius was brought into the altercation and a riot ensued. The
next day, a committee of magistrates called on Porphyrius. The
defensor of the city (a magistrate charged with hearing minor cases
at law in behalf of the poor) presided over the inquest, being
accompanied by the eirenarchs (police magistrates) and the two
executive members of the city council, the duoviri Timothy and
Epiphanius (ὁ δημεκδικῶν μετὰ τῶν εἰρηναρχῶν καὶ τῶν δύο
πρωτευόντων), all of them pagans.[42] The defensor asked: "Why
did you bring a dead man into the city when the ancestral laws
forbid it?" (τῶν νόμων πατρῴων τοῦτο ἀπαγορευόντων).[43] Porphyrius sensed the anger of the deacons Cornelius and Mark, the
latter being an eyewitness to the events of his narrative, and bade

---

[39] V. Porphyrii, Cap. 23.
[40] V. Porphyrii, Cap. 23.
[41] Cod. Theod. 9.17.6. Cf. Trombley, "Boeotia in Late Antiquity," 221f.
[42] V. Porphyrii, Cap. 25.
[43] V. Porphyrii, Cap. 25.

them cooperate. A noisy altercation went on until Baruch recovered his senses, emerged in front of the crowd, and began flailing at them with a wooden plank (ξύλον). He allegedly pursued them as far as the Marneion. For this feat, but more probably because of his near martyrdom, Porphyrius appointed Baruch deacon "worthily and justly".[44] Even if one discounts the tale of Baruch's physical prowess, his emergence from the episkopeion fully alive will have ended the dispute, whether the Hellenes feared ritual pollution, or a new martyr cult as the rallying point for the local Christians.

One did not strike (τύπτειν) urban police officials without the risk of retaliation. It was best to preempt the city officials and get the imperial government on one's side. Sensing the danger, bishop Porphyrius composed a letter to John Chrysostom, the prominent Antiochene homilist who had become patriarch of Constantinople (398–404), requesting him to intercede with the co-emperors Arcadius and Honorius to shut the temples of Gaza. Mark the Deacon acted, by his own account, as *apokrisiarios* of the see to Constantinople, delivered the missive, and secured the appropriate imperial rescript for closing the temples.[45] He also received copies of the edict (τὰ ἀντίγραφα) which he presented to the bishop upon his return to Gaza. Mark does not pretend to quote their text, but observes briefly:[46]

> After seven days the imperial edict (θεῖον γράμμα) was published that the temples of Gaza be closed (κλεισθῆναι) and no longer used, and that Hilarius, a subadjutant of the *magister* [*officiorum*] (σουβαδιουβᾶ τοῦ μαγίστρου) executed the command.

This particular rescript had an entirely local aspect and simply repeated the terms of the more comprehensive laws incorporated into the Theodosian Code. It will be recalled that many of the rulings in Book XVI of the Code were *ad hoc* regulations sent to specific officials. It would not be surprising if many texts like this were not incorporated into the codification in order to avoid repetition, a salient problem with that work in any case. The *subadiuva* arrived with a retinue and seemingly executed his task with promptitude:[47]

> I [Mark] set out from Byzantium three days later and reached Gaza in ten, preceding Hilarius by seven days. I found Porphyrius ailing. I showed him the reply of John of Constantinople and made it known. [Porphyrius recovered from his fever.] Hilarius arrived after seven

---

[44] *V. Porphyrii*, Cap. 25.
[45] *V. Porphyrii*, Cap. 26.
[46] *V. Porphyrii*, Cap. 26.
[47] *V. Porphyrii*, Cap. 27.

days, having with him two *commentarienses* of consular rank, [officials in charge of state documents,] and many assistants (βοηθοί or *adiutores*) from Azotos and Ascalon, and the entire public retinue (πᾶσα δημοσία ὄψις). At once he arrested the three *curiales* of the city and got full satisfaction from them (ἱκανοδοσία), showed them the imperial edict ordering the closure of the idol-temples of Gaza under penalty of capital punishment for the *curiales* of the same city, and having overturned their idols he closed the [temples]. But the temple of Marnas he allowed to function secretly after receiving a large bribe in behalf of this. The idolaters then performed lawless acts anew according to custom.

Stories about bribery, particularly among the *subadiuvae* of the *magistri officiorum*, who were always on the take, abound during this period, and it would be naive or hyper-critical to discount such a possibility in this instance.[48] All this is consistent with Mark's other statements about the prestige, wealth, and scruples of the decurion class of Gaza. The *adiutores* of Ascalon, a city known for the persistence of Semitic pagan cult at this time, evidently made the initial contacts.[49] They would have to deal with decurions of the Palestines after Hilarius had gone.

Mark the Deacon denies us access to the *Weltanschauung* of religious habits and tenets of the Gazan elites except in one case, where, predictably, the person was converted to Christianity. Her name was Aelia, a noble imperial *nomen*, and thus the woman's first name, from the time of Hadrian. Her family belonged to the decurion class (γυνή τις τῶν ἐμφανῶν τῆς πόλεως ὀνόματι Αἰλίας), and was evidently descended from Roman settlers who had founded the *Colonia Gaza* (Κολωνία Γάζη).[50] Bishop Porphyrius converted the woman after an apparent miracle. Aelia's life had been threatened when the fetus she was carrying slipped into an abnormal position across the birth canal and caused a prolonged and dangerous labor. Mark the Deacon observes:[51]

Her parents and husband, having a superstitious fear of their gods (δεισιδαίμονες), made a sacrifice (θυσία) for her every day, and even brought in mantics and persons who performed incantations, thinking she would be helped by them.

[48] Jones, *Later Roman Empire*, 578–580. If some *subadiuvae* could accept bribes from heretics, others will certainly have taken them from pagans. Cf. the case of Priscillian. Ibid., 1057. *Subadiuvae* turn up in the literary and epigraphic sources from c. 400 onwards.
[49] Supra, Ch. III, n. 34.
[50] Hadrian's *nomen*, or middle name, was Aelius (P. Aelius Hadrianus). Albino Garzetti, *From Tiberius to the Antonines: A History of the Roman Empire AD 14–192*, tr. J.R. Foster (London 1974), 378. Cf. Ch. III, n. 9.
[51] *V. Porphyrii*, Cap. 28.

The Greek or Semitic deity invoked by Aelia's family is unknown, but it may have been the local Aphrodite. A growing distrust of its power or of the efficacy of the sacrifices led them to summon magicians to two kinds: incantors (ἐπαοιδοί), who pronounced healing spells and affixed apotropaic devices to the sick, and seers (μάντεις), who no doubt predicted the favorable outcome of Aelia's pregnancy. It is quite probable that Aelia's family purchased the services of the most prominent and expensive magicians to be had. These professions lacked the tradition-bound respectability of the priesthoods of healing deities such as the Semitic Asklepios of Berytus mentioned by Damascius in his biography of Isidore the sophist.[52] Resort to such charlatans betokened nascent atheism in the Hellenic sense, and must have been the first stage in the conversion of many persons to Christianity. Particularly after the amulets and prognoses of the mantics failed there came a second stage of "atheism" leading to Christianity. This religious and cultural mechanism has seldom been appreciated.[53] In the case of Aelia, the matter was resolved when her nurse, a Christian woman who prayed in the martyr-chapels (ἐν τοῖς εὐκτηρίοις οἴκοις) and belonged to bishop Porphyrius' small congregation, acting on the bishop's advice, approached Aelia's family and urged them, because their house was "full of idols" (κατείδωλος), to invoke Christ.[54]

The subsequently successful delivery of Aelia's child brought about the conversion of the entire family and household, which numbered 64 persons in all, a figure which must have included dependent laborers of different kinds and probably many slaves.[55] The exultant acclamation which Mark the Deacon puts into their mouths resembles acclamations addressed to pagan deities: "Great is the God of the Christians, great is the priest Porphyrius" (μέγας

---

[52] ὅτι ὁ ἐν Βηρυτῷ . . . Ἀσκληπιός οὐκ ἔστιν Ἕλλην οὐδε Αἰγύπτιος, ἀλλά τις ἐπιχώριος Φοῖνιξ. Damascius, *Epit. Phot. 348* (Zintzen, 283).

[53] The inscription on a private shrine dedicated to the goddess Agdistis at Philadelphia in Lydia (OGIS 985, 2nd/1st c. B.C.) requires that the person entering the temenos be free from the taint of sorceries, poisonings, love charms, abortion, contraception and so forth: "Let not woman or man who do the aforementioned acts come into this shrine; for in it are enthroned mighty deities." A.D. Nock, *Conversion* (Oxford 1933), 216f. The "second stage of atheism" might be reached when a person seeking divine aid, and disappointed with his sorceries, refused to return to his ancestral gods, but embraced a new cult instead. Christianity became an important option from the fourth century onward.

[54] *V. Porphyrii*, Cap. 29.

[55] *V. Porphyrii*, Cap. 30.

ὁ Θεὸς τῶν Χριστιανῶν, μέγας ὁ ἱερεὺς Πορφύριος).[56] The naming of the bishop is, however, a clear departure from ancient practice.

The conversion and subsequent baptism of Aelia's household will require our attention further on in this analysis, in connection with the growth of the small Christian community at Gaza. The event was unique. Bishop Porphyrius failed completely elsewhere to breach the solid ranks of the decurion class, which kept its faith in the Graeco-Semitic deities to the end, or at any rate until the terminus of Mark the Deacon's narrative.[57]

Mark the Deacon names only one of the landed magnates, a certain Sampsychos (Σαψύχου τοῦ πρωτεύοντος).[58] This Sampsychos and the rest of the city council kept their grip on the public opinion of the urban demos even after the eventual demolition of the Marneion and other temples of Gaza in 402.[59] Mark mentions a dispute which arose between Sampsychos and the *oikonomos* or administrator of revenues of the Gazan church. It "concerned some villages" (χάριν χωρίων), an innocent enough phrase which perhaps conceals too much. He adds in the same context that the pagans were becoming enraged the more they saw Christianity growing (προκόπτοντα τὸν Χριστιανισμόν).[60] The hagiographer avoids detail, and the historian is justified in asking whether, in the course of managing the church lands, the Christian *oikonomos* did not engage in proselytization on the estates of Sampsychos, which may have interlocked with, or adjoined, those of the church. Monks did this sort of thing constantly in northern Syria.[61] At Gaza, it is conceivable that the secular clergy took a hand in such enterprises. The city after all had an aggressive bishop, and Aramaic-speaking monks seem to have been in short supply, as none are mentioned in Mark's account. The countryside was thoroughly pagan, and even if Maiuma had a monastic population, it may well have consisted mostly of migrant Copts from Egypt. Hence an insuperable linguis-

---

[56] Erik Peterson argued that the formula here has a monotheistic sense, as for example: μέγας ὁ θεὸς τῶν Χριστιανῶν, οὐκ ἔστιν ἕτερος θεὸς πλὴν αὐτοῦ. *EIC ΘΕΟC* 197. Pagan parallels to this formula are apparent in a vast number of epigraphic and textual examples. *EIC ΘΕΟC*, 200–210. The most exact of these is the Ephesian acclamation: μεγάλη ἡ Ἄρτεμις Ἐφεσίων (p. 199). But this comes from Christian scripture (*Acts* 19.34).

[57] For similar fifth-century examples at Athens, Alexandria, Aphrodisias and Berytus, see infra, Ch. IV–VI.

[58] *V. Porphyrii*, Cap. 95.

[59] Infra, Ch. III, Sect. 4.

[60] *V. Porphyrii*, Cap. 95. On the demographic features of the growth of Christianity in Gaza, see infra, Ch. III, Sect. 5.

[61] Infra, Ch. VIII, passim.

tic barrier will have arisen between them and the pagan rustics.[62] If
the *oikonomos* did indeed meddle with Sampsychos' properties, the
latter may well have feared a violations of the peace of the gods and
consequent crop failures, not to mention insubordination to his
bailiffs and a breakdown of the entire agricultural regime. Whatever the origin of the dispute, a heated debate ensued between Sampsychos and the *oikonomos* in which the combative deacon Baruch
became embroiled as well. The altercation seems to have occurred
in or near the agora and public buildings, for the remainder of the
city council (οἱ λοιποὶ τοῦ βουλευτηρίου) joined the dispute.
Gaza still had a vocal and potentially seditious demos:[63]

> Many of the citizens approached the councillors, finding in this
> [altercation] an excuse to harm Christians . . . The idol-maniacs
> raged even to the point of taking up swords and clubs, and killed
> seven persons and wounded many others.

In the subsequent street fighting, which proved to be entirely
one-sided, the pagan mob stormed and plundered the episkopeion,
and Porphyrius fled with Mark the Deacon through many houses
(διὰ τῶν δωμάτων), and in such a state of fear that they walked on
free-standing walls (τοιχοβατήσαντες).[64] The men, who seem not
to have countenanced martyrdom in this instance, finally took
refuge in a shack or housetop dwelling to which access was got
through a skylight (διά τινος λυκίσκου), presumably with a pul-
ley. A poor girl aged fourteen resided there. She worked to support
her aged grandmother. They were both of them pagans.[65]

The upshot of this chance meeting will claim our attention later.
Its significance lies in the fact that, just as the large crowd of the
demos (πολλοὶ τῶν πολίτων) which pillaged the episkopeion indicates the existence of a radically pagan and politically vocal artisan
and mercantile class, not to mention the retainers of the decurion
class, there also existed an undoubtedly large number of urban
poor who, it seems, although no longer receiving sacrificial meats
from the temples after their closure, remained adamant in their
allegiance to the old gods and did not defect to Christianity for the

---

[62] This supposition is plausibly consistent with the evidence for rural conditions
discussed infra, Ch. VII–XI.

[63] *V. Porphyrii*, Cap. 95.

[64] *V. Porphyrii*, Cap. 96.

[65] *V. Porphyrii*, Cap. 97. This is one exception to the rule that Constantine the
Great in every instance allied himself to the Christian poor, as must have been the
case with his large gift of estates that went to the Roman churches as endowments.
There were many urban pagan poor who did not avail themselves of Christian
almsgiving, as the *V. Porphyrii* shows. Cf. Peter Brown, *The Cult of the Saints*, 45ff.

sake of free bread. During the stay of Porphyrius and Mark with
the women, the latter served bread, oil, cheese, soaked pulses, and
wine, but doubtless in no more than subsistence portions, for
Salaphtha, the fourteen year-old girl, invited the men to "take it,
my lords, and bless my poverty." There was evidently not enough
food to go around: Mark consumed the cheese and wine, Porphyrius the bread, pulse, and some water.[66] The anti-Christian riot
occurred *after* the final destruction of the Marneion and dedication
of the Eudoxiana basilica on its site in 407. At this time the
ecclesiastical bread dole to the poor probably played second fiddle
to the large disbursements in food, clothing, and specie accorded to
migrants at the *xenodocheion* of the Eudoxiana, which basilica the
empress Eudoxia had subsidized and erected in the old temenos of the
Marneion.[67] Even so, a daily sum of six obols was defrayed to each
poor citizen and foreigner.[68] These foodstuffs and monies evidently
derived from the church's endowment, which will have been provided in the form of agricultural lands.[69] Years later, bishop Porphyrius' will stipulated additionally that each poor man receive on
the fast days during Lent a provision doubtless intended to lure
pagans as well as Christians to the churches.[70] The will perhaps
represents a confession that the ordinary dole had failed to draw
pagans to the churches in sufficient numbers to show the success of
Christianization during Porphyrius' administration of the Gazan
see, after an episcopate of perhaps a decade and a half.[71]

   The riot eventually died down, but Porphyrius and Mark found
it too risky to return to the episkopeion except by night. There they
found the indestructible Baruch, who had come close to dying
(ἐσχάτως ἔχοντα) from the beating he had received. A force of
troops led by a *commentariensis* of the governor of First Palestine
arrived some days later and imposed stern reprisals, although the
number of persons arrested is not given, nor are executions
reported:[72]

---

   [66] *V. Porphyrii*, Cap. 98.
   [67] Infra, Ch. III, Sect. 4.
   [68] *V. Porphyrii*, Cap. 94.
   [69] For Constantine the Great's endowments to the Roman church, see infra, Ch.
III, n. 248.
   [70] *V. Porphyrii*, Cap. 94. Mark the Deacon appears to base his statement on a
knowledge of the actual document.
   [71] The personal and private wealth of the bishop was thus an important factor
in the religious transformation of Gaza, a fact consistent with Raymond Van
Dam's thesis. Supra, Ch. III, n. 2.
   [72] *V. Porphyrii*, Cap. 99.

[The *commentariensis*] punished some, but flogged others with an ox-tendon whip (βουνευρίσας) and then released them, and created no small fear in the city in restoring order.

The decurions can hardly have been among those flogged, for, as has been seen, they enjoyed immense wealth and useful political connections.[73] Nor does Mark the Deacon blame them directly for the riot, which had a spontaneous origin. It is unknown whether any of the pagan Gazan decurions held senatorial rank at this juncture.

In all this one can see the basic leniency with which the law was enforced, and another example of the now-deceased emperor Arcadius' express wish that the Gazans not be alienated, as he observed some years earlier when Eudoxia first broached to him the subject of terminating the secret rites still in progress at the Marneion.[74] Arcadius observed:[75]

I know that the city is given to idolatry, but it is right-minded with respect to taxation and pays much of the public revenue. If we attack them fearfully all of a sudden, [the decurions] will flee and we shall lose much of the revenue, but if it seems appropriate, we shall grieve them partially by taking away the titles of the idol-maniacs and other civil offices, and we shall command that their temples be closed and no longer used. For when we trouble them, we fall short in all areas, and they know the truth of this [dictum].

Gaza, with its seaport of Maiuma, generated great revenue from the imports on the carrying traffic exiting to the Mediterranean from the inland Damascus-'Aqaba trade route. The fiscal realities of this situation required the cooperation of the decurions in some measure. It is possible, as well, that they were punctual in paying the *annona*, the annual tax in kind on the products of their estates, in order to avoid criticism and repression precisely because of their adherence to the old Graeco-Semitic cults. Arcadius' point was simple: suppression meant the forfeiture of the Gazans' coopera-

---

[73] The persons flogged will not have been decurions, but the urban artisans and poor who made up their *clientelae*. City councillors "enjoyed as *honestiores* a number of legal privileges. They could not lawfully be flogged or tortured. . . ." Two laws of Constantius II forbade governors to inflict corporal injuries on decurions, and two more of Theodosius I threatened governors with the severest penalties if they flogged decurions with lashes weighted with lead. Libanius mentions frequent violations of this rule. Jones, *Later Roman Empire*, 749f. We might suppose that Kynegios as an imperial *comes* and *consistorianus* took scrupulous care to avoid offending the imperial will.

[74] *V. Porphyrii*, Cap. 40. Both Bury, LRE 1, 142–147 and Jones, *Later Roman Empire*, 344–346 accept the historicity of Mark the Deacon's account of the negotiations that preceded the empress' request.

[75] *V. Porphyrii*, Cap. 41.

tion. The emperor's surmise proved accurate, for after the final destruction of the Marneion many of the decurion class did eventually migrate from the city.[76]

The riot which arose between Sampsychos and the *oikonomos* of the Gazan see—whose name is interestingly omitted—suggests the large-scale demographic survival of the inner-city pagan population some five years after the destruction of the Marneion. The *stasis* was sufficiently popular to be allowed to run its course, and was thereafter left to the troops of a nearby provincial governor to punish. The eirenarchs, who figure prominently in the earlier part of Mark the Deacon's narrative, are here conspicuously absent. The hagiographer confirms the persistence of the old belief in Zeus Marnas among the inner-city pagans who exhibited a cultic deference toward the marble debris of the Marneion some 15 to 20 years later:[77]

> After the ashes had settled and all the abominations had been destroyed, the bishop [Porphyrius] ordered the remaining debris of the marble work of the Marneion, which the pagans said was sacred (ἱερά) and lay in a place not to be trodden (ἐν τόπῳ ἀβάτῳ), particularly for women, to be used as paving stones in the main street (πλατεῖα) outside the temple, so that they would be trodden upon not only by men, but also by women, and dogs and swine and beasts. This grieved the idolators more than the burning of the temple, wherefore the greater number of them, mainly the women, do not walk on the marbles up to the present day.

Recent excavations at Aphrodisias in Caria, another city which had an intractable pagan population in the fifth century,[78] provides an archaeological example that corroborates the use made of the spolia from the Marneion. At Aphrodisias a vast number of relief sculptures taken from buildings and possibly funerary monuments was used to pave a large courtyard. These materials had quite obviously to be placed face-down with their flat sides upward in order to create a level surface.[79] The artistic value of the relief sculpture did not mitigate its offensiveness to the Christian religion, and so a suitable, and at the same time useful, purpose was found for the blocks. The date of the desposit has not been established, but it can hardly have been earlier than c. 400.[80] Bishop Porphyrius in this instance aimed to insult the cult of Zeus Marnas, but its

---

[76] *V. Porphyrii*, Cap. 63.
[77] *V. Porphyrii*, Cap. 76.
[78] Infra, Ch. VI.
[79] Kenan T. Erim, public lecture, Washington, D.C., March 1986.
[80] Ibidem.

adherents continued to revere the spolia of the ruined temple. We
do not know whether Christians reacted to the stones with analogous dread, or whether to counter this Porphyrius had his workmen
carve crosses and other symbols of Christianization on the
marbles.[81]

In light of this it should not be surprising that Christian monks of
the fifth century like Daniel the Stylite should often have entered
and resided in temples, whose statues had long before been removed, to prove the impotence of the old gods.[82] In some districts
their power was thought to inhere even in marble and stone debris.
The generation at Gaza which had seen its temples destroyed did
not accept the destruction of the Marneion as proof of their gods'
impotence. Of the next generation we know nothing.

III. *The Territorium of Gaza*

Mark the Deacon, like his superior, bishop Porphyrius, was preoccupied with the problem of urban paganism and the issue of finding
means to suppress it. He therefore gives short shrift to the *territorium*
of Gaza. Yet his work contains any number of reports bearing on
religious conditions there. Relations between the *polis* and the
immediately contiguous lands under its direct administration, the
territorium (χώρα), were tightly governed, particularly as the decurion class, the temples of the local deities, and the Christian church
often drew their incomes from villages on estate lands (*fundi*).
Bailiffs (οἰκονόμοι) supervised agricultural labor and improve-
ments on the land, drew up accounts of production, settled disputes
between parties or villages, and much else.[83] Freeholders (δεσπόται),
or owners of their own plots, who sold their agricultural surplus in
the *agora* of the *polis*, also existed in the typical urban *territorium*
along with the tenants and day-laborers who worked on the
estates.[84] Unfortunately little is known about the organization of
the *territorium* of Gaza except that it produced wines of export
quality that found their way to Gaul.[85] Nor are the early arrange-

---

[81] Supra, Ch. II, Sect. 2.

[82] The "church" in question was surely a pagan temple, for the word *naos* is
used. The nearby chapel of St. Michael is by contrast called an *euktērion*. *Vita S.
Danielis Stylitae*, ed. H. Delehaye, *Analecta Bollandiana* 32 (1913), 134, line 12.

[83] See the detailed information in the life of Theodore of Sykeon (c. 582–600),
who served briefly as the bishop of Anastasiopolis in First Galatia. *V. Theodori
Sykeotis*, Cap. 76 in *Vie de Théodore de Sykéôn*, ed. tr. A.-J. Festugière, 1 (Brussels
1970), 63.

[84] Infra, Ch. VIII, and Jones, *Later Roman Empire*, 773–781.

[85] Jones, *Later Roman Empire*, 824 and 850.

ments for the Christianization of the land known either, except for the brief settlement of the hermit Hilarion (291/2–371) there *circa* 330. He was himself born of pagan parents in the village of Thabatha situated some five Roman miles from Gaza, and returned to those parts after studying grammar in Alexandria, where he had come under the influence of St. Anthony the hermit.[86] Hilarion did not proselytize exclusively in the countryside, but is said to have performed cures on victims of incantations in Gaza and to have resisted the cult of Zeus Marnas in the Hippodrome.[87] He performed the notable achievement of converting the family of the later ecclesiastical historian Salaminos Sozomenos, whose well-to-do family lived on a rural estate thereabouts.[88] Hilarion left Gaza permanently thereafter to practice the life of an itinerant hermit.[89] There is thus no evidence for any substantial monastic settlements in the villages of the *territorium* of Gaza, or for the widespread Christianization of the rustics.

Some sixty years elapsed before the arrival of Porphyrius as the bishop-elect of Gaza, which Henri Grégoire and M.-A. Kugener dated to March 395.[90] Porphyrius, accompanied by Mark the Deacon, took the road from Caesarea Maritima to Gaza by way of Lydda-Diospolis, where they spent the night. As the men reached the approaches to Gaza the next day, they met with interference from the rustics who were pagan to a man:[91]

> There were some pagan villages along the road near Gaza. By preconcerted plan the inhabitants spread the entire road with brambles and stakes so that no one could pass, and they poured out slime and made smoke with other foul-smelling materials, so that we were choked by the rotten smell and were imperilled in our eyesight. We entered Gaza at the third hour of the night, hardly having saved ourselves.

Mark advises the reader that this occurred "by preconcerted plan" (ἐκ συνθήματος).[92] The sites are called "villages" (κῶμαι) and the dwellers therein οἰκήτορες, a generic term for "inhabitants" that tells nothing about their economic status, that is, whether they

---

[86] Jerome, *V. Hilarionis*, PL 23, 30f.

[87] Jerome, *V. Hilarionis*, PL 23, 38f.

[88] Sozomen, HE 5.15.

[89] For the chronology of St. Hilarion's life, see: P. de Labriole, *Histoire de l'eglise*, 3 (Paris 1947), 321–324. The author mistakes Hilarion's birthplace for the site of his subsequent activities in and around Gaza.

[90] *V. Porphyrii*, Cap. 17.

[91] *V. Porphyrii*, Cap. 17.

[92] Or, as Grégoire-Kugener (1930) would have it, "sur un mot d'ordre." *V. Porphyrii*, Cap. 17.

were tenants or freeholders. The circumstances suggest, however,
that these folk lived on the estates of the pagan decurions. Some
Gazans had, after all, been present at Porphyrius' election in
Caesarea.[93] It can hardly be doubted that these were prominent
citizens, although Mark the Deacon is silent about their exact
status. These will have been either pagan decurions visiting the
provincial capital of First Palestine on business with the governor,
or their business agents, who would naturally have notified their
employers in the first instance of this new development, which
concerned everyone at old Gaza.[94] At any rate, they objected to
Porphyrius' appointment, sensing in him, because of his monastic
background, a diehard who would threaten the very existence of
the Graeco-Semitic cults.[95] This scenario is fully consistent with the
subsequent conflict between the bishop and the Gazan city council.
Nor is it probable that Mark the Deacon intended to suggest the
existence of a Christian opposition to Porphyrius' appointment.
The point is that, once the bishop and his aide had left for Gaza,
word may have been sent to the bailiffs on the decurions' estates
and perhaps to villages of freeholders to prepare an unpleasant
reception for the Christian prelate. Such acts were not unknown in
the fifth century.[96] The assault on bishop Porphyrius' and Mark's
senses fell short of insult or battery,[97] but demonstrates the ability
of the pagan decurions of Gaza to mobilize large numbers of rural
dependants against the agents of Christianization.

The principal participants in the riot mentioned in the previous
section that was triggered by a dispute "over some villages" (χάριν
χωρίων) may well have been the *clientelae* of the decurions as well,

---

[93] *V. Porphyrii*, Cap. 16.
[94] Business correspondence is well attested in the papyri. *Select Papyri I: Private
Affairs*, tr. A.S. Hunt and C.C. Edgar (London-New York 1932), 346f. and
386–389.
[95] Other die-hards were Marcellus of Apamea (while he lived) and Theophilus
of Alexandria (once aroused). Supra, Ch. II, Sect. 3. Bishops of this kind seem to
have been the exception to the rule.
[96] Cf. the story of Shenute of Atripe's arrival at Pleuit. Infra, Ch. IX, Sect. 1.
[97] But see the commentary on the *Lex Aquilia* in *Digest* 9.2.27 (Ulpian): "On the
other hand, if you have not yet done me any damage but you have such a fire that I
fear you will cause me damage, I think your giving security against threatened
damage should suffice." This ruling seems to apply only to real property. Nor was
the building of the fires to "welcome" bishop Porphyrius the type of "insult"
(*iniuria*) called *clamor*: "Labeo says that to raise an outcry amounts to *iniuria*. An
outcry is said to consist in a tumult or in concerted vociferous abuse. When several
voices come together it is called 'concerted vociferous abuse' when the voices are
indeed concerted against the individual . . . and tends to bring someone into
hatred, ridicule or contempt." *Digest* 47.10.15 (Ulpian). *Digesta Iustiniani Augusti*,
ed. T. Mommsen, 2 v. (Berlin 1970–1963) Tr. excerpted from: Justinian, *The
Digest of the Roman Law*, tr. C.F. Kolbert (London 1979), 84 and 170.

whose patrons could no longer bear the intrusion of an aggressive Christian clergy amongst the agriculturalists on their estates. All this suggests a complex and intractable grouping of agricultural relations and interests spanning the cultural frontiers of the *polis* and *chōra*, all of them dominated by the Gazan decurion class. While Christianity eventually made inroads into the urban population of Gaza, Mark the Deacon offers not a single piece of evidence to suggest that this drive successfully penetrated the *territorium* of the city. It could hardly have been otherwise with the trenchant opposition of the decurions, whose religious conservatism shielded the agricultural regime of their estates and the contiguous villages of freeholders. This hypothesis is fully consistent with the evidence on rural conditions in Bithynia, Syria, and Egypt.[98] The Gazan materials are important here, because they reveal the restrictive influence that decurions often exerted on the Christianization of the countryside, even in the presence of an aggressive clerical regime.[99]

The prevailing hostility to the Christianization of the countryside is illustrated, as well, in the previously mentioned anecdote about the beating administered to the Christian ecclesiastic Baruch:[100]

> When Baruch went out to perform the ecclesiastical canon in a village not far from the city, [he got into a dispute with a pagan]. The unholy (ἀνόσιος) [pagan] called in some farmers, his co-villagers, and they began to strike Baruch with rods, and cast him half-dead into a desert place, having carried him outside the village.

Unconverted villages, whether populated by freeholders or tenant farmers, (γεωργούς τινας ὁμοίους αὐτοῦ συγκωμήτας), lay quite close to the city walls (εἰς κώμην οὐκ μήκοθεν τῆς πόλεως), and were in complete agreement about the measures to be taken against the Christian cleric.

IV. The Polemic against the Pagan Cults of Gaza and Destruction of the Temples in 402

The evidence cited in the two previous sections suggests that the Christianization of Gaza, as it occurred during the episcopate of Porphyrius (395–420), took place in the city proper. Mark the Deacon, who composed his biography of the bishop well before large numbers of urban pagans had converted to Christianity,[101]

---

[98] Infra, Ch. VII–IX.
[99] This may have been the case at Apamea in Second Syria as well. Supra, Ch. II, Sect. 3.
[100] *V. Porphyrii*, Cap. 22.
[101] Infra, Ch. III, Sect. 5.

dwells in particular detail on the destruction of the shrines and
temple buildings of Gaza. All this has the air of a polemical
statement. Mark's delineation of the decurions' impotence in the
face of an aggressive Christian bishop armed with imperial edicts
had the propagandistic intent of convincing his readership, made
up of Aramaic- and Greek-speaking Christians, that the new religion would prevail despite the influence and manipulation of the
pagan landed magnates, who still largely controlled the local politics and economy of old Gaza at the time of the composition of his
work.[102] The story is told in great detail. Mark the Deacon must
necessarily have described the pagan buildings and shrines with
precision, because his readership knew these sites well, witnessed
the sacrifices and processions near them, and stood by during their
final and inexorable demolition. The author had every reason to be
precise.

Mark the Deacon describes the ritual associated with only two of
the Gazan cults, those of Zeus Marnas and the Graeco-Semitic
Aphrodite. The latter can be dealt with briefly. It will be recalled
that an effigy of the female deity stood under a sort of canopy near
the Maiuma gate of Gaza, and that women frequented the spot to
pray for the assistance of the deity in having intercourse with their
husbands. As the hagiographer had it, the dream-oracles which
predicted success were entirely bogus and women "deceived each
other" by embellishing stories about alleged epiphanies.[103] Some
few persons who accepted baptism admitted this; as Mark
observes: "We know these things from those who repelled error and
recognized the truth."[104] All this was grist for bishop Porphyrius'
mill as his polemic against the pagan cults of Gaza intensified.
Porphyrius, or perhaps his disciple Mark, refused to grant that the
supposed dream-oracles were fulfilled even by daimonic power, but
rather ascribed them to a synchronism based on chance (ἀπὸ
συμβάντος τοῦτο γίνεται):[105]

> But some idol-worshippers, unable to bear the misfortunes of the
> hardships which they endured obediently according to the command
> of the pagan god Aphrodite, became vexed and admitted the decep-
> tion. For such are the pagan gods in deception even as to say wholly

---

[102] This is the *prima facie* intent of Mark the Deacon's work. It is argued below in
Appendix I that an *Urredaktion* of the text was edited to bolster Porphyrius'
demand enunciated at the Council of Diospolis in 415 that Maiuma and Gaza be
reintegrated as a single see under, naturally, his own jurisdiction.
[103] *V. Porphyrii*, Cap. 59.
[104] *V. Porphyrii*, Cap. 59.
[105] *V. Porphyrii*, Cap. 60.

nothing truthful. Nor is it possible for them to see the certain, but they feign speciously to appear to those who are enslaved by them. For how can those who are dislocated from the truth speak the truth? Even if they might happen to predict something, it happens by chance, just as often happens with men when someone predicts concerning an event and it happens by chance. We wonder at chance events that happen by chance rarely, and keep silent about chance events that happen continually. This is how it is with the pagan gods and their error.

This demythologization of pagan oracular cult, harking back as it does to Democritus of Abdera's theory (and Epicurus' adaptation of it) about the random collision of indivisible particles (*atoma*) in empty space (*kenos*), was perhaps formulated for catechumens and for the pagan critics of Porphyrius' harsh efforts at conversion. This formulation was meant for anyone who had the slightest knowledge of the Greek *paideia*, where, for example, the activity of chance (τύχη) was a common theme with historians. Christian writers more often than not attacked the theory of chance because it vitiated the idea of divine providence.[106] But here the acknowledgement of τύχη had a catechetical function. Yet Mark the Deacon avoids the word τύχη, substituting a harmless equivalent (ἀπὸ συμβάντος) except in compound words like ἐπιτυχία and ἀποτυχία. The pious converters of pagans would have no more truck with the term τύχη than with the Tyche which the Gazans and most other Hellenized Syrians worshipped in their city's Tychaion. This terminologically sensitive style of argumentation was quite sophisticated and equally uncommon. Christian propagandists more often than not ascribed pagan dream-oracles and the resultant "miracles" (θαύματα) to the activity of *daimones*. With Porphyrius and Mark, however, the deities deceive but rarely act.

The upshot of the polemic against the Gazan cult of Aphrodite was the smashing of the idol. This occurred when a Christian procession led by Porphyrius up from Maiuma entered the city. With the vast quantity of archaeological evidence available from other sites about the smashing of statues, it can hardly be doubted that Porphyrius' followers performed this salutary service.[107] Mark the Deacon provides a mythologized version of the event, designed no doubt to exculpate the Gazan clergy from blame for injuries to two pagan bystanders, one of them fatal:[108]

---

[106] For a rich variety of texts citing *tyche*, see: G.W. Lampe, *A Patristic Greek Lexicon* (Oxford 1961),1422.
[107] See the discussion on the smashing of the statue of Allat in her temple at Palmyra. Supra, Ch. II, Sect. 3.
[108] *V. Porphyrii*, Cap. 61.

> After we disembarked into the city [of Maiuma], as was said, and as
> we reached the place [in Gaza] in which the said idol of Aphrodite
> was (for the Christians were carrying the worthy cross of Christ, that
> is the sign of the cross), the pagan god dwelling in the statue (ἐν τῇ
> στήλῃ), upon seeing the sign and being unable to bear looking upon
> it, departed from the statue in great disorder and cast it down and
> broke it into pieces. Two idol-worshippers happened to be standing
> by the altar at which the idol stood, and upon its fall it sliced off the
> head of one person and broke the shoulder and wrist of the other. For
> both men had been standing there sneering at the holy people.

The author even provides the motive for the acts of mayhem. Many
other instances of a *daimon* supposedly dwelling within a statue, cult
object, or even the building blocks of temples are attested.[109] The
image of the cross, the instrument of Christianization par excellence, was most often carved on statues and their faces simply
knocked off. Here, however, the mere sight of the cross sufficed to
drive out the pagan god (δαίμων). The motive for breaking the
statue into little pieces in this instance lay in the fact that it had the
form of a naked woman, "all of it appearing unseemly."[110] Statues
of Aphrodite did, on occasion, have a truly erotic quality, as for
example that of the birth of the goddess unearthed at Aphrodisias
in Caria, which strikes an almost cheesecake pose.[111] When seen in
this light, Mark the Deacon's myth claims exaggerated status and
power for Porphyrius, and sets him above many other well-known
bishops who demolished temples, but whose followers' chisels and
hammers had to be applied to achieve the result that Porphyrius
got automatically.[112]

The destruction of the statue of Aphrodite took place on 1 May
402, according to Grégoire's chronology, and therefore in the
seventh year of Porphyrius' episcopate. Several days later, a large
imperial military force entered old Gaza. It was evidently the
rumored arrival of these troops that prevented the pagans from
rioting. Kynegios, a member of the imperial consistory and the
holder of unknown offices and titles (and *not* to be confused with the
more famous Praetorian Prefect Maternus Cynegius from the reign
of Theodosius the Great)[113] (Κυνήγιος οὕτω καλούμενος τοῦ

---

[109] Supra, Ch. I, Sect. 3.
[110] *V. Porphyrii*, Cap. 59.
[111] Infra, Ch. VI, n. 7.
[112] This argument was dictated by the requirement of impressing the provincial
bishops' synod at Diospolis in 415. It served the secondary purpose of propping up
Porphyrius' prestige with the Christian congregation of Gaza after the failure of
his cause at the council. Cf. Appendix I below.
[113] Maternus Cynegius' career is fully discussed by Gassowska, "The Allat
Temple in Palmyra," 119–122.

κωνσιστωρίου) commanded the men.[114] With him were the governor (ὑπατικός) and *dux* of First Palestine, with the troops of the province and a body of civil officials (most of them from the *officium* of the governor and no doubt of prosaic rank such as assessors, notaries, and so forth (ἔχων μεθ' ἑαυτοῦ τὸν ὑπατικὸν καὶ τὸν δοῦκα καὶ πολλὴν στρατιωτικὴν καὶ πολιτικὴν χεῖρα).[115] Kynegios was, not surprisingly, "an amazing man boiling with zeal for the faith" (ἀνὴρ θαυμάσιος καὶ ζέων περὶ τὴν πίστην).[116] He bore an imperial rescript which bishop Porphyrius and the metropolitan of Caesarea Maritima had wrung from the emperor Arcadius through the good offices of a friend of John Chrysostom, the *cubicularius* Amantius, who had gotten them an interview with the empress Eudoxia.[117] The edict stipulated the demolition of the temples of old Gaza. Its text survives neither in the Theodosian Code nor in Mark the Deacon's life of Porphyrius. The latter source blandly observes: "The Augusta summoned and ordered him [Kynegios] to raze all the idol temples to the ground and consign them to fire" (παρακαλεσαμένη δὲ αὐτὸν ἡ αὐγούστα παρήγγειλεν αὐτῷ πάντα τὰ εἰδωλεῖα ἕως ἐδάφους καταστρέψαι καὶ πυρὶ παραδοῦναι),[118] a statement that no doubt sums up the formal document drawn up by the quaestor in the presence of Eudoxia Augusta and the prelates.[119]

Kynegios' public proclamation of the edict created a great stir among the pagan Gazans, who submitted before the mailed fist of emperor Arcadius:[120]

> After the tenth day Kynegios arrived, having with him the consular and *dux*, and a large body of soldiery and civil officials. Many idol-worshippers saw ahead, and went out from the city, some to villages and others to different cities. They were the greater part of the wealthy in the city. The said Kynegios requisitioned the houses of those who had fled. On the next day, having called upon the people of the city, with the *dux* and consular governor present, he publicly read the imperial rescript that the idols be overthrown and idol-temples be given over to fire. As soon as they heard, the idol-worshippers lamented with a loud voice that the officials were angry and would send the soldiers against them to strike them with rods and cudgels. But the Christians praised the emperors and magistrates.

---

[114] *V. Porphyrii*, Cap. 51.
[115] *V. Porphyrii*, Cap. 63.
[116] *V. Porphyrii*, Cap. 51.
[117] Bury, LRE 1, 142–148. Jones, *Later Roman Empire*, 344–346.
[118] *V. Porphyrii*, Cap. 51. This clause is repeated in, Cap. 63, when the contents of the edict, as read to the citizens of Gaza, are summarized.
[119] *V. Porphyrii*, Cap. 50.
[120] *V. Porphyrii*, Cap. 63 and 64.

The story that the great part of the landed magnates (ἦσαν δὲ οἱ
πλείους τῶν πλουσίων τῆς πόλεως) migrated to the countryside
or other cities, where they will have had villas and townhouses, is
consistent with known examples of the wide dispersion of estates,
which individual proprietors sometimes had in several provinces.[121]
The economic side of the story makes sense, but the demographic
part lacks plausibility. If many pagan decurions migrated, enough
of them remained in old Gaza to keep the reins of civil power firmly
in their own hands even after the destruction of the temples, as the
previously mentioned incident between Sampsychos and the
Christian *oikonomos* shows.[122] The requisitioning of houses in cities
for billeting troops had become common by this time, and provoked riots at Thessalonike in 392.[123] Kynegios mollified the temporarily overawed populace of old Gaza by accommodating his
troops in the abandoned town houses of the landed magnates. The
later riot which resulted from the altercation between Sampsychos
and the *oikonomos* would reveal what Kynegios already knew well,
that the temper of the *demos* required care. Imperial civil officials
and military men usually exercised tact, so long as they were in
control, but bishop Porphyrius, if left to his own devices, could not
guarantee the same good behavior by the lower clergy.

As mentioned in a previous section, there were eight temples in
old Gaza, those of Helios, Aphrodite, Apollo, Korē, and Hekate,
and the Tychaion, the Heroeion, and Marneion. Except for the
Marneion, these buildings had all been out of service and closed
since the visit of the imperial *subadiuva* Hilarius, who had closed all
the temples of old Gaza in 398, according to Grégoire's reckoning.
The imperial commissioners had allowed the Marneion to go on
functioning secretly in return for a bribe, a common form of connivance at this time, none of which brings surprise.[124] Whether a
mediocre Christian or pagan, the official concerned was certainly
corrupt. The imperial response now lay with a man of different
character, the zealous Kynegios. Mark the Deacon refers to the
buildings as "public idol-temples" (ναοὶ εἰδώλων δημόσιοι), a
term which reflects Julian's short-lived restoration of temple lands
to the cities and the continued use of the buildings thereafter at
Gaza. The hagiographer indicates nothing about their demolition,

---

[121] Jones, *Later Roman Empire*, 781–788.
[122] Supra, Ch. III, Sect. 3.
[123] ἐταράχθη ἡ πόλις διὰ τὰ μητάτα τοῦ στρατοῦ. Theophanes, *Chronographia*,
1 (1883), 72, line 21f.
[124] Jones, *Later Roman Empire*, 407f.

reserving the detailed narrative for the principal temple, the Marneion.[125]

Mark the Deacon's account of the razing of the Marneion, the temple of the Cretan-born Zeus, is the most detailed account of its kind from any period. An impressive building, the story of its destruction added to the prestige of Porphyrius, and therein lies the propagandistic intent of this section. The ecclesiastically sponsored publication of the narrative provided one more sign of the triumph of the Christian God, particularly for Gaza, where the decurions, *demos* and rustics remained adamantly polytheistic.[126] Mark's narrative, then, provided some consolation to the Christians of the old city, obstructed and hedged in as they were by the pagan majority in the decades after 402.

The configuration of the Marneion can be reconstructed from Mark the Deacon's elliptical description:[127]

> It was round, ringed about by two stoas one inside the other, and its center space was a domed baldaschino upraised to a height, and the [temenos] had certain other [shrines] which were suited for idols, well-placed for the defiled and lawless acts performed by the idol-worshippers.

The building probably dated from the second century A.D., and was of the domed Pantheon type.[128] Its roundness, (στρογγοειδές), the concentric stoas (περιβεβλημένον δυσὶν στοαῖς ἀλληλοεσω-τέραις), and domed central space (ἀναφυσητὸν κιβώριον καὶ ἀνατεταμένον εἰς ὕψος) suggest a resemblance to the domed circular churches of the Roman East like that at Bostra in the province of Arabia, whose dome rested upon the inner colonnade. Around the domed space of the Marneion will have stood two concentric galleries divided by a *second* colonnade. The outermost gallery will have been at ground level only, the inner one perhaps with a floorless attic. There is, unfortunately, no archaeological evidence on the Marneion, but to judge from Mark the Deacon's description, it appears to have had a similar layout to San Stefano Rotundo in Rome.[129] A Gazan coin which purports to show the

---

[125] *V. Porphyrii*, Cap. 64.
[126] Cf. the evidence of the Gazan Hellenes' anti-Christian riot discussed in Ch. III, Sect. 3, 4, and 5.
[127] *V. Porphyrii*, Cap. 75.
[128] G.F. Hill, "Some Palestinian Cults in the Graeco-Roman Age" *Proceedings of the British Academy* 5 (1912), 15, n. 1.
[129] For discussion of the architectural features of Santo Stefano, see: Richard Krautheimer, "Santo Stefano Rotondo a Roma e la chiesa del Santo Sepolcro a Gerusalemme," *Rivista di archeologia cristiana* 12 (1935), 54, 55, 59, 81–85, and Tav.

temple indicates a conventional façade, two columns supporting an architrave block with a pediment above, the configuration, probably, of the temple's entrance.[130] The effigy of Zeus Marnas was probably situated under the dome, although there seems to be no firm evidence for the siting of statues from other circular temples. Nor can a plausible scheme be developed for the location of the other statues of the gods within the building. The Marneion had bronze gates (τὰς χαλκᾶς θύρας)[131] and was roofed with wooden beams (ξύλα).[132]

At any rate, Kynegios' soldiers and a mob of Christians from old Gaza and the Maiuma district[133] left the shrine of Aphrodite for the Marneion, but the priests of Zeus Marnas frustrated their advance:[134]

> The soldiers, having turned around with the Christians of the city and of its coastal district, rushed against the idol-temples. They had been advised first to overthrow the Marneion, but were turned back. For the priests of that idol heard in advance and fortified the gates of the inner temple within, having taken to the so-called *adyta* (εἰς τὰ λεγόμενα ἄδυτα) as many sacred vessels as there were in the temple, and hid the small figures of the gods (τὰ ζῴδια τῶν θεῶν) there, and through the same *adyta* fled through other upward exits. For they say that the *adyta* had many such ways up to different places. After being repelled, as I said previously, the Christians turned to the other temples and overthrew them and consigned them to fire, after snatching away all the service vessels in them.

The *adyta* were, of course, the subterranean rooms for receiving oracular pronouncements.[135] The precinct itself was surrounded by a circuit wall (περίβολος) of unknown dimensions and shape,[136] and contained cisterns (φρέατα), one of them quite deep.[137] The

---

I. Spencer Corbett, "Santo Stefano Rotondo," *Rivista di archeologia cristiana* 36 (1960) 256f. The relevant photos and drawing give us some notion of the interior spaces of the Marneion, which was constructed in a similar fashion.

[130] Hill, "Palestinian Cults," 15.

[131] *V. Porphyrii*, Cap. 66.

[132] *V. Porphyrii*, Cap. 70.

[133] The text reads: "its [Gaza's] coastal district" (καὶ τοῦ θαλαττίου αὐτῆς μέρους). Mark thereby fails to recognize the political and administrative independence of Maiuma. This line of reasoning proceeds from the argument made at the synod of Diospolis in 415 that, inasmuch as Gaza and Maiuma had been a single administrative unit, a single *polis*, in the years before 324, they should therefore be recognized as a single ecclesiastical jurisdiction under the bishop of old Gaza. Cf. Appendix I.

[134] *V. Porphyrii*, Cap. 65.

[135] Cf. the adyta of the Serapeum and other temples of Alexandria. Supra, Ch. II, Sect. 3.

[136] *V. Porphyrii*, Cap. 67.

[137] *V. Porphyrii*, Cap. 80.

mob, swollen by soldiers and even foreigners (παρεπίδημοι),[138] spent ten days ransacking the other temples of the city[139] and burning them down.[140] Bishop Porphyrius wished to keep the bullion of the pagan service vessels (σκεύη τίμια) for the church,[141]

> anathematizing in the church every Christian citizen who took anything at all from the idol-temples for his own gain (πάντα Χριστιανὸν πολίτην λαμβάνοντά τί ποτε ἐκ τῶν εἰδωλείων εἰς ἴδιον κέρδος). None of the believing citizens took anything, but the soldiers and foreign residents did. The clerics collected the objects along with the laymen and Porphyrius himself, and cut them up so that no one might appropriate them.

The accrual of this booty to the churches and its protection was an important fiscal aspect of temple conversions, as the parallel case of the destruction of the Serapeum in Alexandria demonstrates.[142] Bishop Porphyrius' jurisdiction extended technically only to the residents of old Gaza. This seems to be the meaning of the anathema directed against "every Christian citizen" (πάντα Χριστιανὸν πολίτην), that is of old Gaza, but not of Maiuma with its separate episcopal see and resident aliens, many of them Egyptian Christians.

Porphyrius and Kynegios did not get to the Marneion until some ten days later, so great was the plunder yielded by the other temples. Considerable discussion ensued as to what should be done with the building, which must have been large enough to house the entire Gazan congregation several times over. Mark the Deacon refuses to tell who said what: "Some said it should be razed (κατασκαφῆναι), others that the place should be burned down, others yet that it should be cleansed and sanctified into a church of God" (ἄλλοι δὲ καθαρισθῆναι τὸν τόπον καὶ ἁγιασθῆναι εἰς ἐκκλησίαν Θεοῦ).[143] In the end, the vow of Eudoxia Augusta to build and endow a new church must have decided bishop Porphyrius and count Kynegios to destroy the old structure and build a new one. The victorious cross and a building of truly imperial grandeur would symbolize the complete destruction—or, rather, *public* destruction—of the cult of Zeus Marnas. Mark the Deacon alleges that the decisive revelation about what to do with the Marneion came through a sort of oracular utterance by a small child after

---

[138] *V. Porphyrii*, Cap. 65.
[139] *V. Porphyrii*, Cap. 66.
[140] *V. Porphyrii*, Cap. 65.
[141] *V. Porphyrii*, Cap. 65.
[142] Supra, Ch. II, Sect. 3.
[143] *V. Porphyrii*, Cap. 66.

Porphyrius had decreed a fast and prayers. Some Gazan Christians, perhaps those of Aelia's family, evidently wanted to keep the
old temple building as a Christian shrine out of civic pride.[144] A
"Christian oracle" was needed to turn public opinion against this
idea, and to compete with the belief of both pagans and Christians
that an oracle emanated from the subterranean chambers of the
Marneion. The Christian oracle is instructive on several counts: [145]

> [A child seven years of age cried out that the Marneion should be
> burned down:] "For many terrible things have happened in it, most
> of all the human sacrifices. Burn it in such a manner: bring moist
> pitch and sulfur and pig's fat, mix the three, smear the bronze gates
> with it, cast fire upon them, and thus the entire temple will be
> burned. Otherwise it is not possible. But leave alone the outer pre-
> cinct with the circuit wall (τὸν δὲ ἐξώτερον ἐάσατε σὺν τῷ
> περιβόλῳ). After the temple is burned, cleanse the place and build a
> holy church there.

The inflammable mixture of pitch and sulfur burned with an
explosive heat, and relied on the pig's fat as a combustible medium
designed to make it adhere to the bronze gates and marble surfaces
of the propylon. (ὑγρὰν πίσσαν θεῖον τε καὶ στέαρ χοίρεον).
Formulae for readily made combustibles are rare in ancient texts.[146]
The precinct which the circuit wall (περίβολος) closed off must
have occupied a block of considerable size in the inner city. This
space would accommodate the Eudoxiana basilica, hostel, and
associated buildings endowed by the empress.

The combustible compound was smeared onto the inner gates of
the temple and caused the Marneion to burn readily.[147] Many of
the provincial soldiers and non-Gazans (ξένοι) ran into the burning building to retrieve whatever metal could be pulled from its
walls and furnishings, including gold, silver, iron, and lead.[148] Even

---

[144] Cf. the case of Athens in Achaea. Infra, Ch. IV, Sect. 2.

[145] *V. Porphyrii*, Cap. 66.

[146] The sulfur and petroleum composition of marine fire, often inaccurately
called "Greek fire", had similar properties. See: John Haldon and M. Byrne, "A
Possible Solution to the Problem of Greek Fire," *Byzantinische Zeitschrift* 70 (1977),
91–99.

[147] The burning of the Marneion has an interesting contrast in the case of the
Zeus temple of Apamea (Second Syria) destroyed at the order of archbishop
Marcellus c. 388. In the latter instance the temple was pulled apart block by block
after the destruction of its colonnade. The columns that supported the roof of the
colonnade were removed after building wooden props to lift off the weight of the
roof. Then the props were ignited, causing the gabled roof to collapse. The stones
of the Zeus temple could then have been reused for other buildings projects,
although we know nothing of their final disposal. Supra, Ch. II, Sect. 3.

[148] *V. Porphyrii*, Cap. 69.

the baser metals got a good price on the scrap market.[149] Mark the Deacon mentions no provision for collecting the metals for the church. The plunder from the Marneion evidently went to reward those who had done their bit over the previous two weeks to facilitate the demolition of the other Gazan temples. Risk and casualties accompanied the looting:[150]

> One of the soldiers' exarchs was there, whom they call a tribune, standing amidst the burning of the temple. He was a Christian by appearance, but by what was unseen by the many, he was really an idolator. Standing by and seeing the conflagration and the pillaging by the soldiers, he gnashed his teeth and, on the pretext of good discipline, mercilessly whipped one man whom he found carrying off some of the spoils. When this was done and the walls were destroyed by fire, suddenly a burning beam fell on the tribune and brought him a double death. For after breaking his head, it burned the rest of his body. [The soldiers and people glorified God and recited a section of Psalm 51.] The temple remained smouldering for many days.

Cryptopaganism was, and would be through the seventh century, a common phenomenon. The tribune (τριβοῦνος), the commander of an *arithmos* of circa 300 men, evidently on bad terms with them, had apparently performed sacrifices after a baptism motivated by the hope of advancement and the damning information became public in the wake of the incident. The crowd's recitation of Psalm 51, 3ff. at the sight of a man burning to death is symptomatic of the bloodthirsty hatred which had arisen between the pagan and Christian Gazans, and Mark the Deacon thought to exploit this fully for the edification of posterity.

The ruins of the Marneion continued to burn and smoulder for many days (ἐπέμεινεν δὲ τὸ ἱερὸν καιόμενον ἐπὶ πλείστας ἡμέρας).[151] It was then that the Christians began systematically to destroy the "idols" found in many courtyards or quadrangles (ἐν πλείσταις αὐλαῖς).[152] It is unclear how many of these effigies were simply free-standing statues and how many belonged the actual shrines. Mark the Deacon was in his statement perhaps thinking about the courtyards of the Gazan decurions' large town houses, which may well have contained shrines, but no doubt also had innocuous and non-religious statuary standing about as well. We have no firm answers to these questions, as no town houses have

---

[149] For the relative price of different metals, see: *Diokletians Preisedikt*, ed. Siegfried Lauffer (Berlin 1971), 15.63–66 (price of various grades of bronze), 30.1–2 (gold), 30.9 (silver), 15.31–40 (various waggons with and without iron parts).
[150] *V. Porphyrii*, Cap. 70.
[151] *V. Porphyrii*, Cap. 24.
[152] *V. Porphyrii*, Cap. 71.

been excavated. The marbles were pulled down and burned, and
their fragments cast into the sewer (εἰς βόρβορον).[153] The so-called
"magic books" discovered at this time may also have come from
the decurions' abandoned town houses:[154]

> They also found books filled with magic, which things [the Hellenes]
> call holy from which they perform mysteries and other lawless acts,
> and similarly these books have an importance equal to their gods.

The destruction of "magic books" often accompanied anti-pagan
riots and forced conversions.[155] One must bear in mind, however,
that while many persons owned books on divination and magical
papyri, they, and the wealthy in particular, will also have filled
their libraries with the standard works of the Greek *paideia*.[156] If
parchment codices of the Homeric poems were illustrated with
drawings of divine and mythical characters, or depicted sacrifices,
they too might have been mistaken for "magic books", particularly
as the ruffians who raided the houses will have had at best no more
than an education in basic grammar.[157] All this led to the immediate conversion of some pagans, who ran to the churches to escape
the prevailing mayhem.[158] The threat of uncontrolled mob violence
thus sufficed as the propaganda of the deed.

The precincts of the Marneion became the site of the planned
Eudoxiana basilica. At the center of the city, it was a most
appropriate place to commemorate the victory of the new religion.
Mark the Deacon's account of the Christian ceremonial that accompanied the transfer of the lot is consistent with the epigraphic and
archaeological evidence for such transactions.[159] Furthermore, the
author's selection of terminology reflects the ongoing war of words
with the pagans of old Gaza in subsequent years. Temple prop-

---

[153] *V. Porphyrii*, Cap. 71.

[154] *V. Porphyrii*, Cap. 71.

[155] This was the case after the destruction of the Serapeum at Alexandria in 391
(supra, Ch. II, Sect. 3), and also a consequence of a house-to-house search for
magic books at Berytus in the 490's (infra, Ch. V, Sect. 5). The behavioral pattern
thus remained quite consistent throughout the fifth century.

[156] The books contained in a typical library can be inferred from the names of
the authors read by Isidore of Pelusium (ob. c. 435), *Epistularum Libri Quinque*, PG
78: *Ep.* 4.91 Demosthenes (1152D–1153A), *Ep.* 2.16 (Hippocrates) (468B), Ep.
4.30 (Homer quoted, *Od.* 22.347) (1081C), *Ep.* 5.546 (Sophocles paraphrased,
Elektra 153) (1633A), etc.

[157] Kurt Weitzmann, *Late Antique and Early Christian Book Illumination* (New York
1977), Pl. 8, where Achilles pours a libation onto an altar with a lustral bowl,
praying to Zeus who is depicted in *imago clipeata*.

[158] *V. Porphyrii*, Cap. 72 and 73. On the demographic implications of this
incident for the Christianization of Gaza, see Ch. III, Sect. 5.

[159] Supra, Ch. II, Sect. 2 and 3.

erties, including agricultural lands, reverted to the imperial *res privata* when confiscated. One can hardly doubt that, although Mark the Deacon omits the legal technicalities, the see of Gaza received the Marneion site as the gift by Arcadius and Eudoxia Augusta of temple properties, now minus the cult buildings that had once stood on it. Some persons in bishop Porphyrius' entourage, whether clerics or laymen we do not know, objected to the use of the Marneion site, arguing that "the memory of the site should be extirpated" (τὴν μνήμην τῆς θέσεως ὀφείλειν περιαιρεθῆναι).[160] Thus the issue of using the site for a church prevailed in Christian counsels only in the end. In all this there exists no hint of any fear of the fallen gods' daimonic powers, but only the pragmatic question of obliterating all memory of the cult, a propagandistic intent. This consideration must have prevailed much more often than urban Christians' supposed fear of haunted buildings, idols, and stones. The example of Gaza is, in this respect, paradigmatic for most eastern Mediterranean cities. That memory did persist. It was noted above that certain Gazan pagans avoided stepping on the marble blocks of the Marneion used to pave the main street (πλατεῖα) in front of the Eudoxiana. It was with some justification that the critics of Porphyrius' intention to use the site feared that the religious awe associated with Zeus Marnas would persist.

Porphyrius and Eudoxia had without doubt agreed in advance to annex the site of the Marneion, for it had already been planned to build the Eudoxiana in the shape of a cross (σταυροειδής) in order to make it fit the available space. A *magistrianus*, an official of the Master of Offices, delivered the building plan (ὁ σκάριφος) from the empress. As donor, she would logically have had some say about its design, which evidently reflected Constantinopolitan taste.[161] The master builder (ἀρχιτέκτων) was a certain Rufinus, an Antiochene and probably an imperial engineer who had handled other such projects for the *res privata*.[162] It was thought best to superimpose a cross-shaped church upon the circular plan of the Marneion for mechanical and technical reasons, and because the temenos, surrounded by other inner-city buildings, could not accommodate a long, rectangular basilica with an atrium.

---

[160] *V. Porphyrii*, Cap. 75.

[161] *V. Porphyrii*, Cap. 75.

[162] *V. Porphyrii*, Cap. 78. Porphyrius supposedly regarded all this as a "revelation" that explained where the basilica should be built. Emperor Arcadius' role as the co-donor with Eudoxia Augusta is suggested by Mark the Deacon's observation: "The heart of the emperor is in the hand of God," that is, in connection with the design and siting of the church. *V. Porphyrii*, Cap. 75.

The church of Gaza formally annexed the temenos after the arrival of the building plan for the Eudoxiana. A detachment of the governor's troops was kept behind to prevent rioting (νεωτερισμός) and to help collect building materials for the church, but the various civil officials departed.[163] The troops will also have broken up any attempts of the pagan populace to disrupt the litanies which accompanied the annexation of the temenos. The ceremonial began with a one-day fast, evening prayers, and an episcopal order for "every Christ-loving man to bring shovels and buckets and other such impliments".[164] The work was to begin at dawn.

At daybreak bishop Porphyrius with the clergy led the procession from the church of St. Irene. He carried a Gospel book. Behind him the deacon Baruch led the laymen of Gaza with a large processional cross (τὸ ἐκτύπωμα τοῦ τιμίου σταυροῦ).[165] Select psalms were recited as the litany progressed toward and entered the Marneion.[166] Soldiers lined each side of the route to enforce good order.[167] Upon entering the temenos the master-builder Rufinus used chalk (γύψος) to outline the foundations of the new church according to the scheme devised by Eudoxia and her architects. The great figure of the cross was thus inscribed upon the surface of the temenos. When Porphyrius gave the order to begin digging, the Christian congregation shouted the familiar: "Christ has conquered!" (ὁ Χριστὸς ἐνίκησεν). Epigraphists have perhaps not appreciated the fact that the Chi-Rho's, crosses, and "Conquer!" expressions found on converted temples derived ultimately from the liturgies that initiated the process, one of which Mark the Deacon records here. Such inscriptions often belong, as it were, to a "personal" liturgy of Christian believers who sought to reassure themselves in the midst of walls, images, and spolia in which the power of the old gods was thought still to inhere. Such inscriptions were often cut officially at the time of temple conversions, but all rock cuttings of this type do not lend themselves to this interpretation.[168]

The digging began with great enthusiasm, and men, women, children, and the elderly all participated.[169] Architects like Rufinus

---

[163] *V. Porphyrii*, Cap. 75.
[164] *V. Porphyrii*, Cap. 76.
[165] *V. Porphyrii*, Cap. 77.
[166] *V. Porphyrii*, Cap. 78.
[167] *V. Porphyrii*, Cap. 77.
[168] For a discussion of this problem, see Ch. II, Sect. 2, and the analysis of the evidence on the Isis temple at Philae in upper Egypt. Infra, Ch. IX, Sect. 3 and 4.
[169] *V. Porphyrii*, Cap. 78.

must have had special procedures for handling unskilled crews, locally recruited by bishops, but Mark the Deacon informs us nothing of this. The trenches for laying the foundation blocks of the church were excavated and dug out in a few days' time.[170] Porphyrius himself laid the first stone of the foundations in a separate liturgy. Many large blocks of an unspecified type of stone used in the construction came from a hill called Aldioma east of the city.[171] It is unclear whether the place was a regular quarry for cutting stone, or if old buildings there provided spolia. The local stone will have gone for the construction of the walls. This done, after about a year, the empress Eudoxia sent thirty-two pillars of Carystian marble (στῦλοι . . . Καρύστιοι) for the ornamentation of the interior space of the church. Their color was green, for they were said to sparkle like emeralds (σμαράγδων δίκην).[172] The pillars will have gone to support either the central dome of the church, or to decorate the aisles of the arms of the cross. In the latter case, the arms would have been quite short, with eight pillars divided into two lines of four on each wing. Mark the Deacon notes that when the ship carrying the pillars arrived, everyone ran down to the seashore at Maiuma: "And leading waggons set in order, they dragged them to the city and parked them within the enclosure of the temple, and again returned and set each pillar in order until they were all arrayed."[173] The operation required exceptional care, lest the pillars be damaged in transit.

The construction work entailed risks to the builders, who, as has been seen, included children. Accidents and injuries were grist for the mill of Porphyrius' pagan and Christian critics, and their allegations required parrying. On one occasion, two boys aged six or seven fell into a deep cistern within the temenos to the west of the Eudoxiana when the planks covering it collapsed.[174] When a man went down the cistern ropes to retrieve their bodies, the boys were found alive conversing with each other, thanks, it was said, to the prayer of Porphyrius.[175] A curious miracle was said to have accompanied their discovery, for each boy bore cross-shaped abrasions on different parts of his body, an evident coincidence that the Christians magnified into a sign of divine approval for the work on the church (σταυροειδῆ σημεῖα . . . ὡς ἀπὸ ξέσματος βελόνης):[176]

---

[170] *V. Porphyrii*, Cap. 78.
[171] *V. Porphyrii*, Cap. 79.
[172] *V. Porphyrii*, Cap. 84.
[173] *V. Porphyrii*, Cap. 84.
[174] *V. Porphyrii*, Cap. 80.
[175] *V. Porphyrii*, Cap. 80 and 81.
[176] *V. Porphyrii*, Cap. 82.

The crosses were well-struck, neither oblique nor crooked, but of a
single measure, so that it was clear that these were divine signs. Nor
did they cause the boys to suffer, nor was there blood, but they were
marked as if from cinnabar.

One can only speculate about how many deaths and injuries
accompanied the work, conducted as it was by initially inexperi-
enced crews. The story of the boys' cross-shaped abrasions perhaps
countered pagan claims that Zeus Marnas' daimonic powers
accounted for their misfortunes. If so, that part of the story has
fallen out of the tradition.

In conclusion, it should be observed that the demolition and
cleansing of the Marneion occasioned bitter political in-fighting not
only with the Hellenes of the decurion class, but also inside the
fragile Christian community. Porphyrius, supported by an imperial
edict, the governor of First Palestine, and some few loyal deacons
like Mark and Baruch, was at pains to justify all his acts not only at
the time of the events analysed above, but afterwards as well,
because the decurions and some interested Christians remained
critical. Porphyrius had well-defined and rather autocratic ideas
along with powerful support from Constantinople, and this
threatened the existing power structure of old Gaza. His clique
undoubtedly survived his death—Mark the Deacon's biography is
proof of that—but no one knows if his successor as bishop sustained
a policy of confrontation with the pagans. This Mark the Deacon
sought to justify in any case. He repeats many stories and versions
of events, including alleged miracles, which Porphyrius' agents
circulated in the wake of events and may derive ultimately from the
bishop's sermons, as for example the mayhem done to the two
pagan-bystanders by the smashing of the statue of Aphrodite.
Porphyrius' need to maintain the support of his imperial patroness
required the explanation of such dubious acts, as did the need to
sustain the solidarity of the tiny Christian community of old Gaza
in the face of pagan claims and criticism. The average reader of
Mark the Deacon's biography might well have repeated the stories
and arguments against Hellenism found in the text when confronted by a fellow citizen of the Hellenic persuasion. If social
relations were difficult in old Gaza, Porphyrius and Mark after him
provided an arsenal of self-justification for their congregation, and
for any bishop seeking to expand his personal power in the face of
entrenched local interests.

V. Conversions and the Growth of the Gazan Church

The propaganda war against the Hellenes of old Gaza sought, apart from Porphyrius' desire to aggrandize the urban real estate of his see at the expense of temple properties, to enlarge the size of his small congregation. The intransigence of the pagan decurions made this difficult, as they controlled much land and material wealth, and also an extensive body of clients both urban and rural. Mark the Deacon provides a running account of the conversions as they took place to the extent of quoting figures. Previous scholars who examined the life of Porphyrius considered them fraudulent, fanciful or exaggerated.[177] Yet, one is struck by the fact that, if taken literally and *in toto*, Mark's data suggest *few* conversions and a *small* Christian community, not a large one, the point being that Mark had need of all the feeble data he could muster, and that he could provide none better than what he reports. If, as argued above, Mark had a local audience initially in mind, it would have been difficult for him to deceive. As a deacon of the Gazan see, Mark would also have had access to the records of recent baptisms, the registers of contributions to the church by local Christians, and the roster of daily bread recipients.[178] The point here is that the hagiographer had access to vast amounts of statistical material, all of it susceptible to exaggeration, but that *the figures as provided suggest anything but mass baptisms*. Let us review these data. It will be necessary in this connection to recapitulate some details discussed in previous sections.

The church of old Gaza proper was quite small, most of the Christians being concentrated instead at the seaport of Maiuma, which incidentally had a considerable Egyptian-Christian population involved in the wine trade. Mark the Deacon numbers his co-religionists in old Gaza at the time of Porphyrius' arrival at 280 men, women, and children, probably some seventy households.[179] It is impossible to estimate the overall population of the *polis* of old Gaza at this time exclusive of its *territorium*, but even a conservative figure of 15–20,000 persons would have relegated Christian laymen to no more than 1.9 persons per thousand inhabitants (0.19%).

---

[177] See, once again, the discussion of Paul Peeters' thesis in Appendix I.

[178] The deacons were, of course, the administrators of the daily affairs of the typical urban see. Jones's discussion of this question is decidedly disappointing in *Later Roman Empire*, 906, 908, 912–913, and 928. On the other hand, Lampe provides an intriguing collection of texts on deacons' ministerial and other duties, all of which suggest a close working relationship with ordinary Christians and catechumens. *Greek Patristic Lexicon*, 352f. (Section II. A–C).

[179] *V. Porphyrii*, Cap. 19.

Although the Gazan see had a number of churches,[180] Mark the
Deacon, who arrived with Porphyrius, refers to only one deacon, a
certain Cornelius, and Baruch, who was at that time a lector or
subdeacon.[181] Baruch and Mark received their appointments as
deacons only later.[182] The first conversions occurred early in Porphyrius' episcopate, at the time when Christian litanies and
prayers were thought to have ended a drought in January and
February 396 that the Hellenes' prayers and sacrifices to Zeus
Marnas, the "master of rainstorms" (ὁ Μαρνᾶς κύριος . . . τῶν
ὄμβρων), had failed to avert.[183] After a rainstorm of five days'
duration arrived, certain pagans (τινὲς δὲ τῶν Ἑλλήνων),
evidently impressed by the synchronism of this phenomenon and
the Christian ritual, came to the church to ask for baptism. They
numbered 78 men, 35 women, and 14 infants, of which five were
girls, 127 persons in all. They came shouting: "Christ the only God
has himself alone conquered" (ὁ Χριστὸς μόνος θεός, αὐτὸς
μόνος ἐνίκησεν).[184] This formula is closely related to that of the
many "One God" inscriptions of Syria and Palestine, most of
which belong to the late fourth and early fifth centuries.[185] The
phrase as used by the Gazan pagans here lends confirmation to the
view that recent converts most often erected these markers as a
personal liturgy. These folk were admitted to the catechumenate at
once, for bishop Porphyrius dismissed them from the church in
peace and "sealed them with the sign of the cross" (σφραγίσας τῇ
τοῦ σταυροῦ σφραγῖδι). Mark the Deacon notes that another 35
persons were converted (προσετέθησαν) during the same year 396,
in addition to the 127,[186] bringing the total number of new adherents to 162. The congregation as a whole grew to 442 persons, an
increase of 57%.

The next significant group of conversions took place, according
to Grégoire, circa 398–401. These came from the family and household of Aelia, wife of a decurion (ἐμφανής), whose nurse had convinced her to summon bishop Porphyrius to pray over her during
an imperiled pregnancy, this after the daily sacrifices to fertility
deities and a flock of incantors and mantics had failed to effect any

---

[180] Infra, Ch. III, Sect. 6.
[181] *V. Porphyrii*, Cap. 23.
[182] *V. Porphyrii*, Cap. 25.
[183] *V. Porphyrii*, Cap. 19.
[184] *V. Porphyrii*, Cap. 21.
[185] Supra, Ch. II, Sect 2, and infra, Ch. X, passim.
[186] *V. Porphyrii*, Cap. 21. This section of the text seems to go back to a roll or list
of baptisms.

improvement in her condition.[187] Porphyrius advised the nurse to tell the woman in front of her husband, parents, and relatives: "Jesus Christ, son of the living God, heals you. Believe on him and you shall live!"[188] Before pronouncing the words, she explained: "A noble physician has sent me to you that you would hear his word, so that after she is healed you would not scorn him." The baby was delivered successfully after Aelia invoked the Christian God.[189] The family then repeated the formula: "Great is the God of the Christians, great is the bishop Porphyrius", and asked for the bishop's "seal in Christ", the ritual which marked them as catechumens. Thereafter they came to the church, received instruction, and were baptized together with Aelia and her baby. The family and household numbered 64 in all,[190] most of them domestic servants and slaves. The overall size of the Gazan congregation thus reportedly rose to 506 persons circa 398–401. Although other citizens must have become Christian as well between the *termini* 396–401, the first five years of Porphyrius' episcopate, Mark the Deacon is silent about them.

The next attested spurt of growth in Porphyrius' congregation came with the arrival of Kynegios with his troops and officials for the purpose of demolishing the eight temples of old Gaza, this in May 402 by Grégoire's reckoning.[191] The grandeur of the spectacle of burning temples, demolished shrines, and troops everywhere triggered many conversions, but hardly enough to make old Gaza a "Christian city". The first act of destruction allegedly occurred when the statue (στήλη) of Aphrodite was said to have exploded automatically as the *daimon* within fled at the sight of the processional cross. The marble fragments decapitated one and injured another pagan bystander.[192] Fear of further injury probably motivated 32 men and seven women, 41 pagans in all, to approach bishop Porphyrius immediately at the church of St. Irene, receive from him the sign of the cross, and thereby become catechumens.[193] Another factor in this set of conversions, at least among the superstitious, was the failure of the deity whose oracles had received popular credence to defend its own shrine. The number of conversions was trifling, considering the importance of the fertility cult to

---

[187] *V. Porphyrii*, Cap. 28 and 29.
[188] *V. Porphyrii*, Cap. 29.
[189] *V. Porphyrii*, Cap. 30.
[190] *V. Porphyrii*, Cap. 31.
[191] *V. Porphyrii*, Cap. 63.
[192] Supra, Ch. III, Sect. 4.
[193] *V. Porphyrii*, Cap. 62.

the Gazan women, for only seven of the defectors were of that sex. The local women seem to have been angry rather than impressed.

It took Kynegios' troops another month to destroy the Marneion and other temples of Gaza. This business, of itself, produced no great number of converts, for Mark the Deacon mentions nothing in that connection. The search of houses for "idols" and "magic books" that followed did induce many conversions, but fear motivated them.[194] As Kynegios' men and the militant Christian populace ransacked the houses and perhaps beat up their inhabitants, some pagans took refuge in the Christian churches and asked for baptism. A dispute then arose inside the church, with some Christians arguing that persons "who approached the church out of fear should not be admitted, but only those who came by deliberate choice" (ὅτι οὐκ ἔδει δέξασθαι τοὺς διὰ φόβον προσερχομένους, ἀλλὰ τοὺς ἀγαθῇ προαιρέσει).[195] Bishop Porphyrius, who was evidently anxious to add to his congregation any way he could, sought to justify their admission. He must have felt some compulsion to display a positive balance sheet to the pious empress Eudoxia, who had invested her money and personal prestige in the success of the enterprise. Mark the Deacon reports the justifications cited by Porphyrius. The bishop observed that "men's virtues include even those based upon critical circumstances" (εἰσὶν καὶ περιστατικαὶ ἀρεταὶ συμβαίνουσαι τοῖς ἀνθρώποις). Using the example of a newly purchased slave who is slapped around until he serves his master well, the bishop pressed his case for the admission of the refugees to the church: "For even if they come doubting, time has the ability to soften them if Christ assents" (εἰ γὰρ καὶ διστάζοντες προσέλθωσιν, δύναται καὶ ὁ χρόνος αὐτοὺς μαλάξαι Χριστοῦ ἐπινεύοντος).[196] Porphyrius' decision did not require immediate baptism. The pagans probably received the initial "seal of the cross" or blessing laid on everyone upon his admission to the catechumenate. These folk received cursory instruction prior to baptism, and continuous instruction thereafter as well. Mark the Deacon sums up the entire business in these terms:[197]

> After persuading the brothers of these things, Porphyrius received all who wished to be baptized, having instructed them not only for many days before baptism, but afterward as well. He taught the word

---

[194] *V. Porphyrii*, Cap. 71.
[195] *V. Porphyrii*, Cap. 72.
[196] *V. Porphyrii*, Cap. 73.
[197] *V. Porphyrii*, Cap. 74.

continuously, not wishing to be remarkable by speaking with grandi-
loquence, but teaching with simple speech and resolving every question from Scripture. They presented the shepherd of Christ about 300
names that year, and from that time onward Christian names [in the
register of the Gazan church] increased at the rate of 100 per annum.

Similar procedures prevailed in the countryside when conversions
occurred en masse.[198]

The statistical data given in the life of Porphyrius are of the
utmost importance because they permit some generalization about
the rate of Christianization in old Gaza over what was a twenty-
five year period, depending on when the episcopate of Porphyrius
ended. Let us tabulate the increments to the congregation between
396–420, working from the supposition that Porphyrius remained
in office until the latter date:

Incident:	Date:	Size of congregation:	Increment:	New Total:[199]
Porphyrius' first year	Jan. 396	280	–	280
Rainstorm	Late winter 396	280	127 (45%)	407
Various	By end of 396	407	35 (9%)	442
Conversion of Aelia	c. 398–401	442	64 (14%)	506
Shrine of Aphrodite destroyed	May 402	506	41 (8%)	547
Post-Marneion house search	June–Dec. 402	547	300 (55%)	847
Aftermath	403–420	847	1,800	2,647 (excluding deaths and births)

The period of the first set of conversions, during the dramatic
events which led to the demolition of the Marneion, lasted eight
years, between January 396 and December 402. During that time,
the Gazan church gained 567 new adherents, an increase of 195%
over eight years, and average annual increment of 24%. This rapid

---

[198] Theodoret of Cyrrhus in his *Historia Philotheos* indicates a similar method of
catechization used by the monk Abraames in a village near Emesa in Phoenicia
Libanensis. Infra, Ch. VIII, Sect. 2.

[199] It is impossible to tell from Mark the Deacon's arrangement of the material
if these "conversions out of fear" are listed separately from those of the people who
approached the church after the destruction of the shrine of Aphrodite. I suspect
that they are. I have listed them separately in order to lend as much impetus as
possible to Mark's argument that "mass conversions" took place, which argument
it is the thesis of this chapter to refute.

rate of Christianization could not, however, be sustained in the
long run, as the catechists chipped away at the hard core of Gazan
Hellenes. After 402, the number of annual conversions was about
100, as Mark the Deacon himself tells us. The meaning of this
figure is unclear at first sight. It evidently represents the mean
annual number of conversions during the remaining years of Porphyrius' episcopate. If our Porphyrius is one and the same with the
bishop who attended the Council of Diospolis in 415,[200] he will have
presided at Gaza no less than another eighteen years. This period
would have yielded another 1800 converts at a rate of 100 per
annum, giving at total of 2,647 Christians by the year 420, an
increase in the congregation of 945% between 395–420.

It will be recalled that anti-Christian rioting broke out in old
Gaza well after the razing of the Marneion and dedication of the
Eudoxiana basilica in 406. The trouble developed after an altercation between the *oikonomos* of the Gazan church and the decurion
Sampsychos "over some villages".[201] The incident suggests a large
inner-city pagan population. Such an interpretation now finds
statistical corroboration in light of the conversion rates established
from Mark the Deacon's data, for even in 420 the c. 2,647 Christians of the city will have been a minority.

This supposition raises one final question about the statistics:
what was the demographic proportion between Hellenes and
Christians in the *polis* by 420, the last year of Porphyrius' episcopate? It was suggested above that Gaza had some 15–20,000
citizens residing within the walls, not an unreasonable guess. On
this supposition, the 2,647 Christians indicated by Mark the Deacon's
account would have amounted to between 13.2 and 17.6%
of the inner-city population in 420. Mark the Deacon wrote his
biography of Porphyrius some time after 415, and the intensity of
his polemic suggests the survival of many pagans in old Gaza even
then. The argument addressed to the local Christian population is
clear: the city was still full of pagans; let the Christian community
derive great satisfaction from its past successes during the heyday
of Porphyrius. Gaza lagged well behind other cities in this respect.
For example, Bostra, the metropolis of the Provincia Arabia, had
roughly equal pagan and Christian populations as early as 362,
according to a letter of its bishop Titus to the emperor Julian the
Apostate (361–363).[202] No evidence exists for the rural *territorium* of

---

[200] Van Dam, "Late Antique Gaza," 6, n. 17.
[201] Supra, Ch. III, Sect. 3.
[202] Julian the Apostate, *Ep.* 41 (Wright 3, 132f.).

Gaza between 396–415 except the feeble record given by Mark the Deacon already discussed above. The countryside probably went the way it did elsewhere, a gradual but incomplete Christianization of villages on an individual basis by c. 475.[203]

One last consideration requires attention, that being the circumstances of "mass" conversion in Gaza between 396–402. The community grew 203% during that time, but could hardly have done so without certain dramatic turns of event that aided the process. Among these were: the Christian processions during the drought of 396, Aelia's successful childbirth, and the destruction of the Gazan temples with the assistance of imperial troops. All this resulted from bishop Porphyrius' opportunism, a willingness to cajole the metropolitan of Caesarea into accompanying him to Constantinople to procure an imperial rescript for the destruction of the temples, the bellicose spirit which Porphyrius inspired in the Gazan diaconate *vis à vis* their pagan fellow-citizens, and a certain flair for showmanship in managing dramatic public processions. His predecessor might easily have attempted the same tactics, but seems to have lacked any spirit of enterprise. Nor, apparently, was Porphyrius' successor as bishop equal to this task. Otherwise Mark the Deacon's reminiscences would have been superfluous.

The persons who accepted baptism after brief instruction had given up their old religious persuasion, but remained vulnerable to other influences. Mark the Deacon describes one of these in great detail, a cell of "Manichaeans" that seems to have made considerable inroads:[204]

> [An Antiochene woman named Julia arrived in Gaza.] She was of the defiled heresy of the so-called Manichaeans. Knowing that certain persons were newly baptized but in no way confirmed in the holy faith, she came stealthily and destroyed them through her magic teaching, but much more by doling out money. For having invented the said heresy, she was unable to entice anyone except by furnishing money. For anyone having common sense, their system of knowledge is filled with every blasphemy and censure and old wives' tales, which

---

[203] The pagan ethos of the villages in the *territorium* of Gaza can hardly have differed too much from that of other un-Christianized districts, except that it was more protracted. In the *territoria* of Antioch and Apamea the epoch of large-scale Christianization was c. 365–425. In the province of Arabia, the Christianization of the Hauran plain and Djebel Hauran covered a longer period, c. 350–550. Even after these dates there remained an occasional pagan village. In the better attested parts of Bithynia and Phrygia the process took place between 375–450, although John of Ephesus and his disciples claimed to have converted an additional 80,000 between about 538–566. For discussion of the evidence, consult infra, Ch. VII, X, and XI.
[204] *V. Porphyrii*, Cap. 85 and 86.

catch women and male children who have weak intellect and insight.
For they synthesized their evil doctrine from different heresies and
Hellenic dogmas, wishing busily and guilefully to catch everyone. For
they speak of many gods, that they would be pleasing to the Hellenes,
but also of birth, fate, and astrology that they might sin with license,
so that one is unable to sin among them, but only out of the necessity
of fate. They confess Christ and say he was incarnate (*enanthrōpēsai*).
For they call themselves Christians by virtue of appearance.

Mark the Deacon goes on to define the specifically Hellenic content
of the "Manichaean" theology of Julia:[205]

I pass over the ridiculous and infamous, lest I fill the ears of those
present with heavy sound and teratology. For they synthesize their
heresy by mixing the ideas of Philistion the playwright, Hesiod, and
the other so-called philosophers with those of the Christians, just as a
painter making a mixture of various colors seemingly brings about a
man or animal or something else for the deception of those who
see. . . . [But the Manichaeans] collect and mix poisons from different snakes and compound a death-dealing drug for the destruction
of human souls.

This striking summary is heavily influenced by Hellenic rationalism.

Julia had migrated from Antioch to Gaza some years before.[206]
The description of her beliefs and practices hardly matches the
traditional picture of the cult which Augustine of Hippo had abandoned not long before these events took place.[207] Mark the Deacon
indicates that bishop Porphyrius had gained a direct knowledge of
Julia's beliefs in an interview to which he summoned her in c. 404,
according to Grégoire's chronology.[208] Antioch in First Syria was at
this time the melting pot of many astrological, automatist, and
theosophical cults.[209] The city had even offended Julian the Apostate some forty years before this for its amorality and the failure of
even its Hellenes to observe traditional Greek religious practices.[210]
Syncretistic forms of Manichaeism like that practiced by Julia will
have arisen easily under these conditions, as Mark the Deacon

---

[205] *V. Porphyrii*, Cap. 86.

[206] *V. Porphyrii*, Cap. 87.

[207] Augustine of Hippo lost his Manichaean faith between c. 375–385. Brown,
Augustine of Hippo 54–81. On the progress of that faith in general, see: Peter Brown,
"The Diffusion of Manichaeism in the Roman Empire," *Journal of Roman Studies* 59
(1969), 92–103.

[208] *V. Porphyrii*, Cap. 85–91.

[209] These numerous religious world-views with their attendant cults still existed
in Antioch 150 years later. *La Vie ancienne de Symeon Stylite le Jeune (521–592)*, ed.
Paul van den Ven, 1 (Brussels 1962), 138 and 144.

[210] Amm. Marc., *Res Gestae* 22.14.1–3.

observes: "They synthesized their false belief out of different heresies and Hellenic dogmas" (ἐκ διαφόρων γὰρ αἱρέσεων καὶ
δογμάτων Ἑλληνικῶν συνέστησαν ταύτην αὐτῶν τὴν κακοδο-
ξίαν).[211] Like many Antiochene cultists, Julia took a mixed clien-
tele wherever she found it. To appeal to Hellenes she spoke of many
gods, genealogy, fate, and astrology (γένεσις καὶ εἱμαρμένη καὶ
ἀστρολογία), but to attract the newly baptized (νεοφώτιστοι) her
followers confessed Christ and opined that he was incarnate
(ἐνανθρωπῆσαι), probably in an effort to ward off accusations of
docetism. The more traditional Manichaean theology would have
precluded the union of the godhead with corrupt matter. The
Gazan "Manichees" had a laxer system of ethics as well: "One is
unable to sin among them except by necessity of fate." Mark's
interpretation here matches the Manichaean tenet that the "hear-
ers" of the cult need not avoid sin because the evil nature of matter
and thus man's carnal nature operates without the control of his
will. Julia had such great personal presence and powers of persuasion that her doctrine was called a "magic teaching" (γοητικὴ
αὐτῆς διδασκαλία). More to the point of Mark's polemic against
her, it was said that adherents came to Julia because of money gifts
(πολλὰ δὲ πλέον διὰ δόσεως χρημάτων). No adequate internal
evidence in the life of Porphyrius explains this economic dimension
of the problem, unless perhaps Julia recruited followers from
among the urban poor of Gaza, a socio-economic reality of the
inner city known from other sections of Mark's narrative.[212]

It will be recalled, finally, that Manichaeism, although the local
churches regarded it as a "defiled heresy" (τῆς μυσαρᾶς αἱρέσεως
τῶν λεγομένων Μανιχαίων),[213] lay under the same legal sanctions
and incurred the same punishments as those meted out for the
pagan sacrifice.[214] This explains the alacrity with which Julia

---

[211] V. Porphyrii, Cap. 85.
[212] V. Porphyrii, Cap. 97–98.
[213] V. Porphyrii, Cap. 85.
[214] The laws respecting Manichaeans are all contained in Cod. Theod. 16.5. The
latest law in the Theodosian Code is that of 30 May 428 given at Constantinople
by Theodosius II and Valentinian III. The law recapitulated previous rulings at a
time when the severity of the punishments against Hellenes was being mollified.
The law of 428 forbade Manichaean religious assemblies, provided for their
expulsion from the cities, voided wills, prevented Manichaeans from building
churches, and refused them positions in the army and civil service except as
common soldiers or lower grades in the officia of the provincial governors. Cod.
Theod. 16.5.65.2. The death penalty laid against them came later, in the time of
Justinian. Earlier laws indicate parallels to the situation in Gaza described by
Mark the Deacon: Manichaeans "attracted people to their conventicles, remodel-
ing their houses to resemble churches." Cod. Theod. 16.5.11. As I have proposed

agreed to meet with bishop Porphyrius and the Gazan clergy. Otherwise he might have sent this intelligence to the governor of First Palestine at Caesarea and brought the full force of the law down upon them. Porphyrius was doubtless anxious to preserve the partially catechized Christians who had been baptized but not yet confirmed in their faith, a ritual that followed the final stage of instruction (μηπω ἐστηριγμένους).[215]

Bishop Porphyrius' conference with Julia and her followers took place after inquiries were made about her doctrine. He held it, in part, to restrain certain pious Christians (τινες εὐλαβεῖς) who wanted to attack the Manichaeans physically. These were presumably persons whose appetite for mayhem and pillage had just been whetted by the burning of the Marneion. Mark the Deacon wrote a separate treatise on the interview in the form of a dialogue:[216]

> Brother Cornelius the deacon, named shortly before, knew the short-hand system of Ennomos, and signified everything said and replied to [by Porphyrius] while Baruch and I wrote from memory. I did not write out the dialogue in full in this book because it was too long and I wished to provide the present work in the form of an epitome, but I set it forth in another book for those who wished to know the wisdom given by God to Porphyrius, and also those old wives' tales which Julia, the teller of marvels and poisoner, told with such foolishness. . . .

Porphyrius spoke while clutching the Gospel books and making the sign of the cross (σφραγὶς τοῦ σταυροῦ), presumably as a precaution against Manichaean "magic", but certainly to signify that the new religion would prevail there too.[217]

Mark the Deacon casts the events of the interview in an eerie light. Julia confronted the bishop, deacons, and certain laymen of the Gazan see (τινες τῶν εὐλαβῶν κληρικῶν τε καὶ λαϊκῶν)[218] at dawn with two men and a number of young women at her side: "They were all young and well-shaped, and all were pale (ὠχροί) . . . All of them came out with statements taken from the secular *paideia* (ἀπὸ λόγων τῆς κοσμικῆς παιδείας), but Julia most

---

above, Manichaeans at times made inroads into newly Christianized congregations, which were particularly susceptible to religious novelties because of their recent catechization: "If any person by a renewed death should corrupt bodies that have been redeemed by the venerable baptismal font, by taking away the effect of that ceremony which he repeats, he shall know such doctrines for himself alone, and he shall not ruin others by his nefarious teaching." *Cod. Theod.* 16.5.5. Translation by Pharr, *Theodosian Code*, 450.

[215] *V. Porphyrii*, Cap. 85.
[216] *V. Porphyrii*, Cap. 88.
[217] *V. Porphyrii*, Cap. 88.
[218] *V. Porphyrii*, Cap. 87.

of all."[219] All Manichaeans presumably had pallors in the hagiographer's mind, but for reasons that we can hardly comprehend. The traditional Hellenic education was, in their hands as with the pagans, a dangerous thing. As previously noted, Mark the Deacon worked up the transcript of the meeting into a separate book. In his biography of Porphyrius he largely limits himself to the weird denouement and demise of Julia:[220]

> Julia began to tremble and her face to be altered, and, remaining in a trance for a long time, she was silent. She was speechless and motionless, keeping her eyes open and fixed on [Porphyrius]. [Everyone present was afraid.] They played with her senses and spoke in her ear, but she had no voice and no hearing. [She expired.] And so she departed into the darkness she honored, after reckoning it to be light. [Porphyrius himself buried her body.]

Mark's description of Julia's symptoms, which resemble those of catatonic schizophrenia, is entirely unique in the literature of anti-pagan polemics and must therefore be based on some real experience or observation, however much exaggerated. It is difficult to avoid suspicion of poisoning, perhaps with a lethal but slow-working drug mixed with opium—a product still being grown in Boeotia at this time[221]—which induced psychotic behavior until the poison took effect. The alternative is some form of taboo-sickness followed by death. The "Manichaeans'" rifling of Porphyrius' catechumenate for their sect was perhaps seen to justify the event, which the deacons immediately bruited as a miracle.

Julia' death led to the conversion of two men and various women in her entourage, and to the rehabilitation of "as many as had been corrupted by her," the latter being recently baptized Christians drawn into the "Manichaean" cell. Porphyrius required them to anathematize Mani, gave them extensive instruction, and "restored them to the catholic church" (προσήγαγεν τῇ ἁγίᾳ καθολικῇ ἐκκλησίᾳ).[222] Few of the converts required baptism, or Mark the Deacon would otherwise have added them to his detailed tallies. The event did bring about some few conversions of pagans. Their number was evidently not high enough to merit recording, and belongs among those recorded elsewhere who accepted Christianity (προφάσει δὲ ἐκείνων καὶ ἄλλοι τῶν ἀλλοεθνῶν μετανοήσαντες ἐφωτίσθησαν).[223]

---

[219] V. Porphyrii, Cap. 88.
[220] V. Porphyrii, Cap. 90.
[221] Trombley, "Boeotia in Late Antiquity," 220.
[222] V. Porphyrii, Cap. 91.
[223] V. Porphyrii, Cap. 91.

The evidence analysed in this section suggests that the urban population of old Gaza adhered to Christianity only slowly, at the rate of about 100 converts per year. When larger numbers came in, it was usually the result of some spectacular piece of showmanship by Porphyrius, such as the procession before the winter cloudburst or the burning of the Marneion, with the latter eventually netting some 300 persons, all of whom had suffered some kind of physical intimidation from the soldiers and Christian mob. This closely resembles the after-effects of the destruction of the Serapeum in Alexandria in 391, concerning which Rufinus of Aquileia seems to exaggerate the number of conversions that occurred under the impact of the death of the old gods.[224] A sort of blessing, the "sealing with the cross", admitted the new adherents to the Gazan catechumenate, a condition which normally—but not in this case—required a year's instruction before baptism, after which another period of instruction followed that culminated in the confirmation ceremony. The Gazan diaconate fully understood the risk of back-sliding by catechumens and the recently baptized during this process of Christianization. The role of Gaza's so-called Manichaeans in this phenomenon should not be underestimated, for they offered a comfortable syncretism and easy ethic which must have appealed to some catechumens who were beginning to understand the strict character of the Christian ecclesiastical canons. Mark the Deacon could less easily admit that some catechumens slipped back into the Hellenic cults whose old ethos lay all around them. The support of Eudoxia Augusta had guaranteed at least a material and administrative victory for the new religion, hence it was impolitic and bad for the morale of the Gazan diaconate to admit even the possibility that the catechumens defected anywhere except to the Manichaeans, whose popular appeal and pertinacity amidst the flux of urban cults Mark the Deacon probably overrates. Old Gaza was not unusual in any respect, except in the relative slowness with which the Christian religion took root there. The transformation of this condition required the coercive methods which bishop Porphyrius instituted to bring his city into the mainstream of religious thought and practice of the early fifth-century Mediterranean basin.

VI. The Local Church Establishment at Gaza

The growth of the Gazan church has been charted from the perspective of its new members during the years c. 396–420. It remains

---

[224] Supra, Ch. II, Sect. 3.

briefly to sum up the physical growth of the church during this period in terms of personnel, buildings, and income in specie.

The diocese that Porphyrius took over in 395 owned a number of buildings in old Gaza. Among them was the bishop's residence or *episkopeion* that figures so prominently in Mark the Deacon's narrative. A church of St. Irene or "Holy Peace" adjoined this building. A legend of Hellenistic origin was attached to the place that when Alexander the Great accepted the surrender of Gaza in 332 B.C., the symbol of capitulation was drawn up there and the place came to be called Eirēnē from then onward. One can hardly doubt that some substance attaches to this piece of local lore. Mark the Deacon asserts that later on, probably in the fourth century A.D., a Christian named Irenion, who was perhaps an early bishop, built a church on the site "because it was honored by the Gazans".[225] He must have been a wealthy man and have owned the lot, or else the Gazans would have prevented him from erecting the church. If Mark's research on the point was accurate—and as deacon he will have had access to the land titles in the church archive—the foundation of St. Irene provides an early example of the Christian practice of sanctifying unused Hellenic sites, whether holy or not, and then merging the ancient toponym with a plausible Christian one. The *episkopeion* complex with this church became the nerve center of Porphyrius' campaign against the old cults of Gaza and a refuge for his clergy during sporadic anti-Christian riots.[226] St. Irene was thus the *katholikon* or bishop's church.

Gaza had two other churches. One of these, built by bishop Asklepas during the era of the persecutions (3rd–4th century) and thus about a century old, lay in the western part of the city just outside the city gate leading to Maiuma.[227] It was evidently constructed at a time when no Christian could purchase property within the walls. Another shrine lay near it, the martyrion of St. Timothy, in which lay also the bones of two other martyrs, Maiour and Thea.[228] The churches, those of St. Irene, St. Timothy, and bishop Asklepas, all lay on the processional route taken by bishop Porphyrius at the time of the great drought of 396, after which the Christian participants found themselves locked out of the city because they had returned "at the ninth hour" or dusk. From this it might be concluded that the martyrion of St. Timothy, unlike the

---

[225] *V. Porphyrii*, Cap. 18.
[226] *V. Porphyrii*, Cap. 99.
[227] *V. Porphyrii*, Cap. 20.
[228] On the veracity of Mark the Deacon's belief in the historicity of the martyrs Maiour and Thee, see Appendix I.

church of bishop Asklepas, lay some distance down the road to Maiuma.

The see of Gaza thus had four buildings in 395: the three churches and the *episkopeion*. These topographical details permit a reconstruction of the growth of church properties in Gaza. The ecclesiastical structure perhaps first established itself outside the west wall on the high road between Gaza and Maiuma. It was the obvious spot for a church. In this way, Christians coming up from the seaport will have met a Christian shrine as their first sight of the old city, and perhaps have performed the necessary prayers and apotropaic rites before entering the pagan city. Bishop Asklepas seems to have erected a bigger church nearer the city c. 300. At a later date, possibly after 363, the Christian Irenion built a church or chapel inside the city walls on his own property and perhaps adjacent to his residence. He was most probably a merchant of Maiuma who had market space in Old Gaza. He apparently willed this property to the nascent Christian church without an endowment, for the life of Porphyrius fails to mention rural lands from which the church drew income. The lack of a firm economic base would explain why the church of Gaza made so few conversions during the fourth century. As Julian the Apostate points out, the Christian churches acquired many new adherents among the urban poor by doling out free bread.[229] The Gazan church lacked the resources for this, and as the urban riots suggest, and Porphyrius' acquaintance with Salaphtha-Irene proves, the urban poor remained unconverted for a long time after his episcopate began in 395.

The size of the Gazan church organization in 395 is difficult to estimate. The deacons of most sees worked closely with their bishops in administering church properties, caring for the poor, arranging for processions, and so forth, while the presbyters, who acted outside the immediate circle of the bishop, performed the liturgy in the smaller urban churches.[230] Mark the Deacon's narrative centers on the *episkopeion* and diaconate. Thus, he informs us in great detail about his own activities, and those of Cornelius[231] and Baruch.[232] No presbyters are known from this time, but one may have conducted the liturgy at the martyrion of St. Timothy outside the walls. Nor did the Gazan church have a great income. Before bishop Porphyrius sailed to Constantinople for the fateful inter-

---

[229] Julian, *Ep.* 22 (Wright 3, 68–71).
[230] See the many relevant text citations on the duties of presbyters in G.W. Lampe, *Patristic Greek Lexicon*, 1130f.
[231] *V. Porphyrii*, Cap. 22, 23, and 88.
[232] *V. Porphyrii*, Cap. 14–15, 22–24, 95, and 99.

view with the empress Eudoxia in 402 (according the Grégoire's chronology), he ordered Mark the Deacon to bring the entire surplus of church funds for the voyage. These assets came to forty-three *solidi* and three books, the latter presumably being sold off for more specie.[233] This was not a large sum in view of the cost of the voyage and, worse, the gratuities required by the court ushers (δεκανοί).[234] In the end it was imperial patronage that effected the great build-up of resources for the Gazan church.

It is not within the scope of this analysis to treat at length the means by which Porphyrius secured the patronage of the *cubicularius* and *castrensis* Amantius, manipulated Eudoxia Augusta, and came away with an endowment from her for the Gazan church, along with an edict from the emperor Arcadius ordering the destruction of the temples. It suffices here to note that the initial contact was made when the ship carrying Porphyrius, the metropolitan of First Palestine, and Mark the Deacon put in at Rhodes and the men visited the monk Procopius.[235] He advised them to speak with John Chrysostom, patriarch of Constantinople (398–404). The latter in turn put them it touch with the eunuch Amantius, who as *cubicularius* enjoyed direct access to the empress.[236] Amantius offered no guarantee at first that the interview with Eudoxia would come off.[237] This proved to be only the first hurdle to the prelates' ambitions, for emperor Arcadius hesitated to crush the Hellenic cults of Gaza for fear that revenue collection there would suffer. Mark the Deacon gives the gist of Arcadius' reply to Eudoxia after she confronted him with bishop Porphyrius' petition. Porphyrius got this bit of information directly from Amantius himself:[238]

> The emperor said: "I know that the city is given to idolatry, but is right-minded with respect to taxation, paying a large amount of public revenue. If we attack them suddenly with fear, they will flee and we shall lose considerable revenue, but if it seems appropriate, we shall aggrieve them partially by taking away the titles of the idol-maniacs and their other civil offices, and we shall command that their temples be closed and no longer used. For when we trouble them, we fall short in all things, and they know the truth of this."

---

[233] *V. Porphyrii*, Cap. 34.

[234] The possibility of an interview with the Augusta was not certain at first. Once it was achieved, Porphyrius received three handfulls of *solidi*, but expended most of them on the court ushers as he left the palace. *V. Porphyrii*, Cap. 40.

[235] *V. Porphyrii*, Cap. 34–36.

[236] *V. Porphyrii*, Cap. 37.

[237] *V. Porphyrii*, Cap. 38.

[238] *V. Porphyrii*, Cap. 41.

The emperor took this position despite the bishops' somewhat ambiguous allegation that:[239]

> The idol-maniacs. . . do unholy things without fear, and tyrannize the Christians, not allowing them to participate in civil office or to farm their fields, out of which they assess public revenue to your authority.

The entire business might have ended here, had not Porphyrius begun to work on the empress' sensibilities. The term of her pregnancy with the infant Theodosius II was in the ninth month. At another interview, after Arcadius' hesitation, Porphyrius promised Eudoxia a son. She would in turn vow to build a church in the middle of Gaza (εἰς τὸ μεσώτατον τῆς πόλεως) if the prophecy proved correct.[240] Porphyrius was invited to bless the baby Theodosius a week after his birth. The bishop used the occasion to tell Eudoxia of a dream he had had in which the empress, standing in the Marneion, handed him the Gospel book and bade him read Matthew 16.18: "You are Peter, and upon this rock I shall build my church, and the gates of hell shall not prevail against it."[241] It seems that Mark the Deacon here had in mind a mosaic of similar theme that was eventually executed in the Eudoxiana cathedral to commemorate its donor. As a result of Porphyrius' machinations, the imperial secretariat, probably on *cubicularius* Amantius' instructions, prepared a rescript for Arcadius' approval which the emperor read out and endorsed in the atrium (πρόθυρον) of an unnamed basilica in Constantinople at Theodosius' baptismal procession.[242] The document (χάρτη) provided "not only for the overthrow of the temples, but also privileges for the holy church and the Christians, and furnished an income. For the holy church was very poor" (. . . οὐ μόνον καταστραφῆναι τὰ ἱερὰ τῶν εἰδώλων, ἀλλὰ καὶ προνόμια τῇ ἁγίᾳ ἐκκλησίᾳ καὶ τοῖς Χριστιανοῖς . . . etc.).[243] The Gazan church now had the resources of wealth at its disposal to Christianize the urban poor.

Mark the Deacon discusses the monies and endowments in detail, listing the amounts and different sources of funds. First came the donation of Eudoxia Augusta:[244]

---

[239] *V. Porphyrii*, Cap. 40.
[240] *V. Porphyrii*, Cap. 42.
[241] It can hardly be doubted that the "Dream of Porphyrius" became the subject of a mosaic or mural in the new church, commemorating its dedication.
[242] *V. Porphyrii*, Cap. 48.
[243] *V. Porphyrii*, Cap. 46.
[244] *V. Porphyrii*, Cap. 53.

Take, father, these two *kentenaria* and build the church I commanded
to be built in the middle of Gaza. Tell me if you want for money still
and I shall send it at once. Build also a hostel for the purpose of
receiving the [Christian] brethren dwelling in your city and furnish
them with three days' expenses. She gave John [the metropolitan for
First Palestine] 1000 *solidi* and suitable [ecclesiastical] vessels for
both establishments. For their expenses she also gave them 100 *solidi*.

Two *kentenaria*, equal to 200 pounds in gold or 14,400 *solidi*, were
envisioned not as the final cost of constructing the new church, but
only as sufficient to hire the stonecutters, carpenters, tool-grinders
and other builders, and to procure raw materials (marble, timber,
metal clamps, etc.), but as cost was no object, more monies would
be provided if necessary. An additional 1,000 *solidi* went to the
metropolitan of First Palestine along with vessels for the new
church and hospice.[245] It was evidently the practice to funnel such
disbursements through the metropolitan, who had cadres of silversmiths at his disposal in the provincial capital and could count on
them to supply vessels (σκεύη) of high-quality workmanship
worthy of bearing the name of an imperial donor. Some of the
vessels may also have been produced in Constantinople.[246] The see
of Gaza also received an endowment from emperor Arcadius:[247]

> The emperor at once ordered the eparchs to pay them twenty pounds
> in gold from the public revenues of Palestine. He also gave them one
> handful (*drax*) for the account of their expenses, which came to 50
> *solidi*. [After three more days they took] the payment of forty pounds
> from public funds, and three days later boarded ship and sailed on
> the twenty-third of the Gazan month Xanthikos, that is 18 April of
> the Roman calendar. The *clarissimus* Kynegios came with us, making
> use of the public post system.

This twenty pounds in gold (1,440 *solidi*) was intended to be the
annual subsidized income of the Gazan church. It would seem that
the officials of First Palestine diverted the monies of the indiction
directly to the bishop of Gaza. This income came as a direct grant
from the imperial revenues rather than lands donated from the *res
privata*, as Constantine the Great had done for the Roman church
during the episcopate of pope Sylvester (314–335). The sum of
1,440 *solidi* for the entire Gazan church was quite modest by

---

[245] The *Liber Pontificalis* lists the gifts of Constantine the Great (sacred vessels,
candlesticks, etc.) in the same sections as those listing the landed estates given as
endowments. Infra, Ch. III, n. 248.

[246] I argue here on the analogy of Constantine's donations to the Roman
church. See n. 248.

[247] *V. Porphyrii*, Cap. 54.

comparison with the endowments that Constantine granted to the individual Roman basilicas.[248] In addition to these monies must be counted the plunder in service vessels (σκεύη τίμια) taken from the Gazan temples during their demolition. It will be recalled that Porphyrius anathematized "every Christian citizen who took anything at all from the idol-temples for his personal gain" (ἀναθεμιτίσας ἐν τῇ ἐκκησίᾳ πάντα Χριστιανὸν πολίτην λαμβάνοντά τί ποτε ἐκ τῶν εἰδωλείων εἰς ἴδιον κέρδος).[249] The monetary value of this lucre is unknown, but it evidently went into a central place for weighing and disbursement. As the Gazan church received the inner-city lot on which the Marneion stood, it seems quite probable that it also got at least a share of the bullion, if not all of it.

The great church built on the site of the razed Marneion was called the Eudoxiana (Εὐδοξιανή) in honor of its donor. It took some five years to complete the structure, and was dedicated, according to Grégoire's calculation, during an eight-day festival at Easter, 14–21 April 407. Mark the Deacon records the festivities whose apocalyptic fervor dismayed the Hellenes (ἐτήκοντο τῇ καρδίᾳ):[250]

> After five years there was completed the work of building the great church called the Eudoxiana from the name of the empress. [The church was dedicated at Easter in the presence of some 1000 monks, but also bishops, clerics, and laymen.] And angelic choirs were seen not only during the ecclesiastical service, but also at the times when they took food. For the altar was not only a perceptible one, but also a spiritual one. A psalm was sung after the [eucharistic] meal and a hymn sung after drinking [the cup]. *The idol-maniacs who saw the event were melted to the heart.* Foreigners came from everywhere to see the beauty and size of the church. It was said to be larger than all the churches of that time.

Eudoxia Augusta did not live to see the dedication of her church, having died of a miscarriage on 6 October 404.[251]

The church endowment allowed bishop Porphyrius to spend money on the urban poor and foreigners as never before. Mark the Deacon will have had access to the documents relating to church

---

[248] *Liber Pontificalis, Pars Prior*, ed Theodor Mommsen (Monumenta Germaniae Historica: Gestarum Pontificum Romanorum 1, Berlin 1898); 47–72. For example, the annual income of the *fundi* and *massae* of the Basilica Constantiniana alone was 4,390 *solidi. LP* 54, lines 12–21.

[249] *V. Porphyrii*, Cap. 65.

[250] *V. Porphyrii*, Cap. 92.

[251] Bury, LRE 1, 159.

receipts and disbursements, and gives a detailed summary of these transactions:[252]

> After he built and dedicated the said church, Porphyrius arranged to give each foreigner living in the city the expenses of one day, and he defrayed to every poor foreigner each day six obols, besides which he himself furnished those who came to him with garments, silver and money, providing to each according to his worth, and no one was separated from the benefits for which he asked for.
>
> On the fast-days of the Pasch, Porphyrius defrayed to each poor man ten obols for the forty days, ordering in his will that the said persons be given ten obols for Lent, after setting aside the fund from which the sum would be paid out. He furthermore decided and ordered in the will that, if the full amount of monies was not defrayed each year, the said excess should go to the holy church of Caesarea. This was done later.

It was after these arrangements began that the pagan riot that resulted from the altercation between Sampsychos and the *oikonomos* of the Gazan church broke out. These doles seem to have attracted the pagan urban poor to the churches, for Mark the Deacon observes immediately thereafter: "The idol-maniacs, the more they saw Christianity growing (ὅσον ἐθεώροον προκόπτοντα τὸν Χριστιανισμόν), raged even more and were eager to harm the Christians and Porphyrius before all."[253] The figure of six obols (coppers with K on the reverse side) per day was generous but not unrealistically high. If a poor man or migrant failed to find employment over a year's time—and it is problematical whether the deacons would have tolerated malingering that long—he might acquire 2,190 obols during a 365-day year, the equivalent of 7.6 *solidi* in gold per annum.[254] This came to about *half* the annual income of a skilled laborer,[255] and thus did not confer too many benefits. Even in Egypt the annual cost of bread fluctuated with the supply of grain, but was often about 1.5 *solidi* for 45 *modii* to feed a single man.[256] Then there was the cost of clothing, some of which the Gazan church supplied, but lodging had to be purchased, as did meat, wine, cheese, and other comestibles. Many of the poor will have had families as well. It is difficult to estimate the number of persons on the ecclesiastical dole at Gaza. At Alexandria, a large and crowded metropolis, the normal figure seems to

---

[252] *V. Porphyrii*, Cap. 94. I have followed the Bonn text in this passage.
[253] *V. Porphyrii*, Cap. 95.
[254] For a convenient equivalency table, consult Bury, LRE 1, 447, n. 1.
[255] John Nesbitt, oral communication (1987).
[256] Jones, *Later Roman Empire*, 445–448.

have been in excess of 7,500.[257] The annual stipend granted to the Gazan church by emperor Arcadius from the revenues of First Palestine, 1,440 *solidi*, would have kept only about two hundred persons fully on the dole at six obols per diem, but the money had to cover other expenses as well, so the figure for regular recipients must be well under two hundred. Doles of this kind were in any case only intended to be *income supplements*, often for seasonally unemployed day-laborers. As indicated earlier, it can hardly be doubted that a good part of the dole went to poor pagan Gazans, and that this was one of the factors that brought about conversions to Christianity, as Julian the Apostate had noticed four decades earlier.[258] The figure produced by Mark the Deacon of c. 100 conversions per year betweem c. 403–420 could well have come from the urban poor and day-laborers who, to judge from the riots that broke out after the completion of the Eudoxiana,[259] skulked about the city in considerable numbers. As if this were not enough, bishop Porphyrius made an additional provision in his will to lure the populace to the Lenten liturgies, as quoted above. Porphyrius aimed the expenditure of his personal funds, it appears, at the poorer pagans of Gaza, the idea being to ensure the ongoing success and completion of the mission that began in 395.

All this is consistent with the story of Irene-Salaphtha (Σαλαφθᾶ), the pagan girl who offered asylum to Porphyrius and Mark the Deacon during the riot triggered by the dispute between Sampsychos the decurion and the *oikonomos* of the Gazan see. Special favors yielded special rewards. After the restoration of public order, Porphyrius ordered the *oikonomos* of the church to pay out to Irene and her grandmother four silver millaresia per diem, the equivalent of 24 obols per diem, *twice the per capita daily dole given to the poor and foreigners* and a considerable sum. Irene's aunt received the lump sum of a *solidus*, the equivalent of 288 obols.[260] All these disbursements preceded their admission to the catechumentate:[261]

---

[257] The figure admittedly belongs to the decade 610–619 A.D., but no reason exists to suppose any wide divergence between conditions c. 400 and that later date, as the Persian War had not yet reached Egypt, and because the demand for Egyptian grain was, if anything, falling because of the Persian conquest of the Syrian and Palestinian seaboard. Leontius of Neapolis, *V. Ioannis Eleemosynarii* in *Leontius' von Neapolis Leben des heiligen Ioannes Barmherzigen Erzbischofs von Alexandrien* (Freiburg im Breisgau-Leipzig 1893), 9, lines 1–2. The population of Alexandria was c. 250–300,000. Jones, *Later Roman Empire*, 1040.
[258] Julian's allotments to the temple of Kybele at Pessinus is discussed supra, Ch. II, Sect. 5.
[259] Supra, Ch. III, Sect. 3.
[260] *V. Porphyrii*, Cap. 100.
[261] *V. Porphyrii*, Cap. 100.

He made the sign of the cross over them, released them, and encouraged them to spend some time praying and in the instruction sessions of the catechumens. He sent Timotheos the pious presbyter and catechist to her house, and ordered him to make the sign of the cross over the girl's grandmother.

All three women subsequently received baptism. It appears that Irene eventually became a deaconess of the Gazan see, for she took ecclesiastical garb and adopted ascetic practices.[262] Her supervisor was the deaconess Photina-Manaris.[263] Irene was still alive when Mark the Deacon wrote his narrative about the life of bishop Porphyrius.

VII. Conclusion

Gaza offers the most complete example of how the Christian episcopal infrastructure manipulated the social hierarchy of the cities in the interest of accelerating Christianization. As will be seen in Appendix I, Porphyrius of Gaza was one of the more politically minded bishops of his time. It is indeed difficult to separate the destruction of the Marneion from the plans he evolved for the aggrandizement of his see. The appendix also reaffirms the historicity and priority of the Greek recension of Mark the Deacon's narrative. This empirical fact was taken as the basis for the foregoing discussion.

It should be immediately obvious that Christianization was not a hermetic phenomenon. Its progress was closely linked to the social structure, economic interests, and cultural pretensions of the cities, and thus varied in duration from place to place. The ancient sources are unanimous in stating that the Marneion ranked in importance with the other shrines of late Hellenic religion. It was quite far from being the last temple of a pagan great god to be destroyed as well: the Serapeum of Alexandria went in 391, but the temple of Artemis Ephesia seems from a variety of chronological indicators to have been destroyed after the episcopate of John Chrysostom (398–407, including exile), with a secure *terminus ante quem* of about 450.[264] The Parthenon of Athens and Aphroditeion of Aphrodisias seem to have been despoiled only c. 481–484. The Isis

---

[262] Irene's diet consisted of bread with salt, soaked pulse, or chopped vegetables. She drank water, abstained from wine, and took olive oil only on festival days. She never tasted anything cooked. *V. Porphyrii*, Cap. 102.
[263] *V. Porphyrii*, Cap. 102.
[264] Supra, Ch. I, Sect. 7.

temple of Philae operated until c. 537.[265] There should be nothing surprising, therefore, about the persistence of clandestine sacrifice at Gaza until 402. The destruction of the Marneion came ten years after the comprehensive law of Theodosius the Great (8 November 392) in a ponderous legal system that seldom acted except in response to petitions that only came to the attention of imperial officials after prolonged effort. One is struck, if anything, by the protracted nature of the wrangling with the court entourage of Arcadius at Constantinople in 401/2 that preceded the action. Christian emperors were bound, like all Roman magistrates, by the principle of equity, and weighed the consequences of temple conversions on the provincial political configuration before acting. It was a far simpler matter when Christian zealots acted first with the connivance of their bishops, as at Alexandria in 391, or when Hellenes came to be identified with sedition, as during Illus' insurgency in 481–488.

Another striking feature of the destruction of the Marneion is that it did not lead to "mass conversions" as Peter Brown has rightly argued.[266] There was often a temporary rise in the number of persons seeking admission to the catechumenate, but this was ephemeral, as Mark the Deacon's figures reveal when given statistical projection. The shock value of the great god's impotence in the face of the Christians' invasion of its temenos and physical intimidation—one might say superstition and violence—explain these conversions, which promptly tailed off once the excitement had died down. The clergy of Gaza questioned the value of packing the catechumenate with such people, a problem whose implications became clear only in the late Justinianic period, when coercion and Christianization of rite masked cryptopaganism or more often a weak sense of allegiance to the new religion. Mark the Deacon's data should make us deeply suspicious about Rufinus of Aquileia's boast that the cults of Sarapis and the Nilotic gods fell to the ground entirely with the demolition of the Serapeum. There was an immediate rush to the churches and some sensational conversions took place as in Gaza, but this was no more than an epiphenomenon.

It is evident from Mark the Deacon's detailed description that there were accepted liturgies, albeit improvised on the spot, that

---

[265] Infra, Ch. IV, Sect. 3 and Appendices II and III. Cf. Ch. VI, Sect. 1–2, Ch. IX, Sect. 3–4.

[266] Peter Brown, *The Cults of the Saints: Its Rise and Function in Latin Christianity* (Chicago 1981), 17f.

accompanied the burning or dismantling of temples. Among these was raising the shout of "One God" and brandishing the cross in the face of the idols as a device to ward off the "daimonic rage" or hostile kratophany of the dispossessed gods.[267] There were also strictly enforced procedures for the collection of bullion from the temples, whether from the images of the gods or simply the clamps binding the blocks of the walls, as we also learn from the case of the Serapeum. Soldiers, public officials, and Christians outside the range of the local bishop's anathemas would break the rules, and so stories about the dire fate of plunderers were circulated. Liturgies of the kind reported at Gaza occurred hundreds of times during the epoch of Christianization, but only some few are reported in detail. By taking different elements from variously reported incidents, one can almost reconstruct a composite liturgy that included "One God" acclamations, the recitation of the psalms, the erasure of the gods' names, the smashing of their faces, the incision of crosses, Christograms, and the Alpha-Omega on temple walls and spolia, the degrading treatment of temple spolia, and, of course, the Christians' keeping a watchful eye as they prayed for the escape of the *daimon* which was often "seen" breaking through the stone as idols were cracked open or filtering away in the smoke of numerous fires.

There is very little in the life of Porphyrius to suggest that "miracles" were an overriding factor in conversions. The safe delivery of Aelia's child is the only convincing case. The real "miracles" as ordinary people saw them consisted of the bishop's defiance of the decurion class of Gaza and of the powers of Zeus Marnas and Aphrodite, whose hostile kratophanies might have been likened to the rage of a patron or matron at the insolent ingratitude of his or her client. Porphyrius made it all better by distributing church monies and bread. Little Irene-Salaphtha and her family enjoyed a privileged position in this respect because of Porphyrius' sincerely paternal feelings for the little girl who was bereft of a father's care and protection. The Christian shepherd's political ruthlessness stood in sharp contrast to the heartfelt concern he could project to people otherwise in the grip of the decurions, who demanded great respect but gave little back in return.[268] In the fifth-century Mediterranean the old gods reminded ordinary people of the decurions to a remarkable degree, much like Xenophanes of Colophon's cows, horses, and lions.[269]

---

[267] Infra, Ch. II, Sect. 1.
[268] This corresponds to the arguments of R. Van Dam. Supra, Ch. III, n. 2.
[269] Xenophanes of Colophon, Fr. 14 and 15 in *Early Greek Philosophy*, tr. J. Barnes (New York 1987), 95.

THE HISTORICITY OF THE GREEK VERSION OF MARK THE DEACON'S LIFE OF PORPHYRIUS OF GAZA

Mark the Deacon's life of Porphyrius of Gaza is the most detailed account of the Christianization of a smaller Greek city that we possess. It is therefore necessary to deal with certain criticisms of its content as a historical document. Henri Grégoire and M.-A. Kugener have addressed many problems of error in detail in the introduction to the 1930 text edition and translation.[1] Their discussion raises few difficulties for the phenomena described in the preceding chapter. There are some scholars who maintain, however, that Grégoire and Kugener did not press the text hard enough to expose Mark the Deacon's fraud.

The debate was seemingly put on a new footing with Paul Peeters' discovery and edition of a late Georgian recension of the life of Porphyrius (6th–7th century) which seemed to derive from a lost Syriac original.[2] The Georgian version, Peeters claimed, was shorter and "less developed", and therefore reflected an earlier state of the text than what has come down to us in the Greek. Peeters regarded the latter as conflated and interpolated with all sorts of historical fictions. Peeters went so far as to argue that the Greek was actually translated from that Syriac *Urtext*. He then assembled a lengthy "historical" introduction to his edition of the Georgian text with his own Latin translation, and attempted to discredit the historicity of Mark's life of Porphyrius *in toto*. I have gone through Peeters' arguments in some detail, and have found them to rest on a variety of assumptions that are untenable.

Peeters' view that a shorter Syriac recension preceded the Greek is based on two faulty axioms: first, that any piece of literature arising from a partially Aramaic-speaking environment like Gaza must necessarily have been composed in "Syriac"; and, second, that by some necessary law early redactions of hagiographic texts are invariably shorter than later ones, which are subject to conflation and pious embellishment.

---

[1] Supra, Ch. III, n. 1.
[2] Ibid.

Let us consider his first point. What were the linguistic realities of early fifth-century Gaza? Did Aramaic, or, as Peeters calls it, "Syriac", have status as an important literary language there? A look at the Late Roman inscriptions indicates that the pattern at Gaza was the same as in the other cities of First Palestine, Arabia, and the two Syrias, namely that Greek predominated straight into the seventh century.[3] Peeters seems to have been ignorant of these inscriptions, although a whole series of them has been published since the late nineteenth century,[4] many of them dated in the era of Gaza (which began 28 October 61 B.C.) with the Macedonian names of the months.[5] The earliest of these, a dated funerary inscription, belongs to a presbyter named Eirenaios (449/50 A.D.), who was perhaps bilingual and had Solomon (Sh*eleimūn* in Syriac) as his Aramaic name, much like little Eirene-Salaphtha (Sh*elaphthā*) in Mark the Deacon's narrative.[6] Persons with Semitic names continued to erect their funerary inscriptions in Greek all through the sixth century, at a time when in northern Syria Syriac inscriptions were becoming a bit more common.[7] Among the Gazan Semites named are Balys (Βαλυς) (literally "kin" or "adherent of Baal") (564 A.D.),[8] Abraamios the deacon ('*Avrahamī*, "kin of Abraham") (540 A.D.),[9] and John Marēabdēnos (perh. 6th century) (probably a village place-name).[10] The bilingual populace at Gaza, as everywhere else, used Greek in its official transactions. Hellenistic and Roman personal names turn up in the Gazan inscriptions as well, attesting the city's traditions as a Hellenistic *polis* and the Roman Colonia Aelia Gaza, as for example Alexander (539 A.D.)[11] and Maximus (5th century).[12] In the third century A.D., expatriates of Gaza residing in Rome saluted emperor Gordian III (238–244) and identified their fatherland with Hellenistic titulature: "the holy city of the Gazans, a place of asylum, subject to its own laws, faithful,

---

[3] For the Palestines, see: Frank R. Trombley, "The Greek Communities of Umayyad Palestine (661–749 A.D.)," *Proceedings of the First International Congress on the Hellenic Diaspora*, ed. J.M. Fossey, 1 (Amsterdam 1991), 261–269.
[4] Martin A. Meyer, *History of the City of Gaza* (New York 1907), 139–151. Inscriptions are cited hereafter by number.
[5] Meyer, *History of Gaza*, 125ff.
[6] SEG 8 (1937), 270.
[7] Collected in: *Publications of the Princeton University Archaeological Experditions to Syria in 1904–5 and 1909, Division IV Section B: Syriac Inscriptions*, ed. E. Littmann (Leiden 1934).
[8] Meyer, *History of Gaza*, nos. 1 and 3.
[9] Meyer, *History of Gaza*, no. 6.
[10] Meyer, *History of Gaza*, no. 26.
[11] Meyer, *History of Gaza*, no. 21.
[12] Henri Leclercq, "Gaza," DACL 6/1 (Paris 1924), no. 30 (p. 718).

pious, splendid, great (erected this statue) at the command of its ancestral god."[13] The deity was no doubt the local Baal, Zeus Marnas (τοῦ πατρίου θεοῦ).

Gaza was bilingual, but the language of culture and administration remained Greek. Nor have any Aramaic inscriptions of Late Roman date turned up at Gaza to dispute this conclusion. Peeters' view that "Syriac" prevailed carries with it the assumption that the Semites of Gaza would have been the immediately intended audience for the story of Porphyrius' deeds. This is quite false. In reality, the principals named in Mark the Deacon's narrative both pagan and Christian have mostly Greek names and must have known Greek because of their social status or professions. The elites, and not the common folk, were the object of Mark's narrative, which has strong polemical tendencies (as will be seen). The only suitable vehicle for this was the Greek language. Furthermore, the language of the see of Gaza was officially Greek. The One God formula that turns up in Mark's narrative is also characteristically Greek.[14] We have epigraphic confirmation of its use at Gaza in a funerary inscription (5th century). It begins: "One God, who gave life to a descendant of Baba son of Maximus" (εἷς, Θεός, ὁ ζῶν Βαβᾶς Μαξίμου ἐγγόνης).[15] Baba was apparently a Semite.

Even if some path should be discovered to circumvent these arguments, Peeters' thesis comes up against an immoveable obstacle in the cultural background of Mark the Deacon. Both the Greek and Georgian recensions contain a statement by the author that he originated from the province of Asia and had practiced the trade of calligrapher prior to his migration to Jerusalem.[16] The use of Syriac as a secondary *lingua franca* in western Asia Minor belongs to the sixth century, but certainly not to the 380's. There is no internal evidence whatsoever to suggest that Mark was anything but a Greek. It is said that Cornelius the deacon recorded the conversation between bishop Porphyrius and the "Manichaean" Julia.[17] We can hardly assume that this was done in anything but Greek. Porphyrius is said to have sent Mark to Thessalonike to undertake the liquidation of the bishop's estates into cash for distribution to the poor in Jerusalem. Mark bore a written *testimonium* (βιβλίον ἐντολῆς) to this effect for use in working out the apportionment with Porphyrius' brothers. The brokerage certainly required the

---

[13] Meyer, *History of Gaza*, no. 36.
[14] This problem in the inscriptions of Syria is analysed *in extenso* infra, Ch. X.
[15] Supra, n. 12.
[16] *V. Porphyrii*, Cap. 5.
[17] *V. Porphyrii*, Cap. 89. Grégoire-Kugener (1930), 136.

document to be in Latin or Greek.[18] There is no reason to doubt the family's Greek ancestry. All Mark tells us is that Porphyrius' family was "noble" (γένος . . . ἐπίσημον), that is, of decurion rank.[19] The Late Antique inscriptions of Thessalonike do not suggest any large-scale settlements by Syrians there, unlike other Mediterranean coastal towns.[20] Whatever we might suppose about the ethnicity of the artisan class or urban poor of old Gaza, the principal characters of Mark's history moved in a Hellenistic milieu, and thought and wrote in Greek.

Peeters proposes the argument that there was much ethnic hatred against Greeks in Gaza and singles out the popular reaction to the soldiery when Kynegios the *consistorianus* arrived in 402 with many troops to keep order during the demolition of the temples. Peeters was anxious to prove the "Syriac" character of the Gazan populace, whose antipathy to "Greeks" found full expression in the story of a soldier (a supposed cryptopagan) who attempted to recover bullion from the burning Marneion, but was killed, this after Porphyrius had anathematized "every Christian citizen" who did this. The inaccuracy of Peeters' argument stems from his failure to consider the Greek version as the original. The problem is best solved by positing just this. In Chapter 70, the Greek text begins: "There was a man, one of the soldiers' officers there, which they call a tribune, who was supervising the burning of the temple. He was a Christian by appearance, but was an idolator in secret for the most part." This same passage comes down to us in the Georgian version, via Peeters' Latin translation, as follows: "Moreover there was present in that place a certain man, who possessed the title of officers, from the troop of Greeks." The Georgian text here is shorter but also vaguer, leaving out "which they call a tribune." How does one account for these "Greeks"? If we accept, as I do, that the original text was Greek, it becomes quite simple. The key passage is "one of the soldiers' officers there" (ἀνὴρ τῶν ἐκεῖσε ἐξάρχων τῶν στρατιωτῶν). When the word "soldiers" was translated from Greek into Syriac, the ambiguous word *rhūmayē* was selected, a term which has a variety of meanings, among them "Romans," "Latins," "*Greeks*," "citizens of the Eastern Roman

---

[18] *V. Porphyrii*, Cap. 6.
[19] *V. Porphyrii*, Cap. 4.
[20] See the many citations in Denis Feissel, "Contributions à l'épigraphie grecque chrétienne de Rome," *Rivista di archeologia cristiana* 58 (1982), 353–382. A single Syrian from the village of Theodeon near Apamea in Second Syria turns up in Thessalonike. Denis Feissel, *Recueil des inscriptions chrétiennes de Macédoine du IIIe au VIe siècle* (Limoges 1983), no. 162.

Empire," and "*soldiers.*"[21] The Georgian translator, who had a
Syriac version in front of him, selected the most obvious meaning of
rhūmayē from the standpoint of a Georgian and rendered it as "the
Greeks" rather than "the soldiers". I suspect that the Georgian
version contains many other such losses of meaning in consequence
of its being based on a Syriac version whose ambiguities lay simply
in the fact that it lacked the precision of the Greek original *vis à vis*
technical terms. From our standpoint here, the fact is important
because local prejudice in Gaza reserved its wrath not for "Greeks"
but rather for the soldiery. Many Syriac texts make this point quite
explicitly.[22] The prejudice was thus not linguistic or cultural, but
one conditioned by soldierly indiscipline and, as it seemed, amoral
defiance of Porphyrius' command. It is worth pointing out that the
soldiery of this period was quite diverse ethnically and not always
"Greek". There were Gothic and Egyptian regiments,[23] not to
mention native formations of Semites organized as *comitatenses* along
the eastern frontier.[24] Arabs who reached officer rank often added
the Constantinian *praenomen* Flavius to their ethnic names.[25] The
"Greek" soldier in Mark the Deacon's narrative may thus well
have been a bilingual Semite or Egyptian like the rest of Gaza's
populace whether pagan or Christian.

There is another obvious objection to Peeters' theory of transmission, and that is the fact that the process of translation in this
period was, as it were, a largely one-way one. There are many
examples of Greek secular and religious literature passing into
tongues like Arabic, Armenian, Georgian, Syriac, Coptic, and
Ethiopic.[26] Admittedly some texts of exceptional merit originally
composed in Syriac were thought worthy of translation into Greek,
the dominant high-cultural language of the eastern Mediterranean
cities, as for example the hymns of Ephraem Syrus (ob. 373) and
some biographical texts about him, but this was not entirely
typical.[27] It should be remembered as well that Syriac literature

---

[21] J. Payne Smith, *A Compendious Syriac Dictionary* (Oxford 1903), 531.
[22] The dislike felt by townspeople and villagers for the soldiery stemmed in part
from the requirement of billeting them and baking soldier's bread for them at their
own expense. *The Chronicle of Joshua the Stylite*, ed tr. W. Wright (Cambridge 1882),
58, 63, 71, 73.
[23] Jones, *Later Roman Empire*, 660–668. Cf. 152.
[24] See the numerous squadrons of *equites indigenae* at the disposal of the Dux of
Palestine in *Notitia Dignitatum*, Or. XXXIV, 23–27, 29 (ed. Otto Seeck, Berlin
1876, p. 73).
[25] Supra, n. 23. Infra, Ch. XI, n. 79.
[26] For an extensive list of Georgian examples, see infra, n. 36.
[27] Anton Baumstark, *Geschichte der syrischen Literatur* (Bonn 1922), 32f., 35f.

was a phenomenon mainly of Roman Osrhoene and Mesopotamia, along with Sassanid Mesopotamia. Palestine was in the late fourth century around Jerusalem highly Hellenized, as we learn from the epigraphic evidence.[28] It is easy to suppose that Porphyrius, as a presbyter in Jerusalem, had dealt with his colleagues and migrant congregation mostly in Greek, as also in Gaza, and not in the least because of his decurion past.

The second axiom of Peeters' method is the assumption that the Georgian text is the better and earlier variant because it is "less developed" (*moins developpé*).[29] The analysis of select sections suggests, however, that the Georgian version is, if anything, an abbreviated product of the original Greek (*plus abregé*). Technical terms, personal names, and whole sections that did not seem relevant to the Georgian translator, if not to his Syriac predecessor, have simply been omitted. Let us consider each of these problems in turn.

Do "more developed" models invariably follow in the process of transmission? For the books of the New Testament this is certainly the case. The earliest codices Vaticanus and Sinaiticus have the so-called Alexandrian text type, which is shorter than the later "Byzantine" recension developed by Lucian of Antioch.[30] In the field of hagiography, H. Delehaye relates the intriguing example of the St. Procopius myth, which in its developed form hardly resembles the earliest variants at all.[31] Hagiographies were often rewritten to suit the needs of later generations. The works of the Metaphrastian series, for example, put the Late Antique narratives in a high sounding rhetoric suited to high cultural life in eleventh-century Constantinople, but omit most official and technical terminology, and are in the main *shorter* than their predecessors.[32] Abundant examples of this latter phenomenon can be discovered through the comparison of texts listed in F. Halkin's *Bibliotheca Hagiographica Graeca* and its supplements.[33] A superb example is found in the later recensions of the life of Theodore of Sykeon,

---

[28] Supra, n. 3.

[29] Peeters, "La vie géorgienne de Saint Porphyre de Gaza," *Analecta Bollandiana* 59 (1941), 74.

[30] Bruce Metzger, *The Text of the New Testament* (Oxford 1964), 215f.

[31] Hippolyte Delehaye, *The Legends of the Saints*, tr. D. Attwater (London 1962), 101–116.

[32] For literature, see: Hans-Georg Beck, *Kirche und theologische Literatur im byzantinischen Reich* (Munich 1959), 570.

[33] François Halkin, *Bibliotheca Hagiographica Graeca*, 3rd ed., 2 vols. (Subsidia Hagiographica 8a, Brussels 1957). Idem, *Auctarium Bibliotheca Hagiographica Graecae* (Subsidia Hagiographica 47, Brussels 1969).

which are all shorter than the original eyewitness account of George the Monk.[34] In the sermons of Asterios of Amasea, the later text variants are abbreviated by the subtraction of a word here or there.[35]

We are not, strictly speaking, dealing with such a problem in the life of Porphyrius. It is rather a case of translation literature which, as I have argued, runs from Greek to Georgian through the medium of Syriac. Two varieties of distortion arise here. First, the translator omitted details that seemed irrelevant to his Georgian-Palestinian monastic audience. Secondly, he avoided certain difficult problems of translation by simply omitting the offending passages from his work. He seems to have had no great capacity for rendering Hellenic philosophical and theological terms into Georgian.[36]

The truly corrupt and derivative character of the Georgian text is evident from a comparison with the Greek. Our task is best served by comparing the three chapters pertaining to the demolition of the Aphrodite shrine. Everything we know about temple conversions tells us that the Georgian version has a poor text, and that the Greek could not have possibly have arisen from the hypothetical Syriac version. The Greek text of Chapter 59 reads:

> As we entered the city at the so-called tetramphodon (= tetrapylon), a marble statue stood which they say was Aphrodite. It is above a stone altar, and the representation of the statue was of a naked woman plainly exhibiting all her unseemly parts.

The Georgian text is quite corrupt in this section, and cannot be the original because the configuration it sets forth for the shrine is archaeologically improbable:

> As we were proceeding to the place of the Marneion, there stood in that place in marble (*lacuna*, which Peeters fills in with "there stood") a statue, supported by four columns (*columnis quattuor innixum*) whose name was Aphrodite.

The crucial expression in the Greek is *tetramphodon* (τὸ καλούμενον τετράμφοδον), which got into the Syriac as "the four-footed statue" or "column" instead of "four-footed stoa" through the addi-

---

[34] *Vie de Théodore de Sykéôn*, ed. tr. André-Jean Festugière, 2 vols. (Subsidia Hagiographica 48, Brussels 1970).

[35] Cf. infra, Ch. IV, n. 61.

[36] The Georgian language itself was capable of translation from Greek theological works, although I am unable to comment on the accuracy of these translations or their consistency with the Greek text, but the example of the Georgian life of Porphyrius is not encouraging in this respect. See for example: Robert P. Blake, "Catalogue des manuscrits géorgiennes de la bibliotheque patriarchale grecque à Jerusalem," *Revue de l'orient chrétien* 3 (1922–23), 345–413; 4 (1924), 190–210.

tion of the letter *nun* to the second word (*'arba'tā 'estūnā* (στῦλος) instead of *'estwā* (στοά)). The Georgian translator had never seen a "four-footed statue of Aphrodite," an archaeological impossibility, and so, assuming the accuracy of the Syriac version he had in front of him, he transmitted the error faithfully. It is surprising that Peeters, who points out this error in the Syriac *Urtext*, refuses to draw the proper inference from it.[37] Instead, he touches up the text in the Latin translation given above, which does not correspond to the hypothetical Syriac. The Greek text contains the very important detail, omitted in the Georgian, about the altar, not only as to its existence, but also that the image stood on a platform behind and implicitly *above* the altar ([στήλη] . . . ἦν δὲ ἐπάνω βωμοῦ λιθίνου). This is not the sort of detail that a pious Christian would insert, but perhaps one that he would omit, as pagan altars were considered to be defiled by the refuse of sacrifices, to attract *daimones*, and to be a constant source of temptation to the catechumenate. Elsewhere the Syrian or Georgian redactor avoided details found in the Greek that might have corrupted the reader's imagination and we should not be surprised if he had done so here as well.[38]

There is another peculiarity about the Syriac or Georgian text of Chapter 59. The Georgian version begins with the phrase "as we were proceeding to the place of the Marneion . . ." (*pervenientibus nobis ad locum fani Maronii . . .*), whereas the Greek indicates entry into the city (εἰς τὴν πόλιν). The latter makes more sense in the context than the former, inasmuch as the first assault on the Marneion is not dealt with until six chapters later, the intervening text discussing the destruction of the Aphroditeion, the reading of Arcadius' edict, and the migration of some Gazan Hellenes. The reference to the Marneion is thus not entirely germane to the subject at hand, whereas the entry into the city is. The Syriac reading or the Georgian translator's handling of it is corrupt. The original will have read "into the city" with the Syriac object prefix *la* (*lam'dīta* as pronounced, but with the *linea occultans* beneath the *nun* in the root *mdnt*). The point was evidently misplaced on the Syriac letter *dalath*, giving *resh* instead, and the *yudh* and *nun* were transposed, giving "to the Marneion" instead (*l'marnaytā*), literally the "house" (*baytha*) of Marnas, or "place of Marnas" (*'athrā Maranayā*), with the god's name appearing in the adjectival form, which has the sense of "the Lord's" or "the Master's". Whether the

---

[37] Peeters, "La vie géorgienne," 173, n. 2.
[38] Infra, Appendix I. Peeters, "La vie géorgienne," Cap. 85–86.

Syriac translator sought to "improve" the text or simply erred in his reading of the Greek cannot be decided. It is also possible that the Georgian translator misread the Syriac out of an *idée fixe* about the importance of this one temple. There are probably large numbers of similar errors throughout the text attributable to transmission from a Greek original. Paul Peeters' treatment of all the possibilities is in this respect deficient.

The Georgian text entirely omits the following Chapter 60.[39] It reports the confession of certain Gazan Hellenes that the dream-oracles of their Aphrodite were fraudulent, and that the fulfilment of these prophecies, when it occurred, happened by chance, and rarely at that. This section is in some sense a digression, but clearly belonged to the original narrative. The Syrian or Georgian translator had difficulty with this passage and with another dealing with Hellenic theology and philosophy. Being more interested in directly narrating events, he omitted Chapter 60 and went on at once to Chapter 61. This fact comes out through a tautology at the beginning of Chapter 61. In the Greek text, Chapter 61 begins by notifying the reader of the resumption of the narrative: "After we had disembarked into the city, *as was said* (καθὼς εἴρηται), as we reached the place where the said Aphrodite was. . . ." The Georgian text retains traces of this, although no need existed any longer for such a phrase because the Georgian text had omitted the digression about oracles and chance in Chapter 60. At the beginning of Chapter 61 the Georgian begins: "Therefore, after we had passed over that way. . . ." The translator has already forgotten his erroneous observation that the procession was moving toward the "Marneion" at the beginning of Chapter 59, a mistake that I have dealt with above. A line-by-line comparison and analysis of the Greek and Georgian versions where the latter is the shorter (*plus abregé*) would assuredly reveal many more traces of the longer but now abbreviated Greek text. For the present, such a study is a desideratum.

The Georgian version omits a second group of references to Hellenic belief in another radically condensed section in Chapters 85–86 of the Greek.[40] It concerns the woman Julia and her cell of "Manichaean" youth seduced from the recently baptized. As I have indicated above, these folk were less Manichaeans than polytheists, who confessed Hellenic beliefs such as destiny, "magic

---

[39] Peeters erroneously combines Cap. 59–60.
[40] Sixteen lines of Georgian as compared with 37 of the Greek.

teaching", casting horoscopes, pagan myth, and so forth.[41] The Syriac or Georgian redactor quite correctly characterizes Julia as an "idol-worshipper" (*quae cultrix erat spurcorum idolorum*). After certain other striking omissions, he states: "Her doctrine was full of every error, of filth, and of fabulous malice. But I omit listing by name (*nominatim recensere praetermitto*) the many forms of this blasphemy and defilement lest the minds of listeners and the tongue of my readers be corrupted." This statement does not appear in the Greek text, which instead enumerates various Hellenic practices and beliefs, and names the poet Hesiod and the playwright Philistion. The Syrian or Georgian redactor admittedly knew these details by name (*nominatim*). He is quite obviously summarizing a list—*the list found in the Greek version*—for his audience, not only because of the offensiveness of these terms, but also on the ground of relevance. What need did a Georgian-speaking monastic community have for such information if it needed translations such as this one? Such things were of interest only to the apologists of the Christian sophistic.

There is good ground, therefore, for supposing that the list of Hellenic practices given in the Greek text is the foundation for the disclaimer given in the Georgian one. I cannot accept the view that the list was invented during the hypothetical "development" of the text posited by Peeters. The list is peculiar and difficult, and not topical like literary commonplaces (*topoi, loci communes*). Why Hesiod and not Homer? Why the otherwise unattested playwright Philistion? Why the attempt to construct Julia's "heresy" as Manichaeism, a well-known religious system, when it incorporated the devices of astrology into its doctrine? Even if this description is aberrant in certain respects, it is still the evident basis of the summary remarks given by the Syriac or Georgian redactor. From the standpoint of strictly literary criticism, the Greek text contains the *lectiones difficiliores*.

There is another possible corruption in the Georgian text out of which Peeters mistakenly makes great capital. This is the mention of the guest-house (ξενοδοχεῖον) for whose expenses Eudoxia Augusta had authorized monies.[42] The Georgian text has it that: "Again, St. Porphyrius built an extensive guest-house near the church for receiving foreign travellers (*rursum prope ecclesiam aedificavit sanctus Porphyrius xenodochium amplissimum ad excipiendos peregrinos*).[43] The

---

[41] This passage is translated supra, Ch. III, Sect. 5.
[42] *V. Porphyrii*, Cap. 53.
[43] Peeters, "La vie géorgienne," Cap. 94.

Greek text, which Peeters regards as more corrupted, is actually more complex and differs considerably: "After the building and consecration of the said holy church, [Porphyrius] ordered the expense of one day's [sustenance] to be given to each foreigner living in the city." The key words in the Greek are: "to each *foreigner living in* the city" (ξένῳ ἐνδημοῦντι). The Greek words given here are susceptible to textual misconstruction, the possible Syriac translation having been *l^eksenūs shaken*, at which the copyist evidently blundered and simply wrote *l^eksenodokīn* instead. His eye probably skipped several letters and then alighted on the final two letters (*kaph* and *nūn*) of *shaken*, a slip that made perfect sense in the context. Thus, "each foreigner living" became *xenodocheion*. Or, if the Syriac was missing a letter or two (Peeters repeatedly indicates such textual corruptions in his notes), the Georgian translator will have simplified the entire business from the obvious sense of the Greek loan word at the start.

Even if we should give all this up and accept *xenodocheion* in the Georgian text as a sound reading, Peeters' contention that the Greek text criminally omits reference to the guest-house provided for by the empress is false. The Greek author implicitly considered this facility to be part of the great inner-city building complex now called the Eudoxiana. The distribution of subsistence monies is proof that the *institutional structure* for receiving foreigners existed in the Gazan church, a fact beyond challenge, and that is the essence of the matter for the social historian (but perhaps not for the philologist).[44]

There are many other peculiarities that differentiate the Greek from the Georgian text in all of which the latter comes off poorly. For example, the Georgian text refers to the patriarch of Constantinople as John "Chrysostom", an expression which was first certifiably in circulation in the *Historia Ecclesiastica* of Sozomen some decades after these events.[45] By contrast, the Greek text sticks with the patriarch's official titulature, calling him for example "the most holy archbishop John" (ὁ ὁσιώτατος ἐπίσκοπος Ἰωάννης).[46] The use of the nickname Chrysostom is certainly a later and less authentic development of the text.

The Georgian text contains a more certain anachronism in the repeated reference to "Borilius patriarch of Jerusalem." At this

---

[44] The Georgian text is perhaps unsound here, having as it does a most peculiar tautology (*xenodochium amplisimum ad excipiendos advenas peregrinos*).

[45] PG 67, 1420C.

[46] *V. Porphyrii*, Cap. 43.

time, of course, Jerusalem was suffragan to the metropolitan of First Palestine, whose see was Caesarea Maritima. Whether we accept Peeters' assertion that the reference is really to Cyril of Jerusalem (c. 350–386) or to Praylius (as in the Greek text) (417–422), the Georgian text is all very stupid because Jerusalem, whatever its claims, was not recognized as a patriarchate until the Council of Chalcedon in 451.[47] The *Urtext* which became the basis of the Georgian version thus has a discernible *terminus post quem* of 451, which is later than that of the Greek version. More importantly, *the Greek version does not have this anachronism* (e.g. "the holy Praylios, the bishop of Jerusalem," ὁσίῳ Πραϋλίῳ τῷ ἐπισκόπῳ Ἱεροσολύμων).[48] This gives the lie to Peeters' contention that the Greek is a "later" and "more developed" form of the text. To the contrary, the Syriac or Georgian text was "corrected" rather carelessly in light of later conditions by someone who knew very little about fifth-century ecclesiastical history. Peeters, who does know the history of this period, passed over this discrepancy with open eyes.

An endless series of similar questions might be asked about the Georgian text and its Syriac predecessor. Such an analysis would require a full-length study, which is impossible in the present context. For example, why does the Georgian text refer to the *consistorianus* Kynegios, who supervised the closing of the temples of Gaza, with the Iranian title *dasturi?*

II. The Historical Context

We must now turn to the objections that Paul Peeters makes against the strictly historical content of the Greek life of Porphyrius. It is not possible in every instance to discuss Peeters' arguments, particularly those that are not well taken. What follows is rather a demonstration of the fact that Peeters' understanding of the historical context of the life of Porphyrius is very narrowly conceived. He posits certain "tests" of historicity and assumptions about the audience of the Greek text that fail. Most important of all, he has ignored a vitally important passage in the *Historia Ecclesiastica* of Sozomen that provides an *exact* context for an early redaction of a Greek life of Porphyrius to have been composed, not indeed the redaction we have today in the Grégoire-Kugener edition of 1930, but a mostly congruent predecessor compiled largely from a concatenation of documents and well-known facts, either

---

[47] Jones, *Later Roman Empire*, 220.
[48] *V. Porphyrii*, Cap. 10, 12.

shortly before or immediately after the bishops' synod of First
Palestine met in 415 at Diospolis.[49]

Peeters first confronts the reader with a list of objections that he
calls *differences par défaut.*[50] The first of these, concerning the plagia-
rism of the introduction from Theodoret's *Historia Philotheos*, will be
dealt with later in connection with the events of 415. The second of
Peeters' objections concerns Porphyrius' "prophecy" during the
interview with Eudoxia Augusta when he requested an imperial
edict to close the Gazan temples, to the effect that the son born to
her, the future emperor Theodosius II, "will live and rule, which
you shall see and enjoy, for many years (,ὅστις ζήσει καὶ
βασιλεύσει σοῦ ὁρώσης καὶ ἀπολαυούσης ἐπὶ ἔτη πολλά).[51] The
prophecy proved to be false, for the empress died on 6 October 404,
some four years after the interview.[52] By contrast, the Georgian-
Syriac text omits the promise of long life implicitly given to the
empress. Peeters considers this a proof that the latter text is "better" because it avoids this historical "error". I find it impossible to
accept this argument. Mark the Deacon did, in fact, know about the
death of Eudoxia Augusta, for he mentions that she had died prior
to the dedication of her great church in 407.[53] Yet, when he was
preparing the Greek text for publication, he did not go back and
edit out the bogus "prophecy". *A quo fine?* On the face of it, this is
an argument in favor of the authenticity of the promise as it
appears in the Greek, for Eudoxia's death proved to be a singular
failure of Porphyrius' prognostic powers. As a tendentious writer,
Mark the Deacon might have been expected to conceal this fact,
and yet he does not. This suggests that the passage in question was
composed before 404, the date of Eudoxia's death (an earlier date
than Peeters could possibly have admitted) and carelessly left in
the text, or that Mark was giving a literally accurate statement of
the words that passed between Porphyrius and Eudoxia as he
remembered them. When a biased writer freely admits criticism of
his subject, it suggests that the fact in question was so widely
known that even an encomiast could not fail to mention it.[54] It

---

[49] I consider Peeters' assertion that a shorter Syriac recension lay behind the
Greek to be impossible, and so that issue is no longer addressed herein.
[50] Peeters, "La vie géorgienne," 74–77.
[51] *V. Porphyrii*, Cap. 42. Peeters erroneously puts the passage in Cap. 22.
[52] Bury, LRE 1, 159. Peeters accepts Grégoire's chronology here in order to
make this argument stick.
[53] This seems to be the point of Mark's calling her "the Eudoxia of eternal
memory" (τῆς ἀειμνήστου Εὐδοξίας). *V. Porphyrii*, Cap. 75.
[54] I am not entirely certain that Gregoire-Kugener's translation or that of
Peeters is accurate. The genitive absolute that expresses Eudoxia's part (σοῦ

should be remembered as well that Porphyrius' "promise" derives from a genre of acclamations that were not intended so much to be accurate predictions as simply polite compliments to imperial officials and their masters the *Augusti*.[55] This consideration deprives Porphyrius' statement of both its "magic" and its "error". Peeters' difficulties with the passage are, in short, imaginary.

The Greek text, like the Georgian, mentions the procession that Porphyrius organized to the martyrion of St. Timothy outside the walls of Gaza. It contains the additional detail that the relics of the martyrs Maior and Theē were also housed there. The Georgian text admits the existence of other martyria, but fails to give their names.[56] Peeters questions the existence of shrines to these two martyrs at Gaza, despite the fact that they are mentioned in the synaxarion of the church of Constantinople. Of these, Maior was executed at Gaza and Theē at Diocaesarea during the Great Persecution.[57] There is no inherent reason why shrines to these local martyrs should not have existed at Gaza, and it is simply perverse of Peeters to suggest otherwise.[58] It seems rather that they were irrelevant to the mind of the Georgian redactor. The truth is that the names of many otherwise unknown or seldom attested martyrs have turned up in epigraphic finds, some of them quite obscure, and that the possibility of Maior and Theē having been interred at the shrine of St. Timothy—a well attested local martyr, and also a well attested *praenomen* among the pagans and Christians of Gaza—cannot be excluded.[59]

No one can seriously pretend that the Greek synaxaries reflect the full extent of the cult of the martyrs, and select inscriptions prove this. The first example commemorates the foundation of a shrine at Sykourion in Thessaly (4th or 5th century): "[Place] of the martyrs John, Luke, Andrew, Leonidas. The martyrion was completed on the 15th day before the Kalends of January. Their slave Soteria built it."[60] These companions are nowhere else attested.

ὁρώσης καὶ ἀπολαυούσης) is, strictly speaking, parenthetical to the main relative clause (ὅστις ζήσει καὶ βασιλεύσει . . . ἐπὶ ἔτη πολλά).

[55] See the examples in Charlotte Roueché, *Aphrodisias in Late Antiquity* (London 1989), nos. 61, 77, 83.

[56] Peeters, "La vie géorgienne," Cap. 20.

[57] *Synaxarium Ecclesiae Constantinopolitanae e Codice Sirmondiano*, ed. Hippolyte Delehaye (Brussels 1902), 467f., 822.

[58] Peeters, "La vie géorgienne," 76f.

[59] Mark the Deacon mentions three Timotheoi, the martyr, a presbyter of the Gazan church, and a pagan decurion. *V. Porphyrii*, Cap. 20, 25, 100. Meyer, *History of Gaza*, nos. 8, 24.

[60] Anna Avramea and Denis Feissel, "Inventaires en vue d'un recueil des

The second example comes from Laodikea Combusta in Phrygia and commemorates a certain Severus: "This memorial contains the wise man, expounder of the wisdom of Christ, the noble athlete, son of a celestial Ancestor (οὐρανίου Γενέτου) Severus, the all-surveying leader of the cities of the sack-wearers, etc." Bishop Eugenius of Laodikea erected the church to honor this victim of the Great Persecution and was buried in it himself (post 340 A.D.).[61] The third example falls closer to home, in the village of Bosana on the northeastern rim of Djebel Hauran in the province of Arabia: "Chostē, wife of Inos the martyr, spent 14 pounds in gold for this house of prayer" (4th century).[62] Inos was a common name at Bosana. The man evidently converted to Christianity and met his death at the hands of fellow villagers. The first reliably dated Christian inscription at Bosana after belongs to 573.[63] These inscriptions demonstrate that one cannot simply dismiss the possibility of the shrines of little-known local martyrs in the regional context.

Following upon this point, Peeters suggests that the "martyria" mentioned in the Georgian text actually belonged to the companion martyrs Eusebius, Nestabos, and Zeno (whose names are, incidentally, mostly Greek). In doing so Peeters does violence to the historical evidence which he cites out of context from Sozomen.[64] First of all, although it is true that the three men were executed in Gaza during the reign of Julian the Apostate (361–63), their relics were *carried* in an earthen pot *to Maiuma*, the seaport of old Gaza and a separate see since c. 324, where Zeno the bishop of Maiuma (who Peeters' careless writing misleadingly suggests was bishop of Gaza) deposited them *in their own martyrion outside Maiuma* during the reign of Theodosius the Great (*inter* 379–395). This cannot have been the same shrine as that of St. Timothy that Porphyrius' procession visited in the winter of 395/6 because the latter was just outside the walls of old Gaza. Peeters has thus translated the relics of Sts. Eusebius, Nestabos, and Zeno from outside Maiuma to Gaza without any justification either in the texts or archaeology. The Georgian version cannot thus be taken to confute the Greek one on the location of the shrine of Sts. Maior and Theē. The

inscriptions historiques de Byzanz: IV Inscriptions de Thessalie (à l'exception des Metéores)," *Travaux et mémoires* 10 (1987), 366f.

[61] *Monumenta Asiae Minoris Antiqua* 1, ed. W.M. Calder (London 1928), no. 171.

[62] W.H. Waddington, *Recueil des inscriptions grecques et latines de la Syrie* (Paris 1870), no. 2249.

[63] Infra, Ch. XI, Sect. 2.

[64] Sozomen, HE 5.9.

Georgian redactor—for that is what he was—evidently failed to see the importance of these little-known martyrs to his audience and simply left their names out, just as he left out the names of the six gods worshipped at Gaza apart from Zeus Marnas and Aphrodite.[65] No critic who reads Sozomen's account can possibly accept Peeters' interpretation, but there it is, in print.

Peeters identifies a second group of "errors" that distinguish the Greek text from the Georgian which he calls "*differences par excès.*"[66] Some of these have been dealt with above, such as the "missing" *xenodocheion* in the Greek text, which is implicitly there after all.[67] Peeters adds two details from later writers to suggest that this guest-house was built later.[68] The first, which is hardly relevant to the argument, comes from the anonymous pilgrim of Plaisance (c. 570) who calls the Gazans *amatores peregrinorum*. The second text has a more portentious content. It is the *Laudatio Marciani*, an encomium composed by Chorikios of Gaza c. 534. This panegyric attributes the construction of the church of St. Sergius and a *xenodocheion* to the bishop Marcian. Peeters has come to the conclusion that these are one and the same as the Eudoxiana basilica and its *xenodocheion* without bothering to allow for the tendentious nature of the *Laudatio Marciani* (a surprising lapse in view of his criticisms of the life of Porphyrius), including the fact that other sixth-century writers claimed buildings for the men they saluted in their panegyrics without respect to historical truth.[69] The "profound forgetfulness" (*un oubli aussi profond*) into which the buildings of Porphyrius had fallen derives from the conscious design of Chorikios of Gaza, who sought to praise Marcian at the expense of all his predecessors. To suggest otherwise is pueril and naive.[70] Neither Grégoire nor Peeters was aware of the archaeological realities of urban church construction at this time. Sites like Gerasa, for

---

[65] Peeters, "La vie géorgienne," 75f.

[66] Peeters, "La vie géorgienne," 77ff.

[67] Peeters, "La vie géorgienne," 78. The Greek text is much more specific about the actual arrangements made to effect the tasks of the *xenodocheion* than the Georgian.

[68] Thus, by Peeters' crooked line of reasoning, the Greek text is historically accurate for *failing* to mention the existence of the *xenodocheion*, something that Peeters has no desire to prove because he puts the construction of this building in the sixth century. But I have dealt with this issue above.

[69] For buildings falsely claimed for Justinian by Procopius, but in reality dating to the reign of Anastasius I, see: C. Capizzi, *L'imperatore Anastasio I*, (Orientalia Christiana Analecta 184, Rome 1969), 206ff.

[70] Peeters did not himself apparently read the *Laudatio Marciani* in detail, but used the summary of F.-M. Abel, "Gaza au VIᵉ siècle d'après le rhéteur Chorikios," *Révue biblique* 40 (1931), 12–23.

example, saw the construction of many churches in the fifth through the seventh centuries.[71] There is no particular reason why the Eudoxiana and basilica of St. Sergius need be one and the same, although it is possible. Churches were in general named for martyrs in the sixth century. It is easy to see how the name "Eudoxiana" could have fallen out of use after the death of Theodosius II, the son of its namesake, in 450. Eudoxia Augusta was best known then, and still is, as the persecutor of John Chrysostom. Peeters seems to be absolutely ignorant of the sheer *necessity* of changing the name of such a building after 450.

Peeters is remiss elsewhere as well. For example, he fails to compare the architectural similarities that are suggested in Chorikios' description of St. Sergius and the plan of the Eudoxiana given by Mark the Deacon. Nor is he right in saying that the use of Karystian marble columns in each building proves that they were the same structure. The life of Porphyrius indicates that *thirty-two* such columns were used in the Eudoxiana, presumably with eight in each leaf of the cross, in which shape the church was built.[72] Chorikios' *Laudatio Marciani* mentions the use of *only four* Karystian columns, and *not in the church*, but in the *propylaia* that led into the atrium, which lay in turn outside St. Sergius to the west of the actual church building.[73] Peeters has built his case here by selecting scattered bits of information without the slightest concern for their meaning in context. Its effect on the reader is nothing less than misleading.

It seems quite probable instead that the Karystian columns of the Eudoxiana so impressed the locals that bishop Marcian, in order to win the esteem of his congregation, simply imported more of that type of marble to signify the importance of the holy edifice that he was building. It seems rather probable in the light of this that the Eudoxiana and St. Sergius' were *not* one and the same building.

The third group of "errors" that Peeters cites are called "*divergences positives*." Not all these objections are of equal merit, and can be set aside if one is convinced at this point in the discussion that there are serious problems with Peeters' thesis about the

---

[71] Carl Kraeling, *Gerasa, City of the Decapolis* (New Haven 1938). Even a relatively small coastal city like Phthiotic Thebes in Thessaly might have four early Christian basilicas. Demetrios Pallas, *Les Monuments paleochrétiens en Grèce de 1959 à 1973* (Rome 1977), 42–54. Peeters demonstrates his naivete about archaeology in supposing the a city should necessarily have only a single church. Other examples abound.

[72] *V. Porphyrii*, Cap. 84.

[73] Abel, "Gaza au VIᵉ siècle," 12f.

Syriac rather than Greek origin of the life of Porphyrius. It is safe to
say that, whatever Peeters tries to make out of the proper names
given in the Georgian version, they are all seriously corrupt. The
statement of the Greek text that Porphyrius was ordained a presbyter by Praylius bishop of Jerusalem (417–422) is simply wrong, just
as is the reading that Peeters suggests instead, that Cyril of Jerusalem (ob. 386) was meant. His argument that the hypothetical
Syriac reading for the bishop's name *Bōrilōs* went back to *Qūrilōs* (for
Cyril) is of course possible. But if, however, we posit that the
translation of the text was transmitted orally from lector to scribe,
it is just as easy to suppose that, as the lector read the first Syriac
letter *pē* in Praylius (giving *Parailōs*), the scribe mistook the plosive
sound of the Syriac *pē* for the letter *beth*, giving rise to the Georgian
Bōrilōs. (Here the Greek -ay- has given way to -ī- in the Syriac or
Georgian.) The confusion of plosives and diphthongs in transliter-
ating from Greek to Semitic languages is patent.[74] Much of Peeters'
argument about the Syriac origin of the Greek text rests on this one
example, but it should be apparent that a Greek original is equally
plausible.

As for the name of Porphyrius' predecessor as bishop of Gaza,
Peeters has come to some very strange conclusions. He seems to
trust the Syriac Ḥabib over the Greek Eirenion for the first of
them.[75] I find it difficult to imagine the bishop of so Hellenized a see
as Gaza with such a thickly Semitic name as Ḥabib at so early a
date. Nor need we suppose that Porphyrius' other predecessor
Aeneas is to be confused with the philosopher and epistolographer
Aeneas of Gaza (ob. 518). If Peeters were honest, he would admit
that many bishops and imperial officials are singly attested in
hagiographic texts, as a perusal of M. Le Quien's *Oriens Christianus*
(3 vols., Paris 1740) will reveal. Is Peeters proposing the purging of
the extant episcopal lists of the *hapax onomazomenoi*? It seems not,
and so his argument cannot be accepted at face value.

In the preceding chapter I have given the transcription Kynegios
for the name of the imperial count and *consistorianus* who supervised
the destruction of the Gazan temples in 402. Peeters sees in the use
of his name an attempt by Mark the Deacon to relate these events
in some fashion to the work of Maternus Cynegius, Praetorian
Prefect of Oriens 384–388.[76] It is, he thinks, a rather stupid forgery

---

[74] Cf. Arabic, which, lacking the plosive "p" entirely, transliterates all Greek
words beginning with the Greek *pi* by using the Arabic *bā* instead, as for example
al-batriq for *patrikios* and *al-batrak* for *patriarchēs*.
[75] Peeters, "La vie géorgienne," 82.
[76] Supra, Ch. II, Sect. 3.

to invest the destruction of the Marneion with such supernal importance.[77] But this can hardly be the case, for Mark identifies this Kynegios specifically as a *comes consistorianus*.[78] The Praetorian Prefect seems to have belonged to the imperial consistory, the supreme advisorial body in the emperor's presence, only when he was *in comitatu* and *not* when on detached duty.[79] His title had in any case singularly greater importance than *consistorianus*, and so we must accept that Mark had a particular count in mind, and not some long-dead Praetorian Prefect.[80] There are many attested *consistoriani* about whom nothing else is known, as for example the list of *comites consistoriani* in the committee that compiled the Theodosian Code, Superantius, Martyrius, Alypius, Sebastianus, Apollodorus, Theodore, and Eron.[81] Even chief notaries (*protonotarii*) were honored with this title.

In one instance where the Greek life of Porphyrius provides an exact synchronism with an external development, Peeters takes it, *mutatis mutandis*, as a sign of inauthenticity! The event in question was the dispatch of Mark the Deacon to Constantinople to make the initial request for the closure of the Gazan temples.[82] His report in the Greek text indicates communication with the *cubicularius* Eutropius and patriarch John Chrysostom.[83] These two men were in fact both in office in the city from 26 February 398 until sometime after 25 July 399, a period of at least fifteen months.[84] If I understand him rightly, Peeters considers it asking too much for a text like the life of Porphyrius to be so reliable. Therefore, it is not, even though it has gotten the dates exactly right.[85] This logic is, of course, a complete inversion of the rules of historical criticism. We prefer to argue that on this one important test the Greek life of Porphyrius is absolutely accurate, and this affects our judgement of Mark the Deacon's other statements in a positive way.

In the Georgian version, Zeus Marnas is almost invariably referred to as Nonos, perhaps an Old Testament epithet of the Gazan god Dagon and meaning something like "of the fishes".[86] He attri-

---

[77] Peeters, "La vie géorgienne," 83.
[78] *V. Porphyrii*, Cap. 51.
[79] Jones, *Later Roman Empire*, 333.
[80] Indeed, Libanius refers to Maternus Cynegius as "prefect" (ὕπαρχος) in *Or.* 49.3 (Norman 2, 462–465).
[81] *Cod. Theod.* 1.1.6.2 (20 December 435).
[82] Peeters, "La vie géorgienne," 83f.
[83] *V. Porphyrii*, Cap. 26.
[84] Peeters gives the wrong date for the fall of Eutropius. Bury, LRE 1, 132, n. 1.
[85] "Nous ne disons pas, et personne ne dira, que cette combinaison chronologique soit impossible. Mais la donner pour naturelle et vraisemblable, c'est

butes this divergence to the Syrian redactor, who was loath to call the deity "Marna" because of the word's resemblance to "*Māran*", "our Lord", a Christian expression (*pour éviter une homophonie presque blasphématoire*). Peeters convicts himself of two errors here. First, if Nonos appeared in the Syriac "original", how does he account for the invariable use of Marnas and Marneion in the supposedly derivative Greek text? Secondly, it seems rather likely that the Syriac did in fact call the god by its local name. We discover upon inspecting the Georgian text that the name "Nonos" often turns up in construction with "temple of". As I have suggested above, the Syriac more probably referred to this building as the "house of Marnas", that is *Marnayā* or *Marnaytā*. This said, it seems more likely that the allusion to Dagon in the Georgian redaction was designed simply to lend the translation a more authoritative air by giving it a bit of Old Testament coloring. The kind of religious scrupulosity Peeters attributes to the Syrian redactor really needs corroboration, but as he fails to supply other examples, it seems that this argument is his own clever invention.

I am less troubled than Peeters is about the names of various civil officials, ascetics, and clerics whose names fail to turn up in the episcopal lists, Greek synaxaries, and other sources.[87] Among the church folk are John the metropolitan of Caesarea, Procopius the monk of Rhodes, the lector Baruch, and little Irene-Salaphtha. As their deeds were not recorded in separate biographies, there was no particular need to add them to the synaxaries. The argument is not strictly relevant anyway, because the compilation of the synaxaries was a late development that occurred long after the Greek tradition about Porphyrius had been codified.[88] The civil officials like Hilarius the *subadiuva* and Kynegios the *consistorianus* were not such "high functionaries" as Peeters imagines. Scores of men will have borne these and similar titles between 395–420. It is not of great import that few of their names have survived, nor should we expect this. The real plausibility of Mark the Deacon's work is found not in the number of names that can be cross-checked, but in what it has to say about the operation of institutions and interactions of social structures and cultural groups. Even if the author gave certain

---

beaucoup demander à l'imagination de celui qui sera chargé de la justifier. Peeters, "La vie géorgienne," 84. Peeters demands more than chronological accuracy. He needs faith!

[86] Peeters, "La vie géorgienne," 82 and passim.

[87] Peeters, "La vie géorgienne," 84f.

[88] The *Synaxarium Eccelsiae Cp.* contains entries about persons of the early medieval period, and is thus quite a late compilation.

persons "coded" names, which is possible, there is no particular reason to doubt the social behavior that he describes, whether it was the collection of bullion from the destroyed temples (as happened also at Alexandria),[89] the slow rate of Christianization inside Gaza (a fact supported by analogous developments in Athens and Aphrodisias),[90] or the continued existence of rural temples.[91]

I have already discussed one aspect of the encounter with Julia the "Manichaean" above. It is quite clear that Mark the Deacon had in mind a cult that was syncretistic in character and more Hellenic than dualistic. I have shown that traces exist of a longer account by the Syriac or Georgian redactor. The Greek version of the meeting between Porphyrius and Julia is not a caricature (*insignificante caricature*, pace Peeters), but an attempt to come to grips with a real set of practices. Both Grégoire-Kugener (1930) and Peeters express the belief (it is little more than that) that Mark the Deacon, or pseudo-Mark, cribbed some of the Hellenic terminology from the *Panarion* of Epiphanius of Salamis (ob. 403), a supposition that incidentally fails to affect the early *terminus post quem* that I am assigning to the *Urredaktion* of the Greek text. Even so, neither editor can point to a *specific and detailed passage* that was directly cribbed, and so their argument is deprived of all force.[92]

It is in questions of historical interpretation about the "Manichaean" episode that Peeters runs widest of the mark.[93] He supposes that "Julia" is simply an allegorical homonym to represent Julian the Apostate. This argument is completely untenable, as there are no parallels in the Julianic corpus. Nor did his critics ever suggest that he had ever corrupted Christian youth.[94] Different varieties of the name turn up in the nomenclature of the decurion class of Antioch, as for example Julianus.[95] It may have been a common *nomen* there. Nor was the *locus* of Julian's last period of administration at Antioch a compelling reason for Mark the Deacon

---

[89] Supra, Ch. II, Sect. 3.

[90] Infra, Ch. IV and VI.

[91] Infra, Ch. VII–XI.

[92] Peeters, "La vie géorgienne" 86. Grégoire-Kugener (1930) lxxxviif. Peeters' argument that Mark the Deacon saw the necessity of having a Manichaean episode does not affect the *terminus post quem* either. He is unable to demonstrate a positive reliance on a supposedly similar story told about bishop Cyril of Jerusalem (ob. 386), and so confines himself to a passing reference to the tale.

[93] Peeters, "La vie géorgienne," 87f.

[94] A problematical inference of this kind might have been drawn from Julian's law against Christian sophists' teaching in the schools, but Peeters missed this argument, which is specious anyway, because the law had little time to act before Julian's death ended the problem.

[95] Libanius, *Or.* 48.42 (Norman 2, 456f.).

to invent an Antiochene origin for Julia. The apostate emperor's stay in that city was anything but a political success. He found public opinion in this largely Christian city against him, and he disgraced himself even in the eyes of admiring Hellenes like Ammianus Marcellinus because of the excessive number of sacrifices he performed.[96] Peeters wants to have it both ways, for he claims that this Julia also resembled Hypatia, the Neoplatonist philosopher of Alexandria who was murdered by Christians in 415.[97] The stories are entirely dissimilar both as regards the philosophical abilities of the women (Julia had none) and the story of their deaths.

This last point enables Peeters to bring in Cyril of Alexandria (412–444), whom he sees as the foil for Porphyrius of Gaza in Mark the Deacon's narrative, both as regards the destruction of Julia and Hypatia, and also the closure of the temples. Here Peeters blunders crassly. He identifies Cyril of Alexandria with the destruction of the Serapeum, an event that took place during the patriarchate of his uncle Theophilus in 391, *fully twenty-one years before Cyril became patriarch in 412.*[98] This is not simply a slip of the pen, for Peeters repeats the error again (*les deux épisodes*).[99]

Peeters then argues that Mark the Deacon sought to show, in contrast to Cyril's (*sic*) activities in Alexandria, that at Gaza the closure of the temples took place "without disorder or violence" (*sans désordre ni violence*),[100] the only case being the cryptopagan tribune who looked for bullion in the burning Marneion.[101] Peeters has forgotten a great deal in making this statement: the fire lit at the approaches of Gaza upon Porphyrius' arrival (Cap. 17), the closure of the city gates against the Christian procession in 395/6 (Cap. 20), the nearly fatal beating of the lector Baruch (Cap. 22), the beating of the deacon Cornelius and two other Christians (Cap. 23) (to whom Porphyrius remarked: "Be bold brothers, for the time of martyrdom is at hand"), Baruch's beating of many pagans (Cap. 25), the killing of two pagans when the shrine of Aphrodite was demolished (Cap. 61), the resistance of the priests of Zeus Marnas to the burning of the Marneion (Cap. 65), the plundering of the Hellenes' townhouses for "idols" and "magic books" (Cap. 71), the conversion of some pagans out of fear of violence (Cap. 72–73), fear

---

[96] Ammianus Marcellinus, *Res Gestae* 22.13.
[97] Peeters, "La vie géorgienne," 87.
[98] Peeters, "La vie géorgienne," 87.
[99] Peeters, "La vie géorgienne," 88.
[100] Peeters, "La vie géorgienne," 87.
[101] Peeters, "La vie géorgienne," 87f.

of rebellion in the city after the incineration of the Marneion (Cap. 75), the killing of Julia (which may have been effected by poison, although a natural explanation akin to taboo-death or hysteria followed by exhaustion cannot be excluded) (Cap. 90),[102] and the great anti-Christian riot that nearly cost Porphyrius and Mark their lives, and in which seven Christians were killed and many others injured, and in which the deacon Baruch was a second time nearly beaten to death (ἐσχάτως ἔχοντα) in the *episkopeion* (Cap. 95, 96, 99). Peeters' assertion that the Christianization of Gaza took place without mayhem is thus entirely frivolous (e.g. . . . *et qu'elle ne fit pas d'autres victimes qu'un officier païen, tué par un accident, qui semblait un châtiment du Ciel*").[103] There is little in Mark the Deacon's narrative to suggest what Peeters says of Porphyrius' *"nonviolence"*: "*Il exhorte à la mansuetude et leur en donne l'exemple.*" This is nothing but a summary fabrication.

The question remains as to how either Mark the Deacon or Porphyrius could have seen himself as a competitor with the patriarch of Alexandria. Gaza was a suffragan see of Caesarea Maritima in First Palestine, which lay under the jurisdiction of the patriarch of Antioch until 451 when the Palestines passed to the control of the newly created patriarchate of Jerusalem. Gaza had no claims even to relative prestige in this ecclesiastical power configuration. Peeters is thus rather naive about these realities. In the next section below I shall establish a more plausible motive for the composition of the *Urredaktion* of the life of Porphyrius.

Peeters then moves on to questions of chronology.[104] It is, of course, no small thing to expect the perfect recapitulation of dates even in chronographical works from this period.[105] It is difficult to understand why Peeters has applied such a high standard for Mark the Deacon. I shall for this reason direct my remarks more to the historical side of this issue. For example, minor anomalies in the internal chronology do little to vitiate the evidentiary merit of Mark's narrative.[106]

Peeters makes great play of Mark's failure to mention the great massacre ordered by Theodosius the Great at Thessalonike in 390,

---

[102] See Sigmund Freud's observations about "taboo sickness' in *Totem and Taboo*, in *The Origins of Religion*, ed. Albert Dickson (The Penguin Freud Library 13, London 1985), 79ff.

[103] Peeters, "La vie géorgienne," 87f.

[104] Peeters, "La vie géorgienne," 88ff.

[105] The chronology of John Malalas' *Chronographia* is, however, quite sound for this period. For his sources, see: *The Chronographia of John Malalas*, tr. E. Jeffreys (Melbourne 1986), xxiii.

[106] Peeters, "La vie géorgienne," 89f.

as Mark is thought (by Grégoire's reckoning) to have visited the city in 392 to collect Porphyrius' share of his father's estate in cash for distribution to the poor of Jerusalem.[107] It is unthinkable to Peeters that the hagiographer should have omitted this important historical event, and is inconceivable that one or more of Porphyrius' brothers should not have perished in the mass executions.[108] This subjective judgement by Peeters about what Mark the Deacon should have included in his narrative does not strictly speaking affect the historicity of his account. Was Peeters expecting a sort of moralistic complaint about the calculated barbarity of Theodosius the Great, the father of the same Arcadius who had authorized the destruction of the Gazan temples? This is all really quite naive in view of Porphyrius' political debts to the Theodosian dynasty. For all his criticism, Peeters failed to identify this most obvious reason for Mark the Deacon's calculated silence. Peeters has also confused his literary genres here: Mark's work is not a world chronicle, but the biography of a bishop who worked hand in glove with the Theodosian dynasty and could be expected to give a favorable judgement about it, as it does for example to Eudoxia Augusta, the much-reviled persecutor of John Chrysostom. The idea was to convey information that was *not* widely known, in contrast to the events at Thessalonike, which had already been reported.[109] It cannot be proven that Porphyrius' brothers *should* have been in the city on the day of the massacre, when 7,000 men, women, and children were killed, and so Peeters' case is moot. It must be borne in mind as well that Thessalonike had been replanned under the Tetrarchy as an imperial residence, and was quite a large city. Hence the 7,000 dead represented perhaps fifteen percent of the inner-city population. Peeters' sneer should really be thrown back in his own face: "In real life, things happen differently."[110] There is quite a good chance that Porphyrius' brothers avoided harm. The massacre was in any case old news by 392, and certainly by 415, when, as I shall suggest below, the first redaction of the life of Porphyrius was assembled.

Peeters engages in a drawn-out criticism of Porphyrius' first "miracle of the rain" that fails because of a crucial mistranslation of the Greek.[111] Let us first translate the passage:

---

[107] *V. Porphyrii*, Cap. 6.
[108] Peeters, "La vie géorgienne," 90f.
[109] Sozomen HE 7.25, Theodoret HE 5.17, etc.
[110] Peeters, "La vie georgienne," 90.
[111] *V. Porphyrii*, Cap. 19.

In that year, there occurred a want of rain, and all those in the city *ascribed the matter to the arrival of the blessed (man)*, saying: "An oracle was given by Marnas that Porphyrius is *unfortunate* (not: ". . . has the evil eye," as Grégoire would have it) for the city." As the god has remained unwilling to grant rain during the first month, that called Dios, and (now) yet also the second, that called Apellaios, all the (citizens) were distressed.

The crucial passage is: "(they) ascribed the matter to the arrival of the blessed (man)," and the key words in Greek are: ἐπέγραφον . . . τὸ πρᾶγμα τῇ εἰσόδῳ. Peeters has translated τῇ εἰσόδῳ as a dative of point of time,[112] when it is in fact simply the dative complement of the verb.[113] In consequence, Peeters imagines there was supposed to have been a drought at the time of Porphyrius' arrival, and a second one in October through late December 395. The passage makes no sense in the way Peeters has taken it, as is made clear by Grégoire and Kugener in their translation. Peeters has created an illusion of philological competence by flinging the Georgian and quasi-Syriac texts into the face of the classicists. The Georgian text agrees entirely with the Greek if understood properly. It states in summary fashion: "Moreover, in the year of our arrival . . ." (*hoc autem anno adventus nostri*). This derives, of course, from the Syriac or Georgian summary of a longer passage. Peeters' criticism that Mark the Deacon mistook the spring dry season for a "drought" is thus exploded.[114] The Georgian text is also wrong about the year. The Greek refers to "this year", *meaning the Gazan year*, which began on 28 October. The Gazan year was, incidentally, based on the ancient Egyptian year—one aspect of Gazan life that Porphyrius did not Christianize.[115] Its first two months were Dios (28 October–26 November) and Apellaios (27 November–26 December), exactly as the Greek text states the matter. The use of the Gazan era and old Dorian months in the city is confirmed by the epigraphy.[116] The dates using this scheme in the life of Porphyrius[117] thus correspond to indisputable documents of fifth- and sixth-century origin in the local context, a strong argument in favor of the Greek rather than the Georgian text. The Georgian

---

[112] Herbert W. Smyth, *Greek Grammar*, rev. G.M. Messing (Cambridge, Mass. 1956), 352f.
[113] Cf. the ancient example of Herodotus, *Histories* 8.9 (τοῖς θεοῖς τὸ ἔργον), an almost identical construction.
[114] "Le narrateur n'y a pris pas garde." In this case the critic's sarcasm has rebounded against him.
[115] Meyer, *History of Gaza*, 125f.
[116] Meyer, *History of Gaza*, 132–136.
[117] Listed by Meyer, *History of Gaza*, 126f.

redactor apparently "corrected" the false impression given by the use of the Gazan year by simply converting the chronology to the Roman calendar, whereby Porphyrius arrived in late March and the drought took place in November through late December, all in the same Roman calendar year that Grégoire computed to be 395, but in the year *after* Porphyrius arrived according to the Gazan era. The correct translation given to the Greek text above, which avoids Peeters' error, frees it from internal inconsistency. It is indeed shocking that Peeters should have made such strident statements in ignorance of the local calendar and, what is worse, of a rather simple bit of Greek grammar.

There is one other point of chronology that Peeters criticizes, and that is the formula used by Mark the Deacon to characterize the years of Porphyrius' episcopate after the completion of the Eudoxiana cathedral in 407. The participial phrase runs: ". . . he lived on (or "survived") a few more years after the dedication of the holy church" (ἐπιζήσας ἄλλα ὀλίγα ἔτη).[118] This is difficult to reconcile with the date of Porphyrius' death given later in the chapter: 12 Dystros in the year 480 of the Gazan era, that is 26 February 420. How can some 14 years be characterized as "a few"? And why is Porphyrius' role at the Synod of Diospolis omitted from the last part of Mark's narrative? Both these questions posed by Peeters deserve discussion, especially because he was himself unable to come up with a satisfactory explanation except the trite and unconvincing argument that Mark the Deacon was incapable of truthful testimony (*un témoin véridique*).[119] This assertion falls not far short of a historical lie, for Peeters did not read all the sources bearing on the Synod of Diospolis with serious intent. Put briefly, Mark the Deacon had every reason to conceal Porphyrius' role at the council because he suffered a catastrophic political defeat there, one that called into question the entire achievement of his episcopate. The Greek expression "lived on" or "survived" (ἐπιζήσας) refers to Porphyrius' career between 406–415. The "death" hinted at is to be taken more in the sense of *discredit*.

III. Porphyrius of Gaza and the Synod of Diospolis in 415

These suppositions bring us into some few fragments of evidence about Porphyrius' episcopate found outside Mark's biography and,

---

[118] *V. Porphyrii*, Cap. 103.
[119] Peeters, "La vie géorgienne," 93f. Peeters goes on: "Comment expliquer cette omission . . ." etc. A little effort would have enabled him to answer his own question.

in fact, to finally confronting the reason why Mark the Deacon took up the pen in the first place and the audience for whom he wrote. The explanation was anticipated in Peeters' scholarship, but has probably been, unfortunately, delayed by the turgid obfuscations of the historical and philological evidence found in his introduction to the Georgian text.[120]

Signs of Porphyrius' work turn up in other sources, although he is not mentioned by name. There are, for example, two direct reports about the fate of the Marneion in the letters of Eusebius Hieronymus (St. Jerome) dating the event to the first decade of the fifth century. In his letter to Laeta dated 400/1, he observes: "Marnas is in mourning at Gaza, shut in, and shakes with fear for the destruction of his temple" (*Marnas Gazae luget inclusus et eversionem templi iugiter pertremescit*).[121] This corresponds precisely to the status of the temple in that year according to Grégoire's chronology. The *subadiuva* Hilarius had arrived at Gaza in 398 with a retinue of officials bearing an imperial edict that closed the temples. Mark adds: "But he allowed the temple of Marnas to give oracles (or "to function") *secretly* in return for a bribe" (τὸ δὲ ἱερὸν τοῦ Μαρνᾶ εἴασεν λεληθότως χρηματίζειν).[122] The sense one gets from Hieronymus' letter is that the priests of Zeus Marnas knew it to be just a matter of time before the Marneion would be destroyed. Since the government had clandestinely tolerated the cult and was allowing the priesthood to keep its service vessels in the temenos,[123] the threat came from elsewhere. The life of Porphyrius identifies the "elsewhere", the *episkopeion* of an aggressive, ascetic bishop with a mentality like that of Marcellus of Apamea.[124] Later, in his commentary on Isaiah, which dates from about 407, Hieronymus observes: "The Serapeum of Alexandria and the Marneion at Gaza have arisen (again) as churches of the Lord" (*Serapium Alexandriae et Marnae templum Gazae in ecclesias Domini surrexerunt*).[125] The commentary is thought to have been completed between late 408 and the beginning of 410.[126] The destruction of the Marneion in 402 and raising of the Eudoxiana in 407 (Grégoire's dates) conform to the chronology apparent in Hieronymus' writings, which invest these events with an almost eschatological significance. It is not difficult

---

[120] Peeters' ridicule of Gregoire's attempt to come to grips with the text is difficult to understand.

[121] Hieronymus, *Ep.* 107, PL 23, p. 870.

[122] *V. Porphyrii*, Cap. 27.

[123] *V. Porphyrii*, Cap. 27.

[124] Supra, Ch. II, Sect. 3.

[125] *Comm. in Isaiam prophetam* 7.17, PL 25, 241D.

[126] Grégoire-Kugener (1930), xlvi.

to discover the hand of at least a quasi-Porphyrius in these reports.

Two other notices about this quasi-Porphyrius have surfaced in the literature. The first is the bishops' list of the Synod of Diospolis (December 415), the local council of First Palestine summoned by Eulogius of Caesarea.[127] There are two Porphyrii in the list, but none of the suffragan bishops are identified with their sees. It is circumstantially possible that one of them was our Porphyrius.[128]

The second report is very important and seems not yet to have been linked with Porphyrius of Gaza. Sozomen, whose ecclesiastical history goes down to about 425, five years after Porphyrius' supposed death, writes:[129]

> One of the bishops of Gaza in our own times was eager to put both clergies under himself after the bishop of the Maiuman church died, saying it was not lawful that two bishops should preside over one city. When the Maiumitans protested, a synod of the province resolved the issue and appointed another bishop [for Maiuma], having decided that it was entirely proper that those deemed worthy of just things because of their piety should not have the privileges given them among the episcopal sees and in the rank of churches taken away, even though they exercised that office through the decree of a Hellenist emperor Julian the Apostate.

Sozomen's "own times" (καθ' ἡμᾶς) were the first three decades of the fifth century. Michael Le Quien discusses the affair at length.[130] The *termini* of this incident are the death of bishop Zeno of Maiuma, which Le Quien puts after c. 400 (*obiit probabiliter ineunte saeculo quinto*) and 431, when bishop Paulianus of Maiuma signed the decree of the Council of Ephesus.[131] With these *termini* in view, it seems rather probable that the unnamed bishop was our Porphyrius, whose supposed episcopate (395–420) overlaps with *two-thirds* of that period, and who was a contemporary of Sozomen. Sozomen made it a deliberate point not to give the name of this bishop of Gaza. His silence must be seen in the context of another statement. After praising the career of bishop Zeno of Maiuma in exceptional detail, Sozomen observes:[132]

> But I have commemorated the bishops at that time for the purpose of example, as it would be an arduous task to recount the story of all, *since the greater number were good men.* And God witnesses their lives, listening to their prayers and performing many miracles.

---

[127] Grégoire-Kugener (1930), xlv.
[128] Infra, n. 129.
[129] Sozomen, HE 5.3 (Hussey 2, 444, lines 1–17).
[130] M. Le Quien, *Oriens Christianus* 3, 621–624.
[131] Le Quien, *Oriens Christianus* 3, 624.
[132] Sozomen, HE 7.28 (Hussey 2, 774–776).

The critical sentence is: ". . . since the greater number were good men" (οἱ πλείους ἀγαθοὶ ἐγένοντο). Quite obviously there were some few, or perhaps one in particular, whom Sozomen wanted to exclude from this category, including an unnamed bishop of Gaza whose episcopate fell sometime between c. 400–425. As will be seen, Sozomen had good reasons for refusing to publicize this man's name.

Before tying together the implications of these disparate texts, it will be necessary to examine one last text that explains Sozomen's attitude toward the see of Maiuma. In his discussion of the persecution of Christians during the reign of Julian the Apostate, Sozomen digresses about the fourth-century history of his own family:[133]

> Although [Julian] did not persecute them, the Christians in the cities and villages fled. Many of my forefathers took part in this flight, even my grandfather. He was of a pagan father, but he and his entire household and those of the family of Alaphion were the first to become Christians in Bethelia, a Gazan village that was populous and had temples holy to the people living there by reason of antiquity and ornamentation, and in particular the Pantheon, inasmuch as it lay on an artificially constructed hill on the akropolis and overtopped the village from every direction. I suppose that the village got its name from this temple, which is translated from the Syrian tongue to Greek as "the house of the gods," and so therefore as the temple of the *pantheon*.

Sozomen's family had thus accepted Christianity a decade or two before Julian's reign, and perhaps owed its conversion to the work of St. Hilarion, who seems to have operated mostly in the countryside around Maiuma, which became an independent *polis* sometime after 324. As a successful Christian sophist and advocate from one of the first Christian families of Bethelia (for rural conversions were quite rare before 363),[134] Sozomen had a vested interest in what was said and *in what was written* about the greater Gazan district, which included the old pagan city and its Christian seaport. He was at pains, for example, to discuss the careers of two brothers of decurion rank in Maiuma, Ajax and Zeno, all of it done in glowing terms. The latter became bishop of the city around the time of Theodosius the Great's death in 395 and seems to have lived on past 400.[135] He thus began his episcopal career at the same time as our quasi-Porphyrius. Sozomen's special notice of Zeno's life suggests a specific motive: to extol a good man whose achievements had been overshadowed in the public eye by his ruthless and

---

[133] Sozomen, HE 5.15.
[134] Infra, Ch. X and XI.
[135] Sozomen, HE 7.28.

longer-lived competitor, that despicable bishop of Gaza who sometime after Zeno's death sought to abolish the good man's legacy by
repossessing Maiuma for his own see in the years after 400. Sozomen's silence about this fellow's name is indisputably deliberate
and meaningful, particularly as he was well-informed about Gazan
affairs. The name suppressed was that of Porphyrius, bishop of
Gaza in First Palestine.

Having analysed these texts, it is now time to return to Mark the
Deacon's narrative to see how neatly it all fits into the context of
Sozomen's polemic.

The principal theme of the life of Porphyrius is the overthrow
of the pagan cults in a city that was overwhelmingly polytheistic for
at least the first three decades of the fifth century.[136] Mark the
Deacon suppresses practically all the other issues confronting the
see of Gaza between 395–420, as though some necessity were
guiding his selection of material. Porphyrius certainly abhorred the
Semitic and Hellenistic cults of Gaza, but was powerless to execute
his program of closing the temples. His sole source of support was
his superior, the archbishop of Caesarea Maritima. Porphyrius can
hardly be blamed for wanting to make the task easier on himself
and his slender political assets. The moment of opportunity came
when Zeno, bishop of Maiuma and a man of great ascetic sanctity,
died shortly after 400. It will be recalled that Constantine the Great
had divided Gaza and Maiuma into separate municipalities to
ensure the free practice of Christianity in the latter. Julian the
Apostate later reversed this scheme by reuniting the cities into a
single *polis*. Gaza and Maiuma had nevertheless continued to retain
their separate bishops until 395, when Porphyrius and Zeno became bishops of the two places. It would hardly be surprising if,
after Zeno's death, Porphyrius had not raised the issue of reunify-
ing the episcopate of Gaza-Maiuma by simply taking over Zeno's
clergy, estates, and mercantile Christian population. This would
have given him the resources needed to counteract to power of the
Gazan city council more effectively. This is, in any case, what
Sozomen says happened sometime between c. 400–425.

This brings up, in turn, the matter of the personal embassy that
Porphyrius and the metropolitan of Caesarea conducted to Constantinople in 402. As ecclesiastical legations go, this was quite a
high-ranking affair, for it was more typical to send an *apocrisarius*
instead, as Porphyrius had done in 398 to secure at least the formal

---

[136] Supra, Ch. III, Sect. 5.

closure of the Gazan temples. The suspicion exists that Porphyrius went to Constantinople to gain more than the incineration of the Marneion and other temples. With Zeno of Maiuma superannuated and ill (if not already dead), the Gazan bishop may have been seeking nothing less than the termination of the Maiuman episcopate and the extension of his own jurisdiction over greater Gaza. He will have been aided in this by the metropolitan of Caesarea, who sensed a useful ally in Porphyrius and was perhaps fearful of political eclipse, as the rising claims of Jerusalem to the status of a patriarchate grew. The edict of emperor Arcadius granting unconditional destruction of the Gazan temples made for good press, but was perhaps given, along with the endowment of the Eudoxiana cathedral, as a consolation prize. Porphyrius would be allowed to advance his aim of eradicating paganism, but not at the expense of the existing order. The reason for this is easy to see. The subdivision of Gaza and Maiuma had the virtue of antiquity as a Constantinian measure. Arcadius had the legislative competence to reverse it, but refused in principle. When Mark the Deacon came to write his account of the embassy of 402, he deliberately suppressed the story of the negotiations concerned with the dismal failure of this fine bit of chicanery, and concentrated instead on the public success of the decree on the temples. This hypothesis will, we hope, satisfy the pupils of Paul Peeters, who agree that there is much that Mark the Deacon fails to tell.

The issue was not buried, however, in Porphyrius' mind. We know nothing, unfortunately, about the Maiuman episcopate until 431. Porphyrius evidently waited around until the next bishop died and raised the issue at the provincial synod. This was certainly after the death of emperor Arcadius (1 May 408). If we accept the argument from statistical probability that the typical episcopate lasted about fifteen years, it is not impossible that the next opening for this scheme came in early 415. The matter might have come up in any case on the agenda of the Synod of Diospolis in 415. The reigning emperor Theodosius II (408–450) was still an adolescent. A petition from the provincial synod might have gained the approval of his elder sister Pulcheria Augusta, who acted as regent between 414–416.[137] Cyril of Alexandria got all he wanted from Pulcheria during these years, including being excused for the anti-Jewish rioting and murder of the philosopher Hypatia, all of which he tolerated or indirectly instigated.[138] The argument that Porphy-

---

[137] Bury, LRE 1, 214ff.
[138] Bury, LRE 1, 218–220.

rius lodged his request at the Synod of Diospolis is reinforced by Mark the Deacon's silence about the event. The point is that Mark had *good reason* to be silent because, as Sozomen tells us, the Gazan bishop saw his proposal rejected, as I have argued, a second time.

Sozomen provides an important hint as to the line of argument Porphyrius of Gaza used at the Synod of Diospolis. He contended that "it was unlawful for two bishops to preside over one city" (μὴ θεμιτὸν εἶναι λέγων, μιᾶς πόλεως δύο ἐπισκόπους προεστάναι). The provincial synod (ἡ τοῦ ἔθνους σύνοδος) rejected this claim and decreed instead that "it was entirely proper for those deemed worthy of just things because of their piety . . . *even though they exercised that office through the decree of a Hellenist emperor* (διὰ δὲ κρίσιν Ἑλληνιστοῦ βασιλέως ἄλλως πράξαντας). The Gazan bishop's argument lay in the accepted rule that a *polis* should have only one bishop. It is apparent that when Julian the Apostate reincorporated Maiuma with Gaza, he made a specific exception to this rule, which he probably regarded as otiose, and allowed the seaport to keep its own bishop. He probably thought it better in any case to segregate Hellenes from Christians, as historical forces were running quite strongly in favor of the new religion. His successor in the East, Valens, did not modify this arrangement. The claims of old Gaza lay dormant, it seems, until Porphyrius argued anew for the historical rights of his see, as we have suggested, in 402 and again in 415. This has an important connection with the composition of Mark the Deacon's narrative. He could hardly discuss the Synod of Diospolis directly, as it reflected, according to this hypothesis, a second defeat for the claims of the Gazan see. This was *not* a consequence of the author's incompetence or lack of knowledge about the career of the "real" Porphyrius, as Peeters suggests, but a deliberately executed suppression of the truth about a disastrous political failure.

This raises the question, finally, of the date and intended audience for the life of Porphyrius. An examination of the Greek text reveals rather careful attention to official titulature and protocol. Mark lists all bishops and civil officials by their correct titles and is most anxious to show that Porphyrius worked through proper channels during the legation to Constantinople in 402 and in all else, including the use of military force to suppress the great pagan riot (*post* 407). This was supposed to obviate the supposition of his critics that he practiced the sort of schemes for which Theophilus and Cyril of Alexandria were legitimately scorned and distrusted. John Chrysostom's *carte blanche* for the closure of the temples gave all Porphyrius' enterprises a certain justification. The number of

Christians in Gaza is deliberately played down, just as the strength
of the pagan city councillors is exaggerated. If taken at face value, it
justified Porphyrius' resort to the *force majeure* of the imperial authorities in Caesarea and Constantinople. The emphasis on protocol, as I have said, suggests an ecclesiastical audience. To what
end? The bishop of Gaza had gone to the provincial synod of First
Palestine to overturn a special concession granted to Maiuma by
the "Hellenist" emperor Julian. It served the prelate's purpose to
posture as the greatest local antagonist of the old religion since
Theophilus had closed the Serapeum in 391. This view was in wide
circulation in Palestine when, as we have seen, Hieronymus was
writing his commentary on Isaiah in 408–410, and since his testimony implicitly buys into this propaganda, it reflects a fairly
popular view of the situation. The story reflects the Gazans' implicit claim that all the political and religious devices of Hellenic
religion should be demolished vigorously, not only the temples but
also the ruling of Julian the Apostate on the see of Maiuma. It is
obvious who the immediate beneficiary would have if the provincial
synod had ruled differently.

    The life of Porphyrius was in all probability circulated in an
early redaction a few years after the provincial synod had rejected
the Gazan bishop's claims. It is difficult to say whether this took
place before or after Porphyrius' death in 420. It dwelt in great
detail on Porphyrius' monastic credentials, his fictitious early associations with the current bishop of Jerusalem Praylius (417–422),
who is falsely said to have ordained him a presbyter c. 392, and of
course the closure of the temples. The original Greek *prooimion* of
this redaction has not survived, and the events during the last
decade of Porphyrius' episcopate are hardly treated because of his
political failures. Porphyrius' supposed association with Praylius in
the narrative is not accidental. The latter perhaps sympathized
with the claims of Gaza during his episcopate, which incidentally
began *two years* after the Synod of Diospolis.

    The rapprochement between the sees of Jerusalem and Gaza in
all probability lasted beyond the deaths of Porphyrius in 420 and
Praylius in 422. The latter was succeeded by Juvenal, who gained
recognition for his see as the fifth patriarchate at the Council of
Chalcedon after nearly three decades of painstaking political
manipulation.[139] Prior to 451, however, the bishops of both Gaza
and Jerusalem had to live with inherited traditions of aggrievement

---

    [139] Ernst, Honigmann, "Juvenal of Jerusalem," *Dumbarton Oaks Papers* 5 (1950),
209ff.

over denied historical claims to status and power. It would have been natural for them to cooperate at some level.

The extant Greek redaction of the life of Porphyrius is a later one. It belongs to the period right before the Council of Chalcedon. The reasons for this are twofold. First, the *prooimion* of this redaction seems to have been cribbed partly from Theodoret of Cyrrhus' *Historia Philotheos* or "Lives of the Syrian Monks," whose publication date Pierre Canivet has put at no earlier than 444.[140] On the other hand, the bishop of Jerusalem is referred to throughout the Greek as simply "bishop" (ἐπίσκοπος) (and not "patriarch" as in the Georgian), without any qualification or allusion to the state of affairs after 451. This new or second redaction, which is the present Greek one edited by Grégoire and Kugener (1930), was therefore concocted on the eve of the Council of Chalcedon in the latter part of the terminal years 444–451. The new redaction saw few changes, but they were significant. The more dignified *prooimion* was written to lend force to the importance of the subject, the closure of the Gazan temples. It relied on the *Historia Philotheos* of Theodoret, who had been deposed from his see at the Latrocinium in 449, but whose theology gained stock after the summoning of the Council of Chalcedon in 450–451. Mark the Deacon had probably died long before this. The redactor probably lived in First Palestine, and our suspicion is that Juvenal of Jerusalem sponsored the work. The *prooimion*, with its allusions to a recent and popular work of Theodoret, sought to put its sponsor Juvenal somewhere in league with the revisionists who would not only overturn the Latrocinium but would also make Jerusalem the fifth patriarchate. The other editing was of a minor order. The text was generally left in its original form except in Chapter 103, where Mark the Deacon refers to Porphyrius as "surviving a few more years" after the construction of the Eudoxiana cathedral in 407. A formulaic statement giving the date of Porphyrius' death was clumsily juxtaposed to this phrase.

If this rationale is accepted, what motive can be assigned to the redaction of 444–451? It will be recalled that Hieronymus in 408–410 was inclined to think that the closure of the Serapeum in 391 and that of the Marneion in 402 were events of a similar order and importance. Juvenal of Jerusalem perhaps considered it essential to publicize the great success of a Palestinian see in the struggle against Hellenic religion. Jerusalem could then, in a certain sense,

---

[140] Théodoret de Cyr, *Histoire des moines de Syrie*, ed. tr. Pierre Cavinet and Alice Leroy-Molinghen 1 (Paris 1977), 30f.

even if the argument was not entirely cogent, boast with the other eastern patriarchates that great events lay in the recent past, thanks in part to Praylius of Jerusalem, Porphyrius' associate and supporter, and perhaps Juvenal's mentor. Constantinople had seen to the cleansing of the Artemision of Ephesus sometime after 400, Antioch the destruction of Apollo's shrine in Daphne, and Alexandria that of the Serapeum. It seems possible that in the prestige games that preceded the Council of Chalcedon, Juvenal's agents hawked copies of the redaction about, particularly in Constantinople, to win civil and ecclesiastical sympathy for their cause. The subject greatly interested the emperor Marcian who summoned the oecumenical council. He published an edict later that year, given in Constantinople to Palladius the Praetorian Prefect of Oriens (14 November 451) that dwelt anew upon the continued use of recently closed temples for sacrifice. It cannot be entirely excluded that the publication of the life of Porphyrius at this time increased the resolve of the government to suppress the elements of Hellenic cult that had persisted despite the publication of the Theodosian Code and Third Novel of Theodosius II in 438.[141]

There remains one last question to be answered: why did Sozomen withhold the name of the bishop of Gaza who sought to repossess Maiuma for his see? If he had not, our Porphyrius would probably not have ended up as a quasi-historical personality, but either a very real one or a non-existent one. To discover the answer, we must have a further look at Sozomen's personal background. As we have seen, his family was one of the first in the Gazan countryside to accept Christianity. They had done this without the coercion of imperial edicts or troops, and had become migrants during the Julianic "persecution", which will have taken place mainly at the hands of the Gazan city councillors. As happened with most Christian intellectuals c. 400, Sozomen will himself have become a Christian sophist and advocate only after much controversy with the conflicting claims of the Hellenic educators in the schools *vis à vis* the Greek *paideia* and sacrifice.[142] Both he and his family thus had strong anti-Hellenist credentials. They evidently knew the decurion family from which Ajax and Zeno, bishop of Maiuma c. 395–400, had arisen. The latter had these credentials as well, having probably come from a Hellenist family and later building a shrine near Maiuma for three Gazan martyrs of Julian's Hellenic revival, Eusebius, Nestabos and Zeno.

---

[141] Supra, Ch. I, Sect. 5.
[142] Cf. infra, Ch. V *passim*.

It is to be strongly suspected that this well-entrenched Christian aristocracy greatly resented the fanfare that accompanied Porphyrius' schemes after 395. They will have regarded him as a dangerous interloper bent on getting credit for Christianizing Gaza and, even worse, of overthrowing the autonomy of the Christian families of Maiuma in selecting their own bishops, men who like Zeno had risen to considerable local repute. Mark the Deacon's narrative creates any number of false impressions, as for example that the *territorium* of Gaza was entirely polytheist c. 395, a supposition contradicted by Sozomen's observations about the conversion of his own family between c. 340–360. The emphasis that Sozomen puts on the career of Zeno and the threats to the autonomy of the Maiuman see relate not only to the publicity that accompanied the Gazan bishop's grab for power, but quite possibly as well to the circulation of the earlier recension of the life of Porphyrius that was published, as we believe, after 415. Sozomen is quite obviously trying to give the second side to an already well-known story with self-conscious irony. Everyone knew the name of the Gazan bishop in question, whether from his constant hankering after imperial edicts and endowments, or from Mark the Deacon's pen. The withholding of a well-known person's name in a context of criticism is usually to be taken as a form of tacit insult. There were some persons in Jerusalem who acknowledged Gaza's historical claim at the time Sozomen was writing, as we have argued above. It is difficult to conclude otherwise than that Sozomen's bishop of Gaza was in fact Mark the Deacon's Porphyrius. Even if "Porphyrius" were to be understood as an encoded name, it is almost impossible to avoid the conclusion that a bishop very much *like* this fellow closed the temples of Gaza between 400–410.

I have avoided addressing Peeters' conclusions in any detail because most of the premises contained in the "empirical" section of his introduction to the Georgian life of Porphyrius seem to be questionable, if not perverse, in light of the analysis given above. I have instead offered a historical context for the Greek text that is more nearly appropriate. The basic difficulty with Peeters' objections to the general or approximate authenticity of Mark the Deacon's narrative lies in his failure to see it in the context of ecclesiastical politics in early fifth-century Palestine. It is not really such a naive text as he supposes. The conventions of ecclesiastical rhetoric never really allowed for such plays of free association of names and events as Peeters imagines when he assigns the text to the sixth century. The ecclesiastical politics of that time were simply too ruthless to allow for such carelessness in matters of detail. In this respect Peeters accepts the rather common fallacy that Late Antique men were rather simple-minded compared to twentieth-century scholars. It seems unlikely that this will be the last word written on the subject, but a provisional case relying on hitherto unexamined—*or carelessly examined*—texts was considered essential to the treatment given the Porphyrius text in this history.

CHAPTER FOUR

ATHENS AND ATTICA

The origins of the religious transformation in Athens has few
credible witnesses. The earliest testimonia are Christian inscriptions which hardly suggest a die-hard ecclesiastical structure c. 300
that brooked no compromise with the prevailing Hellenic social
and religious ethos. The Athenians prided themselves on the temples, altars, statues and shrines of every sort. These signs of the old
religion abounded not only in the narrowly concentrated, built-up
area around the Akropolis, but along the routes leading up from the
Peiraeus, the seaport of inland Athens, and elsewhere.[1] The impression of a pervasive, even antiquarian Hellenic religiosity given
by Marinus of Neapolis' biography of the Neoplatonist philosopher
Proclus (ob. 485) suggests continuous development from the days
when Pausanias composed his itinerary (2nd century A.D.), notwithstanding the damage inflicted by Alaric's Visigoths in 396.[2]
The typical criteria for assessing the extent and pace of the Christianization of Athens are lacking, as there exists no hagiographic
life of a bishop who closed the temples, nor have the Christian
inscriptions been published in large numbers.[3] The extant literature falls mostly into the high-cultural mode: one can hardly guess
from Eunapius of Sardis' (ob. 414) *Lives of the Sophists* and Marinus
of Neapolis' *Life of Proclus* that the primitive Christian community
of Athens had made serious inroads into the old religious ethos,
albeit at the expense of some syncretism and borrowing of terminological and conceptual features of the old beliefs. To our authors,
hardly anyone was worthy of note except the Hellenic sophist or
student of rhetoric, unless he were a shipmaster who shanghaied
pupils for certain teachers, as Eunapius relates about his own

---

[1] For preliminary discussion, see: Henri Leclercq "Athènes," DACL I/2, ed. F.
Cabrol and H. Leclercq (Paris 1924), 3039–3104.
[2] Infra, Ch. IV, Sect. 2.
[3] Charles M. Bayet, *De Titulis Atticae Christianis Commentatio Historica et Epigraphica* (Paris 1878). Bayet in fact prepared the *editio princeps* of many of the texts
now conveniently found in *Inscriptiones Graecae 3/2: Inscriptiones Atticae Aetatis Romanae*, ed. W. Dittenberger (Berlin 1882). This series is hereinafter abbreviated as IG
and given in brackets after the citation from Bayet's corpus.

arrival in Athens.[4] The object of our inquiry will be the religious transformation of Attica, and the continuity of cult made obvious in Marinus' *Life of Proclus*. The judgements will, however, be of a less quantitative nature than those made about Gaza in First Palestine.

I. The Christianization of Attica and the Epigraphy

Apart from the notices in the Acts of the Apostles and references to a Christian episcopate and rhetors in Eusebius of Caesarea's ecclesiastical history,[5] the earliest record of the Christianization of Athens lies in the epigraphy. No early Christian inscription bears a date, however, until the late seventh century.[6] Thus, a probably pre-Constantinian funerary inscription (3rd–4th century) reads: "Maurus by name, son of Victorinus . . . [an Athenian?] by birth, a faithful Christian, rests in this place, having reached the age of twenty-one years."[7] The inscriptions which securely belong to later centuries (late 4th to 6th) invariably have crosses incised around them and use the word "place of sleep" (κοιμητήριον) for the tomb, a dating criterion indicating the relative antiquity of the Maurus text. The expression "a faithful Christian" would necessarily derive from a time when adherence to the new religion was unusual and a mark of differentiation. The inscription lacks the cross and Chi-Rho christogram of the post-Constantinian texts. Examples of this phenomenon—the term *Christianos* without the

---

[4] Eunapius, *Lives of the Sophists* (Wright, 478f.).

[5] Eusebius of Caesarea provides the vaguest hints about an early Christian community in Athens, the supposed first bishop being Dionysius the Areopagite, a suffragan to the archiepiscopal see of Corinth (HE 3.4.11). The archbishop of Corinth, another Dionysius, is said to have written an epistle cautioning the Athenian congregation against apostasy to Hellenic religion c. 136–180 after the execution of their bishop Publius in a persecution of seemingly local origin (HE 4.23.2). The community survived thereafter under the leadership of bishop Quadratus (HE 4.23.2–3). The incidence of Latin names in the episcopate suggests the growth of Christianity amongst slaves and freedmen who were ethnic Greeks, but received their names from the *gentilicia nomina* of city councillors who had attained Roman citizenship and civic renown during the era of Herodes Atticus (i.e. Titus Claudius Atticus Herodes, fl. c. 140 A.D.), the great public benefactor. The Christian philosopher Athenagoras of Athens (2nd c.) is reliably believed to have composed an apology for his faith addressed to Marcus Aurelius (161–180) and to have published a treatise on the resurrection of the dead. *Athenagorae Libellus pro Christianis. Oratio de Resurrectione Cadaverorum*, ed. Eduard Schwartz (Leipzig 1891).

[6] A.K. Orlandos and A. Vranousē, *Ta Charagmata tou Parthenōnos* (Athens 1973), no. 34, the earliest Christian episcopal inscription, that of Andrew dated 693. But many of the other inscriptions in Orlandos' collection are certainly no later than the sixth century, to judge from their letter forms (e.g. no. 25).

[7] Bayet, no. 75 (IG 3/2 3435). The rounded epsilon, sigma, and omega uncials are typically 2nd–4th c.

symbols—are characteristic of third- and fourth-century inscriptions in Asia Minor and Syria as well.[8] Underlying this format lay a desire not to offend the opinion of Hellenes whose tombs and monuments at times shared the same *nekropoleis*, or to avoid provoking defacement. Another early but undated inscription with the Constantinian symbols reads (4th century): "Sambatis and Demarchē lie in this place, Christians. Ρ Ω Ρ Α Ρ."[9] The owners of the tomb found it necessary to advertise their cult, once again, when few Christians were about in Athens, even after the Constantinian victory in the East in 324.

These inscriptions suggest two premises: first, that in the crucial period between c. 284–337 the adherents of the new religion were something of a rarity; and, secondly, that conversions at this time were, as it were, "complete", and paid little tribute to the intensely pagan ethos of Athens. No chic Hellenic euphemisms for the Christian God appear. Rather, the dead are *Christianoi* pure and simple. The dead "rest" and "lie", but do not die, an implicit affirmation of the Christian resurrection which avoids the usual pagan lamentations about cruel fate and the wretched state of the dead.[10] All this suggests a cult that rigidly resisted the torrents of rhetoric that poured from the high-cultural philosophical schools, funerary epigrammatic conventions, and the poetic traditions of the city of Athens. The Christians rather verbalized their sentiments from the Septuagint and New Testament books.[11] This tendency had undergone some modification by c. 400. A new Christian militancy had crept into the epigraphy: "(Cross) Christ has conquered. May it happen. Amen." (+ ὁ Χ(ριστὸ)ς ἐνίκησεν, ἀμὴν γένοιτο).[12] This expression invariably turns up in towns where the local bishop or monks engaged in converting or demolishing temples, or manifested the intention to do so.[13]

Parallel to this tendency, however, came the admission of increasing numbers of Athenian pagans to the Christian catechumenate who would not, or could not, forsake their ties to Hellenic culture. It is sometimes supposed that the Neoplatonic scholars of

---

[8] See, for example, the texts collected by W.M. Calder, "Philadelphia and Montanism," *Bulletin of the John Rylands Library* 7 (1922–23), 336–354, some of which are securely dated to the third century.

[9] Bayet, no. 75 (IG 3/2 3525). Cf. Bayet, no. 76.

[10] An exception to this rule is found on an inscription cut c. 400 at Tanagra in Boeotia. For discussion, cf. Trombley, "Boeotia in Late Antiquity," 225f.

[11] Ibid., 224f. and infra.

[12] Bayet, no. 92 (IG 3/2.3544). The uncials (e.g. A) and leaves suggest a 4th–5th c. date.

[13] Supra, Ch. II, Sect. 2.

Athens and their students lived in some splendid religious and
cultural isolation from the artisan, notarial, and laboring classes,
but the inscriptions do not bear this out. The "well-born" or
Eupatrid families, whose conception of the immortality of the soul
drew in great measure upon the prevailing tenets of the Neoplatonic schools, had begun to convert to Christianity by c. 400, and it
shows in their funerary verse inscriptions: "Nicephorus, a well-
born man (εὐγενής), lies here, having left behind many friends.
The earth has hidden [him], who left his wife a widow and grieving
infant children."[14] Bayet reckoned the inscription to be Christian
because the characteristic phrase "here lies" (ἐνθάδε κῖτε) does
not occur in the pagan epigraphy of Roman/Late Roman Attica.[15]
The noble name Nicephorus occurred amongst the great families,
one having held a *prytanis* and many others having been admitted to
the ephebate.[16] References to the earth concealing the body (γεῖ
κέκρυπτε) and grief (ἄχεα/ ἄχαια) were of pagan provenance. The
adherence of the upper classes to the Greek *paideia* required such
touches. A second inscription (4th–5th century) offers graphic
proof of the influence of Neoplatonic thought concerning the soul:[17]

> Photius, son of Photius, . . . was born of Demostratē [his mother], the
> daughter of Zoilos. The earth hides a body here, but the soul was
> carried up into the aether and abides with those [who came] before it.
> (Alpha) (Cross) (Omega) . . .

The ascent of the soul into the upper air (ἀλλ᾽ εἰς αἰθέρα ψυχὴ
διέπτη καὶ σύνεστιν οἷς τὸ πρίν) at death was a fundamental
Neoplatonic tenet,[18] but was not inconsistent with Christian notions of an afterlife. Such formulations are exceedingly rare in
Christian funerary epigraphy except in Athens. The traditional
name Demostratē, once again, suggests lineage in the local
aristocracy.[19] A third Christian metric inscription borrows extensively from Hellenic models:[20]

> (Cross) The earth took and seized the new mother when her children
> needed milk, the good Attic woman Athenodora, the religious wife of
> Thaumasios who had begotten children and was nurturing infants.

---

[14] Bayet, no. 98 (IG 3/2.1385).
[15] Cf. IG 3/2.1307–3434.
[16] IG 3/2.1112, 1119, 1160, 1165, 1177, 1199, 1202.
[17] Bayet, no. 38 (IG 3/2.1386).
[18] Infra, Ch. IV, Sect. 3.
[19] Cf. the occurrences in the local aristocracy of the male variant Demostratos,
with its bearers listed as holders of the prytanis, office of archon, the ephebate, etc.
IG 3/2.676, 679, 907, 1020, 1041, 1202, 1231, 1283.
[20] Bayet, no. 41 (IG 3/2.1384). IG 3/1–2 contains many examples of the
theophoric Athenodora.

Athenodora was, once again, the feminine variant of a local aristocratic name. The stele marks well her Attic heritage, and pays
tribute to that of her husband as well. She bore the theophoric
name meaning "gift of Athena", the sort of name that few Christian
parents would confer on their children or a bishop permit as a
baptismal name. Athenodora evidently came of pagan parentage
and converted to the new religion later, with her elders or husband,
or both. The existence of theophoric names in Christian funerary
epigrams invariably indicates conversion in adulthood, or the conversion of one's parents during a person's childhood, but in any
case many conversions. The letter forms on the stele might suggest
a date c. 400.[21] Athenodora was "religious" (φιλένθεος), a term
which in the Orphic hymns has the sense of one whom the god Pan
had "inspired by divine frenzy".[22] The Orphic texts were, of
course, a well-travelled topic among the fifth-century Athenian
philosophers like Proclus (ob. 485), who was well known for his
interest in, and the study of, the so-called sayings of Orpheus (τὰ
λόγια 'Ορφέως), Orphic theology,[23] and Orphic ritual purifica-
tions (καθάρματα 'Ορφικά).[24] Thus, well-worn terms with specific
and intensely felt Hellenic meanings found their way into Christian
parlance when other terminological conventions[25] fell weak by comparison, as for example θεοσεβής, a common term for "religious"
that recurs in pagan and Christian texts alike and which Marinus
of Neapolis used to characterize Proclus' cult practices (θεοσέβεια).[26]
These funerary epigrams are consistent with the increasing trend
among the aristocracies of provincial towns to convert to Christianity in the decades after the death of Julian the Apostate in 363.[27]

In some cases the Christian funerary inscriptions make clear
departure from orthodox Christian notions of the spiritual world.
One, belonging to a certain Asklepiodotos (another pagan
theophoric name meaning "gift of Asklepios"), refers to the Neoplatonic immortality of the soul (ψυχῆς ἀθανάτης), a doctrine

---

[21] Bayet, Plate II, no. 7.
[22] Orphica 11.5 (ed. Eugen Abel, Leipzig - Prague 1885, p. 64). Said of Pan, the
two lines address him as: "Blessed, leaper, running around, enthroned with the
Hours, goat-limbed, filled with Bacchic frenzy, lover of divine frenzy, cave-
dwelling, etc." Ibid., line 4f.
[23] Marinus of Neapolis, Vita Procli 26, ed. Iohannes F. Boissonade (1814; repr.
Amsterdam 1966), 20.
[24] Marinus, Vita Procli 18 (Boissonade, 15).
[25] G.W. Lampe omits φιλένθεος from the entries in A Patristic Greek Lexicon
(Oxford 1961). The term seems to have had no considerable use even among the
writers of the Christian Sophistic.
[26] Marinus, Vita Procli 9 (Boissonade, 8).
[27] Trombley, "Boeotia in Late Antiquity," 222.

which, strictly speaking, implies the soul's pre-existence to the body. The inscription also refers to the activity of Fate (ἡ μοῖρα) in human affairs:[28]

> Friend, I Asklepiodotos see well the sacred beauty of the body and immortal soul. For nature gazes at a single undefiled beauty in both. If Fate snatches one away, it does not subdue it. In dying alone it does not die. It has not forsaken drink, and, if it leaves, it looks down even now on [the body] from heaven and dances and keeps watch.

The inscription lacks even the barest hint of Asklepiodotos' cult, except in its syncretistic view of the soul, and is yet one more example of the mixing of theologies that resulted from the conversion of the Athenian decurion class. The soul drinks, dances, keeps watch, and partakes of equal beauty with the body—a weak attempt at humor perhaps, but also a set of notions that had a local Hellenic origin. The text is Christian only in the sense that pagan funerary epigraphy usually avoids references to the soul and immortality. A striking exception to this rule is the funerary epigram of Proclus the Neoplatonist, which Marinus of Neapolis transcribed for the philosopher's biography:[29]

> I was Proclus, a Lycian by race, whom Syrianos nourished here, a recipient of his teaching. This common tomb received the bodies of both. May one place also receive their souls.

Proclus had, early in his career, studied Aristotle's rationalistic *On the Soul*.[30] His epigram is therefore, and not surprisingly, free of any suppositions about the ascent of the soul into the aether or its subsequent observation of earthly phenomena while sporting above. This form of speculation was left to the unlearned and less critical, including the newly converted Christians who adopted the Neoplatonic cant. Proclus expresses the sentiment, by contrast, that their souls would abide in some common place (χῶρος) of an indeterminate character. All this indicates a common but somewhat differentiated *Weltanschauung* among the educated aristocrats of Attica c. 400. Ideas about the nature of the spiritual world transcended private opinion about religious cult, ritual, saving

---

[28] Bayet, no. 118 (IG 3/2.1383).

[29] Πρόκλος ἐγὼ γενόμην Λυκίος γένος, ὃν Συριανὸς ἐνθάδ' ἀμοιβὸν ἑῆς θρέψε διδασκαλίης. ξυνὸς δ' ἀμφοτέρων ὅδε σώματα δέξατο τύμβος. Αἴθε δὲ καὶ ψυχὰς χῶρος ἑεὶς λελάχοι. Marinus, *Vita Procli* 9 (Boissonade, 2f.).

[30] Cf. Proclus' Aristotelian studies with the sophist Olympiodorus and study of Aristotle's *Peri Psychēs* with the Athenian Neoplatonist Plutarch, son of Nestorius. Marinus, *Vita Procli* 9 and 12 (Boissonade, 7, 10).

gods, temple versus church architecture, and so forth. Areas of agreement such as this, combined with a deeply felt sense of Attic-Athenian heritage, led to an easy tolerance that accounts for the relatively late closure of the Parthenon and Asklepieion, in the 480's,[31] ineluctable events which solidarity amongst the local decurions averted for a time. The absence of such a cultural factor explains why Gaza in First Palestine lost its temples earlier, in 402.

Passing from the decurion classes, teachers of philosophy, and rhetors to the ordinary Athenians, let us consider the progress of their Christianization. The new religion had made deep inroads into the population by Proclus' day (ob. 485). When Proclus' biographer Marinus of Neapolis' name was put in nomination for the office of *diadochos* or director of the Academy, Theagenes the archon vetoed this on the ground that the Christian population would take Marinus' too strident Hellenism as a direct challenge.[32] This will hardly have troubled the civil peace except that the Christians by this time will have numbered several tenths of the population more than the Hellenes. Theagenes himself bore the imperial title of *patricius* and the epithet of "the Herodes Atticus of his day" because of his expenditures on secular buildings in Athens.[33] Although a Hellene himself, Theagenes well knew the potential climate of local and imperial opinion against himself and his fellow Hellenists, should the statements of a pagan on the chair of the Academy become a *cause célèbre*.[34]

The presence of Hellenic theophoric names on the funerary inscriptions of ordinary Christian Athenians suggests the conversion of many adult pagans during the period 350–450 for the reasons given above.[35] The persons commemorated often bore the names of deities with locally popular shrines. Among these folk were Askleparion,[36] Atheneos the housebuilder,[37] Nike,[38] Asklepia,[39] and

---

[31] Infra, Appendix II.
[32] Damascius of Damascus, *Das Leben des Philosophen Isidoros*, tr. Rudolf Asmus (Leipzig 1911), 94. On Theagenes, see: E. Groag, *Die Reichsbeamten von Achaia in spätrömischen Zeit* (Budapest 1946), 76f. and infra, Ch. IV, Sect. 3.
[33] Groag, *Reichsbeamten von Achaia*, 76.
[34] Damascius, *Vita Isidori* (Asmus, 96).
[35] For preliminary discussion, see: Timothy E. Gregory, "The Survival of Paganism in Christian Greece," *American Journal of Philology* 107 (1986), 239f.
[36] IG 3/2.3521.
[37] Bayet, no. 25 (IG 3/2.3454).
[38] Bayet, nos. 27 and 49 (IG 3/2.3458 and 3484).
[39] Bayet, no. 72.

Dionysia.[40] The cult of Asklepios had many adherents among the decurion class, as will be seen, and among the ordinary folk as well, all of whom took their petitions to the Asklepieion on the south slope of the Akropolis to seek cures as late as c. 480 from the saving god, whose cult had become more significant in an everyday sense than that of other deities.[41] The cult of the tutelary Athena, whose temple dominated the skyline of the city, seems to have had as its adherents mainly philosophers like Proclus, Syrianus, and Lachares, who sought an increase of wisdom for professional purposes.[42] Marinus of Neapolis even calls her the "philosopher goddess" (ἡ φιλόσοφος θεός).[43] The cult of Athena was closely linked to civic life as well, being celebrated with the procession of the boat at the Panathenaia, a great festival that continued to be celebrated in the fourth and fifth centuries, probably until the removal of the image of Athena from the Parthenon.[44] The temple of Nike also stood on the Akropolis, and shrines of Dionysus were round about. The theophoric Dionysius and Dionysia were not common in Christian nomenclature, despite the prestige of the name in its New Testament context with the conversion of Dionysius the Areopagite.[45] Other theophoric names among the Christians of Athens included Hermophilos ("friend of Hermes"),[46] Oinophilos ("friend of Wine"), which is probably a Dionysiac epithet,[47] and Kalliope, the name of a muse.[48] One also encounters a Samuel, son of Pythas.[49] Here the convert Samuel either took a Hebraic name, or his father Pythas, bearing the theophoric of the Pythian Apollo at Delphi, kept his own name after baptism, but picked his son's name from the Septuagint.[50]

Christian slaves existed as domestic workers in the households of

---

[40] Bayet, no. 57 (IG 3/2.3477). The personal names Dionysios and Dionysia were not common in Christian nomenclature, despite the prestige of the early convert Dionysios the Areopagite (Acts 17.34). On the other hand, they are *very* common in pagan Attic epigraphy during the Roman imperial period.

[41] Infra, Ch. IV, Sect. 3.

[42] Marinus, *Vita Procli* 11 (Boissonade, 9).

[43] Marinus, *Vita Procli* 30 (Boissonade, 24), and infra.

[44] Cf. Himerius, *Oratio 47* in *Declamationes et Orationes*, ed. Aristides Colonna (Rome 1951), 194f. Marinus, *Vita Procli* 30 (Boissonade, 24), and infra.

[45] Acts 17.34. Cf. the names of the correspondents of Nilos of Ankyra. There is one Dionysiodorus (1.283), one Dionysius (4.55), and one Dionysius the monk (2.93). PG 79, 185B, 576A, and 241C.

[46] Bayet, no. 36 (IG 3/2.3448).

[47] Bayet, no. 19 (IG 3/2.3468 and 3469).

[48] Bayet, no. 69 (IG 3/2.3461).

[49] Bayet, no. 125 (IG 3/2.3450).

[50] The name Pythas is entirely lacking among the correspondents of Nilos of Ankyra. Cf. supra, Ch. IV, Sect. 1.

wealthy Hellenes, as one inscription (4th–5th century) indicates: "Funerary monument of Dionysius the silk-worker, a domestic servant of the proconsul Plutarch the *clarissimus*" (+ Μνημόριον Διονυσίου συρικαρίου οἰκαίτη (= οἰκέτου) τοῦ λαμπροτάτου Πλουτάρχου ἀνθυπάτου).[51] Groag puts Plutarch's tenure as proconsul of the province of Achaea c. 375–425.[52] The governor and his extended family appear to have been pagan, if the supposed relationship amongst the different Plutarch inscriptions of Attica is accurate.[53] The proconsul, whose official residence was in Corinth, had estates and industrial shops in Attica, whose considerable work force included slaves. These facilities lay at a site outside Athens near Trachon, where the inscription was discovered.[54] The presence of Christian slaves in pagan households had always been quite common.[55] The man's theophoric name Dionysius suggests, however, that the new religion had begun to find converts even in the rural estates of Attica where Christian churches and clergy hardly existed. The man may have been purchased elsewhere for his special skills, or perhaps his workshop had at one time stood in Athens where he was exposed to the influence of the new religion.

The demographic features of the Christianization of Athens in the fifth century are difficult to document because of the paucity of the evidence, but some generalizations are possible. In the period before the death of Julian the Apostate the church and its adherents were inward turning and made few compromises with the religious culture of the city, but after c. 365 everything was in flux. Aristocrats, artisans, and slaves began to accept the new religion and brought their cultural baggage with them, enjoying an easy tolerance from the bishops, who had themselves probably come from Eupatrid families and were themselves Hellenists in some sense, particularly after church properties began to increase, basilicas to be built, and the prestige of holding the episcopate rose. The historian would probably not go wrong in drawing one conclusion from a comparison between Athens and Gaza, namely that, because of the prestige of the local cults and influence of the schools of philosophy, the regular increment of new Christians was no more than a trickle, perhaps one or two hundred per annum. The Neoplatonic cant and epithets of the local gods belonged to the average

---

[51] Bayet, no. 102 (IG 3/2.3513).
[52] Groag, *Reichsbeamten von Achaia* 59.
[53] Ibid., 59–62.
[54] Bayet, no. 102.
[55] Cf. the female Christian slave of the pagan matron Aelia of Gaza. Supra, Ch. III, Sect. 2.

Athenian's everyday vocabulary, and these tendencies colored the
popular theology of the church. That church was "liberal" by
fifth-century standards because of its Hellenic tone. The decisive
blow against the old cults certainly came c. 481–84 with the removal of the statue of Athena from the Parthenon and the demolition of
the Asklepieion. The closure of the temples in Gaza in 402 has a
paradigmatic significance for the early fifth century. Large numbers of erstwhile pagans rushed to the Christian churches as soon
as workmen laid their hands on the pagan shrines, but the exact
circumstances in Athens are unknown.

The clergy of the Athenian church, or the church itself in its
official role, carried over much of the terminology of the old religion
when it converted temples. These transactions occurred toward the
end of the fifth century, probably between 481–488 as will be seen
below.[56] One example appears on the Erechtheion, a temple on the
Akropolis which served several deities and displayed the Karyatids
on its south porch: "Mother of God, mistress of believers, save the
cross (?) and protect your suppliant Dionysius John, a humble man
and psalmist of the catholic church of Athens."[57] Here the deliberately Christian vocative "Mother of God" (θεοδόχε) is deliberately
juxtaposed with the Hellenic "mistress" (δέσποινα), a name of
Hekate and Artemis, but particularly of the chthonic Demeter of
Eleusis.[58] The expression "save the cross" (τὸ κέρας σῶζε) would
refer to the recent erection of the Christian symbol on the sacred
home-ground of Hellenism and hints at fear lest the adherents of
the old religion remove the cross. Similarly the Hellenic "suppliant" (ἱκέτης) is juxtaposed with the Christian clerical attribu-
tive "humble" (ταπεινός). The see of Athens found it necessary to
express its public position in language that all would understand,
namely that a quasi-divine female figure, in the mind of Hellene
and Christian alike, guarded the newly erected cross, the symbol of
Christian victory.

III. Hellenic Religion c. 400

At the beginning of the fifth century Athens had to all appearances undergone little or no religious transformation. Although a
small Christian community had been in existence for several cen-

---

[56] Infra, Ch. IV, Sect. 3.
[57] *Ephemerides*, p. 1809, no. 3467. Quoted by Leclercq, "Athens," 3062.
[58] Supra, Ch. II, Sect. 4. See also Orlandos-Vranousē, *Charagmata tou Panthenō-
nos*, nos. 25, 87, 212.

turies and had grown considerably since the time of Constantine the Great (324–337 in the East), reminders of the Hellenic religion stood everywhere: the temples on the Akropolis dominated by the Parthenon, the Asklepieion on the south slope, the other temples, and innumerable shrines dedicated to lesser deities, to the Hellenic heroes, and to the ancestors of the aristocratic families which still put up candidates for the office of archon eponymous, staffed the city council, and supervised the great public processions like the Panathenaia, which included the dragging of the sacred boat of Athena from the Peiraeus to the Parthenon. Civic rituals of this kind were strictly tolerated by the Christian emperors.[59] Only one significant difference struck those whose remembered the old days: if the air was still scented with incense, the billowing smoke which carried the smell of sacrificial meats round the base of the Akropolis was lacking. The Christian emperors had handed down successive laws proscribing public sacrifice, and so the urban poor will have presented themselves in increasing numbers at the churches for daily bread instead of waiting for the sacrificial meats distributed at the festivals. So too an occasional Christian litany led by the bishop will periodically have threaded its way through the streets in bodies of people too small to suggest the religious transformation that was about to take place in Athens.[60]

Asterius of Amasea (ob. 410) provides a full, if hostile, survey of the popular cults still practiced in Attica probably no earlier than 390–400 in his *Encomium on the Holy Martyrs*, a work which defends the cult of martyrs against pagan critics who ridiculed Christians as worshippers of myriad dead men:[61]

> Did you not reflect on Demeter and Kore in your dementia? Did you not build two temples to female deities and honor them with sacrifices, and make the *proskynesis* with every kind of rite? Is not the acme of your worship the mysteries at Eleusis, and does not the Attic *demos* and all Hellas assemble, that they might worship the most vain things? Is there not in that place a dark stairway, and are there not sacred rites of the hierophant with the priestess, him alone with her? Are not the lamps extinguished, and do not the considerable and innumerable people think the acts accomplished by the two in darkness to be their salvation? Do you not make *proskynesis* to the Theban Dionysus as a god (I speak of his fatherland, that you might know the human being [rather than supposing him a god]), a viticulturist and

---

[59] Supra, Ch. I, Sect. 2.
[60] The case of Gaza between 395–402 provides a good example of a Christian procession in a predominantly pagan city. Supra, Ch. III. Sect. 2.
[61] Asterios of Amasea, *Homilia X in SS. Martyres*, PG 40, 324A–D. Cf. Idem, *Homilies I–XIV*, ed. C. Datema (Leiden 1970), 140, for a more developed text.

lover of wine and reveller who plays drunken tricks, who leads a *demos*
slurred with drunkenness, doing those things which make them licentious profligates, and who behaves drunkenly with old man Silenos,
and spends time with the Satyrs who are fond of capering, and who
provides a history of drunkenness for a way of life? Do you not
conduct sacrifices to the man Heracles, as though he were a god, a
strong man who happened to have a powerful and virile body? Do
you not worship that man because he had virtue in many [great
deeds] and escaped from many animals? Why did you admire and
worship Asklepios, who carried many things around in a cane and
iron box? Do you not despise the fact that you do this? For the
temples everywhere in the *oikoumene*—I speak of the Asklepieions and
Herakeions—have stood refuted for vanity.

Conspicuously absent is Athena, whose cult had become largely a
civic function by this time, except among the professors of philosophy, and had perhaps become so dangerous to celebrate as to
ossify in the public imagination. On the other hand, the savior,
benefactor, agrarian and underworld deities rated high esteem
among the Athenians: Asklepios with his medical chest whose
temple in Athens remained a site of prayers and incubation until
c. 481–488;[62] Dionysus, whose cult was linked to the wine cycle
between September and December in the Mediterranean lands,
and had special shrines in Athens near the Akropolis;[63] Heracles,
who must have had a place among the shrines dedicated to heroes
that the Neoplatonist Proclus visited,[64] along with those of
Achilles;[65] and Demeter, whose formal cult (but not the popular
one) became extinct late in the lifetime of Eunapius of Sardis (ob.
414) after the old priestly families had died off and an aristocrat
from Thespiae in Boeotia received the office of hierophant.[66] Asterius, like many other Christians, may have visited Athens as a
student, although firm evidence is lacking.[67] As a resident of
Amasea, he might have railed about the worship of the Mother of
the Gods and other local Anatolian deities, but instead confined his
remarks to Attica, an argument that he had a different audience in

---

[62] Infra, Appendix II and III.

[63] Dionysus was still being invoked during the Brumalia, the final stage of the
wine cycle in December, when the fermented fluid was poured into bottles for
distribution and consumption, c. 691, when the Council in Trullo was convened in
Constantinople. Frank R. Trombley, "The Council in Trullo (691–692): A Study
of the Canons Relating to Paganism, Heresy, and the Invasions," *Comitatus* 9
(1978), 5f.

[64] Marinus, *Vita Procli* 36 (Boissonade, 28).

[65] Zosimus of Panium, *Historia Nova* 4.18.2–4. Infra, Ch. IV, footnote 111, for
editions used.

[66] Eunapius, *Lives of the Sophists* (Wright, 436–39).

[67] Cf. the case of John Chrysostom, infra.

mind. A strictly antiquarian critique of the Athenian cults would have required some mention of Athena, Zeus, and Pan, but this is lacking, and hence the contemporary relevance of his encomium.

The old cults and practices were still deeply rooted in Athenian society and culture c. 400. This rule applies not only to the philosophers and rhetors of the Academy and other schools, but also to the decurion class drawn from the Attic aristocracy. This group provided candidates for the archonship, sat in the city council, and held the different priesthoods. A man with suitable connections might at times have combined several of these offices in his own person. The post-Julianic aristocracy is known mostly from scattered notices in inscriptions and literary sources. The earliest of these turns up in George of Alexandria's seventh-century life of John Chrysostom, who is reputed to have visited Athens briefly to study.[68] The authenticity of the historical data in this text has been periodically challenged and does in fact pose many difficult problems, which are dealt with in an appendix below.[69] The time of Chrysostom's visit would have been between July 367 when he completed his rhetorical studies with Libanius in Antioch, and Easter in 368, the earliest date at which he could have accepted baptism.[70] George of Alexandria's account appears to go back to real historical evidence. His description of social relations is of the utmost significance for understanding the Christianization of Attica.

In the winter of 367/8 the city council of Athens consisted almost entirely of Hellenes. At the apex sat the archon eponymous, whom George of Alexandria styles as the father of the city (πατὴρ πόλεως).[71] The man was a Hellene, as were the landed magnates (οἱ μεγιστᾶνες) that made up the city council.[72] They are described as "landowners and archons of the city and of its *territorium*" (τῶν κτητόρων καὶ ἀρχόντων τῆς πόλεως καὶ τῆς περιοίκου αὐτῆς).[73] The rhetors and sophists of the schools were also of the old religious opinion. Eunapius of Sardis' survey of their careers in the *Lives of*

---

[68] The relevant sections of George of Alexandria's life are found in *Douze Récits byzantins sur Saint Jean Chrysostom*, ed. François Halkin (Subsidia Hagiographica 60, Brussels 1977), 76–88. Hereinafter cited as *Vita Chrysostomi*.

[69] Cf. infra, Appendix II.

[70] Robert E. Carter, "The Chronology of Saint John Chrysostom's Early Life," *Traditio* 18 (1962), 357–364.

[71] George of Alexandria, *Vita Chrysostomi*, 79, line 6f. Cf. Nilos of Ankyra, *Ep.* 2.36, who reports a certain Demosthenes, who served as "father of the city" (πατὴρ πόλεως) of an unnamed *polis*. PG 79, 213C–D.

[72] George of Alexandria, *Vita Chrysostomi*, 79, line 28f.

[73] Ibid., 78, line 29f.

the Philosophers and Sophists discloses only one Christian amongst the scores of Athenian professors, a certain Prohairesios, who was incidentally Eunapius' praeceptor when the latter studied in Athens.[74] Eunapius must have omitted the biographies of many minor figures out of personal spite or political dislike.[75] One of these was perhaps a certain Anthemius, another Hellene whom the biography of Chrysostom asserts dominated the intellectual life during the early post-Julianic period, to the extent, it is said, of having a statue with an honorific inscription (στήλη) erected for him in Athens and also in Rome.[76] At the bottom of the social structure lay the people, the ordinary citizens of Athens, among whom Christianity had begun to make inroads, and the resident aliens. Among the latter numbered the students in the schools, many of whom like Gregory of Nazianzus, one of the founders of the new Christian sophistic, and Julian the Apostate were Christians. It can hardly be doubted that many adherents of the new religion lived among the shipmasters and businessmen of the Peiraeus, just as they did in Maiuma, the seaport of Gaza in First Palestine, a city which was otherwise almost entirely pagan in 367.

The conditions prevailing at Athens emerge from George of Alexandria's narrative about the public reception given Chrysostom by the city council. It is said that he was conveyed to the bouleutic chamber in a special chariot (ὄχημα) reserved for ceremonial occasions,[77] and that the archon bade him sit in the middle (ἐν μέσῳ) where not only the local officials but also the sophists and rhetors might greet and question him. The event is not improbable in the context of praefectural and local provincial politics, nor in the realm of late fourth-century intellectual life. Chrysostom was himself the son of Secundus, *magister militum per Orientem*, who had had all the military formations of the eastern frontier under his command. The man had acquired immense wealth in the course of his career, in large measure through his marriage to Anthusa, a woman of the landed aristocracy and decurion class of Antioch.[78]

---

[74] Eunapius, *Lives of the Sophists* (Wright, 476ff.).

[75] For example, Eunapius makes short shrift of Libanius and Porphyrius of Tyre. *Lives of the Sophists* (Wright, 518–27 and 352–63, respectively). Eunapius condemns Libanius' style of rhetoric as "feeble, lifeless, and uninspired," and as pre-puerile (Ibid., 522f.). His verdict on Porphyrius is more positive. The reason for Porphyrius' brief treatment perhaps lay in the fact that he had rejected sacrifice to the gods in connection with his adherence to Pythagorianism. Apart from his polemic against Christians, Porphyrius' writing proved most useful to the Christian polemic against Hellenic cult and theology. Cf. infra, Ch. V, Sect. 3 and 4.

[76] George of Alexandria, *Vita Chrysostomi*, 78, lines 22–25.

[77] Ibid., 79, line 8. Cf. IG 14.1072.

[78] George of Alexandria, *Vita Chrysostomi*, 73. Jones, *Laker Roman Empire*, 599.

Sufficient money had been left to the widow after Secundus' prema-
ture death to finance John Chrysostom's studies under Libanius,
one of the most prominent rhetors of the late fourth century.[79] It
was after the completion of his studies with that man in July 367
that the young scholar, still a catechumen, appears to have sailed
for Athens, perhaps to overcome the taint of provincialism and to
exchange views with his contemporaries, the *sine qua non* for rounding out his somewhat Hellenistic education.[80] Chrysostom was, on
the other hand, well connected politically and a student of the great
Libanius (of whom Eunapius incidentally makes short shrift), and
was hardly travelling *incognito*. The provincial aristocracy of
Athens, some of whom must have attained senatorial rank, had
everything to gain by regaling the son of a senior contemporary
whose political acquaintances had undoubtedly included the co-
emperors Valens and Valentinian I before their elevation to imperial power. Furthermore, even if Eunapius makes short shrift of
Libanius in the *Lives*, one can hardly conclude that Athenians at
large shared such sentiments about his status as a professional.
Thus, when the sophist Anthemius reputedly complained about the
prominent seat given Chrysostom in the bouleutic chamber,[81] the
archon Demosthenes retorted:[82]

> It is necessary, O philosopher, that you act and speak and behave in
> a manner befitting a philosopher. You have neither the title nor the
> right to perform acts or make speeches in a manner apart from
> custom in the middle of this colloquium, or to do the same as the
> demesmen and cry out like certain rustics who drive animals out on
> the plains or like those who are set upon by brigands. Even if this
> wise John has been honored by us, we could not accomplish anything
> for him outside the customary, just because he is in the first place the
> son of a man who became the great *magister militum* in Antioch and it
> was fitting to render him honor because of his rank.

Chrysostom certainly had the rhetorical credentials to speak in this
company as well.
    In the subsequent interview, the discussion between Chrysostom
and his interlocutors is said to have devolved upon matters of

---

[79] The authority for this datum is Socrates, HE 6.3 (PG 67, 665A), who was a
near contemporary, I find A.J. Festugière's wavering scepticism on this question
unnecessary, *Antioche païenne et chrétienne: Libanius, Chrysostome et les moines de Syrie*
(Paris 1959), 409f.
[80] George of Alexandria, *Vita Chrysostomi*, 78. Such an interpretation is consistent with the low esteem as a rhetorician in which Libanius was held by his peers.
Supra, Ch. IV, n. 75.
[81] George of Alexandria, *Vita Chrysostomi*, 80, lines 5–23.
[82] Ibid., 80, line 29 to 81, line 2.

religious opinion. It can hardly be doubted that he had already refused to partake of sacrificial meats and the round of polytheistic rites that the open shrines made available to visitors in Athens during the tolerant reign of the co-emperors Valens and Valentinian I,[83] including many a Christian catechumen.[84] Chrysostom would thus have been well known by the time he came before his audience, and had probably already vented his views on the pervasive character of the Athenian cults. To these he shows no mercy in the diatribe reported by George of Alexandria in the bouleutic chamber. He is said to have denounced Apollo, Zeus, Kronos, Hermes, Aphrodite and Hera as "dead gods" (θεοὶ νεκροί), despite the existence of their shrines in Athens.[85] Many Hellenes would doubtless have agreed here, for the cult of the Olympians was dying out everywhere by this time, and had been for centuries earlier. Their names persisted mostly in non-Greek cults which had adopted their onomastics during the Hellenistic period and given them to local gods that had equivalent functions. Thus at Gaza the Cretan-born Zeus still received ardent worship, as did a Semitic fertility goddess conveniently called Aphrodite.[86] So too did the Egyptian Kronos.[87] Chrysostom supposedly noted as well the continuing devotion to Athena and Artemis, whose statues, particularly the chryselephantine Athena of the Parthenon, still stood (στῆλαι), and whom the Christian rhetor called "little whores".[88] As has been already noted, the cult of Athena had by this time become a civic festival amongst the ordinary citizens, but the philosophers, rhetors and sophists, whom Chrysostom had in mind, continued to worship her as the "philosopher goddess". He adds that their cults led to "acts of magic and poisoning" (μαγεία καὶ φαρμακεία), a probable reference to the theurgy which had become popular among philosophers like Maximus of Ephesus, who had cultivated the female deity Hekate.[89] Also objectionable to Chrysostom were the "statues of every sort of wild beast, made of stone and wood, and by every material technique" (στήλας

---

[83] Supra, Ch. II, n. 46.

[84] For Christian catechumens who performed sacrifices c. 490, see infra, Ch. V, Sect. 2–4. Among them was the future monophysite leader Severus of Sozopolis. This was *not* an isolated instance.

[85] The survival of the Hellenic gods' shrines in Athens until c. 484, along with the Parthenon and Asklepieion, is implicit in Marinus *Vita Procli*. Infra, Ch. IV, Sect. 3.

[86] Supra, Ch. III, Sect. 2 and 4.

[87] Infra, Ch. IX, Sect. 1.

[88] καὶ ὡς θεοῖς λατρεύουσιν αὐταῖς πορνικοῖς γυναικαρίοις. George of Alexandria, *Vita Chrysostomi*, 82, line 27f.

[89] Supra, Ch. I, Sect. 3.

κνωδάλων παντοίων καὶ θηρίων ἐν ξύλοις καὶ λίθοις καὶ πάσῃ ὑλικῇ τεχνουργίᾳ γενομένων).[90] He was perhaps thinking here of the sphinxes that graced so many Greek shrines. Chrysostom denounced *in fine*, "the profane literature of Greek mythology, which relates the story of indecent and licentious persons, webs of *daimones*, the rites of magicians and of those who make incantations, and the soul-destroying evil arts" (ἡ γὰρ τῶν Ἑλλήνων βέβηλος συγγραφὴ μυθολογίας, γοητῶν τε καὶ ἐπαοιδῶν τελετὰς καὶ ψυχοφθόρους κακομηχανίας).[91] These words will hardly have earned the assent of the assembled crowd in the bouleutic chamber, which included not only archons, councillors, sophists, rhetors, and philosophers, but also an interested portion of the populace (πᾶς ὁ λαός), many of whom had a rudimentary schooling in the Greek *paideia*.[92] At any rate, Chrysostom's invective is said to have drawn shouts of approval from the Christians present.[93] This is not impossible in light of the Christian funerary inscriptions discussed above, some of which belonged to families of high social standing. It must be admitted that Chrysostom's contentions are formulated in the manner of a school-boy's composition, and lack the sophistication of argumentation already seen from the pen of Mark the Deacon, Asterius of Amasea, and even the quaestorial staff that drafted the laws of Theodosius the Great and the co-emperors Arcadius and Honorius.

The archon Demosthenes and Anthemius the sophist are said to have delivered rebuttals which chided Chrysostom for ingratitutde to his benefactors in the bouleutic chamber and accused him of abominating the local gods. Anthemius' reply is a particularly forceful version of the sophistic reply to the blows of the new religion against the dying polytheism in Athens:[94]

> Every man who comes to the school of this city imparts honor and service to the gods by going up to the temple of the great goddess Athena and, falling before her, by asking her to make his reasoning wise for excellence in the sciences. Wherefrom happening upon [this excellence] through her help, they turn back in order to acknowledge her for very many benefactions in their own affairs. This John alone, having come here, was taught thoroughly all the wisdom of grammar to the summit by the power and care of Athena, and has now been honored by your excellency and the citizens in a manner beyond all those who have preceded him in the school. He did not impart the

---

[90] George of Alexandria, *Vita Chrysostomi*, 82, lines 17–19.
[91] Ibid., 82, lines 10–12.
[92] Ibid., 78, line 29.
[93] Ibid., 83, line 5f.
[94] Ibid., 83, line 26 to 84, line 10.

fitting and necessary thanks and recompense to the city and his
benefactors, but he even insulted the gods of the city, even abominating
the sacred teachings and reckoning them myths. And furthermore all
those departing the temple of the great Athena were carried off by him to
his teaching [the Christian religion]; and all the ancient objects of awe
shall be downtrodden by the Christians.

The prevalence of the cult of "great goddess Athena" amongst the
grammarians and philosophers, including the trek up to the Parthenon (εἰς τὸ ἱερὸν τῆς μεγάλης θεᾶς Ἀθηνᾶς) recurs. The
worship given her was viewed in terms of the peace of the gods, for
without her help (ἐπικουρία) the excellence of the sciences
(μαθήματα) taught in Athens might decline. This section of the
narrative is fully consistent with the beliefs and practices of Proclus
a century later. Elsewhere the sophist Anthemius makes the more
traditional arguments about the *pax deorum*:[95]

Christ does not nourish us, but the earth gives bloom to fruits when it
is well-cultivated and sown by farmers. And the air increases and
nourishes them by the ordinance and foresight of the gods.

This argument had a particular relevance for Attica, which had not
been agriculturally self-sufficient since the early fifth century B.C.[96]
Anthemius' peroration indicates one additional thing: Chrysostom, although only a catechumen, or rhetors like him, had perhaps
been proselytizing among the grammarians and sophists. Anthemius' words express the fear that defections from the old religion
and the abandonment of all the ancient cult practices (πάντα τὰ
ἀρχαῖα ἡμῶν σεβάσματα) might lead to the closure of the temples
with the waning of local support. The latter was already an accomplished fact in cities where many conversions had taken place
amongst the decurion class, the preservers of the old order. Gaza,
Aphrodisias, and Athens were, by 367/8, three important exceptions to the tendencies of the age, so that an Athenian Hellene c.
367 might well have feared this eventuality. It would be interesting
to know what public position, if any, Gregory of Nazianzus and the
other Christian scholars had taken *vis à vis* the old religious opinions a decade earlier during their educational stay in Athens. One
suspects that their comments were rather more muted than those of
Chrysostom, particularly as many of them came from ordinary
decurion families.

The greatest danger to any local Hellenic religious establishment

---

[95] Ibid., 85f.
[96] Trombley, "Boeotia in Late Antiquity," 217. This is also implicit in Eunapius, *Lives of the Sophists* (Wright, 382f.).

consisted in the emergence of a *cause celèbre* about the old religion. It might come about by anti-Christian riots (as at Alexandria), the exclusion of Christians from local social and political life (as we saw in the case of Gaza), or bitter recriminations between the Christian and pagan intelligentsia. Whatever drew the attention of the government at Constantinople to local divergences from past imperial edicts against pagan cult held great danger for its adherents. These laws were held in abeyance under the co-emperors Valens and Valentinian I, but remained on the books. Furthermore, the danger always existed of new edicts. It is possible, in fact, that the co-emperors did issue edicts bearing on this question in response to local conditions that the Theodosian codification omitted. The archon Demosthenes is said to have reprimanded Anthemius with this in view. George of Alexandria's biography of Chrysostom gives the gist of Demosthenes' precautionary invective:[97]

> Our revered emperors are Christians and have published edicts that no one sacrifice to any other god than the one Christ whom they worship and believe in. Those who devote themselves to Hellenic worship having learned this accomplish it secretly, and those who do this here, if they become known to the emperors, are ruined and destroyed by them, since they have despised their imperial and inexorable command. Cease, Anthemius, to expatiate at length, lest this discourse reach their worthy ears, and the limited and secret worship of the gods get not only from our midst, but we be set upon by perils and fatal punishments, because each human being and every land that is in truth under their authority worships Christ and all revere him.
>
> Today their empire and glory have even subjected many barbarian nations. The latter have submitted their necks to them from the time when the Roman emperors put their trust in Christ. Even I was associated with their faith before I came to this magistracy. Be satisfied with this and keep silent in what you say about this.

The existence of cryptopagans in the Athenian city council c. 367 would be consistent with the times. Many persons who converted to Christianity in the face of Constantius II's harsh policies—not to mention those who did so for the sake of political advancement—will have thrown off the façade when Julian received the oecumenical imperium in 361, only to lapse afterward into cautious or secret practices (ἡ μικρὰ καὶ κρυπτὴ τῶν θεῶν λατρεία), including sacrifice, in the uncertain times after his death. One need not have been baptized to have maintained the façade. Demosthenes' phrase that he "associated" or "communicated" with the Christian emperors'

---

[97] George of Alexandria, *Vita Chrysostomi*, 84, lines 11–29.

faith (κἀγὼ δὲ αὐτὸς ἐκοινώνησα τῇ πίστει αὐτοῖς) before his magistracy may simply indicate the acceptance of his catechumenate by the bishop of Athens, a practice characteristic of many serious Christians at this juncture and of Chrysostom himself. Demosthenes' admission hardly constitutes proof, in itself, that the decurion class of Athens had accepted Christianity in any great measure.[98] It will be seen that this social stratum remained at least partly Hellenic pagan even in the late fifth century. Demosthenes' statement reflects the fact, above all, that c. 367 the laws against sacrifice were only loosely enforced, and that a discreet person might continue to practice the Hellenic cults with impunity.

The life of Chrysostom goes on to describe the alleged conversion of the archon Demosthenes and Anthemius the sophist. This section of the narrative has a certain late fifth-century flavor and its veracity must be largely excluded.[99] It is said that the bishop of Athens admitted Anthemius and his household to the catechumenate with the seal of Christ (ἡ ἐν Χριστῷ σφραγίς), probably a blessing like that administered by bishop Porphyrius of Gaza.[100] Contacts certainly existed between Christians who knew the Greek *paideia* and the pagan intelligentsia. Two generations later, Nilos of Ankyra (ob. c. 430) numbered two possibly pagan philosophers among his correspondents,[101] three rhetors.[102] and two possibly pagan sophists.[103] These contacts at times led to conversions. Nilos knew an ex-rhetor become a monk who could not bring himself to give up his "Hellenic books"[104] and a certain Lucian whom he found it

---

[98] It is worth noting that the emperor Valentinian I got credit for the successful campaign of Jovinus, *magister equitum per Gallias*, against the Alamanni in 365/6. (Ammianus Marcellinus, *Res Gestae* 27.1–2). This restored prestige to the Christian empire after sundry defeats dating back to 363, and gave rise to the official claim that the Christian God had once again conferred victory on the empire. When the victories ceased in the early fifth century, this confidence was weakened again in the Latin-speaking West. Augustine of Hippo composed the *De Civitate Dei* expressly to fill the resulting void in Christian morale. The implicit reference to the victorious Valentinian I and Valens in the *Vita Chrysostomi* with this particular synchronism, 367 being about a year after Valentinian I was acclaimed *Alamannicus*, suggests that George of Alexandria did not invent the Athenian interlude, but drew upon a source that had real reference points in the history of the fourth century. See also Brown, *Augustine of Hippo*, 299–329.

[99] Cf. Appendix II.

[100] Supra, Ch. III, Sect. 5.

[101] Nilos of Ankyra, *Epp.* 2.264 and 2.280. PG 79, 333D (Aphrodisios Philosophos) and 340C–D (Aeneas Philosophos).

[102] Nilos of Ankyra, *Epp.* 1.75, 1.184, and 2.291. PG 79, 116A–B (Apollodoros), 152D (Amphiktyōn), 345A (Leonidas).

[103] Nilos of Ankyra, *Epp.* 2.42 and 2.145. PG 79, 216C (Chryserōs) and 268A (Eulampios).

[104] Nilos of Ankyra, *Ep.* 2.73. PG 79, 232D–233A.

necessary to address as "Christian sophist" (σοφιστῇ Χριστιανῷ).[105] Two statements mar the historicity of George of Alexandria's narrative, however: the assertion that Anthemius fell possessed after his attack on Chrysostom in the bouleutic chamber,[106] and the claim that the archon, landed magnates, and much of the demos rushed to the bishop's residence after this and requested baptism. This was manifestly improbable in the pre-Theodosian period of the late fourth century, as the example of Gaza suggests as well.[107] On the other hand, the acclamation supposedly shouted by the archon and all present in the bouleutic chamber after the debate requires note, whatever its date and provenance, because it resembles the one used at Gaza:[108]

> Great is the God of the Christians, who alone performs wonders. What God is able to perform such signs as the Christ whom the Christians worship? Great is their faith! Truly we have erred in worshipping gods unable to help or harm anyone!

It is, once again, manifestly improbable that the archons, city council, and demos should have recited this c. 367. On the other hand, a Christian faction in the chamber may have done so, this at the risk of worsened social and political relations with their fellow citizens. It was certainly possible under proper conditions. There are, for the present, no firm answers to all the problems raised by this difficult text. It suffices to say here that much of the narrative is consistent with late fourth-century conditions, but that it is contaminated with data or suppositions from a later period, c. 481–488.[109]

The next witnesses to the state of the Athenian cults turn up in the writings of Eunapius of Sardis (ob. 414) and Zosimus (6th century). Eunapius composed the already mentioned *Lives of of the Philosophers* and also a *Universal History*, the latter of which survives only in fragments.[110] Zosimus, an imperial count and financial officer, summarized the contents of the latter work in his *Historia*

---

[105] Nilos of Ankyra, *Ep.* 2.224. PG 79, 317A–B.

[106] George of Alexandria, *Vita Chrysostomi*, 86, line 3ff.

[107] It is also said that the bishop refused baptism to the archon Demosthenes because he had once been baptized (διὰ τὸ ἅπαξ βαπτισθῆναι αὐτόν). The bishop is said to have allowed him to communicate after instructing him in the ecclesiastical canons. Ibid., lines 23–27. The possibility that this Demosthenes will have become Christian for the sake of expediency during the reign of Constantius II (337–361) cannot be entirely excluded.

[108] Ibid., 86, lines 30–34.

[109] For discussion of the so-called Justinianic law, cf. supra, Ch. I, Sect. 6 and Appendices II and III.

[110] Cited supra, Ch. I, n. 72

Nova.[111] As Eunapius resided in Athens before the time of the events
c. 375–396 under consideration next, Zosimus' work constitutes the
concise digest of a secondary account. Two notices in the *Historia
Nova* pertaining to late fourth-century Athens reflect the continuity
of the old religion.

The occasion of the first instance was the great earthquake of 375
which struck the Balkan peninsula, but Crete, the Peloponnese,
and central Greece in particular. Athens and Attica largely escaped
destruction, in contrast to some nearby districts. Whatever the
explanation for their survival in terms of earth tectonics, some
pious Athenians ascribed it to the city's tutelary deities and circulated a version of the story heard by Eunapius:[112]

> Nestorius, who was at that time appointed as hierophant, saw a
> dream commanding him to honor the hero Achilles with public
> honors. For this was to be the salvation of the city. When he made the
> dream known to those in office [the archons], they reckoned that he
> was talking nonsense such as the very old do, and did what he said in
> nothing. [Nestorius], reasoning what had to be done in his own
> manner and instructed by god-like conceptions and having fashioned
> a model of the hero in a small temple, set it below the statue of
> Athena that sits in the Parthenon, and [then] completed for the
> goddess the usual rites proper to himself [as hierophant]. And he
> performed for the hero what was made known to him according to
> law.
>
> After the prescription given in sleep was completed by a work
> (*ergon*) in this manner, it fell out that only the Athenians were saved
> when the earthquake struck, with all Attica partaking of the benefac-
> tions of the hero. That this is true one can learn through the things
> the philosopher Syrianus related when he wrote a hymn on this hero.

Nestorius held the office of hierophant (ἱεροφαντεῖν τεταγμένος)
of the mysteries of Demeter and Persephone at Eleusis. It will be
recalled that toward the end of the fourth century the Eumolpids,
the last of the two priestly families presiding there, died out, and
that the office of hierophant fell to a man of Thespiae, who held the
rank of *pater* in the Mithraic cult.[113] Nestorius was evidently one of
the last Eumolpids, who must have been landowners of decurion
rank. Nestorius' knowledge of Attic religious lore and arcana
allowed him to formulate new rituals even when asleep, during the
dream vision. It is unclear whether he thought he saw Achilles or

---

[111] All citations are taken from: Zosimus of Panium, *Historia Nova*, ed. Ludwig
Mendelsson (Leipzig 1887). See also: Zosime, *Histoire nouvelle*, ed. tr. François
Paschoud, 3 vols. in 5 (Paris 1971–89).

[112] Zosimus, *Historia Nova* 4.18.2–4 (Mendelsson, 173, lines 4–20). For commentary, cf. F. Paschoud, 2/2, 367–369.

[113] Eunapius, *Lives of the Sophists* (Wright, 436–439).

some other apparition. It made little difference whether Nestorius was senile or not.[114] The cults celebrated on the Athenian Akropolis lay outside his sphere of activity in any case. The archons and priests refused his request for public honors to the hero Achilles (τὸν Ἀχιλλέα τὸν ἥρωα δημοσίαις τιμᾶσθαι τιμαῖς) because it required sacrifices in their official domain and, to judge from the upshot of all this, the construction of a small shrine. This business hardly falls under the category of "civic religion", as F. Paschoud suggests; it was a civic apotropaic measure (ἔσεσθαι γὰρ τοῦτο τῇ πόλει σωτήριον) in the mind of its sponsor, and required, so he thought, real religious ritual to be efficacious. The council rejected Nestorius' petition not in principle, but ostensibly because of its implausibility. Even if the co-emperors Valens and Valentinian I were then making allowances for local Hellenic religious preferences, new cult images, temples, and sacrifices might have triggered a *cause celèbre* that could have led to unfortunate consequences.[115]

At any rate, Nestorius accomplished in miniature what the archons and priests denied him when he laid the image of the hero at the foot of the chryselephantine Athena in the Parthenon (εἰκόνα ἥρωος ἐν οἴκῳ μικρῷ δημιουργήσας ὑπέθηκε τῷ ἐν Παρθενῶνι καθιδρυμένῳ τῆς Ἀθηνᾶς ἀγάλματι). Two sets of rituals accompanied the votive offering: the usual rites performed for Athena (τῇ θεῷ τὰ συνήθη), but also rites made known personally to him in the ordinance received in the dream vision (τῷ ἥρωϊ τὰ ἐγνωσμένα οἱ κατὰ θεσμὸν ἔπραττε), which came in the form of "god-like notions" or "conceptions" (ταῖς θεοειδέσιν ἐννοίαις παιδαγωγούμενος),[116] and which he performed "in his own manner" or "in the manner of a personal service" (κατὰ ταὐτόν). Nestorius' behavior in this instance provides decisive proof for the survival of personal religion in the Hellenic priesthoods on the eve of the Theodosian legislation, and that the old public rites went on as usual, but in private or muted form. It will be seen that the Neoplatonist Proclus continued to visit the shrines of heroes even in the late fifth century.[117] Furthermore, unless Nestorius himself had artisan skills, he was able to procure the services of silversmiths,

---

[114] The expression used by Zosimus suggests that Nestorius was *acting like* a *senile* man in raising the issue, but not superannuated (οἷα δὴ ὑπέργηρων ὄντα). Zosimus, *Historia Nova* (Mendelsson, 173, line 9).

[115] Supra, Ch. II, Sect. 3 on the Serapeum of Alexandria.

[116] Zosimus, *Historia Nova* 4.18.3 (Mendelsson, 73, line 11).

[117] Infra, Ch. IV, Sect. 3.

ivory-cutters, or the like to have idols fashioned.[118]

A second instance of the cult of Achilles is implicit in Zosimus'
account of Alaric's unsuccessful siege of Athens in 396. His source
Eunapius had it on good authority that the ephiphany of Pallas
Athena and Achilles had at the critical moment in the siege fright-
ened Alaric into concluding an armistice:[119]

> After the Thebans had escaped [destruction], [Alaric] went on to
> Athens, thinking the city would be easy to take and impossible to
> defend by the populace within because of its great size; and further-
> more, because the Peiraeus was gripped by a shortage of supplies,
> the besieged would surrender after no great time. But if Alaric was
> caught up in these hopes, the ancient character of the city was about
> to get a measure of divine providence for itself and so remain unsack-
> ed, even in impious times.
>
> It would be unworthy to pass over in silence the cause (*aitia*)
> through which the city was saved, which was something befitting the
> divine and called those who heard the story to piety. Upon
> approaching the city with his entire army, Alaric saw Athena Prom-
> achos inspecting the walls just as she is to be seen in the statues,
> armed as a hoplite and about to resist attackers. He also saw Achilles
> the hero standing in front of the walls such as Homer shows him
> before Troy when he fought in his wrath to avenge the death of
> Patroclus. Unable to bear this sight, Alaric refrained from any
> attempt against the city . . . (lacuna in text), but sent an embassy
> instead.
>
> After [the negotiators] had mutually accepted statements and had
> given and received oaths, Alaric entered the city with some few of his
> men. After meeting a friendly reception and going to the baths and
> having shared a public dinner with the select men of the city (the
> archons, priests and sages), and furthermore after receiving gifts, he
> left the city unharmed. . . .
>
> And so just as Athens was alone saved in the earthquake which
> shook all Greece during the reign of Valens in the manner I spoke of
> in the previous book, and now came into extreme peril once again, it
> escaped. Alaric left Attica unplundered out of fear of the spectral
> figures that had appeared and went on to the Megarid, took it by *coup
> de main*, and kept up the march into the Peloponnese without meeting
> any opposition.

The notion that such an apparition would have daunted a Roma-
nized Christian Visigoth is patently absurd.[120] On the other hand,
the great image of Athena Promachos that stood on the Akropolis
on the way up to the Parthenon from the Propylaia may still have
been *in situ* and a dominating feature of the skyline. Some defenders

---

[118] Zosimus' expression "having fashioned" (δημιουργήσας) can refer either to
the artisan (efficient cause) or the donor.
[119] Zosimus, *Historia Nova* 5.5.8 to 5.6.3 (Mendelsson, 222f.).
[120] Cf. Zosime, *Histoire nouvelle* 3/1 (Paschoud, 97).

of the wall will, as Hellenes and patriotic Athenians, have invoked her palladium. The credulous doubtless fancied that her image terrified the invader. Eunapius' interest in the philosophers' supposed ability to conjure theic epiphanies elsewhere makes one suspect the intellectual elite of such practices during the siege.[121] The apparition of Achilles will have justified the hierophant Nestorius' aforementioned personal devotion to the hero. His friends, who evidently knew Eunapius, probably invoked Achilles' power and later related the supposed effects to Eunapius. The story quickly became the talk of the Athenian Hellenes, achieving a wider circulation and propagandistic intent through the pen of Eunapius, and that of Zosimus a century later.[122]

There is no convincing argument *per se* against the proposition that many participants in the siege of 396 believed the story or that they sacrificed before the effigies of the hoplite gods during the poliorcetic terror. One can imagine Alaric making ironic inquiries about the city's ubiquitous statuary during his tour of Athens with his lieutenants after the conclusion of the armistice. His escorts, the "select men of the city" (τοῖς ἐν τῇ πόλει λογάσι) who led him to the baths and threw a public dinner on his behalf (λουσάμενος τε καὶ κοινωνήσας ἑστιάσεως), were none other than the archons, many of whom still adhered to the old religion and held priesthoods. One can well imagine the yarns spun by this crew after the Visigoth and his hordes had safely scuttled over the western hills in the direction of Eleusis and the Megarid.[123]

III. The Mid-Fifth Century

The anti-pagan legislation of the emperors Arcadius (395–408) and Theodosius II (408–450) has left no imprint whatsoever on the surviving history of the old cults in Athens except in the sphere of the public sacrifices now abandoned. Two seldom studied texts, Marinus of Neapolis' *Life of Proclus* and Damascius' *Life of Isidore*, both of them written in the years after 485, indicate that the elimination of Hellenic cult from public life came well after 450, and that the old religion thereafter went underground, losing little of its strength amongst true believers.[124] The task of the historian is

---

[121] On the supposed conjurings of Maximus of Ephesus, cf. supra, Ch. I, Sect. 3.

[122] I cannot accept Paschoud's view that the Goths destroyed "paganism" in Greece. Zosime, *Histoire nouvelle* 3/1 (Paschoud, 97).

[123] Zosimus, *Historia Nova* 5.6.4–5 (Mendelsohn, 223, lines 17–29).

[124] For text editions, cf. supra, Ch. I, Sect. 3. Historical analyses of these texts are sparse. H.J. Blumenthal, "529 and Its Sequel: What Happened to the

somewhat complicated because Damascius' *Life of Isidore* survives only in scattered fragments. All the same, these texts must be considered together, as they cover a roughly synchronous period and mention not only the surviving cults, but also name many of their adherents.

Proclus is himself known for his commentaries on the works of Plato, Homer, Hesiod, and for various works on physics and theology. The object of the discussion here is not so much Proclus' religious thought or theology, but rather his everyday cult practices and those of the other Hellenes in his social milieu, which included not only the Athenian philosophers and rhetors, but also members of the decurion class. The pagan sacrifice still existed along with other ritual acts, as did the traditional devotions to the age-old deities of Attica, including Asklepios, Athena, and Dionysus. Different systems of theurgy and divination survived as well. Let us consider the more striking cases of these phenomena.

The prevalent Athenian cult, to judge from the extent of the notices that survive in fifth-century sources, remained that of the physician god Asklepios, whose shrine the Asklepieion occupied a site on the south slope of the Akropolis. The temenos included not only the temple with its altar and images, but also a fairly extensive complex of dormitories where persons seeking cures might reside until healed by the god in a dream vision.[125] The temple certainly continued to receive suppliants of the god in the 450's, and probably through the 460's and 470's as well, being closed sometime before Marinus composed his *Life of Proclus*.[126] This reality would suggest the continued employment of priests, assistants (διάκονοι), doorkeepers (θυρωροί), physicians, surgeons, and medical assistants as well. Proclus often invoked Asklepios and other savior deities in behalf of his friends:[127]

> If one of his acquaintances was caught in illness, first Proclus besought the gods fruitfully in his behalf with works and hymns, then visited the sick man in a caring manner and led in the physicians, urging them to accomplish their art without delay.

The "works and hymns" (ἔργοις τε καὶ ὕμνοις) can hardly have

Academy?" *Byzantion* 48 (1978), 369–385. Idem, "Marinus' Life of Proclus: Neoplatonist Biography," *Byzantion* 54 (1984), 469–494. Garth Fowden, "The Pagan Holy Man in Late Antiquity," *Journal of Hellenic Studies* 102 (1982), 33–59.
[125] Gregory, "Paganism in Christian Greece." 238.
[126] Infra, Appendix II and III.
[127] Marinus, *Vita Procli* 17 (Boissonade, 14).

excluded sacrifices. Marinus here uses compressed phraeology, but is more specific in the introductory chapter to the *Life of Proclus*:[128]

> But now, being unable to compare my own [diction] with that [of Proclus], I take heart that those who approach the altars for sacred [rites] do not perform their rituals out of equal means. Some furnish themselves suitably with bulls or goats or other such offerings in behalf of communion with the gods at their altars, and complete some hymns with great refinement in meter and other hymns without meter. But others can effect none of these [works], but, sacrificing only a round-cake and a grain, if possible, of frankincense, and making the invocations with some short address, they enjoy no less a favorable hearing than the others.

The writer has, in comparing his biography to a poor man's sacrifice in the present tense, revealed the existing state of cult: a decurion might sacrifice an animal to the tune of metric hymns (τοὺς ὕμνους . . . ἐν μέτρῳ), but cakes and incense with a short invocation ensured the peace of the gods for the common man (πόπανον δὲ μόνον καὶ χόνδρον, εἰ τύχοι, λιβανωτοῦ θύοντες).[129] Proclus was himself known to partake of sacrificial meats at regular religious festivals.[130] On one occasion Proclus, whose house lay near the Asklepieion, visited the temenos to pray for Asklepiegeneia (a theophoric name meaning "born of Asklepios"), daughter of his friend the archon Archiadas and wife of Proclus' personal benefactor the archon Theagenes.[131] The incident apparently took place in the mid-450's when Proclus was about forty-two years of age:[132]

> Taking along the great Perikles, who is from Lydia, quite a man and a philosopher as well, [Proclus] went up to the Asklepieion to pray to the god in behalf of the suffering girl. For the city at that time had the good fortune of this [god's presence], and still had the temple of the savior unsacked. After he prayed in the more ancient manner, a suitable change appeared in the girl, and she was suddenly relieved. For the savior [Asklepios] heals easily, as befits a god.

The Asklepieion had thus remained inviolate for over half a century after the incineration of the Marneion at Gaza in 402 (καὶ γὰρ ηὐτύχει τούτου ἡ πόλις τότε, καὶ εἶχεν ἔτι ἀπόρθητον τὸ τοῦ σωτῆρος ἱερόν). Sacrificial rites (τὰ ἱερά) accompanied the hu-

---

[128] Marinus, *Vita Procli* 1 (Boissonade, 1).
[129] Ibid.
[130] "He tasted them only for the sake of the holy" (μόνον ἀπεγεύετο καὶ τούτων ὁσίας χάριν). Marinus, *Vita Procli* 19 (Boissonade, 15f.).
[131] Marinus, *Vita Procli* 29 (Boissonade, 23).
[132] Marinus, *Vita Procli* 29 (Boissonade, 23f.).

man drama, and Proclus earned the epithet "savior" (σωτήρ) for
his effort. Well might Proclus have accomplished this in secret, for
his unnamed enemies may have included Christians of decurion
rank with connections to the imperial government who took all this
badly.[133] Proclus' ties to his patron (εὐεργέτης) Theagenes, the
husband of Asklepiegeneia, may have required a particularly de-
monstrative appeal to Asklepios the savior with all the attendant
risks of creating a *cause célèbre* of the kind that the Hellenes of Athens
had sought to avoid during the early post-Julianic period.

There is less certainty about the cult of Athena. The priesthood
of the Parthenon still seems to have existed when Proclus arrived in
Athens, sometime before the death of Plutarch in 431 or 432, a
holder of the chair of Platonic philosophy (διαδοχή) at Athens,[134]
for when Proclus first reached the city he went up to the Akropolis
(εἰς τὴν ἄκραν) but found his way barred by the doorkeeper
(θυρωρός), a minor temple official[135] who was about to lock the
gates either of the Propylaia or of the Parthenon proper (ἤδη τὰς
κλεῖς ἐπιτιθέναι μέλλων ταῖς θύραις).[136] A law of Theodosius I
and his co-emperors given on 30 November 382 to the *dux* of
Osrhoene and incorporated into the Theodosian Code had provided that temples might be left open continuously and their images available for public inspection if the effigies had high artistic
value.[137] Discretion was left to the local authorities as to whether to
lock the buildings. Pheidias' chryselephantine statue of Athena still
stood in the Parthenon, being removed much later, probably at the
time when the Asklepieion was sacked, shortly before the death of
Proclus in 485.[138] Marinus reports a tale probably circulated by
Proclus himself connected with the removal of the great statue. It
gives rather less information than one would hope for about the
incident:[139]

> Thus he became beloved to the philosopher goddess. His choice of life
> was suitably disposed in philosophy, such being done so much as
> reason suggested. For the goddess made it plainly clear when her
> image, still situated in the Parthenon, was carried away by those who

---

[133] Infra, Ch. IV, Sect. 3.
[134] For the date, see: A.C. Lloyd, "Athenian and Alexandrian Neoplatonism,"
The Cambridge History of Later Greek and Early Medieval Philosophy, ed. A.H. Arm-
strong (Cambridge 1967), 302. Blumenthal concurs in "Marinus' Life of Proclus,"
473.
[135] Marinus, *Vita Procli* 10 (Boissonade, 9).
[136] Ibid.
[137] Supra, Ch. I, Sect. 2.
[138] Infra, Appendix III.
[139] Marinus, *Vita Procli* 30 (Boissonade, 24).

move even what should not be moved. It seemed to the philosopher that a certain well-dressed woman came to him in a dream and announced that it was necessary for him very quickly to prepare a residence for her in advance. "For the mistress of Athens," she said, "wishes to stay with you." He had previously shown his friendship with Asklepios, when an epiphany of the god persuaded us he was in a state of fatal illness. Being between sleep and wakefulness, he saw a serpent creeping around his head, from which time the disease had the beginning of its remission, and thus from the time of the epiphany he perceived a certain ceasing of the disease, and, unless a willingness and much desire for death hindered it, he would have deemed his body worthy of suitable care and, I think, he would finally have become healthy again.

The incident is quite possibly contemporaneous with the final suppression of the urban pagan allies of the rebels Leontius and Illus, after Roman armies shut them up in the Isaurian mountain fortress of Cherries in the fall of 484.[140] If so, it will have been the proconsul of the province of Achaea with the troops of his *officium* and interested urban Christians who tore down the chryselephantine Athena, "those who move even what should not be moved" (τῶν καὶ τὰ ἀκίνητα κινούντων, where ἀκίνητα has the sense of "sacred things to be kept inviolate").[141] Imperial decree will thus have ended the extraordinary status of the Athenian temples, a sequel not unlike that which occurred at Gaza in First Palestine, but where once again the text of the decree is lost.

Athena was the "philosopher goddess" (ἡ φιλόσοφος θεός)[142] and the object of regular cult practices among the Neoplatonist philosophers:[143]

It was evening time. While they conducted the dialogue the sun went to the western parts and the [new] moon appeared for the first time after the conjuction. They attempted to send away the young [Proclus] as a foreigner, that they might have leisure time for themselves to worship the goddess. [Proclus] came forward a little, and also seeing from the house that the moon was appearing, he unloosed his sandals while all looked on, and embraced the goddess. Lachares was struck by the boldness of the youth, and told the philosopher Syrianus that this saying was divinely spoken by Plato about great natures: "This man shall be a great good or its opposite." And such signs, to mention a few of the many, came to the philosopher from God while he resided in Athens.

---

[140] Bury, LRE 1, 398f. and n. 5.

[141] Marinus' use of this phrase is a direct reminiscence of Herodotus' account of Miltiades' attempt to plunder the temenos of Demeter the Lawgiver on Paros. *Hist.* 6.134.

[142] Marinus, *Vita Procli* 30 (Boissonade, 24).

[143] Marinus, *Vita Procli* 11 (Boissonade, 9f.).

Proclus celebrated the cult in this manner shortly after his arrival
in Athens (*terminus ante quem* 431/2) at the house of Syrianus, his
praeceptor in philosophy. It is difficult to determine the importance
of the dying civic and popular cult of this tutelary deity amongst
the educated Athenian Hellenes of the non-philosophic professions.
The men here must have performed certain rites but their character
is unknown. We know from Damascius' *Life of Isidore* that metric
verses were often considered a sufficient thank-offering to the gods,
and this may have been the essence of the New Moon service.[144]
Many gods and *daimones* were thought to preside over philosophy,
but Athena was considered the chiefest of them (ἡ τῆς φιλοσοφίας
ἔφορος).[145]

Socrates probably fell among the lesser deities or *daimones*, for a
shrine dedicated to him (ἱερὸν χωρίον), the Sokrateion, lay outside
the city gate on the road up from the Peiraeus (ἐπὶ τὴν πόλιν). A
statue of Socrates marked the site (ἡ Σωκράτους στήλη), which
also had a sacred spring not far away (οὐδὲ γὰρ πόρρω ἦν ἡ
πηγή). Various rites were performed at the Sokrateion. Marinus of
Neapolis refers to them as "honors" (τιμαί), but Zosimus of Panopolis uses that expression as a euphemism for sacrifices.[146] It was
here that Proclus drank Attic water (Ἀττικὸν ὕδωρ) for the first
time upon his arrival in Athens, and entered the city after making
the *proskynesis* to the deity.[147]

The evidence for the popularity of other traditional Attic deities
is less than satisfactory for the mid-fifth century. One can at times
hardly tell from Marinus' narrative whether Proclus engaged in
antiquarian and arcane practices connected with otherwise popular
cults, or whether the cults were dead to all but a few Hellenic
theologians and cognoscenti of his stamp. The cult of Dionysus
provides an instance of the former, for as late as the Quinisextum or
Council in Trullo (691–692) the cult of this agrarian earth deity
prevailed in the rituals connected with the wine cycle.[148] The
Canon unfortunately fails to indicate where these practices went
on. If Asterius of Amasea's description of the Attic cults is accurate,
the Theban Dionysus still had a public following c. 400, and there
is fundamentally no reason to doubt this. At any rate Proclus is
reported to have celebrated certain mysteries of Dionysus "according to its primary principles" (περὶ τὰ πρῶτα ἐβάκχευε καὶ
αὐτόπτης ἐγίνετο τῶν ἐκεῖ μακαρίων ὄντως θεαμάτων). He did

[144] Damascius, *Vita Isidori* (Asmus, 125).
[145] Marinus, *Vita Procli* 10 (Boissonade, 8).
[146] Supra, Ch. IV, Sect. 3.
[147] Marinus, *Vita Procli* 10 (Boissonade, 9).
[148] Trombley, "Council in Trullo," 5.

this by avoiding the "wand-carrying" aspects of the cult (τὰ ναρθηκοφόρα), an allusion to Proclus' tendency as a Platonist to avoid the popular or apocryphal aspects of cults and to "grasp at virtue and the patterns in the divine mind" (τὰ ἐν τῷ θείῳ νῷ παραδείγματα) in his practices.[149] Marinus of Neapolis provides an admirable *précis* of Proclus' method, which entailed theologizing about both Athenian and foreign cults:[150]

> The philosopher, working according to this principle, easily saw into all Hellenic and barbarian theology, and all theology that is overshadowed by mythical affectation; he led those who wished or were able to follow him to the light, and, inspired by God, taught all and led it to harmony. Having traversed all the writings of the more ancient authors, he penetrated as much as was fertile in them with discrimination. If he found anything longwinded, he discarded it as something disgraceful and refuted with much inquiry whatever stood contrary to the good, this after investigating each thing anew and ably in the colloquia [with students and colleagues], and writing down everything in his books.

This was, Marinus remarks, "pious wisdom" (σοφία).[151] It appears that the knowledge of ritual which Proclus passed on to the priesthoods of Lydia during a year-long visit there (sometime after he reached the age of twenty-eight) was of the Dionysiac variety.[152]

Attica and the Peiraeus in particular had always been a melting pot for the cults of alien gods, and Proclus himself worshipped an extensive pantheon. Of these the Mother of the Gods or Kybele had a prominent place. Her cult, which was indigenous to Asia Minor, persisted long after the time of Proclus in Caria and Lydia, but evidence is lacking for Attica.[153] Proclus once again practiced a highly theologized variant of the cult: "He strictly observed the Roman Metroaikai every month, and even the ascetic practices once attended to by the Phrygians."[154] The "Phrygian" rituals were those practiced at Pessinus in Galatia, where the temple cult of Kybele had a priesthood and waning popular following in the time of Julian the Apostate.[155] Proclus consumed sacrificial meats in connection with the cult,[156] but the other rituals had died out or

---

[149] Marinus, *Vita Procli* 22 (Boissonade, 17f.).
[150] Marinus, *Vita Procli* 22 (Boissonade, 18).
[151] Ibid.
[152] Marinus, *Vita Procli* 15 (Boissonade, 12f.).
[153] Trombley, "Paganism in the Greek World," 344.
[154] Marinus, *Vita Procli* 19 (Boissonade, 16).
[155] Julian the Apostate, *Ep.* 22 (Wright 3, 66–73).
[156] Marinus discusses the Metroaikai in connection with Proclus' consumption of animal meats "only for the sake of piety" (μόνον ἀπεγεύετο καὶ τούτων ὁσίας χάριν). Marinus, *Vita Procli* 19 (Boissonade, 15f.).

gone underground in Athens and elsewhere, as Marinus of Neapolis indicates in a particularly prolix section of Proclus' biography:[157]

> But if I wished to go into detail for everyone and tell of his love for Pan son of Hermes, and narrate fully the blessing and salvation (*eumeneia kai sōteria*) which came from the god for Athens, and still more the good fortune (*eumoiria*) that was gotten from the Mother of the Gods, on which he throve and rejoiced greatly, I would be perhaps talking idly to those I met and speaking unbelievable things to some. For many and great things were accomplished and spoken to him by the goddess [Kybele] on as many days as exist, of which . . . I now have no complete memory. If anyone desires to see that capability of his in full, let him take into his hands the book of [Proclus] about Kybele. For one can see that it is not possible to speak the entire theology of the goddess without divine possession, as well as the other myths he disclosed about her and Attis, and what was done and said philosophically, so that no longer will one's hearing be disturbed by the discordant dirges and other things spoken secretly there.

Proclus' "philosophical" book on Kybele (ἡ μητρῳακὴ αὐτοῦ βίβλος), which is lost, perhaps owed something to the work of Julian the Apostate on the same subject.[158] The decline of the "discordant dirges" and "other things spoken there secretly" (ὡς μηκέτι θράττεσθαι τὴν ἀκοὴν ἐκ τῶν ἀπεμφαινόντων θρήνων καὶ τῶν ἄλλων τῶν ἐκεῖ κρυφίως λεγομένων) indicates the elimination of the threnodic and orgiastic behavior in Athens, as happened in all cities. Proclus must have known that pockets of Kybele worshippers still existed in Asia Minor, particularly in the countryside, and that they practiced "possessed" behavior and even self-castration.[159] These data, and that pertaining to the Dionysiac cult, suggest quite clearly that Proclus turned his attention *primarily to extant cults*. If they had great antiquity, Proclus was careful to preserve their ritual amidst all his philosophizing and theologizing. His behavior towards the deities was thus not simply antiquarianism, but a sophisticated version of popular practice.

A very considerable amount of ritual accompanied Proclus' celebration of these rites and mysteries. His consumption of sacrificial meats has already been noted, as was the existence of, and Proclus' composition of, various hymns. He accorded songs of praise to Semitic and Egyptian deities as well:[160]

---

[157] Marinus, *Vita Procli* 33 (Boissonade, 26f.).
[158] Julian the Apostate, "Hymn to the Mother of the Gods" (Wright 1, 442–503).
[159] Trombley, "Paganism in the Greek World," 344.
[160] Marinus, *Vita Procli* 19 (Boissonade, 16).

The matter of his hymns included not only encomia of the gods honored among the Greeks, but also of hymning the Gazan Marnas, the lion-grasping Asklepios of Askalon, Theandrites, another god much honored among the Arabs, and *the Isis still honored at Philae*, and plainly all the others. For the god-fearing man always held the phrase ready and said that it befitted the philosopher to be a worshipper of the ancestral gods not in just a few places or his own city, but to be hierophant of the whole cosmos in common.

Late evidence (late fourth through sixth centuries) survives about the ongoing cults of three of these deities. Mark the Deacon's narrative discussed in the previous chapter demonstrates that the adherents of the cult of Zeus Marnas remained in Gaza through the first several decades of the fifth century, and Antonius of Alexandria seems to have continued the cult privately into the late fifth century.[161] Similarly the cult of Theandrites turns up in the rural epigraphy of the late fourth-century Provincia Arabia, in villages populated by Hellenized Arabs.[162] Furthermore, the cult of Isis at Philae in upper Egypt was finally suppressed only under the emperor Justinian c. 537.[163] The priesthood erected many inscriptions there in honor of Isis in the temenos during Proclus' lifetime, c. 449–468.[164] At the time Marinus of Neapolis was writing, after Proclus' death in 485, only the temple at Philae still remained in service, but knowing the longevity of the other cults, it would not be surprising if they had great operative and vestigial strength in the mid-fifth century, including the worship of the Semitic lion-grasping Asklepios of Askalon in First Palestine (Ἀσκληπιὸς Λεοντοῦχος Ἀσκαλωνίτης), which is mentioned nowhere else.

The Greek words τιμή and τιμάω, which literally refer to acts of honor, often connote sacrifices. Marinus employs this root to describe the rites at Philae (Ἶσις ἡ καὶ τὰς Φίλας ἔτι τιμωμένη), whereas the inscriptions in the temenos itself use the term *proskynema* which quite probably means offering or sacrifice in that context.[165] Theandrites was, similarly, a much-honored or "much sacrificed-to god among the Arabs" (Θυανδρίτης ἄλλος Ἀραβίοις πολυτίμητος θεός). Like other rural cults, it probably lasted well into the sixth century.[166] Thus, the hymns to the Greek, Semitic, and Egyptian gods were not solely academic exercises. Proclus'

---

[161] Supra, Ch. II, Sect. 3.
[162] Infra, Ch. XI, Sect. 1.
[163] Infra, Ch. IX, Sect. 3–4.
[164] Infra, Ch. IX, Sect. 3.
[165] Ibid.
[166] This subject is discussed *in extenso* in Ch. VII–XI infra.

circle of rhetors and philosophers, and presumably his decurion friends as well, found suitable occasions to recite them. These occasions included not only the times designated for sacrifices,[167] but also personal crises such as sickness and self-doubt:[168]

> [Proclus] ignored the pains [of illness]. Indeed, he bore them gently when they fell upon him, ... He made the distance of his soul from all these sufferings quite clear, even during his final illness. For when weighed down with this [illness] and accompanied by great pains, he attempted to evade the sufferings. He called upon us every time to sing hymns. After the hymns were uttered, there occurred relief from every suffering and *ataraxia*. What is even more surprising than this, he retained what was recited in his memory, although hardly noticing the people nearby when the disease fell heavily upon him. When we began to sing, he completed the hymns and most of the Orphic verses. For we read even these aloud when we were present.

Hymns of Proclus or their fragments survive to Helios, Aphrodite, the Muses, the Lycian Aphrodite, Hekate and Ianos, Athena Polymetis, and Dionysus, as do his *Orphica*. There is also a "Common Hymn to the Gods".[169] These texts, once again, reflect popular belief and practice in variable degree, being the sort of metric hymns one might expect to hear at a rich sacrifice.[170] The statements in Marinus' biography of Proclus about the character and persistence of sacrifice seem all the more plausible in the mid-fifth century context, as Proclus himself wrote a work on sacrifice as well.[171]

Proclus made use of various rites of purification, some of them nocturnal. These included apotropaic acts, lustral sprinklings, and other varieties (νύκτωρ τε καὶ μεθ' ἡμέραν ἀποτροπαῖς καὶ περιρραντηρίοις καὶ τοῖς ἄλλοις καθαρμοῖς χρώμενος), some of them Orphic, others Chaldaean. He would go down to the sea to bathe at least once a month. In these rituals inhered the aim of purifying the soul, that it would achieve its end and become like unto a god (πρὸς τὸν θεόν).[172] This suggests a synthesis of philosophic Neoplatonism and theology. This lustral sprinkling (περιρραντήριον) can hardly have died out any sooner than the

---

[167] As in Marinus, *Vita Procli* 1 (Boissonade, 1).

[168] Marinus, *Vita Procli* 20 (Boissonade, 16f.).

[169] See *Eudociae Augustae Procli Lycii Claudiani Carminum Graecorum Reliquiae*, ed. Arthur Ludwich (Leipzig 1897), 115–158. Cf. *Procli Hymni*, ed. Ernest Vogt (Wiesbaden 1957), with scholia and commentary.

[170] Marinus, *Vita Procli* 18 (Boissonade, 1).

[171] Proclus, *De Sacrificio et Magia*, in *Analecta Graeca*, ed. W. Kroll (Greifswald 1901), 5–11.

[172] Marinus, *Vita Procli* 18 (Boissonade, 15).

lustral sacrifices still performed in temples and private houses in the fourth and fifth centuries, whose continuation is reflected in a provision in the Theodosian Code.[173]

Calendar customs also belonged to the traditional round of practices, and Proclus celebrated these as well:[174]

> He strictly observed the Roman Metroakai every month, and even the ascetic practices once attended to by the Phrygians, and he kept the unlucky days of the Egyptians better than they themselves did, and fasted by himself on certain days for the sake of display. He avoided banqueting and bread the first day of the month and the day before, just as he celebrated the New Moon splendidly and in a manner beseeming the sacred, and also the most distinguished festivals and ancestral rites: these he completed lawfully. He did not perform these things, as others allege, as an excuse for rest or to banquet, but with all-night assemblies and a hymnody and the like.

The celebration of the New Moon (τὰς νουμηνίας λαμπρῶς ἐπετέλει καὶ ἱεροπρεπῶς) was deeply embedded in the Hellenic mentality. It suffered proscription at the Quinisextum or Council in Trullo (691–692) and again in John of Damascus work *On Heresies* (8th century),[175] as did many processions and rites listed as calendar customs.[176]

Another aspect of the cults practiced in Proclus' circle in Athens was theurgy, magic, and divination. As noted in a previous chapter, philosophers regarded the mastery of these arts as a requisite part of their discipline. It will be recalled that Maximus of Ephesus, a friend of Julian the Apostate later executed for magic and conspiracy, had gained notoriety for theurgy even among Hellenes.[177] Proclus practiced all these arts as well. This often entailed his summoning Hekate, the goddess of theurgy, just as Maximus of Ephesus had:[178]

> He had converse with luminous apparitions of Hekate that he saw himself, as he has recalled in his own book somewhere. He set clouds in motion after moving spells of a suitable nature and thereby freed Attica from extraordinary droughts. He imposed amulets against earthquakes, and was experienced in the mantic activity of the tripod, and he cast out metric lines about his own destiny.

---

[173] *Cod. Theod.* 16.2.5. Supra, Ch. I, Sect. 2. The repetition of the law in this codification indicates continuity of practice.

[174] Marinus, *Vita Procli* 19 (Boissonade, 16).

[175] Canon 65 of the Council in Trullo of 691–692 in: Périklès-Pierre Joannou, *Discipline générale antique (IIe–IXe s.)* (Rome 1962), 203.

[176] Canon 62, Joannou, *Discipline générale*, 198–200.

[177] Supra, Ch. I, Sect. 3.

[178] Marinus, *Vita Procli* 28 (Boissonade, 22f.).

Unlike certain other contemporary theurgists, Proclus employed his arts for the public welfare of Attica. The practice of sorcerers driving clouds from place to place in order to mitigate the effects of drought on tilled lands (ὄμβρους τε ἐκίνησεν ἴυγγα τινα προσφόρως κινήσας, καὶ αὐχμῶν ἐξαισίων τὴν Ἀττικὴν ἠλευθέρωσεν) was common in popular magic as well. Folk called "cloud-drivers" (νεφοδιῶκται) are attested in the fourth-century Pseudo-Justin, *Quaestiones et Responsiones ad Orthodoxos*:[179]

> If the clouds send rain to earth by divine nod, how do the so-called cloud drivers move the clouds wherever they wish by certain invocations, in order to cast immoderate rain and hail?

Resort to cloud-drivers was condemned once again at the Quinisextum.[180] The unpredictable nature of the seasonal Mediterranean rains meant a constant demand for these services, particularly after local temple cults like that of the Cretan-born Zeus at Gaza had disappeared.[181] These practices became so prevalent that the monks adapted them to local needs through *Ritenchristianisierung*.[182] Popular theurgy also included the making of amulets (φυλακτήρια) to fend off a variety of evil phenomena including disease and the supposed activity of sorcerers, but here Proclus received the request to design these devices to avert earthquakes like the great one that struck central and southern Greece in 375.[183] Proclus will have composed the invocations, and then have farmed out the work of writing the texts on papyrus or inscribing them on metallic discs or sheets to readily available artisans, who also cut representations of the deities or *daimones* summoned on these media.[184] Proclus' use of the tripod to cast oracles harks back to the debacle of the THEOD oracle during the reign of Valens (364–378) that resulted in the execution of Maximus of Ephesus and many other Hellenes.[185] It demonstrates the continuity of proscribed and potentially criminal practices through the mid-fifth century.

Proclus' theurgic activities belong to the time around his fortieth birthday (c. 450). He learned certain invocations and mantic tech-

---

[179] PG 6, 1277C–D.
[180] Canon 61, Joannou, *Discipline générale*, 196f.
[181] Supra, Ch. III, Sect. 2–4.
[182] Implicit in Trombley, "Paganism in the Greek World," 340f.
[183] The earthquake is mentioned in Zosimus, *Historia Nova* 4.18 (Mendelsson, 172f.).
[184] Cambell Bonner, *Studies in Magical Amulets Chiefly Graeco-Egyptian* (Ann Arbor 1950), passim.
[185] Supra, Ch. I, Sect. 3.

niques from Asklepiegeneia, daughter of Plutarch, *diadochos* of the Neoplatonic academy in Athens, including the use of the "voiceless magic spinning tops" (τοῖς θείοις καὶ ἀφθέγκτοις στροφάλοις ἐκέχρητο).[186] Michael Psellos, writing in the eleventh century, provides a description of this practice based on the *Chaldaean Oracles*. Proclus himself seems to have had access to this work in some form.[187]

> A top of Hekate is a golden sphere enclosing a *lapis lazuli* in its middle that is twisted through a cow-hide leather thong and having engraved letters all over it. [Diviners] spin this sphere and make invocations. Such things they call charms, whether it is the matter of a spherical object, a triangular one, or some other shape. While spinning them, they call out unintelligible or beast-like sounds, laughing and flailing at the air. [Hekate] teaches the *taketēs* to operate, that is the movement of the top, as if it had an ineffable power. It is called the top of Hekate because it is dedicated to her. For Hekate was a goddess among the Chaldaeans. In her right hand she held the source of the virtues. But it is all nonsense.

Thus Proclus' interest in the mantic arts. He also had his horoscope cast. Marinus of Neapolis reproduces it in full with some brief observations that need not detain us here.[188] The study of genealogy (γένεσις), astrology, horoscope-casting, and "sky-worship" continued and throve throughout the fifth century unabated despite the penalties attached to them in the Theodosian Code, but these practices lay outside the sphere of the traditional Hellenic cults, as the jurists who codified the law realized, and are thus omitted from further discussion here.[189]

The death of Proclus in 485 caused Marinus of Neapolis to compose a long description of the cults of heroes, ancestors, and philosophers, whose souls received honor at various sites around the Akropolis in Athens. Knowledge of the traditional Athenian funerary rites had survived until this time as well. Proclus' death moved Marinus' emotions deeply. These emerge somewhat through the veneer of Atticist convention:[190]

---

[186] Marinus, *Vita Procli* 28 (Boissonade, 22).
[187] Michael Psellus, *Expositio ad Oracula Chaldaica*, PG 122, 1133A–B.
[188] Marinus, *Vita Procli* 35 (Boissonade, 28).
[189] For example, in a law given at Aquileia by Theodosius II and Valentinian III on 17 July 425, astrologers (*mathematici*) are grouped with Manichaeans, heretics, and "every sect inimical to the Catholics." *Cod. Theod.* 16.5.62 (Pharr, 462).
[190] Marinus, *Vita Procli* 36 (Boissonade, 28f.). The rites mentioned in this passage seem to have entailed sacrifice. Cf. Marinos of Neapolis, *The Extant Works*, tr. A.N. Oikonomides (Chicago 1977), 79.

He died in the 124th year after the reign of Julian (485 A.D.), when
Nikagoras the younger was archon eponymous in Athens, on the 17th
of the Athenian month of Mounichion, April 17 according to the
Roman calendar. His body was deemed worthy of care in accordance
with the ancestral customs of the Athenians and as he had himself
ordered when still alive. For the blessed man had, if any other did,
the knowledge and concern for the execution of rites for the dead. At
no time did he omit their customary services, but every year on the
defined days he visited the monuments of the Attic heroes and
philosophers, and of those who had become his friends and acquaintances. He performed the customary rites, doing them himself and
not through proxies.

After the service for each, he went down to the Academy and in a
certain demarcated place appeased the family-protecting souls of his
forefathers. In a separate place a libation was poured for the souls of
all the philosophers in common. The most pious man [Proclus]
demarcated another third place and performed rites of purification
for all the souls of dead persons.

His body was, as said before, clothed in accordance with his
directions, carried by his companions and buried in the more eastern
suburbs of the city at Lykavettos where the body of his professor
Syrianos lies. For that man had given him this command while still
alive, and because of this had had the double sarkophagos made.
After Syrianos' death, when once the most holy Proclus debated
whether this was proper, he was heartened by Syrianos threatening
him in a dream, and by only this. On the monument was inscribed a
four-lined metrical epigram which he composed for himself thus:

"I was Proclus, a Lycian by race, whom Syrianus nourished here,
a recipient of his teaching. This common tomb received the bodies of
both. May one place also receive their souls."

The funerary procession and many of Proclus' devotions and rites
can only have been performed publicly.[191] The sarkophagi and
monuments (μνήματα) lay, of course, outside the walls of Athens in
accordance with imperial law.[192] The customary services of the
dead (ἡ εἰωθυία αὐτῶν θεραπεία) involved sacrifices of a minor
order.[193] Many tombs of the Attic heroes (τὰ τῶν ἀττικῶν
Ἡρώων) probably still stood in the Kerameikos. On the other
hand Proclus' contemporaries, including his mentor Syrianus, were
interred at a nekropolis on the slopes of Mount Lykavettos. A
Christian nekropolis also grew up there,[194] but one that contained
the undated markers of poorer folk, many of them steles that refer
to the grave as a "place of sleep" in the misspelled form

---

[191] Pagan funeral processions were still public occasions in the 370's Cf. supra,
Ch. I, Sect. 3.
[192] *Cod. Theod.* 9.17.6.
[193] Supra, Ch. I, Sect. 2, for the evidence provided by the epigrams of Gregory
of Nazianzus (4th c.).
[194] Bayet, nos. 24–33.

κυμητήριον instead of κοιμητήριον, and have small incised crosses, an occasional Chi-Rho christogram,[195] or an Alpha-Omega.[196]
The inscriptions are quite short, unlike the florid texts erected over
the tombs of Christian decurions.[197] Only one stele identifies the
trade of the owner: "(Cross) Tomb of Atheneos (sic) the house-
builder" (+κυμητήριον Ἀ[θ]ηνέου οἰκοδόμου).[198] The rest were
perhaps hired day-laborers, including a migrant from Thessalonike
([Θεσ]αλονι[κέως])—the inscription is only fragmentary.[199]
Pagans and Christians had apparently begun to share the Mt.
Lykavettos area in the early fifth century.

On the other hand, shrines for the rites of the souls (ψυχαί) of all
the dead, ancestors, and philosopher colleagues stood within the
city limits at the Academy (εἰς τὴν Ἀκαδημίαν) in three demarcated spots. The prescribed acts could be performed without the
ritual contamination thought to accompany contact with the dead
even in the legislation of Christian emperors.[200] Marinus of Neapolis makes it quite clear that the monuments and sarcophagi of
Proclus' friends and acquaintances, the philosophers and Attic
heroes, lay in one place outside the city walls, whereas the shrines
dedicated to the souls of his family and the philosophers lay at the
Academy. When Proclus made his customary tour of the funerary
monuments, then, he will have first gone to the *nekropoleis*, including
Mt. Lykavettos where Syrianus lay, and from there to the
Academy. Proclus was a Lycian. The family tombs, including those
of his parents, must have been located outside his home town of
Xanthos.[201] The Neoplatonic theology of the soul apparently permitted one to honor his ancestors' and friends' souls in a special
shrine distinct from the tomb, whether the sarkophagos lay just
outside the city or hundreds of miles away. By way of contrast, the
local Athenian philosophers commemorated in the shrine at the
Academy often had their tombs only a short distance away. This
theology of honoring souls, for which no evidence seems to exist
outside Athens, stands in sharp contrast to the Christian cult of
martyrs, which required the actual presence of the relics. Finally, it
is of interest to know that memorial rites at tombs could be performed by proxy, although Proclus performed the ritual himself

---

[195] Bayet, no. 28.
[196] Bayet, no. 31.
[197] Supra, Ch. IV, Sect. 1.
[198] Bayet, no. 25 (IG 3/2.3454).
[199] Bayet, no. 26 (IG 3/2.3529).
[200] Supra, Ch. IV, n. 191.
[201] Proclus' parents, although residents of Constantinople when he was born,
moved back to Xanthos in Lycia. It was here than Proclus received his early
education in grammar. Marinus, *Vita Procli* 6 (Boissonade, 5f.).

whenever possible (οὐ δι' ἑτέρου, ἀλλ' αὐτὸς ἐνεργῶν). It is unclear by what arrangements and through what persons the proxies acted in these situations.

Marinus of Neapolis' biography of Proclus provides incontrovertible evidence about the survival of Hellenic cults at Athens in all their forms: the numerous shrines and temples stayed open through about 481–488, private sacrifices were performed, and an entire subculture of theurgy and divination persisted little altered from the late fourth century. Moreover, the adherents of these practices suffered little interference from imperial officials until late in Proclus' life, perhaps c. 484/5, when the Parthenon, Asklepieion, and other temples were demolished or closed along with the elimination of their public, non-sacrificial cults. The *Life of Isidore* composed by Damascius in the early sixth century provides a corroborating picture of these tendencies.

Isidore, a Neoplatonist philosopher and *diadochos* of the Academy after Proclus, moved in the same milieu in Athens as his predecessor. His biography, which survives mainly in the form of fragments and extracts scattered through the *Suda* dictionary, is more discursive than that of Proclus, but differs little from it in the tenor of its remarks about the ongoing Hellenic practices. This rule applies in particular to the cults of the traditional Attic deities. The Panathenaia along with the processions and banquets that accompanied it still drew subsidies in the fifth century, although the games connected with the Great Panathenaia, which had in Antiquity been celebrated every fourth year, had certainly disappeared by the mid-fifth century.[202] The biographer of Isidore makes an oblique reference to the Panathenaia:[203]

> This man [Archiadas the decurion] manifested what kind of soul he had. For after much of his property had been plundered [during Attila's raid against northern Greece in 447], when he perceived that Theagenes, then still a small boy, was grieved at what had been destroyed and despoiled, he said: "O Theagenes, you must dare to confess to the gods [their] saving blessings in behalf of our material bodies, and not be disheartened over money. For if Athena Polias commanded these [funds] to be expended on the Panathenaia, how much expense would we have gone to? As it is, one must reckon the present contest (*agōn*) [of financial hardship] more brilliant and pious than any other, even the Panathenaia.

---

[202] Cf. Himerius' account of the Panathenaia (4th c. A.D.). Supra, Ch. I, Sect. 2. For the Olympia celebrated at Chalcedon, cf. infra, Ch. VII, Sect. 1.

[203] Damascius, *Vita Isidori*, Fr. 273, (Zintzen, 217).

The simple past condition in which the penultimate sentence is given is, of course, capable of synchronous interpretation c. 447.[204]

If some ambiguity surrounds the extent of the cult of Athena, the same cannot be said for that of Asklepios. The Asklepieion remained a site of Hellenic incubation as late as c. 484,[205] as a detailed narrative about the philosopher Plutarch reveals:[206]

> For Asklepios at Athens delivered the same oracular cure to Plutarch the Athenian and Domninus the Syrian, the latter after spitting blood . . . the former, I do not know what ailed him. The cure entailed being sated with pork. Plutarch could not, however, stand medicine of this kind even though it was not illicit for him in accordance with ancestral custom. Upon being awakened from sleep and then leaping upon his elbow on the pallet, he gazed at the statue of Asklepios (for he happened to be sleeping in the forecourt of the temple) and said: "O master! What would you command to a Jew who was ailing with this sickness? You would not order him to consume pork, would you?" He said this, and Asklepios at once *sent forth out of the statue a certain very harmonious voice* and prescribed another treatment for the malady.

The image of Asklepios (τὸ ἄγαλμα τοῦ ᾿Ασκληπιοῦ), like the chryselephantine Athena, remained an object of cult perhaps as late as 484. The Asklepieion was itself equipped with dormitories that fronted onto an elongated central courtyard that led in turn to the temple proper. The suppliants often chose to lie instead in the forecourt beneath the gaze of the statue (ἐγκαθεύδων τῷ προδόμῳ τοῦ ἱεροῦ).[207] The dormitories were quite possibly reserved for the non-Athenians who had travelled far and spent much money to reach the shrine. One can hardly doubt that a share of the cooked pork given to Plutarch was offered to Asklepios in sacrifice, but it is impossible to tell from the text whether the offerings were burnt within the temenos or at a private residence.

Damascius makes no clear reference to the cult of Aphrodite, which lacked indigenous roots in Attica, but remarks that her statue, which he had himself seen (ὅτι φησὶν ὁ συγγραφεὺς ἄγαλμα τῆς ᾿Αφροδίτης ἰδεῖν ἱδρυμένον) was still standing in the Odeion. The work had been the votive offering (ἀνάθημα) of Herodes Atticus (2nd century A.D.). The statue exerted a powerful influence on the observer, but in this instance not an erotic one, the latter being a factor which often triggered Christian revulsion and

---

[204] Herbert W. Smyth, *Greek Grammar*, rev. G.W. Messing (Cambridge 1956), 515 (=Sect. 2292).
[205] Infra, Appendix III.
[206] Damascius, *Vita Isidori*, Fr. 218 (Zintzen, 183f. Asmus, 80f.).
[207] For the term πρόδομον, cf. CIG 2754.

led to the destruction of many such works.[208] Damascius enumerates the peculiar characteristics of the statue of Aphrodite in the
Odeion:[209]

> Upon seeing the statue I perspired under the influence of astonish-
> ment and surprise. And thus I got my animate soul into such a state
> of joy that I could not dismiss the matter at home, but often there-
> after went out to return to the sight. The sculptor blended much beauty
> into it, nothing sweet or erotic, but dignified and masculine, man-
> ifesting joy in hoplite armor as if restored from a victory.

Here at least Damascius makes no speculations about the divine
"conception" of the image causing frenzy in the mind of the
observer.

IV. The Social Background to the Survival of the Athenian Cults

It is unfortunate that hardly a shred of evidence survives about
the popular appeal of the Athenian cults except to the decurion
class. Little information even about the latter would have come
down to us either, except for the interest of the scholars of medieval
Constantinople in Proclus' commentaries on Plato and the hit-or-
miss excerpting of the *Life of Isidore* by the compiler of the Suda
dictionary. The philosophical schools thus became the key not only
to the survival of many local Hellenic cults, but to information
about them as well. One can only lament the disappearance of a
similar record in the other eastern Mediterranean cities and suppose that somewhat analogous conditions prevailed.

The task of reconstructing social conditions in Athens has a

---

[208] Cf. the destruction of a mosaic representing the "story of Aphrodite" at
sixth-century Amasea in Asia Minor: "A certain young man, learned in the craft of
the mosaicist, was making one such in the house of Chrysaphius of blessed
memory, in the city of Amasea. While he was tearing down an ancient mosaic from
the wall which had on it the story of Aphrodite (for the said man wished to make
the house into a chapel of the archangel . . .), and the mosaicist dug out the form of
the unclean Aphrodite, the *daimon* abiding in it stuck the hand of the craftsman."
Eustratius of Constantinople, *Vita S. Eutychii* PG 86, 2333D–2336A. Cf. supra, Ch.
III, Sect. 1, for the destruction of the Aphrodite of Gaza. An early sixth-century
mosaic inscription at Thebes in Boeotia mentions a man who gave up the cult of
the "obscene goddess". This should be taken as a late reference to the worship of
Aphrodite, and not Artemis or Athena, as in Trombley, "Boeotia in Late Antiquity," 223. The *editor princeps* has inexplicably accented the word for "goddess" (θεά)
on the wrong syllable, making it "spectacle" (θέα) instead. Cf. Demetrios Pallas,
Les Monuments paleochrétiens en Grèce de 1959 à 1973 (Rome 1977), 16, n. 30.
[209] Damascius, *Vita Isidori*, Epit. Phot. Fr. 87 (Zintzen, 122). There is a second-
century A.D. example of this "masculine-looking" but sublime Aphrodite with
serene facial features from the facade of the theatre at Aphrodisias in Caria. K.T.
Erim, *Aphrodisias: City of Aphrodite* (London 1986), 84. On animate statues—which
that seen in Athens was not—see supra, Ch. I, Sect. 3.

twofold aspect: the elucidation of the atmosphere of public freedom in which the archons and philosophers expressed religious opinion and practical Hellenism, and an inferential discussion of how extensively the public at large adhered to the old practices. Little doubt exists about the first of these groups. The Hellenic aristocracy lived much as it had in the days of Herodes Atticus. We learn of two prominent figures in this group, Archiadas and his son-in-law Theagenes. Both men maintained close ties with the philosophical schools and actively pursued local political careers.[210] Theagenes held the office of archon eponymous and was called the "Herodes Atticus of his time".[211]

Archiadas was Proclus' elder contemporary, and already an important man in Athens when the philosopher arrived there (*ante* 431/2). A convinced Hellene—Marinus of Neapolis refers to him as "the beloved of the gods" (Ἀρχιάδας ὁ τοῖς θεοῖς φίλος)— Archiadas made considerable outlay for the civic and religious ceremonies connected with the Panathenaia.[212] Archiadas held the office of archon eponymous (intra 438–450). One can hardly conclude otherwise from the fact that Proclus persuaded him "to preside over the common [welfare] of his own city and to serve as benefactor to everyone by using his own [property]" (ὅλης τε τῆς ἑαυτοῦ πόλεως προΐστασθαι κοινῇ προτρεπόμενος, ἕκαστον ἰδίᾳ εὐεργετεῖν).[213] Public munificence went with holding high local office. The vagueness of Marinus' rhetoric conceals the precise nature of Archiadas' activities, which included the refurbishment of certain public buildings (εἰς ἔργον δὲ δημόσιον).[214] Epigraphic evidence from nearby Megara suggests what this might have entailed. The inscription dates from c. 400–450 and must be considered typical of the period:[215]

> This is the work of the most magnificent count Diogenes, son of Archelaos, who cared for the Hellenic cities as if they were his own household, and furnished even to the city of the Megarians 100 *solidi* for the refurbishment of towers; 150 additional *solidi* and 2,200 feet of marble for the renovation of the bath-house, considering nothing more honorable than being a benefactor to the Greeks and restoring their cities.

---

[210] Groag, *Reichsbeamten von Achaia*, 75–77.

[211] Ibid., 76. Groag merely summarizes the contents of the *Vita Isidori*.

[212] On the preparations for, and execution of, the Panathenaia, see supra, Ch. I. Sect. 2. Damascius, *Vita Isidori*, Fr. 273 (Zintzen, 217=Asmus, 96).

[213] Marinus, *Vita Procli* 14 (Boissonade, 11f.).

[214] Marinus, *Vita Procli* 14 (Boissonade, 12).

[215] IG 7.26. Quoted by Groag, *Reichsbeamten von Achaia*, 77f. I have taken *chrysinoi* to be *solidi*.

Archiadas practiced old-fashioned public munificence, if not emulation, on this model (τιμιώτερον οὐδὲν ἡγούμενος τοῦ τοὺς Ἕλληνας εὐεργετεῖν ἀνανεοῦν τε τὰς πόλεις).[216] Archiadas' activities in behalf of citizens (ἀστοῖς) and foreigners (ξένοις) can only be conjectured, but the amount of expenditure was said to be so great that "he displayed himself superior to the ownership of money."[217] Archiadas assigned certain lands of his extensive estates (κτήματα) to the public domain of Athens and also to that of his city of origin, Xanthos in Lycia.[218] Although it was common for landed magnates to draw income from estates scattered throughout many provinces,[219] one can hardly doubt that Archiadas had considerable holdings in Attica, or that the villages thereon can hardly have undergone Christianization at the initiative of the owner or his bailiffs (οἰκονόμοι), as analogous conditions in rural Bithynia, Syria and Egypt prove.[220] The income from city-owned lands went not only to the repair of walls, cisterns, and aqueducts, but to the maintenance of the temples, their priesthoods, and cultus. The Asklepieion and Parthenon appear not to have been closed until c. 484, and the imperial government can hardly have tampered with them before that date. This being the case, Archiades' heterogenous donations will probably have strengthened the economic underpinnings of the Athenian cults, and have postponed the Christianization of the colonate and renters on the estates mentioned in the legacy.[221]

Archiadas supposedly drew inspiration for his acts of piety and public munificence from Proclus' teaching. The philosopher, at that time preoccupied with the *Politics* of Aristotle and the *Republic* and *Laws* of Plato, had little time for urban politics (πράττειν . . . τὰ πολιτικά), but tried to inspire Archiadas with the political virtues and methods (αἱ πολιτικαὶ ἀρεταὶ καὶ αἱ μέθοδοι) treated in these texts.[222] Civic and religious virtues were closely allied in the

---

[216] Groag, *Reichsbeamten von Achaia*, 78.

[217] Marinus, *Vita Procli* 14 (Boissonade, 12).

[218] ταῖς πόλεσι καταλέλοιπε κτήματα, πατρίδι τε τῇ ἑαυτοῦ καὶ ταῖς Ἀθήναις. Ibid., 12.

[219] Cf. the example of Paulinus of Pella, who had estates scattered through the provinces of Achaea, Epirus Vetus, and Epirus Nova. Jones, *Later Roman Empire*, 782.

[220] Infra, Ch. VII–IX.

[221] The Christianization of rural Lycia was still in progress in the early and mid-sixth century. Trombley, "Paganism in the Greek World," 337–339. Idem, "Monastic Foundations in Sixth-century Anatolia and their Role in the Social and Economic Life of the Countryside," *Greek Orthodox Theological Review* 30 (1985), 55–58.

[222] Marinus, *Vita Procli* 14 (Boissonade, 11).

Hellenic mind. Speaking of that man's son and namesake, Marinus observes:[223]

> Archiadas [the younger] on the whole differed not a little from his father and the many in virtue by taking up the study of philosophy. Inasmuch as he was unlearned and not liable to flattery because of his ancestral properties, he displayed a holy life as much as anyone else [ever] did, and acquired by practice great experience in sacred works and words, but nothing greater than his father [had accomplished].

The younger Archiadas flourished in the period down to 484/5.

Proclus himself took a hand in urban politics after the death of the elder Archiadas, having received the requisite rhetorical education at Alexandria and experience at the bar in Constantinople by the age of twenty (c. 430).[224] He sat in the city council or bouleutic assembly of Athens, and perhaps served as archon eponymous. Marinus of Neapolis sums up the political phase of Proclus' career in these terms:[225]

> The philosopher himself sometimes took up political counsels, being present at the public discussions in behalf of the city and introducing opinions sensibly, meeting with the archons and solliciting them not only in behalf of justice but compellingly and in a bold manner for a philosopher the apportionment of what was fair to each person. He cared for the decorum of his professors and made sobriety a way of life for them, teaching not with mere reason *but being capable of the actual task* through all his life, as if becoming the prototype of sobriety to the others. He displayed the Herculian form of civic virtue.

Proclus made enemies who compelled him to leave Athens and reside in Lydia for a peiod of one year. The nature of the dispute is unknown. Marinus' biography merely indicates that the philosopher got into a difficult situation with certain predatory men (ἐν περιστάσει τινῶν γυπογιγάντων).[226] Although the city council certainly contained many Christians and must have taken a hand in the deportation, the act can hardly have been the result of local prejudice against Prolus' well-known religious Hellenism, for the old religion prevailed everywhere and the Christian decurions of Athens sympathized with it, to judge from their funerary inscriptions discussed above. On the other hand, there was always a risk of local political enemies' trumping up charges about Proclus' zeal and thereby attracting an investigation. If such were the case,

---

[223] Damascius, *Vita Isidori*, Fr. 353 (Zintzen, 287f.).
[224] Marinus, *Vita Procli* 8 (Boissonade, 7).
[225] Marinus, *Vita Procli* 15 (Boissonade, 12).
[226] Ibid.

CHAPTER FOUR

withdrawal would have been prudent. If this was the case, it is ironic that Proclus spent his time in Lydia officiating at pagan rites.[227] To clinch the argument, Proclus while there is said to have observed the Pythagorean maxim: "Live and escape notice" (λάθε βιώσας).[228] Proclus may have attained the office of archon eponymous after his return to Athens, as he reportedly gave orders to the board of archons regarding the apportionment of grain allowances and other public duties (καὶ τοὺς ἄρχοντας ἀπαιτῶν σιτηρέσιά τε καὶ τὰς ἄλλας κατ' ἀξίαν ἀπονέμειν ἑκάστῳ τιμάς).[229] He was known for a harsh temper which could however change to mildness, for it was said that his anger "was turned to wax with the spinning of an ostrakon". (καὶ ὀστράκου περιστροφῇ κήρινον ἀπεδείκνυ τὸν θυμόν).[230]

Proclus' administrative talents and prestige as a philosopher enabled him to effect his policies without any marriage connections to the influential Athenian families of preferred birth and wealth (γένος τε καὶ πλοῦτος) that offered him their daughters in marriage. If Proclus provided his good friend the elder Archiadas with theoretical inspiration, Archiadas schooled him in practical affairs. The philosopher's urgent sense of justice and love of mankind (τὸ φιλάνθρωπον) exceeded that of many of the decurions, for he permitted his more capable household slaves (οἱ ἐπιτηδειότεροι τῶν οἰκετῶν) to inspect his provision for them in his will.[231] His properties were probably not small, as his father Patrikios had apparently risen in law and the imperial administration at Constantinople before the family returned to Xanthos in Lycia.[232] Proclus became known in his later years as the "ornament of the city-state" (Πρόκλος ὁ κόσμος τῆς πολιτείας) having the friendship of the gods (θεοφίλεια), a man blessed in all things (ὁ τὰ πάντα εὐδαίμων).[233] This view spoke as much for Proclus' profession of philosophy and Hellenic theology as it did for his political career.

---

[227] Marinus, *Vita Procli* 15 (Boissonade, 12f.).
[228] Marinus, *Vita Procli* 15 (Boissonade, 13).
[229] Ibid.
[230] Marinus, *Vita Procli* 16 (Boissonade, 13f.).
[231] Marinus, *Vita Procli* 17 (Boissonade, 14).
[232] Marinus, *Vita Procli* 6, 8 (Boissonade, 5, 7). His parents' affluence also explains Proclus' education in Alexandria with such luminaries as the sophist Leonas and the grammarian Orion (who came from an Egyptian priestly family). Proclus' wealth also enabled him to make the acquaintance of a certain Theodore, who held a magistracy in Alexandria. Ibid., 6f. Proclus thereafter studied in Athens with the Aristotelian philosopher Olympiodorus and the god-fearing (θεοσεβής) Heron. Marinus *Vita Procli* 8–9 (Boissonade, 6f.).
[233] Marinus, *Vita Procli* 32 (Boissonade, 26).

V. Conclusion

The remainder of Greece and the Aegean islands became Christianized in rather obscure circumstances between c. 300–600.[234] It is nearly impossible to set a chronology for these events of the kind that exists for northern Syria and Arabia, where one can often date the arrival of the new religion at towns and villages within about a quarter of a century.[235] This is due in part to the local convention in Greece about funerary inscriptions that forbade including the clumsy dates of local eras. One therefore has to fall back on the analysis of themes and letter forms, which is often a rather ambiguous procedure. Still, it is possible to make a few conclusions and generalizations by taking the epigraphy of Attica as the standard.

At Melos, an island lying to the southeast in the Cyclades, the new religion had gained a foothold by the beginning of the fourth century, as we learn from the funerary inscription of a family that supplied three presbyters and a deacon to the local church. All of them have Hellenic names including theophorics like Asklepis and Asklepiodotos. These folk were the first Christian generation for all the familiar reasons.[236] The stone-cutter adjures the passer-by in the name of the presiding Christian angel to leave the tomb inviolate (ἐνορκίζω ὑμᾶς τὸν ὧδε ἐφεστῶτα ἄνγελον). He has of course replaced the name of the katachthonic divinity or local temple god in the formulary. The inscription begins "in the Lord" (ἐν κ(υρί)ῳ) and invokes Christ to help the stonecutter and his family.[237] Two of the daughters either died young or else embraced Christian virginity (παρθενεύσασα). This clergy all came from a single family, and may well have been the entire clergy of the island at this time. According to this scheme Christianity will have become dominant at Melos town only from the late fourth century onward, but not in the countryside, whose Christianization is a historical blank. Somewhat later in time comes a funerary inscription at Patras at the northwestern corner of the Peloponnese that calls upon "those who are Christians and fear God" (Χριστιανοὶ ὄν[τ]ες καὶ τὸν [θ](εὸ)ν [φο]βούμενοι) not to disrupt a tomb (koimēlērion).[238] The stress on this distinction puts the burial in the

---

[234] Gregory, "The Survival of Paganism in Christian Greece," passim, and Trombley, "Boeotia in Later Antiquity," 221–226.

[235] Cf. infra, Ch. VIII, X, and XI.

[236] Cf. infra, Ch. IV, Sect. 1.

[237] M. Guarducci, *Epigrafia Greca IV: Epigrafi sacre pagane e cristiane* (Rome 1978), 368f. IG 12/3 *Inscriptiones Insularum Maris Aegaei, Fasc. III: Inscr. Symes . . . Meli*, ed. F. Hiller von Gaertringen (Berlin 1898), no. 1238.

[238] CIG 4 9298.

first half of the fourth century when Hellenes still dominated the
seaport and its *territorium*. Large Christian communities of the fifth
century are difficult to identify because of the limited epigraphic
evidence. One exception to this is Aidepsos on the island of
Euboia.[239]

Outside Athens the temple conversions and other epigraphic
testimonia to the Christian victory seem to be chronologically in
step with developments elsewhere in the *oikoumene*. One thinks here
of bishop Iovianos and his church at Palaiopolis on the island of
Kerkyra which contains a ringing proclamation composed in the
language of the Christian sophistic:[240]

> (Cross) I, Iovianos, having the confidence of the emperor as the
> helpmate of my purposes, built this sacred church (Cross) for you,
> blessed Ruler on high, having sacked (Cross) the altars and temple
> precincts of the Hellenes, a wedding gift to the Lord from my own
> worthless hand.

The language is almost entirely Epic. Christ has the titulature of
the now dead Hellenic gods: "blessed" (μάκαρ), the "ruling on
high" of Zeus (ὑψιμέδον), and "Lord" (ἄναξ), also of Zeus. The
church had replaced the old shrines (Ἑλλήνων τεμένη καὶ
βωμούς) as the new "sacred temple" (ἱερὸν ἔκτισα νηόν).[241] At
Lindos, where the pagan priest Aglochartos dedicated a grove of
olive trees to Athena c. 300, various pagan dedications were built
into the walls of the church that displaced the temple.[242] The signs
of the new religion began to appear elsewhere as well. A Christian
of Sparta in the Peloponnese incised a cross and a six-leaf in a circle
over the face of a very early Spartan decree.[243] On the island of
Delos, the home of Apollo, Christ became the "new Dionysus" with
the incision of his name on the base of a wine press: "(Cross) Christ,
help your servant (Cross) Peter."[244] This replacement of the old
gods of the olive harvest and the wine cycle was taking place in
northern Syria and North Africa as well.[245] Acts of substitution

---

[239] IG XII/9: *Inscriptiones Insularum Maris Aegaei prater Delum, Fasc. IX*, ed. Eric
Ziebarth (Berlin 1915), nos. 1232–1241.

[240] Guarducci, *Epigrafia Greca* 4, 347f.

[241] Iovianos was not, of course, the emperor Jovian (ob. 363), but the bishop of
the city, as a newly discovered inscription reveals. Ibid., no. 6.

[242] *Inscriptiones Graecae XII/1: Inscriptiones Insularum Maris Aegaei Praeter Delum*, ed.
F. Hiller von Gaetringen (Berlin 1895), nos. 851, 855, 777, 847. Cf. supra, Ch. II,
Sect. 1.

[243] *Inscriptiones Graecae 5/1: Inscriptiones Laconiae Messeniae Arcadiae*, ed. Walther
Kolbe (Berlin 1913), no. 1.

[244] SEG 34 (1984), 789.

[245] Cf. supra, Ch. X, Sect. 1.

went on during the Greek middle ages. Thomas of Malea seems to have expelled such tutelary divinities. It is said that his prayer once made a new Christian spring gush from the ground on Mount Malea in the Peloponnese.[246] The direction was sometimes reversed. The Athenian inscription of Askleparion and Hesychia had its cross deleted. The stone was evidently reused in some fashion and the offending sign erased.[247]

Hellenic religious ideas were deeply embedded in the psyche of native Greeks, as the examples cited by John Cuthbert Lawson reveal. They seem to have come down to the Neohellenic period largely intact by oral transmission in the folklore without any great distortion by literary anachronism. But even if this were not the case, it is difficult to explain the popular interest in the old divinities that still prevailed in the late nineteenth century. It quite obviously met important cultural needs. Although much of Greece had been formally Christianized by c. 529, the indigenous religious traditions had great strength. It would therefore be dangerous to regard Proclus' beliefs and practices as a sharp exception to the popular religiosity.[248] The most notable feature of this is the survival of the Late Antique recategorization of the Hellenic divinities into a whole variety of *daimones*.[249] This groping Christianization is reflected in the funerary inscription of a certain Euphemia who was interred at Panaiania in Attica (5th–6th c.?):[250]

> (Cross) Euphemia's place of sleep (*koimētērion*). If anyone should at any time or in any manner plaster over (this inscription) and set a foreigner or local person or relative of hers (in this place), he shall have to deal with God the Pantokrator and with the powers in heaven and with those in the air and those in the earth and with the subterranean powers, and they shall take a contribution (from him), with those who told, and crucify him. (Cross) And the God-loving clergy shall also have to deal with the aforesaid powers if they allow (any act) against this seal and have someone buried as you say (?) or transfer those lying here to another place.

The critical phrase, which is full of solecisms, is the reference to "the powers in heaven and . . . those in the air and in the earth and . . . the subterranean powers" (κὲ πρὸ[ς] τὰς ἐν οὐρανῷ

---

[246] *Menologion*, PG 117, 529B-C. *Synaxarium Ecclesiae Constantinopolitanae e Codice Sirmondiano*, ed. Hippolyte Delehaye (Brussels 1902), 803.

[247] IG 3/2 3521.

[248] See my own definition of "popular religion" in *Oxford Dictionary of Byzantium*, ed. Alexander Kazhdan et al., 3 (Oxford 1991), 1698f.

[249] Lawson, *Modern Greek Folklore and Ancient Greek Religion*, 66–69.

[250] SEG 29 (1979) 250. See also the commentary: Denis Feissel, "Notes d'épigraphie chrétienne (IV)," *Bulletin de Correspondance Hellénique* 104 (1980), 159–175.

δυνάμις, [κὲ] πρὸς τὰς ἐν ἀέρι κὲ ἐν [γῆ] κὲ κατα[χθ]ονίας δυ⟨νά⟩μις). The formula is pre-Christian. It has something in common with the Neoplatonic taxonomies that put the gods in the firmament, and the angels and *daimones* in the lower air.[251] Indeed the word "power" (δύναμις) had a certain currency in Hellenistic times as a synonym for *daimon*.[252] But the powers in the earth can only have been the underworld deities Demeter and Persephone, and the katachthonic powers the furious divinities thought to stand guard over tombs.[253] One would expect some anachronism and Hellenic color in an Attic funerary inscription, as was seen previously,[254] but the present text expresses real belief. The curse is applied to the local Christian clergy as well. A well-taught Christian might have been expected to regard the cross, Christogram, and "One God" formula as superior to these powers, which the new theology degraded to mere *daimones*. Here at least the idea of the "life to come" as symbolized by the use of the term *koimēterion* is subordinated to Hellenic taboo fears that had remained quite strong. The old gods may have become *daimones*, but their localities of operation were still discreetly remembered.

Proclus speaks best for the Hellenic faith of the intellectuals. Of the less sophisticated folk, some revised their earlier beliefs in light of Christian teaching, but others failed to make the transition to the new religious culture *in toto*. During the millenium that followed, it was the people of the Hellenic homeland who reflected this trait most strongly.

---

[251] Iamblichus, *De Mysteriis*, Bks. 1–2 (Des Places 38ff.).
[252] *A Greek-English Lexicon of the New Testament and Other Early Christian Literature*, ed. W. Bauer, tr. W.F. Arndt and F.W. Gingrich, 5th/2nd ed. (Chicago 1957), 208.
[253] Infra, Ch. VII, Sect. 2.
[254] Supra, Ch. IV, Sect. 1.

DID JOHN CHRYSOSTOM VISIT ATHENS IN 367/8?

George of Alexandria's life of John Chrysostom, written c. 620, mentions a visit by the latter to Athens after he had completed his studies in grammar and rhetoric with Libanius in Antioch.[1] Chrysostom Baur disregards the supposed incident, taking it as something that George simply invented as an encomiastic appreciation of John Chrysostom's rhetorical brilliance.[2] This interpretation is difficult to understand. For one thing, as Baur himself admits, George of Alexandria was little more than a compiler, and so the invention of such an oddly detailed account with a certain Attic flavor about it is rather surprising. The second objection is that George has fitted the incident quite precisely into a perfectly plausible space in the established chronology of John Chrysostom's life. Let us consider the chronology first, and then the content of the narrative.

Robert E. Carter in a 1962 article worked through the chronologies of Chrysostom's early years proposed by C. Baur, S. Schiwietz, A. Moulard, and others, and established convincingly that the saint finished his education with Libanius in July 367, and received baptism at Easter 368.[3] In between was a period of about nine months which cannot otherwise be accounted for. It is here that George of Alexandria inserted the narrative about Chrysostom's visit to Athens. There can be strictly speaking no objection to it on the ground of material possibility or motivation. For one thing, John's visit was quite short. The sailing season was still suitable for a swift passage from Antioch to Achaea in late July or August, although a return would not have been easy until the westerly March tradewinds. It is said that he left not long after the attack on Hellenic religion made in front of the archon Demosthenes because

---

[1] The relevant sections are found in *Douze récits byzantins sur Saint Jean Chrysostom,* ed. François Halkin (Brussels 1977), 76–110. Hereinafter cited as *V. Chrysostomi.*

[2] Chrysostomus Baur, "Georgius Alexandrinus," *Byzantinische Zeitschrift* 27 (1927), 3.

[3] Robert E. Carter, "The Chronology of Saint John Chrysostom's Early Life," *Traditio* 18 (1962), 357–364.

the bishop of Athens wanted to ordain him.[4] But if John left "secretly" (λάθρᾳ), as George of Alexandria's narrative indicates, the young scholar may have returned to Antioch by an unplanned route on land or sea or both.[5]

George of Alexandria's biography indicates that Chrysostom went to Athens "wishing to complete the rest of his education" (πληρῶσαι θέλων τὰ λείποντα τῆς παιδεύσεως).[6] His monastic biographer Palladius knew him only in later life. Robert Carter has shown that his account of Chrysostom's youth is hazy about chronology and not entirely trustworthy.[7] Even if Palladius had known of the visit to Athens, he would have found it difficult to believe that the mature Christian intellectual that Chrysostom had become had ever harbored the desire to improve upon the rhetorical skills that had made him one of the most prolific Greek writers of the Christian sophistic. The young man often has ambitions that the old man looks back upon with a spirit of disdain or amusement. It would be naive to suppose that Chrysostom was a mature Christian homilist and exegete even in his youth, or to deny that youthful ambition inspired by Libanius' teaching once glowed within him. He may, in fact, have been under considerable family pressure to emulate the career of his father Secundus, who had attained the rank of *magister militum per Orientem*. As A.H.M. Jones has pointed out: "The service was often in practice hereditary. . . ."[8] By 367, to be sure, with the demise of Julian the Apostate in the past, Christian sophists will have been more common even in Athens, although it was the professional competence of the teacher rather than his religion that decided students to study with him.[9] Basil of Caesarea's studies in Athens are proof of this, as is the fact that Eunapius of Sardis' tutor, Prohaeresius, was a Christian (ante 363). There is nothing, strictly speaking, against Chrysostom's having gone to Athens on the ground of plausibility. The problem lies, rather, in the seeming lack of veracity of George of Alexandria's narrative.

We may safely regard the story of the pagan rhetor Anthemius' possession by a *daimon* in front of the Athenian council for affirming the Hellenic peace of the gods as a later invention, although it is not impossible that Hellenes riding the fence over their religious allegiances sometimes suffered the physical symptoms of taboo hysteria

---

[4] Supra, Ch. IV, Sect. 2. *V. Chrysostomi*, 87f.
[5] *V. Chrysostomi*, 88, line 12.
[6] *V. Chrysostomi*, 78, line 12.
[7] Carter, "Chronology," 357.
[8] Jones, *Later Roman Empire*, 599.
[9] Infra, Ch. V, Sect. 3.

inflated by the evident power of the new religion and its God.[10] But it is difficult to disconnect many of the other details as entirely improbable. The criticisms of Hellenic religion put into Chrysostom's mouth by the hagiographer are quite weak, as for example his calling female divinities "little whores". On the other hand, the early years of the co-emperors Valens (364–378) and Valentinian I (364–375) were quite free from the religious persecution of Hellenes, and this will have permitted some rather brusque exchanges of viewpoint in Athens, where Hellenic culture and belief were still strongly entrenched. The pagan sophists and city councillors were mainly anxious to avoid some *cause celèbre* that might result in the demolition of their temples. George of Alexandria's narrative is accurate in attributing such anxiety to the city magistrates and a degree of fanaticism to the pagan sophist Anthemius. The problem with our source is in reality the lurid light in which the description is given and certain anachronisms that point to a date of composition in the late fifth century not long after the law against Hellenic religion that I have attributed to the emperor Zeno in the years 481–484, when the living memory of John Chrysostom was a thing of the past.

There are certain peculiarities of language and content in George of Alexandria's narrative that correspond to realities of life in Athens as attested in the Roman Imperial and Late Antique inscriptions. Some of them are sufficiently striking to merit more than passing notice.

There are, first of all, very precise allusions to the co-emperors Valens and Valentinian I and their inscriptions. Thus the archon Demosthenes avers that "our august emperors happen to be Christians" (οἱ σεβάσμιοι ἡμῶν βασιλεῖς Χριστιανοὶ ὑπάρχουσιν).[11] George of Alexandria quite correctly infers the existence of co-emperors in 367/8 through the use of the present tense. It is improbable that he was improvising here. In fact, the surviving inscriptions of Greece name both co-emperors during their joint reign and that of successors,[12] as for example at Thespiae not far from Athens in Boeotia: "The city (set up statues of) our masters the Augusti Flavius Valentinianus and Flavius Valens" (in

---

[10] This is what Sigmund Freud describes as "taboo sickness" in *Totem and Taboo*, published in *The Penguin Freud Library 13: The Origins of Religion*, ed. Albert Dickson (London 1985), 79f.

[11] *V. Chrysostomi*, 84, line 11.

[12] IG 4, 674: "In behalf of the emperors Claudii Valentii Caesares" (in Greek). IG 4, 1109: "Valentinian and Valens Augusti" (in Greek) (Nauplion) IG 4.674. Later emperors: IG 7, 24 (Megara). Alison Frantz, "A Public Building of Late Antiquity in Athens (IG 2,² 5205)," *Hesperia* 48 (1979), 198.

Greek).[13] Only a person knowledgeable about the official nomenclature, and perhaps of Achaea, would have been aware of this
practice. George of Alexandria cannot have simply invented this at
so late a date as c. 620. Demosthenes also observes that "each man
and every land" under their authority worships Christ (ἕκαστος
ἄνθρωπος καὶ πᾶσα χώρα), and again that they had conquered
many barbarian nations (πλεῖστα βάρβαρα ἔθνη).[14] Chrysostom
concurs in his reply that Christ is worshipped "from the farthest
point of the oikoumene to its (opposite) boundaries."[15] This somewhat echoes known inscriptions of Athens and Megara from the
joint reign of the sons and grandsons of Theodosius the Great. One
prologue iterates:[16]

> In behalf of the safety and victory and eternal permanence of the
> masters of the oikoumene, Flavius Arcadius and Flavius Honorius and
> Flavius Theodosius (the younger), the eternal and trophy-holding
> Augusti.

John uses the term oikoumene known from the imperial inscriptions,
restating Demosthenes' "each man and every land" with a painful
precision that turned the minds of his listeners to the imperial
edicts. The "victory" of Valentinian I and Valens was spelled out
quite emphatically in their titulature, which included the names of
conquered enemy nations.[17]

George of Alexandria has also gotten the chronology of the
Parthenon's closure right. The pagan sophist Anthemius observes
that "every man who comes to the school of this city imparts honor
and service to the gods by going away to the temple of the great
goddess Athena... (ἀπιὼν εἰς τὸ ἱερὸν τῆς μεγάλης θεᾶς
Ἀθηνᾶς), and falling before her, asks her to make his reasoning
wise for excellence in the sciences."[18] This is a direct reference to
Pheidias' chryselephantine statue of Athena in the Parthenon. The
description of the ritual is all quite accurate, but the procedure,
implicit for example in Marinus' biography of Proclus, is explicitly
stated in no other source. George of Alexandria nowhere mentions
the closure of the Parthenon, as he might have been tempted to do,
nor is there any anachronism in his treatment of the subject. This

---

[13] IG 7, 1849 (Thespiae). See Infra, n. 15.
[14] V. Chrysostomi, 84, lines 11, 22f., 25.
[15] V. Chrysostomi, 84f.
[16] IG 7, 24 (as above). Also: "Our master the unconquered Flavius Constantine
Augustus," where the last word is Σεβ[αστόν]. IG 7, 1848 (Thespiae).
[17] Hermann Dessau, Inscriptiones Latinae Selectae (=ILS) nos. 762, 763, 765, 770,
and especially 771.
[18] V. Chrysostomi, 83, line 27f.

circumstance seemingly puts the date of the account he used before the actual closure of the Parthenon.

The most striking feature of George of Alexandria's account is a series of faint echoes of, or allusions to, the two quasi-Justinianic laws that I have dated to the reign of Zeno. Anthemius is told: "*Go to the church* before our holy father the bishop. And he will teach you what is necessary for your own benefit." Or again: "Anthemius returned to his house and *took his wife and children, boys and girls, and went to the bishop.*" And then: "Delaying nothing, he (the bishop) catechized them all and *deemed them worthy of holy baptism*, teaching them to keep the commands of the Lord and no longer to approach the unclean idols, but rather *to spend time* (σχολάζειν) *in the holy church and read the divine scriptures.*" And finally: "The eparch and landed magnates . . . and much of the *demos . . . went at a run* (δρομαίως) *into the church* to the bishop and persuaded him to make them Christians." Since Demosthenes had already been baptized, the bishop "*instructed him* in following *the ecclesiastical canons.*"[19] The phrases italicized are all of them logical or literal echoes of the two quasi-Justinianic laws.[20] Since George of Alexandria's source had no knowledge of the closure of the Parthenon, but knew seemingly more than a little about the law in question, it is probable that this source upon which he drew belonged to the brief period between the beginning of Illus' rebellion in 481 and the closure of the Parthenon in about 484. If so, it was a tendentious document suggesting that tolerance of Hellenic belief and practice, and the leniency about sacrifice that prevailed in Valens' early reign, perhaps guaranteed some conversions, but that in the end only coercion and the strict enforcement of the imperial edicts could destroy the grip of the old religion; in the context of the civil insurrection of 481–488, only harsh methods could ensure the survival of the Christian empire. If this hypothesis be accepted, it is one more bit of corroboration for the host of synchronisms pointing to 481–484 for the two quasi-Justinianic laws. George of Alexandria was drawing upon a source not entirely lacking in political sophistication. It was perhaps intended, as well, to lecture the fifth-century patriarch of Constantinople, the politically pliant Acacius (471–489), on the evils of complacency toward Hellenic religion by contrasting the present state of affairs with his predecessor Chrysostom's youthful defiance of propriety before the Athenian Council of 300.

---

[19] The passages are scattered over *V. Chrysostomi*, 86f.
[20] *Cod. Iust.* 1.11.9 *prooem.* and *Cod. Iust.* 1.11.10, clauses 1, 3, and 5.

There are some other historical points in George of Alexandria's life of Chrysostom that have an Attic color. Among these are bits of information about the Athenian constitution. It is known from the inscription honoring Rufius Festus, the proconsul of Achaea (324 or later), that the Council of the Areopagus, Council of 300, and demos of the Athenian people were still recognized civic bodies.[21] There seems little doubt that the office of archon eponymous survived along with these institutions. Demosthenes will have held this office, although George's text styles him as the "eparch of the city".[22] His name was incidentally quite a common one at Athens (2nd–3rd century A.D.).[23] The civil officials who met Chrysostom are styled as "archons", and it is indicated that they had jurisdiction over the *territorium* of Attica (τῆς περιοίκου).[24] George mentions *nomothetes* elsewhere in a general context.[25] Men holding this office are mentioned in the inscriptions of the Roman Imperial period[26] and were, of course, members of the archontal college.[27] The city councillors are characterized as land owners (τῶν κτητόρων) and magnates (οἱ μεγιστᾶνες).[28] Most striking of all is George's use of the Attic technical term "demesmen" (δημόται) for the ordinary folk.[29] These constitutional terms have considerably greater significance through their association in the strictly Athenian context of George's narrative. It can hardly be accidental.

The story of the rhetor Anthemius' arguments and supposed possession evoked the contempt of François Halkin, the editor of George of Alexandria's text: "*Personnage inconnu. Tout ce long chapitre, d'ailleurs, est propre à Georges d'Alexandrie—et suspect.*"[30] There is no Anthemius mentioned in Eunapius of Sardis' *Lives of the Sophists*, but this is hardly relevant because Eunapius seems to have left Athens after the Julianic law banning Christian lecturers from expounding the Greek *paideia*, for his tutor Prohaeresius was a Christian. Eunapius is thus not well informed about the later 360's, when Anthemius is supposed to have taught. Like the majority of sophists there, Anthemius was a foreigner, inasmuch as his name is

---

[21] IG 3/2 635.
[22] *V. Chrysostomi*, 79, line 6f.
[23] Eighteen examples in IG 3/2. 1031, 1040, 1052, 1077, etc.
[24] *V. Chrysostomi*, 78, line 29f.
[25] *V. Chrysostomi*, 82f.
[26] IG 3/2 1085, 3849.
[27] *V. Chrysostomi*, 78, line 29.
[28] *V. Chrysostomi*, 79, line 28f.
[29] *V. Chrysostomi*, 80, line 32.
[30] *V. Chrysostomi*, 78, n. 7.

entirely unattested in the Attic epigraphy.[31] There are certain plausible details given, as for example that "a stele (i.e. a statue) had even been erected for him in Athens and in Rome" (καὶ στήλην αὐτῷ ἀνεγεῖραι ἔν τε 'Αθήναις καὶ ἐν 'Ρώμη).[32] The term "stele" is quite common in Attic epigraphy, but the honor is less significant than George of Alexandria implies. For example, in the third or fourth century, a group of students (οἱ σχολάσαντες) erected a stele of their professor (ὁ καθηγητής), Alexander of Phaleron.[33] The only steles of sophists in Italy that I have discovered belong to funerary monuments, those of Sekkios Trophimos of Side (Aesquiline Hill, Rome), Herkleitos of Laranda (in vinea Moroni), and probably Hermokrates of Tarsus (Rome).[34] These instances certainly prove that easterners migrated to Rome to teach the Greek *paideia*, and Anthemius probably belongs in this category. The single largest group of foreigners attested in the Athenian epigraphy of this time are migrants from Antioch. Even in the fourth century a person like John Chrysostom could have counted on finding the friendship of young Antiochenes, like himself aged eighteen. This hometown bond helped unify the Christian students who confronted the Hellenes of Alexandria a century later.[35] Foreign residents in Athens (called *xenoi* by George of Alexandria) were invariably known by their city names,[36] whereas locals were identified by their deme names.[37] George of Alexandria's use of the term δημόται hints that this nomenclature lasted until the fourth century A.D., as does Eunapius of Sardis' invariable mention of the professors' cities of origin in his *Lives of the Sophists*. The practice began to die out only with the increasing Christianization of the city and its *territorium*.[38]

The rush of the Hellenes to the churches to receive baptism in George of Alexandria's life of Chrysostom is exaggerated, as this sort of behavior really belonged to the period of violent temple conversions in the 380's and later.[39] There was nevertheless a drift towards henotheism or perhaps monotheism in Athenian religious life. This is apparent from the foundation of a temple of Men

---

[31] The occurrence of the name "Anthimos" in the lists of the ephebes is certainly not a relevant phenomenon. IG 3/2 1112, 1119, 1132, etc.

[32] *V. Chrysotomi*, 78, line 24f.

[33] IG 3/2 773.

[34] IG 14 1702, 1928, 1589.

[35] Infra, Ch. V, passim.

[36] IG 3/2 2202, 2959.

[37] IG 3/2 1471–2201.

[38] Infra, Ch. IV, Sect. 1.

[39] Cf. supra, Ch. II, Sect. 3, and Ch. III, Sect. 4.

Tyrannos c. 200 A.D.,[40] various offerings to the "Highest God",[41] and those to Isis as well.[42] The *taurobolia* celebrated in honor of Mithra in the later fourth century are relevant to this trend as well.[43] More than a few Athenians in the late 360's discovered a capacity to identify the Christian victory confessed by Demosthenes the archon with their own deities, particularly if the latter went by the name of "highest" or "unknown" God.[44] The mythical beasts of Athenian statuary like sphinxes were still standing in 367/8 (στήλας κνωδάλων παντοίων καὶ θηρίων),[45] but were being degraded to the status of *daimones* through both Neoplatonist and Christian recategorization. Yet even the Christian confession put into the mouth of Anthemius was derived from Hellenic polytheism: "I confess that there is no god either in heaven or in the earth except the God of the Christians" (ὁμολογῶ μὴ εἶναι θεὸν μήτε ἐν οὐρανῷ μήτε ἐν τῇ γῇ πλὴν τοῦ θεοῦ τῶν Χριστιανῶν).[46] There is a parallel and more complete example of this formula cited above at the end of Chapter IV, the funerary inscription of Euphemia at Panaiania in Attica. This latter inscription shows that Anthemius' confession derived from an originally longer list of gods or *daimones*. It included not only those in heaven and in the earth, but also those of the lower air and the subterranean ones as well. We have a polytheistic formula here that was reduced in scope to make it suitable for the confession of the Christian God. This text is one more corroboration of the hypothesis that George of Alexandria's account of Chrysostom's visit to Athens was taken from a literary source whose author had authentic knowledge of the Athenian milieu. This seems quite certain, even if the historicity of the story is rejected.[47]

The story was concocted between 481–484 for the tendentious purpose of rousing Acacius of Constantinople to cooperate with the government by ordering his bishops to advise the civil authorities as to the identity of the Hellenes in the cities of the patriarchate like

---

[40] IG 3/2 73, 74.

[41] IG 3/2 152–155.

[42] IG 3/2 140. Cf. Trombley, "Prolegomena to the Systemic Analysis of Late Hellenic Religion," passim.

[43] IG 3/2 172, 173.

[44] Cf. the attestations of the latter as late as the third century A.D. in Bauer, *Greek-English Lexicon of the New Testament*, 12, under "*agnōstos*".

[45] *V. Chrysostomi*, 82.

[46] *V. Chrysostomi*, 86, line 13f.

[47] Cf. also Anthemius' correctly formulated characterization of the peace of the gods and his certainly authentic acclamation: "Great is the God of the Christians!" etc. *V. Chrysostomi*, 85f. and 86.

Aphrodisias, where pagan support for Illus' rebellion was quite strong.[48] This obligation of the bishops' informing is stipulated in the first quasi-Justinianic law.[49] It was evidently thought necessary to prod Acacius with the historical example of the most eminent scholar and anti-Hellene of the century to occupy the patriarchal throne, John Chrysostom. Acacius, like the *philoponoi* of Alexandria, seems to have favored voluntary conversions without coercion.

[48] Infra, Ch. V, Sect. 4.
[49] *Cod. Iust.* 1.11.9. Supra, Ch. I, Sect. 6.

THE CLOSURE OF THE ASKLEPIEION AND PARTHENON IN 481–484

Different historical synchronisms of the events of 481–484 have been discussed in their local contexts throughout this work. Marinus of Neapolis' life of Proclus suggests rather baldly that the closure of the Parthenon came not long before the philosopher's death in 485.[1] I append the list of the other synchronisms for the convenience of readers.

1. The two quasi-Justinianic laws found in the *Codex Iustinianus* rather more probably go back to the emperor Zeno's attempts to suppress the pagan factions backing Illus' rebellion that lasted 481–488.[2]

2. George of Alexandria's clear allusions in his life of John Chrysostom to both these edicts, but omission of details about the closure of the Parthenon, puts the *terminus post quem* of the laws in 481 (the beginning of the rebellion) and the *terminus ante quem* in 485 at the latest (the date of Proclus' death). The long-feared *cause cèlébre* had come at last and led to the final act against the chryselephantine Athena and the Asklepieion. It was politically inspired, but, contrary to everyone's expectation, the impetus came from outside Attica.[3]

3. The temple of Aphrodite at Aphrodisias seems to have been dismantled around the same time. The archaeologists have had little on which to base their dating arguments for this except the stylistic features of the marble panels used in the "temple church" emplaced within the temenos.[4] Since a Hellenic "resistance" to the emperor Zeno arose in both Athens and Aphrodisias, there is every reason to suppose that the temple closures had the same motivation: the suppression of seditious civic patriotism that went hand in

---

[1] Cf. the conclusions reached by Timothy Gregory in "The Survival of Paganism," and Alison Frantz, "From Paganism to Christianity in the Temples of Athens," *Dumbarton Oaks Papers* 19 (1965), 187–205.
[2] Supra, Ch. I, Sect. 6.
[3] Supra, Ch. IV, Sect. 2 and 3, and Appendix II.
[4] Infra, Ch. VI.

hand with Hellenic belief and practice. The opposition at Aphrodisias centered in the circle of Asklepiodotos the elder, a wealthy decurion.[5] The Hellenic writers of Athens are rather elusive about the subject of the rebellion. It seems probable therefore that the scholars of the Neoplatonist academy, including Proclus himself and his friends among the city councillors, were in sympathy with Illus' program because of his promise to restore Hellenic rites to the temples that were still standing.[6]

4. It is not entirely clear whether Zeno moved against the temples immediately to break the resolve of Illus' sympathizers, or whether he acted afterwards in reprisal. The former of the alternatives is the more pragmatic and therefore the more probable.

5. Timothy E. Gregory has argued quite strongly for the rapid conversion of the Asklepieion site into the healing shrine of St. Andrew.[7] His thesis is perfectly consistent with the arguments framed above on Christianization of rite, temple conversions, and the recategorization of Hellenic divinities into *daimones*, all of which will have comforted recent converts in their new religious surroundings and perhaps have attracted new ones.[8] It would not be surprising if many pagan Athenians converted to Christianity after the demise of their gods. Such an outcome is consistent with the rapid conversion of temples into Christian shrines elsewhere. The instances of the Serapeum of Alexandria and Marneion of Gaza are the most obvious.

6. George of Alexandria's stories about the cryptopaganism of the archon Demosthenes and the conversion of the sophist Anthemius are more consistent with behavior after temple conversions than of pagan-Christian polemics around 367/8. The author of this section of George of Alexandria's compilation perhaps drew on the actual events of 481–484 in shaping his account. On the other hand, he may have fabricated the actual conversion stories simply as a device to show what effect the imperial edicts of 481–484 would have if carried out properly by Acacius of Constantinople and his suffragan bishops. In either case the stories derive from an Athenian milieu.

7. There is no particular reason to suppose that a church was not built in or around the Parthenon shortly after 481–484. This

---

[5] Infra, Ch. V, Sect. 4.

[6] Rudolf Asmus, "Pamprepios, ein byzantinischer Gelehrter und Staatsmann des 5. Jahrhundert," *Byzantinische Zeitschrift* 22 (1913), 320–347.

[7] Gregory, "Survival of Paganism" 238f. Frantz, "Paganism to Christianity," 194f.

[8] Supra, Ch. II, Sect. 1–3.

would have been consistent with the alterations done to the nearby Asklepieion. A. Frantz' argument that fear of the daimonic power of the gods will have prevented this is not consistent with the vast body of evidence discussed in this book to the effect that incised crosses, Chi-Rho's, Alpha-Omega's, One God formulae, and the veritable presence of Christian holy men, whether bishops or monks, were thought to counteract such hostile kratophanies. It is true that the stones of demolished temples evoked religious awe, as at Gaza, but it was pagans rather than Christians who harbored such notions.[9] The violation of sanctuaries by the raising of the cross and the translation of martyr relics was thought in general to prove the impotence of the old gods, but on a more practical level made the temenos unsuitable for performing sacrifices or receiving oracles because of the ritual pollution entailed in placing a corpse there.[10] The first Christian inscription to appear on the Parthenon dates from 693,[11] but there is no reason to suppose that Christians feared to approach the building before that date. *Daimones* bearing the names of the old gods were certainly believed in after the events of 481–484 and in time became part of Christian Greek folklore. The apotropaic devices used against *daimones* in Greece c. 1900 had their origin in Late Antiquity, and were perceived to have generally the same force then as in the early twentieth century.[12]

---

[9] Supra, Ch. III, Sect. 4.
[10] Infra, Ch. V, Sect. 4.
[11] Orlandos-Vranousēs, *Charagmata tou Parthenōnos*, no. 34.
[12] E.g. Lawson, *Modern Greek Folklore and Ancient Greek Religion*, 155f.